NORTH CAROLINA
STATE BOARD OF COMMUNITY COLLEGES
LIBRARIES
WAKE TECHNICAL COLLEGE

1000 MOST PRACTICAL WORDS

1000 MOST PRACTICAL WORDS

Norman W. Schur

Originally published under the title "Practical English: 1000 Most Effective Words"

Facts On File Publications
New York, New York • Bicester, England

1000 MOST PRACTICAL WORDS

Norman W. Schur

Originally published under the title "Practical English: 1000 Most Effective Words"
Reprinted by permission of Ballantine Books,
A Division of Random House, Inc.

Copyright © 1983 by Eric Weber and Norman W. Schur

All rights reserved. No part of this book may be reproduced or utilized in any form or by any means, electronic or mechanical, including photocopying, recording or by any information storage and retrieval systems, without permission in writing from the Publisher.

Library of Congress Cataloging in Publication Data

Schur, Norman W.
   1000 most practical words.

   1. Vocabulary.   I. Title.   II. Title: One thousand most practical words.
PE1449.S453   1984   428.1   83-25372
ISBN 0-87196-868-1

Printed in the United States of America

10 9 8 7 6 5 4 3 2 1

Preface

Variety is the spice of language. The words listed in this book are not intended to replace those that most people use most of the time. Rather, they are variations on the theme. We tend to use the same old words over and over again, to limit our powers of expression by limiting our vocabulary. There is nothing wrong with the "old words," but why not enhance your speech and writing by learning to use "new" ones from time to time as alternatives?

How often have you spoken of having an *accident*? Why not use the alternative *mishap* once in a while? Everyone talks of the *usual* thing to do or expect. Might not one, to enrich his speech, speak of the *customary* thing? Or why not occasionally describe a situation as *aggravated* instead of *worsened*?

Don't throw away the "old words." Vary them with the "new words." English is an especially rich language, and often there are delicate shades of difference between two words that are generally regarded as equivalent or synonymous. Thus, a *mishap* is not merely an *accident*; it is an *unfortunate* accident. (There can be fortunate accidents, like bumping into an old friend you haven't seen for years and whose address you've lost.) So, in using *mishap* instead of *accident*, you must be sure of the distinction. Again, you'd never say "as customary" rather than "as usual," because the latter phrase has become part of the language. But wouldn't it sometimes be pleasant and perhaps more interesting to describe a kind act by someone as having been done with his *customary* rather than his *usual* thoughtfulness? Other examples: *fragrant*, for *smelling good*, or *having a nice smell*; *morsel*, for *bit*; *wayward*, for *disobedient*; *deft*, for *skillful* or *clever*.

No doubt a good many words in the list will be familiar to you—but do you use them, or do they remain the "property" of others? They are included to introduce variety, and, more often than not, subtle shades of meaning into your speech and writing. Try to make these words your own, as companions or friendly rivals of the ones you have managed within the past. Let them compete, and make your language all the richer.

Many words have more than one meaning. In such cases, I have given the meaning or meanings most likely to be used in everyday speech, omitting the rest. As an example, the word *docile* means not only "easily led" or "manageable," but also "easily taught" or "teachable." (*Docile* comes for the Latin *docilis*, whose first meaning is "teachable," and is based on the Latin verb *docere*, meaning "to teach," a form of which, *doctus,* meaning "taught," gave us our word *doctor.*) In this book, only the meaning "easy to manage or lead" is given, because the other use ("teachable") is very rare in everyday English usage. Or take *ghastly,* which means "ghostlike" as well as "horrible, dreadful" (as in *a ghastly accident* or *a ghastly mistake*). The first meaning is sufficiently rare, for the purposes of this book to warrant omission.

In setting forth pronunciation, only one special symbol has been used—the *schwa,* represented by an upside-down *e,* thus: ə. It indicates the indefinite *uh* sound—almost none at all—of a vowel in an unaccented syllable, as in these examples: the *a* in *ago* or *woman,* the first *a* in *escalator* or the second *a* in *palace* or *solace;* the *e* in *open* or *agent;* the *i* in *admirable, edible* or *pencil,* or the second *i* in *imperil;* the *o* in *gallop* or *scallop;* the *u* in *focus* or both of them in *hocus-pocus.* The placing of an *h* after an *e* or *i* when the vowel is not followed by a consonant indicates that the vowel is "short" like the *e* in *get* or the *i* in *it* (example: *symmetry*—sim ih tree).

The best way to demonstrate the meaning of a word is by example. I have in many cases chosen to amplify my own examples with quotations from past masters of literature, whether prose or poetry. In this I had a dual purpose: Great writers use words not only precisely, but imaginatively and dramatically, in such a way as to fix them in the mind; and there is in addition the hope that the excerpts may serve to introduce readers to aspects of literature they may not have considered previously, and to stimulate them to seek further acquaintance with the works and authors quoted. When a foreign author is quoted, it should be understood that the quotation is a translation from the original.

It may happen that one of the *1000 Most Effective Words* appears in the explanatory comment under an entry. If you run across an unfamiliar word in the text, look it up first in this book; if you can't find it here, look it up in *1000 Most Important Words,* and if you still don't find it, look for it in your *Random House Dictionary.*

Use this book as a reference work, or browse through it when you get a moment, and some of it will stick. Your language will improve, and, since we think in words, so will your thinking.

Norman W. Schur
Hawkhurst, Kent, England, 1983

Acknowledgment

I must express my heartfelt thanks to my good friend and Random House editor Eugene F. Shewmaker for his creative attention to the manuscript, and to my friend and amanuensis Lilian F. Loveday, who went far beyond the call of duty in the correction and typing of the manuscript.

abduct (ab duct´) *vb.* To *abduct* is to kidnap, to take someone away illegally, using force or fraud or any other means, and to keep that person confined against his will. Such conduct is, of course, against the law and severely punishable. The act is called *abduction* (ab duk´ shən). There are many situations in which, after a divorce, the parent to whom custody was not awarded *abducts* a child or children and all sorts of complications develop. In 1782, Wolfgang Amadeus Mozart (1756-1791) wrote an opera entitled (in English translation) *The Abduction from the Seraglio*. (A *seraglio* is a *harem*.) One of the most famous cases of *abduction* was the kidnapping of the Lindbergh baby by Bruno Richard Hauptmann in 1932.

abolish (ə bol´ əsh) *vb.* To *abolish* something is to do away with it completely, to put an end to it. The word is used especially in legal circles to indicate the annulment of a law. The noun is *abolition* (ab ə lish´ ən), and we are all familiar with the word in connection with the *abolition* of slavery in the United States and the conflict between the *abolitionists* (those in favor of putting an end to the shameful institution) and those in favor of slavery which led to the Civil War. Thomas Jefferson (1743-1826) wrote, in the Declaration of Independence (July 4, 1776): " . . . whenever any form of government becomes destructive to these ends [life, liberty, and the pursuit of happiness], it is the right of the people to alter or to *abolish* it. . . . " The English philosopher Alfred North Whitehead (1861-1947), whose lectures the author attended at Harvard, wrote in his *Dialogues*: "The English never *abolish* anything. They put it in cold storage." Bad laws and systems should be *abolished,* good ones observed and encouraged.

abort (ə bort´) *vb.* To *abort* something is to cut it short. Plans are made for a complicated undertaking, and everything seems set to go. Then something turns up in last-minute checking requiring an adjustment, and the program is *aborted* so that corrections can be made and trouble prevented. We have often seen the lift-off of a missile or satellite *aborted* for just this reason. If trouble looms during a pregnancy, it is *aborted,* and the process is known as an *abortion*. The adjective is *abortive* (ə bor´ tiv). An *abortive* attempt is one that comes to nothing. Halfway up Mt. Everest, severe weather changes make the climbers give up, resulting in an *abortive* climb. If all the effort put into the agitation in favor of the Equal Rights Amendment to the United States Constitution fails to gain adoption by the required (two-thirds) number of states, the movement will be said to have been *abortive*.

abound (ə bound´) *vb.* This verb can be used in two ways. Anything that *abounds* somewhere exists there in large quantities. Thus, insects *abound* in the tropics, as do parasites, snakes, and other unpleasant inhabitants. *Abound* can also be used with a preposition, particularly *in* or *with*: Some forests *abound with* deer and other game; some lands *abound in* rich ores yielding various minerals. Not only physical things, but also abstract ones can *abound*: In Shakespeare's *Henry VI, Part 2* (Act II, Scene 4), the King's Uncle Humphrey, Duke of Gloucester, says to his servant: "And after summer, evermore succeeds/Barren winter . . . /So cares and joys *abound,* as seasons fleet." And in his *Henry VIII* (Act III, Scene 2), Cardinal Wolsey speaks of "perils" which "*Abound* as thick as thought could make 'em." *Abundant* (ə bun′ dənt) is the adjective, meaning "plentiful," and *abundance* (ə bun′ dəns) is the noun, meaning a "large quantity" or "supply." Our Victorian forefathers ate food in such *abundant* quantities that their stomachs grew larger and their lives shorter. Money isn't everything, but an *abundance* of it helps. When there is a lot of something, it can be said to exist *in abundance*.

abrupt (ə brupt′) *adj.* This useful word can be used in a variety of ways. Its commonest meaning is "sudden," as when one comes to an *abrupt* stop, or makes an *abrupt* turn in the road. A very steep hill, like a precipice, can be described as *abrupt*. The general idea in the use of *abrupt* is unexpectedness: Someone enters a room, then makes an unexpected about-face and a quick exit. Such an action would be best described as *abrupt*. There can be an *abrupt* change in the weather—sudden and unexpected—the kind that spoils your picnic plans, or an *abrupt* decline in the stock market—the kind that may change your vacation plans. The word is often coupled with *departure*: In *Henry VI, Part 1* (Act II, Scene 3), the messenger of the Countess of Auvergne asks Lord Talbot: " . . . my lady craves/To know the cause of your *abrupt* departure." *Abrupt* can also have the flavor of *curt*, or *brusque*: An *abrupt* reply can describe a sharp retort, the upsetting, unsettling kind. It is the opposite of a *soft answer*, the kind that turneth away wrath (Proverbs 15:1).

abscond (əb scond′) *vb.* To *abscond* is to run away and hide, to leave hastily and secretly. The word is usually associated with the image of someone, like a partner or member of the gang, running off with the money. In gangster movies, especially, one of the gang often *absconds* with the loot, and that leads to interminable chase scenes. With or without loot or money, criminals often *abscond* in order to escape the law. Brazil, which never signed an extradition treaty with the United States (or any other nation, so far as is known), seems to be a favorite place to *abscond* to. Then, there is the silly story about the feeble-minded accountant who *absconded* with the accounts payable.

abstain (əb stane′) *vb.* When you *abstain* from something, you do without it voluntarily; when you *abstain* from doing something, you refrain from doing it. We hear the term often in reports on what's doing in the United Nations General Assembly: So-and-so-many nations vote for the resolution, so-and-so-many vote against it, and the cop-outs *abstain*. The First Epistle General of Peter (2:11) commands: "*Abstain* from fleshly lusts, which war against the soul." George Eliot (1819–1880), in *Impressions of Theophrastus Such*, wrote: "Blessed is the man who, having nothing to say, *abstains* from giving in words evidence of the fact." *Abstinence* (ab′ stə nəns) is the noun; it refers, usually, to food or drink, or other earthly pleasures. *Total abstinence* describes the discipline of the teetotaler. Edmund Wilson (1895–1972) spoke of "*abstinence* from the movies." Samuel Johnson (1709–1784) said: "*Abstinence* is as easy to me as temperance would be difficult." Apparently, that great man favored the cold-turkey route.

abundant (ə bun′ dənt) *adj.* See **abound**.

abyss (ə bis′) *n.* An *abyss* is a chasm, a bottomless depth. Literally, it describes a fissure of great depth in the earth's surface, but it is most commonly found in the figurative sense of "measureless depth," in phrases like *abyss of despair, abyss of shame.* President Kennedy, in an address to the United Nations in 1961, spoke of "that dark and final *abyss*" which would be man's fate in nuclear war, and Churchill, in a 1940 speech to the House of Commons, said that if the Battle of Britain were lost, the world would "sink into the *abyss* of a new Dark Age." (The physical *abyss* resulting from the explosion of a 100-megaton H-bomb would be the least of it.) A little-used variant is *abysm,* from which we get the adjective *abysmal* (ə biz′ məl), meaning "wretched in the extreme, immeasurably awful." The *abysmal* poverty of much of the Third World should shock the conscience of the developed peoples. The *abysmal* ignorance in which the people are kept is one of the strongest weapons of dictators.

access (ak′ ses) *n. Access* to a place is a way of getting to it; *access* can also mean "admittance" to a place. *Access* to something (other than a place) is the right to utilize it. Examples: *Access* to John's house is by way of Murphy Lane. *Access* to headquarters requires a special pass. *Access* to certain medications is by prescription only. Things to which *access* exists are said to be *accessible* (ak ses′ ə b'l). One of the advantages of the ruins of the ancient Greek temples in Sicily is that they are so easily *accessible*. *Accessible* usually implies easy approachability: It is hard to get in to see some bosses; others are quite *accessible*. A place impossible to get to is described as *inaccessible,* like the summit of Mt. Everest until Sir Edmund Hillary (born 1919) made it to the top in 1953.

accessory (ək ses′ ər ee) *n.* See **accomplice**.

acclaim (ə klame′) *n., vb. Acclaim* is loud, enthusiastic approval, and to *acclaim* a person or an accomplishment is to greet him or it with a show of enthusiastic approval and endorsement. Heroes returning from battle are *acclaimed*; successful candidates, athletes, and actors are *acclaimed*; victories, as well as winners, are *acclaimed*; so are great performances and discoveries. We *acclaimed* Jonas Salk (born 1914) for his great breakthrough in the fight against polio, and we *acclaim* the vaccine itself. *Acclamation* (ak lə may′ shən) is the noun that describes the act of *acclaiming*. The noun is often used to describe a voice vote, without an actual count, when someone is elected at a meeting, or a resolution is adopted. At the end of a long political convention, after numerous ballots, the delegates often make it unanimous, adopting the nominee by *acclamation*.

acclimate (ak′ lə mate) *vb.* When you become *acclimated* to new physical surroundings or new circumstances, you get accustomed to them and accept them without further question or unease. This happens, for instance, when you move out of the old familiar neighborhood, or move into a new job, and usually takes time. The word *climate* covers not only the prevailing weather conditions of a particular place, but figuratively, the prevailing conditions of any situation affecting your life generally, like what goes on in a particular job or community. *Acclimate* refers literally to *climate* or *weather* (life up north after years in the tropics); but its more general use is in connection with the problem of getting settled in a new environment, whether community or position or anything else, like the switch from bachelorhood to blessed matrimony. People vary: Some find it hard to adjust; others have no trouble in getting *acclimated*. *Acclimatize* (ə klyˊ mə tize) is a variant, used mainly by the British.

accomplice (ə komˊ pləs) *n*. An *accomplice* is a partner in crime, usually one in a position subordinate to the ringleader. If I help you do something lawful, I am your assistant; if I assist you in an unlawful enterprise, I am your *accomplice*. An *accessory* (ak sesˊ ər ee) is one who helps in the commission of an illegal act though absent. He can be an *accessory before the fact* or *after the fact*, aiding the criminal in the preparatory stages, or helping him to evade the law after the crime is committed. An *accomplice*, on the other hand, is on the scene, lending a helpful hand to what the police would call the chief "perpetrator."

accomplish (ə komˊ plish) *vb*. When you *accomplish* something, you succeed in doing it. To *accomplish* a given task is to complete it. In his play *Wilhelm Tell* (Act III, Scene 3), the German poet Friedrich von Schiller (1759–1805) wrote: "Who reflects too much will *accomplish* little." (Apparently, Schiller didn't think much of looking before you leap, and how about "Fools rush in . . . "?) A feat accomplished is called an *accomplishment* (ə komˊ plish mənt). The usual idea is to indicate success and achievement. Sir Edmund Hillary's scaling of Mt. Everest was an extraordinary *accomplishment*. Putting men on the moon was an incredible *accomplishment*. The British statesman and author Lord Chesterfield (1694–1773), famous for his *Letters*, wrote in one of them (May 8, 1750): "Knowledge may give weight, but *accomplishments* give luster. . . . " *Accomplishment* is also used in another way, to describe a skill, usually one acquired by hard work. In this sense, playing a musical instrument well is an *accomplishment*; so is fluency in several languages. In this usage, the term is often used in the plural: It is high praise to be spoken of as a person of many *accomplishments*. The form *accomplished* has a special use as an adjective meaning "skilled, proficient." Thus, we speak of an *accomplished* pianist, reporter, candlestick maker, etc., to indicate a skilled practitioner. An *accomplished fact* is something over and done with, like the case of a dentist's pulling the wrong tooth. Some people feel that it is always better to face people with an *accomplished fact* (like, for instance, an elopement) rather than ask permission or argue about it.

accord (ə kordˊ) *n., vb*. As a verb, to *accord* is to grant, to concede. When heroes return from a great achievement, they are *accorded* a rousing welcome. But the word is more commonly used as a noun, meaning "agreement," and is often found in the expression *in accord*. After all sides have stated their points of view, and a consensus is reached, all parties are said to be *in accord*. When I'm *in accord* with you, we're in agreement. To do something *of one's own accord* is to do it voluntarily, willingly, without having to be asked, the way thoughtful people anticipate another's needs or wishes.

accrue (ə krooʹ) *vb.* Anything that *accrues* is the result of a natural growth or development. In financial matters, interest on a loan or a bank deposit is said to *accrue* as time goes on. The *accrued* interest at any given moment is the interest that has accumulated up to that day even though it is not payable until a later date. The noun is *accrual* (ə krooʹ əl), which can refer either to the mere act of *accruing*, or to the amount itself. However, *accrue* is used in other than financial matters: If you own a piece of land, the right to build on it (subject, of course, to zoning regulations) *accrues* as a matter of law. The word is often used in the phrase *accrue to one's advantage*; thus, if you get a bye in a tournament, as the result of the draw or incapacity of your opponent (poor chap), that chance happening can be said to *accrue* to your advantage. In Shakespeare's *Henry V* (Act II, Scene 1), the rascal Pistol says: ". . . I shall sutler be/Unto the camp, and profits will *accrue*." (A sutler was one who followed an army to sell provisions to the soldiers; now we have the PX.)

accurate (akʹ yər ət) *adj.* That which is *accurate* is exact, precise, error-free. Thomas Jefferson (1743-1826) said in 1787 of John Adams (1735-1826) that "he is profound in his view; and *accurate* in his judgment." Oscar Wilde (1854-1900), in *The Importance of Being Earnest,* has Lady Bracknell say (Act III): "No woman should ever be quite *accurate* about her age; it looks so calculating." Objects, as well as people, can be described as *accurate.* To avoid tickets for speeding it is well to have an *accurate* speedometer; to know how to dress for the day, better have an *accurate* thermometer. The noun is *accuracy* (akʹ yər ə see). Thucydides (470-401 B.C.), the great Greek historian who wrote the classic *History of the Peloponnesian War,* said that his *History* rested on "partly what others saw . . . the *accuracy* of the report being always tried by the most severe and detailed tests possible." When tests are given, it is often stated that "answers will be marked for neatness and *accuracy.*"

achieve (ə cheevʹ) *vb.* To *achieve* something is either simply to succeed in doing it, or to reach or attain it by one's own efforts. Agatha Christie (1891-1976) *achieved* the writing of a very large number of detective stories; she *achieved* success, fame and a knighthood, to say nothing of financial rewards. If I set myself a goal and am successful in attaining it, I can say I have *achieved* my goal. The noun *achievement* (ə cheevʹ mənt) covers not only the act of *achieving*, but the thing *achieved.* An *achievement* is a feat, and the word usually implies exertion and perseverance, as in Sir Edmund Hillary's *achievement* in 1953 of being the first to climb Mt. Everest. It has become fashionable in educational circles to describe students as "early *achievers*" or "late developers," as the case may be.

acrid (ak´ rid) *adj.* This term is applied to anything stinging or irritating to one's taste or smell, and is often applied to the smoke of burning buildings. It has a figurative use as well, describing words that are stinging or bitter to the point of inflicting real hurt. Oliver Wendell Holmes (1809–1894), in his poem *The Moral Bully,* described the subject as feeling ". . . comfort while his *acrid* words/Turn the sweet milk of kindness into curds." It is hard to get along with people who have *acrid* dispositions. It was the *acrid* denunciation by the American news commentator Edward R. Murrow (1908–1965) of Senator Joe McCarthy (1909–1957) that initiated the latter's decline.

acumen (ə kyoo´ mən, ak´ yoo mən) *n.* Those blessed with *acumen* are notable for their keenness and quick understanding, and their shrewd and deft handling of situations as they arise. A prominent advertising agency once cried up its wares (a Samuel Johnson [1709–1784] usage for *boasting* about one's product) with the slogan "A blend of creative flair and business *acumen.*" The political *acumen* of Lyndon B. Johnson (1908–1973) deserted him when it came to his overview of the Vietnam War. It takes more than mere *acumen* to win on Wall Street; it takes luck as well.

acute (ə kyoot´) *adj.* An *acute* person is keen, shrewd, quick to get the point. The English statesman Edmund Burke (1729–1797), in his second speech on Conciliation of America, said: "In no country . . . is law so general a study . . . this study renders men *acute,* inquisitive . . . full of resources." The word can be used in other ways: Good hearing can be described as *acute.* Feelings of pain can be called *acute*; emotions like jealousy or distress can be so characterized. A short but severe attack of an illness can be labeled *acute* rather than chronic. A severe shortage of workers or material can be described as *acute.* A special usage in geometry reserves *acute* to describe an angle of less than 90 degrees. An *acute* accent in some foreign languages, especially over an *e,* as in *canapé,* is one that leans over to the right (the one that leans the other way is called a grave accent). (This last is a matter of linguistics; in other matters things that are *acute* are usually also grave.)

adamant (ad´ ə ment, -mant) *adj.* An *adamant* person just won't give in; he takes a position and will not relent or yield. In the olden days *adamant* described a supposedly unbreakable type of stone. The English poet Thomas Hood (1799–1845) was a specialist in puns:

> When Eve upon the first of Men
>   The apple press'd with specious cant,
> Oh! what a thousand pities then
>   That Adam was not *Adamant*!

To be *adamant* is to be more than merely stubborn; when a man is *adamant* he is inflexible, like resolute Churchill in the face of those tremendous odds. The brave defenders of the Alamo (1836) were *adamant* in their position to hold or die.

adapt (ə dapt´) *vb.* When you *adapt* something, you change it to make it fit a new situation, or adjust it to new circumstances. Novels are often *adapted* for the stage. Machinery is *adapted* for new uses. One sometimes has to *adapt* his language to suit a particular audience. More drastically, one may have to *adapt* oneself to new circumstances, like a move to a different place, or a new job, or the loss of a loved one. The verb can be used by itself, without an object: Man has had to *adapt* to one change after another in his way of life as a result of new technological development. (Some call it progress.) John Marshall (1755-1835), Chief Justice of the United States, described our Constitution as "intended to endure for ages to come, and consequently, to be *adapted* to the various crises of human affairs." Our poet Robert Frost (1874-1963) wrote, in 1962: "It takes all sorts of in and outdoor schooling/To get *adapted* to my kind of fooling." The adjective *adaptable* (ə dap´ tə b'l) describes an object that can be adjusted to suit various uses; when used of a person, it implies that he can adjust to changing circumstances without too much difficulty. Do not confuse *adapt* with **adopt**.

adept (ə dept´) *adj.* An *adept* person is skilled, proficient to a high degree, and may be considered an expert at whatever occupation he pursues. One does not describe a person simply as "adept"; one specifies whatever the person is *adept at*, or *in*. Albert Einstein (1879-1955) was (to put it mildly) *adept* at physics; Louis Armstrong ("Satchmo," 1900-1971) at the trumpet; Babe Ruth (1895-1948) at the bat. Primitive peoples are often *adept* in handicrafts. *Adept* can be used not only to describe people, but also to characterize skillful acts. Thus, one may speak of an *adept* play at third base, or, in hockey, an *adept* save. Shakespeare was (again, to put it very mildly) *adept* at the writing of plays, and in the tragedies particularly, was capable of *adept* shifts to moments of comedy to relieve the tension.

adequate (ad´ ə kwət) *adj. Adequate* describes persons or things that are good enough for the requirements of the particular moment or situation. It must be used carefully, for it is a term of faint praise all too often used in a somewhat derogatory way. Persons and things described as *adequate* are barely suitable, just about acceptable, and entirely unremarkable. The term can be used more literally, in a phrase like *adequate grounds* (e.g., for a lawsuit), or *adequate provisions* for a short camping trip. But to say that an actor's performance was *adequate*—well, 'twere better left unsaid. *Inadequate* is, of course, the negative form, but used alone of a person marks him as not up to snuff generally. It's hard to say whether one would rather be called *adequate* or *inadequate*.

adhere (ad heer´) *vb.* When you *adhere* to something or somebody, you stick fast and stay attached. The word is used literally to describe what happens when you apply a Band-Aid, or a coat of paint under proper weather conditions. Figuratively, the word is used to describe loyalty in the support of a leader or a principle, and one who does so is known as an *adherent* (ad heer´ ənt). People who don't think for themselves tend to *adhere* to the political party of their forefathers, as well as their religious beliefs. The noun *adherence* (ad heer´ əns) means "attachment," particularly to a person, cause, belief, or program. *Adhesion* (ad hee´ zhən) is usually used in a more literal sense, to indicate the sticking together of two things, like the *adhesion* of things that are glued together. To make your language more interesting it would be well to *adhere* to the principle set forth in the Preface of this book.

admirable (ad´ mər ə b'l) *adj*. An *admirable* person or thing is first-rate, excellent, and, as the word itself indicates, worthy of *admiration* (ad mə ray´shən). Every schoolboy is familiar with George Washington's *admirable* confession that it was he, with his little hatchet. . . We all respect the *admirable* courage and achievements of the Resistance movement during World War II. The careers of the heroes in the novels of Horatio Alger (1834–1899) are models of conduct *admirable* in the extreme. The adverb *admirably* (ad´ mər ə blee) can be used literally: Florence Nightingale (1820–1910) acted *admirably* under the most adverse circumstances. However, the word is often used merely as an intensive, a variation of *extremely*: Teflon is *admirably* well suited to the needs of non-stick cooking utensils. Sir James Barrie (1860–1937) wrote a play entitled *The Admirable Crichton*. What was *admirable* about Crichton, the butler to a family of wealthy ne'er-do-wells, was that when they were all shipwrecked on a desert island, Crichton could do all those Robinson Crusoe-like things that the useless family couldn't. (Naturally, the flighty daughter fell madly in love with Crichton—but it was all over when they were rescued.)

adopt (ə dopt´) *vb*. In the literal legal sense, to *adopt* a person is to take him into your family and bestow upon him all the rights of a child. The word is useful, however, in several other connections. When you *adopt* an idea or a theory, you follow it, take it up and make it your own; the same is true when you *adopt* a plan or course of action. At conventions, political parties *adopt* platforms. At corporate meetings, stockholders and directors *adopt* resolutions. When you *adopt* a child, you became its *adoptive* (ə dop´ tiv) parent. Whatever is *adopted*—whether child, theory, plan, or resolution—that act is called *adoption* (ə dop´ shən). When you *adopt* a new idea, you may have to *adapt* to it, and if you *adopt* new ideas often enough, you may become *adept* at it—but do not confuse these three words.

advantageous (ad vən tay´ jəs) *adj*. This word is obviously derived from the familiar word *advantage*. Anything *advantageous* is profitable and beneficial; it is so because it gives you an *advantage* in that it improves your position. A fair contract is *advantageous* to all parties. A treaty of mutual assistance is usually more *advantageous* to the weaker country (we were thinking of Liechtenstein and the United States, for example). More and more these days, professional malpractice suits appear to be resulting in unusually *advantageous* financial settlements. In any struggle it is *advantageous* to keep the other fellow guessing.

adverse (ad vurs′, ad′ vurs) *adj.* *Adverse* is most frequently used in the sense of "unfavorable," and is commonly found in the phrase *adverse circumstances*. High interest rates are *adverse* to the best interests of the building industry. Japanese manufacturing efficiency and the high price of imported oil have produced an *adverse* balance of trade for the United States. *Adverse* winds reduce the speed of sailing vessels. From this word we get the nouns *adversity* (ad vur′ sə tee), meaning "misfortune," and *adversary* (ad′ vər ser ee), meaning "opponent," whether in war, sports, or other endeavors. In I Peter (5:8), we are told: "Be sober, be vigilant; because your *adversary*, the devil, as a roaring lion walketh about seeking whom he may devour." Failure to heed this advice might result in *adverse* circumstances. Do not confuse *adverse* with **averse**.

advocate (ad′ və kət) *n.*, (ad′ və kate) *vb.* An *advocate* is one who takes a position in support of a person or a cause. Lawyers are *advocates*; that is what they are called in the Channel Islands, and the *Faculty of Advocates* is the Scottish bar. (*Avocat* is French for "lawyer"; the Italian is *avvocato*, the Spanish *abogado*.) Emile Zola (1840–1902), in *J'accuse*, was the *advocate* of Alfred Dreyfus (1859–1935), the French army officer falsely convicted of treason and later acquitted, whose *advocates* (supporters) were called *Dreyfusards*. Abraham Lincoln was the great *advocate* of abolition. *Advocate* is also a verb: To *advocate* something is to argue in its favor. Union leaders *advocate* higher salaries and shorter hours. Mahatma Gandhi (1869–1948) *advocated* passive resistance rather than violence.

affirm (ə furm′) *vb.* When you *affirm* something, you state it in positive terms, and declare it to be true. In taking a loyalty oath, you *affirm* your allegiance to your country alone. In reciting the Apostles' Creed, one *affirms* his beliefs in the principles of Christianity. Quakers are exempted from taking oaths; when they take the witness stand they are permitted to *affirm* rather than swear. In law the word has a special use: When, on appeal, the Appellate Court agrees with the decision of the lower court, the Appellate Court *affirms* it, and this act of the higher court is called an *affirmance* (ə furm′ əns). An *affirmation* (af ər may′ shən) is the act of *affirming* or the thing *affirmed*. An *affirmative* (ə fur′ mə tiv) statement is one that is positive. "Yes" is an *affirmative* reply, and when one says yes he can be said to be answering "in the *affirmative*."

affront (ə frunt′) *n.*, *vb.* When you *affront* someone or subject him to an *affront* you are insulting him openly and intentionally and offending his dignity. Not only individuals, but also nations and racial groups can be *affronted*; for this reason it is high time to put an end to ethnic jokes. Iranian slurs are an *affront* to the American people. Yassir Arafat's not-quite-concealed revolver, worn when he addressed the United Nations, was an *affront* to it and the civilized world generally. The English poet William Cowper (1731–1800) wrote: "A moral, sensible, and well-bred man/Will not *affront* me, and no other can." Lord Chesterfield (1694–1773), the authority on manners, wrote: "Those who now smile upon and embrace would *affront* and stab each other if manners did not interpose."

afoot (ə foot´) *adj., adv.* Apart from its literal meaning of "on foot," as distinguished from transportation by car, oxcart, rickshaw, ship, plane, etc.—or any means other than shanks' mare—*afoot* means "astir, in progress, happening, going on": "What's *afoot*?" is a rather elegant way of asking "What's happening?" or "What's cookin'?" or "What gives?" There are times when a sensitive person, without being able to point to anything specific, just knows that there is *trouble afoot*. In Shakespeare's *Julius Caesar* (Act III, Scene 2), after Marc Antony has made his great "Friends, Romans, countrymen" speech and got the populace all stirred up, as he intended, he cries: "Now let it work. Mischief, thou art *afoot*,/Take thou what course thou wilt!" In other words, he has started trouble, and will let the chips fall where they will.

aggravate (ag´ rə vate) *vb.* To *aggravate* is to worsen, to make more serious, to make bad matters worse. That is the proper way to use this word: The U-boat blockade *aggravated* England's food shortage during World War II. However, *aggravate* acquired a second meaning, at first colloquial, but now acceptable as standard English: to "annoy, exasperate," and that is the way it is most often used now: Noisy children *aggravate* their elders. Mahatma Gandhi (1869-1948), the Hindu nationalist, found that nothing *aggravated* the British more than passive resistance. What is more *aggravating* than the whispering of people sitting behind you in the theater? Yet, purists feel that the use of *aggravate,* and its noun *aggravation* (ag rə vay´shən), should be confined to its original meaning of "worsen," and words like **exasperate** (ig zas´ pə rate) and *annoy* and their nouns should be used when the situation involves somebody's getting peeved about something.

aggrieve (ə greev´) *vb.* To *aggrieve* someone is to wrong him, to do him harm, to cause him pain and sorrow, to distress him. The word is based on the noun *grief* (greef), which is deep sorrow, and the verb to *grieve* (greev), which is to mourn, to feel acute sorrow and distress, and is most commonly found in the form *aggrieved,* meaning "wronged." A related noun is *grievance* (gree´ vəns), a term meaning "ground for complaint": A person with a *grievance* feels that he has been treated unjustly. In law, the *aggrieved party* is the one who has been wronged by being denied a legal right, and is now seeking compensation. To feel *aggrieved* is to feel wounded by having been done wrong, to feel abused. One feels *aggrieved* at the disloyalty of a supposed friend who turns out otherwise, who fails, for instance, to keep a confidence, or who turns on one, who joins the other side. In Shakespeare's *Julius Caesar* (Act III, Scene 1), Julius Caesar's anguished "Et tu, Brute?" ("You too, Brutus?") is the most dramatic cry in literature of an *aggrieved* giant about to fall by the hand of an old and trusted colleague. See also **grievous.**

aghast (ə gast´) *adj.* It is unpleasant to be *aghast,* for this word can express any one of a number of emotions, none of them agreeable: When you are *aghast,* you are either terrified, bewildered, disgusted, or shocked—or all of them. (*Ghast* is a Scottish form of *ghost,* and seeing one of those can cause all of them.) This adjective is almost always used in the predicate; one doesn't speak of an *aghast* person, but says of someone that he is or was or will be *aghast at* something or other. Each generation seems to be *aghast* at the morals, or conduct generally, of the next generation. One is *aghast* at the revelations of what went on in the Nazi concentration camps. The word is often used in the expression to *stand aghast*: The American people *stood aghast* at the Iranian seizure of the hostages. These days one finds oneself *standing aghast* at the prices in the supermarkets (and lots of other places). Cf. **ghastly**.

agile (á jəl—*a* as in *hat*) *adj.* It is a good thing to be *agile* in both mind and body, for to be *agile* is to be quick and lively, nimble and deft. To be *agile* in body is to be quick and smooth in your movements, and the noun *agility* (ə jil' ə tee) implies gracefulness as well. Ballet dancers and gymnasts are *agile*, but one can be *agile* in one's movements without engaging in either of those activities. We think of antelopes and deer as *agile* creatures, and the lively hare as opposed to the slow-moving turtle (though the hare lost the race, but that's another story). An *agile* mind is the mark of a quick-witted person, one who thinks rapidly and gets the point directly, in a keen and lively way. It is inspiring to be in the company of a man of *agile* wit, like Adlai Stevenson or Winston Churchill.

alienate (ale' yə nate, ay' lee ə nate) *vb.* When someone is *alienated*, he becomes estranged, unfriendly, or even hostile to someone to whom he was previously attached. Selfishness can *alienate* your friends. Failure to understand what is really on the voters' minds can *alienate* them and lose their support. After a divorce, a parent will sometimes engage in the unfortunate practice of attempting to *alienate* the children from the ex-spouse through continuous propaganda. *Alienate* has an entirely distinct meaning in law: to "transfer ownership" (of property) to someone. If something can be transferred, it is said to be *alienable* (ale' yən ə b'l, in ay' lee ə nə b'l); if not, it is *inalienable*. The Declaration of Independence states that "all men . . . are endowed by their Creator with certain *unalienable* rights, that among these are life, liberty and the pursuit of happiness." (The authors of that document preferred *un-* to *in-*.) *Alienation* (ale yə nay' shən, ay lee ə nay' shən) is the noun. *Alienation of affections* is the legal term for the wrongful act of luring a person away from his or her spouse and causing estrangement.

allot (ə lot') *vb.* To *allot* something is to parcel it out, usually among a number of recipients. Funds are *allotted*, for instance, by foundations to deserving people or groups to enable them to carry on projects of one sort or another. In making up a program of activities, a committee will *allot* time to each of the various items on the agenda. Seats at sports events or performances of one kind or another are often *allotted* to chosen persons or groups. When a group assigns a task, the leadership *allots* to each member the particular task for which he is best suited. The thing *allotted* is called an *allotment* (ə lot' mənt). *Allot* and *allotment* can be used figuratively about things that are not material: Some people have received a more than average *allotment* of common sense. We must be content with whatever happiness and success life has *allotted* us.

allude (ə lood′, -lyood′—*oo* as in *boot*) *vb*. When you *allude* to something, you are referring to it in an indirect or casual or suggestive way. A person now well off, telling a story about slums and wretched conditions, is probably *alluding* to the poverty of his early days. In the presence of a deformed person, it would be well not to mention physical disabilities lest he think you are *alluding* to his deformity. The act of *alluding* is *allusion* (ə loo′zhən, ə lyoo′zhən); the indirect reference itself is an *allusion*. *Allusions* in writing are lost on people who have not shared the experience to which the *allusions* are being made. An *allusion* to a now forgotten event adds nothing to a reader's understanding or interest; it is best to consider whether the *allusion* will mean anything to him. T. S. Eliot (1888–1965), writing about poetry and poets, said: "Poets in our civilization . . . must be more difficult . . . more *allusive*, more indirect, in order to force . . . language into its meaning." Do not confuse *allusion* with **illusion**.

allure (ə loor′, -lyoor′—*oo* as in *book*) *n., vb.*; **alluring**, *adj. Allure* is both noun and verb. As a noun, it describes the power to fascinate and entice, and is often found in the longer form *allurement*. Applied to women, it is the equivalent of what was called "it" in the 1920s, and somewhat more recently, "sex appeal," also known as "s.a." As a verb, to *allure* is to entice, tempt, fascinate, with the suggestion of some great reward at the end of the road; but in that sense it generally gives way to the shorter form *lure* (discussed under that heading), and is most often found in the adjectival form *alluring*. People enter risky ventures because of *alluring* prospects of financial gain or some other satisfaction, like fame. *Alluring* is often applied to women in history and literature, all the way from Delilah and Cleopatra to Mata Hari. There is a hint of danger in the word *alluring*. The Roman poet Lucretius (99–55 B.C.) wrote of the sea: "Never trust her at any time, when the calm sea shows her false *alluring* smile." Faraway places, remote and mysterious, like the islands of the South Pacific or the casbahs of North Africa made famous by Charles Boyer and Hedy Lamarr, are often described as *alluring*. It is a term overworked in glossy travel brochures.

aloof (ə loof′—*oo* as in *boot*) *adj., adv*. An *aloof* person is one who stands apart, removed, at a distance, in the spiritual sense, from what is going on around him, indifferent to both people and things. To stand *aloof* is to be indifferent to those around you, their opinions, their interests. Samuel Taylor Coleridge (1772–1834), in his *Ode to Tranquillity* (1801), wrote:

> *Aloof* with hermit-eye I scan
> The present works of present man—
> A wild and dream-like trade of blood and guile,
> Too foolish for a tear, too wicked for a smile!

(The world hasn't changed much!) *Aloof* suggests haughtiness, but that may be misleading; spiritual self-removal is the key, based on indifference. Peace-loving people stand *aloof* from a fray—let the combatants fight it out! Serious art lovers remain *aloof* from the passing fads. For a good physical representation of *aloof-*

ness, take a good look at the next camel you come across; if you can't find a camel, look for a giraffe.

alternate (ol′ tər nət) *n., adj.,* (ol′ tər nate) *vb.* As an adjective, *alternate* describes things that succeed each other in rotation, like the red and white stripes on the Star-Spangled Banner. One can say that those stripes are *alternately* red and white. Some buildings are built of *alternate* layers of cement and brick. Winter and summer are *alternate* seasons. As a noun, an *alternate* is a replacement, a substitute, someone ready to take someone else's place in case of need. After a jury is chosen, a number of *alternates* are selected to stand by and fill in if one or more jurors should be incapacitated. To *alternate* (the verb; note the last syllable, pronounced *-nate*) is to take turns, to occur one after the other. Night *alternates* with day, winter with summer. Sometimes, on a given day, rain *alternates* with sunshine. The mood of a maniac depressive *alternates* between high spirits and deep despair. *Alternation* (ol tər nay′ shən) is the noun; the Changing of the Guard at Buckingham Palace is an example. We are familiar with *alternating* current, which reverses directions at regular intervals. Do not confuse the noun and adjective with **alternative**.

alternative (awl tur′ nə tiv) *n., adj.* As an adjective, *alternative* describes anything that offers a choice between two (or among more than two) possibilities. One can travel by a direct route, or take an *alternative* route which is more scenic. There are often *alternative* methods of arriving at the same result. The noun *alternative* can be applied to either the choice between or among possible courses of action, or to one of the possibilities itself. If, for example, there are two or more possible ways of getting somewhere (for example, by car or by train), you have that *alternative,* and each of the methods may itself be described as an *alternative.* President Kennedy, in a speech to the United Nations on September 25, 1961, said: "... in the development of this organization rests the only true *alternative* to war." Under certain circumstances, *alternative* is used to describe a *remaining* choice: After rejecting one possibility after another (whether, for example, to treat a sore back by operating, osteopathy, or medication), the doctor might say, "There is an *alternative*: simple rest." Do not confuse *alternative* with **alternate**,

altruist (al′ troo ist) *n.* An altruist is a person who unselfishly devotes himself to the needs and interests of others. He is the very opposite of an *ego(t)ist.* The hooded, barefoot monk treading the dusty road and doing good works is an *altruist.* The good Samaritan, giving help and sympathy of his own accord to the distressed and needy (Luke 10:30-37), is the classical example of an *altruist.* The adjective is *altruistic* (al troo is′ tək); the noun, *altruism* (al′ troo izm). The entire life of Albert Schweitzer (1875-1965) among the lepers in Africa is a shining example of *altruism.* On a less dramatic scale, every time you put a coin into a blind man's cup you are being *altruistic*; gratuitously, spontaneously, without hope or motive of self-gain, you are acting solely for the good of another.

amazon (am′ ə zon, -zən) *n.* In classical mythology, the *Amazons* were a nation of female warriors. Hence, the term came to be applied to any tall, muscular, masculine woman, and is usually written with a lowercase *a*. Shakespeare used the word: In *Henry VI, Part 1* (Act I, Scene 2), the Dauphin of France says to Joan of Arc as they fight: "Stay, stay thy hands! thou art an *Amazon*. . . ." (Joan may have been little, but she fought like a man.) Female Olympic shot-putters are almost always *amazons*. *Amazonian* (am ə zoe′ nee ən) is the adjective. The term *amazonian* can well be applied to those powerful ladies who specialize in weight lifting and professional wrestling, but the term can be used to describe any powerful aggressive woman, like the ones who fight on to victory during the opening minutes of a department-store sale. (The *Amazon* is, of course, the South American river which is the longest river in the world.)

ambit (am′ bət) *n.* The *ambit* of a person or thing is his or its scope, extent, sphere of activity, limit, or bounds of influence. Literally, an *ambit* is a circuit or circumference, the physical limits around a place; but it is generally used to describe one's sphere of action or influence. If you're lucky, the person you engage as secretary will be helpful well beyond the usual *ambit* of that position. No one has ever been quite able to define the *ambit* of a Vice-President of the United States; to many his main function is that of understudy, to stand by in case the President dies. *Ambit* is a nice word to substitute for *limit* or *scope* or *extent* in the proper situation. Do not confuse *ambit* with **gambit**.

amble (am′ b'l) *n., vb.* To *amble* is to walk along at a leisurely pace; often found in the expression *amble along*. To *amble* is to saunter, to stroll. It's pleasant to be ahead of time for an appointment and rather than have to hurry and hustle, *amble* on one's way. *Amble* is the technical description of a horse's gait when it moves at a smooth pace by raising both legs on one side, then alternating to the other side. Hence, an *amble* is any smooth, easygoing walking pace. One often observes the *amble* of a holiday crowd along a boardwalk on a hot, sunny day.

amend (ə mend′) *vb.* To *amend* is to change, especially to change for the better, to improve. People are told to *amend* their ways, i.e., to improve their conduct. *Amend* has a special use in connection with phraseology; it is often well to *amend* a remark or an observation. *Amend* has a use familiar to those who follow legal or legislative developments; one often reads of *amending* a statute or a constitution. The noun is *amendment* (ə mend′ mənt); we are all familiar with the various *Amendments* to our Constitution. When a person "takes the Fifth," he is resorting to the Fifth *Amendment* to our Constitution, preserving our right against self-incrimination. The plural noun *amends* (ə mends′) is quite another story: One *makes amends* for having committed a wrong like inconsiderateness, selfishness, or rudeness. It is related to the verb *amend* in that *making amends* usually does change the situation for the better.

amiable (ay′ mee ə b'l) *adj.* An *amiable* person is good-natured and likable, is easygoing and shows the world a pleasant disposition. One can speak of an *amiable* gathering, or an *amiable* disposition, as well as of an *amiable* individual. Joseph

Addison, the English essayist and poet (1672-1719), wrote: "Good nature . . . gives a certain air to the countenance which is more *amiable* than beauty." The phrase *amiable weakness* has appeared again and again in literature: The novelist Henry Fielding (1707-1754), in *Tom Jones*, used that expression; the historian Edward Gibbon (1737-1794), in *Decline and Fall of the Roman Empire*, mentioned the "*amiable weaknesses* of human nature"; and Richard Sheridan (1751-1816), in *The School for Scandal*, excuses a character with the sentence, "It was an *amiable weakness*." They were all speaking of a minor defect of character, quite forgivable, that made the person in question all the more human, all the more likable. *Amiably* (aȳm ee ə blee) is the adverb, as in "We chatted *amiably* about old friends." *Amiability* (ay mee ə bil' ə tee), the noun, is a quality much to be admired and cultivated, and makes for happy relationships. Do not confuse *amiable* with **amicable**.

amicable (am' ə kə b'l) *adj.* An *amicable* discussion is a friendly one; an *amicable* settlement is the best way to end a dispute. Anything *amicable* has in it the element of goodwill. *Amicable* relations with neighbors make for a pleasant environment. *Amicable* is a term much used in the context of "friendly" divorces, especially in the expression *amicable arrangement*. (They all too often start out that way and, alas, turn bitter somewhere along the route.) *Amicably* (am' ə kə blee) is the adverb, as in "The dispute was settled *amicably*." *Amicability* (am ə kə bil' ə tee) is the noun, and is a quality devoutly to be wished. Do not confuse *amicable* with **amiable**.

amid (ə mid') *prep.* *Amid* is another way of saying "among," or "in the middle of." *Amidst*, another form, is the equivalent of *in the midst of*. *Amid* and *amidst* can refer either to tangible things or people, like trees or crowds, or to intangible things, like strife, dangers, or joyous tidings. Some people get nervous when they find themselves *amid* huge crowds, or walking on a narrow street *amid* enormous skyscrapers. One admires those, like nurses, who can attend to the needs of others *amid* their own pressing, personal problems. Bertrand Russell (1872-1970), the English philosopher, said: "*Amid* such a world [as ours] . . . our ideals henceforth must find a home." *Amid* can also express the idea of *in the course of*: *Amid* all the strife throughout the world today, we must still continue the struggle for peace.

amiss (ə mis') *adj., adv.* When something has gone *amiss*, it has gone *wrong*. *Amiss*, whether as adjective or adverb, expresses the idea of an error, a fault, something out of kilter. When the person or the letter you're expecting is very late in arriving, you fear that something's gone *amiss*; there's trouble somewhere. *Amiss* is always used in the predicate: A situation can be *amiss*, but you cannot say "an *amiss* situation." People usually go *amiss* in dropping out of school. After making a tactless remark, one might ask oneself, "Have I spoken *amiss*?"—i.e., "Did I say the wrong thing?" *Amiss* is often used with a negative, to express a positive idea: A speaker, or someone at a conference may say, "A few remarks at this point may not be *amiss*. Here, *amiss* is the equivalent of *uncalled for*, and *not amiss* means "in order," or "appropriate." When Robert Burns (1759–1796) wrote, "The best laid schemes o' mice an' men/Gang aft a-gley," he was using *a-gley* as the Scottish equivalent of *astray* or *amiss*.

amity (am′ ə tee) *n*. *Amity* is friendship, and expresses the idea of friendly, peaceful relations between nations ("international *amity*"), groups, or sects. *Amity* implies toleration of opposing views, which the two sides, though they differ, accept out of goodwill. Harmony and accord are ingredients of *amity*. The American diplomat George F. Kennan (born 1904) wrote, of relations with the U.S.S.R.: "If we are to regard ourselves as a grown-up nation . . . we must . . . put away . . . self-idealization and the search for . . . absolutes [like] absolute *amity*. . . ." In Shakespeare's *King John* (Act III, Scene 2), King Philip of France talks to King John of England about " . . . deep-sworn faith, peace, true *amity*/Between our kingdoms and our royal selves." And in his *Antony and Cleopatra* (Act II, Scene 2), the good Agrippa advises Antony to marry Octavius's sister and thus create a bond between the two squabbling men: "To hold you in perpetual *amity*/To make you brothers, and to knot your hearts/ . . . take Antony/Octavia to his wife. . . ." *Amity* is a lovely quality; let there be more of it in the wrangling world!

amoral (ay mor′ əl) *adj*. An *amoral* person is neither moral nor immoral; he is without moral principles, incapable of distinguishing between right and wrong; he thinks and acts without moral or ethical restraints or standards. It is said that all babies are *amoral*; how can they distinguish between right and wrong? The inability to make that distinction is one of the tests of insanity; thus, insane people, like babies, are *amoral*. This does not mean that all *amoral* people are insane; they just lack moral judgment, and act as their passions, appetites, and needs dictate. *Amoral* people who act badly are not conscious of the harm they do. That requires *immorality*, which is a very different thing: wickedness, knowingly committed. The *a-* in *amoral* is from the Greek prefix *alpha-* (their *a*), meaning "without," as in *asexual* (having no sex), and is to be distinguished from the *im-* in *immoral*, meaning *not*, which is a form of the Latin prefix *in-*, meaning "not," as in *impossible*.

ample (am′ p'l) *adj*. What is *ample* is spacious, abundant, not only enough for the purpose, but in certain contexts, more than enough. "Is there enough gas in the tank?" "*Ample!*" (signifying "enough, and to spare"). The word is used, rather jokingly, in the description of a portly person as having an *ample* frame. It was fashionable, in the 1890s, to have an *ample* bust. A picture window gives an *ample* view. An *ample* picnic basket is a comforting sight as the family sets out on the day's journey. The noun *amplitude* (am′ plə tood, -tyood—*oo* as in *boot*) is used oftener than *ampleness*. *Amplitude* usually refers to abstract things: William Wordsworth (1770–1850), in his poem *The Prelude*, spoke of "clearest insight, *amplitude* of mind," and the English writer John Pudney (1909–1977) wrote of "an *amplitude* of noble life." In *The Comedy of Errors* (Act V, Scene 1) Shakespeare has Antipholus, one of the twins of Ephesus, implore Duke Solinus to give him *"ample* satisfaction" for the indignities he has suffered. It is to be hoped that you will devote *ample* time to this book to derive *ample* benefit from it. The related verb *amplify* (am′ plə fye) means "to increase, to make more *ample*, to develop,'' the way one strengthens a point by giving proof, examples, and arguments. Lawyers are careful to *amplify* a point in an argument or brief by supporting it with details, statistics, and reasoning. The related noun is *amplification* (am plə fə kay′ shən).

analyze (an′ ə lize) *vb.* When you *analyze* something, you examine it closely so as to learn all you can about it. You look at all its aspects in details, to determine its nature, use, tendencies, etc. Sociologists *analyze* society in its various aspects; economists *analyze* the production and distribution of wealth, finance, and related matters; chemists *analyze* organic and inorganic materials. The noun is *analysis* (ə nal′ ə sis); the activity is described as *analytical* (an ə lit′ ə k'l). Careful lawyers *analyze* a situation very carefully before giving an opinion; skilled physicians *analyze* the patient's symptoms and background before reaching a decision. Grammarians and linguists *analyze* language, examining its component parts and formation. *Analyze* and *analysis* have become fashionable shortenings of *psychoanalyze* and *psychoanalysis*. *In the last analysis* is a rather pompous expression for "all things considered," or "after all is said and done." *Analysis* takes things apart and examines them in order to understand the whole. It is the opposite of *synthesis* (sin′ thə sis—*th* as in *things*), which puts things together to make up a whole.

anarchy (an′ ər kee) *n*. *Anarchy* is the technical term for complete absence of government, the elimination of all official law and order. The Russian and French revolutions were followed by periods of *anarchy*. It is commonly used figuratively, to describe total disorder generally, like the goings-on among children in a classroom when the teacher leaves for a moment, or what happens in the life of commuters when railroadmen call a wildcat strike. In this use, *anarchy* is the equivalent of *chaos*. The basic concept of *anarchy*, whether in the literal political sense or the figurative general sense, is the lack of rules, regulations, or restrictions. One can speak of the *moral anarchy* of amoral people, or the *intellectual anarchy* of people unable to reason. The English poet Ben Jonson (1572–1637) wrote of "Those that merely talk and never think/That live in the wild *anarchy* of drink." An *anarchist* (an′ ər kist) is literally one who subscribes to the theory that all government should be abolished and is ready to promote *anarchy* by violent means. Here too, the word may also be used in a figurative sense, to describe anyone who instigates disorder generally by ignoring and flouting rules of orderly conduct. Not all *anarchists* have the whiskers and bombs popularized by cartoonists. *Anarchism* (an′ ər kizm) is the theory, supported by some smooth-shaven bombless intellectuals, that full liberty and justice are attainable only through the abolition of government. Things may be bad, but can you imagine what the world would be like if they had their way?

annex (an′ eks) *n.,* (ə neks′) *vb.* An *annex* is, generally speaking, an addition; its usual use is to describe a wing of a building, or a nearby structure used as a supplement to the main building. As a verb, to *annex* something is to join it to the main part, the way one *annexes* a new wing to an existing building, or a rider to a contract. This word is used mainly about territories *annexed* by a country, with or without legal sanction. By purchase from Mexico, Texas was *annexed* to the United States. Israel has *annexed* parts of Egypt, Jordan, and Syria. The word is sometimes used so as to imply that the *annexation* (an ək say′ shən) is not exactly lawful: In that use, to *annex* is to obtain by questionable methods. A cultured thief might, with tongue in cheek, display to a "fence" certain articles that he just happened to "*annex*." (He joined them to himself; that is, he appropriated them; or to be blunt about it, he swiped them.)

anonymous (ə non′ ə məs) *adj. Anonymous* literally means "nameless." The commonest use of this word is to characterize something written by a person whose name is unknown or withheld. Many writings and sayings are *anonymous*. Nobody knows who first said "A fool and his money are soon parted," or "Open, sesame!" or "The Campbells are comin', oho, oho." All these, and many more, are *anonymous*; often abbreviated *anon.* in anthologies. Hence the witticism: "Who is the most prolific author?" "*Anon.*" *Anonymous* can be used as a somewhat derogatory term, like *nameless* and *faceless*: The American novelist Sinclair Lewis (1885–1951) spoke of "a sea of *anonymous* faces" and "a district of brown *anonymous* houses." Here, *anonymous* is used to indicate a lack of distinction. How often do you get a dig in the ribs from some rude, *anonymous* fellow? *Anonymity* (an ə nim′ ə tee) is the quality of being *anonymous*. Norman Thomas (1884–1968), the American socialist and political writer, wouldn't debate with men who "hid behind *anonymity*." The English novelist James Hilton (1900–1954) wrote of the "vast and kindly *anonymity* of London life." Franklin Roosevelt spoke of "men with a passion for *anonymity*." Most newspapers won't print *anonymous* letters to the editor.

antagonize (an tag′ ə nize) *vb.* When you *antagonize* someone, you rub him the wrong way and make him hostile to you. Something you do, or some unpleasant characteristic, like constant grouchiness or rudeness, will *antagonize* those around you. The hostility so created is *antagonism* (an tag′ ə nizm). *Antagonism* can exist between classes, like the rich and the poor, labor and capital, city people and country people. George Kennan (born 1904), the American diplomat, wrote (about relations between Russia and the West): ". . . there is no international relationship between sovereign states . . . without . . . *antagonism*. . . ." An *antagonist* (an tag′ ə nist) is an opponent, an adversary. Edmund Burke (1729–1797), the Irish writer and politician, wrote (about the French Revolution): "He that wrestles with us strengthens our nerves. Our *antagonist* is our helper." But on a less lofty plane, *antagonizing* people doesn't help; it can cause the *antagonizer* a lot of harm. All kinds of things can *antagonize* people: selfishness, loudness, flashy clothes, bad breath. How often your career may be set back by the *antagonism* caused by things you may do or say, or characteristics you may exhibit, that just happen to *antagon-*

ize those in a position to affect your future! The adjective *antagonistic* (an tag ə nis' tək) is generally used of people or things that are opposed to each other: Slavery and democracy are *antagonistic*; monopoly and free trade are *antagonistic*; city people and country folk often seem naturally *antagonistic*; so do sailors and motorboat owners, and little girls and little boys until they grow up. (But later. . . !

anticipate (an tis' ə pate) *vb.* This word has many uses. Its common meanings are to "expect, look forward to, foresee." After all the picnic preparations are made, you *anticipate* a pleasant day by the river. When you *anticipate* an adversary's next move, however, whether in sports, a lawsuit, or a business maneuver, you foresee it and forestall or prevent it by taking appropriate action in advance. To *anticipate* a request or a wish is to guess it and perform it before it is made or expressed. A careful secretary will *anticipate* the boss's every need. *Anticipation* (an tis ə pay' shən) is looking forward to something. It is commonly said that *anticipation* is better than realization; the actual event may turn out to be disappointing. In this sense, *anticipation* is the equivalent of *expectation*. Benjamin Disraeli (1804-1881), Queen Victoria's Prime Minister, said: "What we *anticipate* seldom occurs; what we least expect generally happens." *Anticipation* can be used as well in the sense of foreseeing something disadvantageous or damaging and acting to prevent it. A successful boxer will *anticipate* his opponent's every move. Thus, *anticipation* can be mere passive expectation or action to protect oneself by neutralizing someone else's action. (Don't just sit there and *anticipate* trouble; do something—*anticipate* it!)

antonym (an' tə nim) *n.* See synonym.

appall (ə pol') *vb.* To *appall* someone is to horrify him, shock him, fill him with dismay. The verb is usually found in the forms *appalling* (it was an *appalling* sight!) and *appalled* (people are *appalled* by the scenes of suffering in the Nazi concentration camps). The -*pall* in *appall* is related to *pale* and *pallid*, which is the way people—especially ladies in Victorian novels—are supposed to grow when they are *appalled*. One may speak of having witnessed an *appalling* accident. History is all too full of *appalling* disasters, like earthquakes, floods, and famines. *Appalling* may be applied to much less world-shaking events or things: "We had the most *appalling* meal at Jennifer's!" "What an *appallingly* dull couple they are!" Here, *appalling* is nothing more than a fashionably exaggerated way of saying "terrible" or "awful" in the figurative sense. The poet Charlotte Perkins Gilman (1860-1935) wrote a little verse about people:

> The people people have for friends
> Your common sense *appall*,
> But the people people marry
> Are the queerest folk of all.

In Shakespeare's *Macbeth* (Act III, Scene 4), after the murdered Banquo's ghost appears and terrifies Macbeth at the banquet table, his wife asks, "Are you a man?"

and he answers, "Aye, and a bold one, that dare look on that/Which might *appall* the devil."

apprehend (ap rə hend´) *vb. Apprehend* has two main distinct uses: When the police *apprehend* a person, they seize and arrest him. When you *apprehend* something (an idea, or suggestion, a concept), you grasp its meaning. It is also used, but not so commonly, to express a feeling of foreboding: One can *apprehend* an exam, in the sense of dreading it or thinking about it with great anxiety. The noun *apprehension* (ap rə hen´ shən) can reflect all these uses, so as to mean "arrest" or "understanding" or "foreboding"; but its common use is the last: a feeling of alarm, anxiety, fear of trouble lurking around the corner. In Shakespeare's *Measure for Measure* (Act III, Scene 1), Isabella says to her brother Claudio: "Dar'st thou die? The sense of death is most in *apprehension*." Police, on television, like to talk of "*apprehending* the perpetrator" (as though mere *catching* were too good for him). We find the use of *apprehend* in its more literary meaning of "understand" or "conceive" by John Milton (1608–1674) in his pamphlet on the freedom of the press, *Areopagitica*: "He that can *apprehend* and consider vice with all her . . . seeming pleasures, and yet abstain . . . is the true . . . Christian." The English philosopher Alfred North Whitehead (1861–1947) used *apprehend* in the same way, defining *intelligence*, in his *Dialogues,* as "the quickness to *apprehend* as distinct from ability, which is capacity to act wisely on the thing apprehended."

appropriate (ə proe´ pree ate) *vb.*, (ə proe´ pree ət) *adj.* To *appropriate* is to take as one's own, often with the implication that the taking is without permission, and improper. When a guardian *appropriates* his ward's money, he is running afoul of the law. Public money appears to have been *appropriated* for the embellishment of President Nixon's estate at San Clemente. *Appropriate* can also be used to describe the perfectly lawful act of setting aside certain funds for a particular use or purpose. *Appropriation* (ə proe pree ay´ shən) is the noun and the *Appropriations Committee* of Congress is the body that *appropriates* the funds to provide the expenses of carrying out legislative programs. Congress can vote for a bridge or a dam or a social program, but the money must be *appropriated* by that committee before anything can happen. As an adjective (note different pronunciation) *appropriate* means "suitable, fitting." It is *appropriate* for a man to raise his hat when greeting a woman. John Marshall (1755–1835), Chief Justice of the United States, wrote, in a famous opinion: "Let the end be . . . within the scope of the constitution and all means which are *appropriate* . . . are constitutional." Enough discussion of *appropriate*; it is *appropriate* to end it now!

arbitrary (ar´ bə trerr ee) *adj.* This adjective can apply to persons and to their acts, judgments, decisions, and agreements. It can mean "discretionary," but its more common use is in the sense of "capricious," i.e., based on whim or notion without reference to rules or restrictions. Some people make *arbitrary* decisions without reasoning and without thinking about the consequences. The great liberal U.S. Supreme Court Justice Louis D. Brandeis (1856–1941) wrote that in government, "the deliberative forces should prevail over the *arbitrary*." The journalist Walter Lippmann (1889-1974) said: "The denial that men may be *arbitrary* in human transactions is the higher law." Parents should not be *arbitrary* in bringing up children; they should take the trouble to explain the reasons for the rules. *Arbitrarily* (ar bə trer´ ə lee) is the adverb. Despots like Adolf Hitler and Idi Amin acted *arbitrarily* (to put it mildly), and look where it got them. See **arbitrate**, a word related to *arbitrary* in sound, but with an entirely contrary emphasis.

arbitrate (ar´ bə trate) *vb*. To *arbitrate* a dispute, or submit it to *arbitration* (ar bə tray´shən) *n*., is to settle it by having the parties state their cases to a chosen tribunal (whether one person or a board) which will render a decision. A person so deciding, or forming part of such a board, is an *arbitrator* (ar´ bə tray tər). *Arbitration* is common in collective bargaining negotiations. The American *Arbitration* Association is an institution which many prefer to the courts, and contracts often contain a clause requiring the submission of controversies to that body. The United Nations was formed as a forum for the airing and *arbitration* of grievances as an alternative to force or war. (Its record in that department has thus far been undistinguished.) "Now, who shall *aribitrate?*" wrote Robert Browning (1812-1889) in his poem "Rabbi Ben Ezra," about the confusion caused by men's differences of opinion and taste: ". . . whom shall my soul believe?" In Shakespeare's *Richard II* (Act I, Scene 1), where Bolingbroke and Mowbray are accusing each other of treason before the King, Mowbray says: "The bitter clamour of two eager tongues / Can *arbitrate* this cause betwixt us twain. . . ." But arguments cannot do the trick: At the end of their furious debate, King Richard gives up and says: "At Coventry . . . / There shall your swords and lances *arbitrate* / The swelling difference of your settled hate. . . ." (Some *arbitration!*)

arid (ar´ id—*a* as in *hat*) *adj*. This is the word commonly used to describe dry, barren land having insufficient moisture for agricultural use. In its figurative sense, it means "uninteresting, dull, monotonous," and can be used in the way we use *dry* in its figurative sense. Some lectures are interesting, some are *arid* and dry. Long legal documents are, to the layman, *arid*, dull, uninteresting, dry. To one person, etymology, the study of the origins of words, may be fascinating; to others it may be the most *arid* subject in the world. There is nothing better calculated to produce a major attack of yawning on a fine Sunday morning than an *arid* sermon. There is the rarely used noun *aridness*, but *aridity* (ə rid´ ə tee) is the common term.

arrogant (ar´ ə gənt—*a* as in *hat*) *adj*. *Arrogant* people are unpleasantly full of self-importance; they are haughty, imperious, and overbearing. This characteristic is called *arrogance* (ar´ ə gəns). In a speech made less than a month before he died, President Kennedy said: "When power leads man toward *arrogance,* poetry reminds him of his limitations." The poet Marianne Moore (1887-1972) referred to man as ". . . small dust of the earth / That walks so *arrogantly*. . . ." Edmund Burke (1729-1797), the Irish writer and statesman, wrote: "The *arrogance* of age must submit to be taught by youth." In *Henry VI, Part I* (Act I, Scene 2) after Woodville, Lieutenant of the Tower of London, tells the Duke of Gloucester that the Cardinal of Winchester has forbidden the Duke to enter the Tower, the Duke refers angrily to the Cardinal as *"arrogant* Winchester, that haughty prelate." *Arrogant* may be used to describe not only persons, but attitudes. Thus, one may speak of someone making *arrogant* claims or *arrogant* demands, striking an *arrogant* pose, or responding with an *arrogant* answer. Avoid *arrogance*; the *arrogant* will never inherit the earth!

articulate (ar tik´ yə late) *vb.*, (ar tik´ yə lit) *adj.* When you *articulate,* you speak clearly and pronounce carefully and distinctly. To be *articulate* (note difference in pronunciation of the adjective) is to be able not only to pronounce distinctly but to be able to *express oneself* clearly and make sense. The noun *articulation* (ar tik yə lay´ shən) is the *way one speaks* and pronounces. *Articulateness* (ar tik´ yə lit ness) is the art of *expressing oneself* clearly. Examples: John *articulates* very well (he speaks clearly and distinctly). John is *articulate* (he expresses himself well). John's *articulation* is excellent (his manner of speaking is excellent). John's *articulateness* does him credit (his ability to express himself clearly is commendable). The Scottish historian Thomas Carlyle (1795-1881) wrote: "In books lie . . . the *articulate* audible voice of the past. . . ." If you want to get your message across, it is important to *articulate* well and clearly (pronounce carefully), and to be *articulate* (arrange your thoughts, use suitable words, and express yourself in a way that makes sense and leaves no room for doubt). An *inarticulate* (in ar tik´ yə lit) person is one who cannot express himself clearly and effectively, and is unable to present his ideas or feelings in an understandable and effective way. Shy people are often *inarticulate.* Good writers are sometimes *inarticulate* speakers. Rage can sometimes make a usually *articulate* person *inarticulate.*

ascertain (as ər tane´) *vb.* To *ascertain* something is to learn or find it out definitely, once and for all, with certainty. When it comes to *ascertaining* the facts, hunches are not enough; *certainty* (a related word) must be established. Doctors do their best to *ascertain* the cause of an illness. Jewelers have certain tests to *ascertain* the purity of precious metals. A good many pages of detective stories are devoted to the hero's painstaking examination of all the suspects in order to *ascertain* their whereabouts at the moment of the commission of the crime. Military experts carefully examine maps of the countryside to *ascertain* whether a surprise attack can be made from any direction. One *ascertains* the facts by examination, trial and error, experiment, or any other means at hand.

ascribe (ə skribe´) *vb.* We *ascribe* things to their supposed causes or origins. The earliest alphabet is usually *ascribed* to the Phoenicians, an ancient Mediterranean people who lived in what now is Syria, Lebanon, and Israel and who invented a mode of writing by the eleventh century B.C. or earlier. Sleeping sickness is *ascribed* to the bite of the tsetse fly. In Shakespeare's *All's Well That Ends Well* (Act I, Scene 2), Helena soliloquizes: "Our remedies oft in ourselves do lie/Which we *ascribe* to heaven. . . ." The English poet Isaac Watts (1674-1748) was so proud of his Christianity that he wrote: "Lord, I *ascribe* it to Thy grace/And not to chance, as others do,/That I was born of Christian race. . . ." (One wonders about Christian *"race"*—but Watts had to find a rhyme for *grace*!)

ashen (ash′ ən) *adj.* *Ashen,* literally the gray color of ashes, is used figuratively to mean "pallid, drained of color," describing the face of one who is startled, terrified by an apparition or the sudden appearance of someone or something he dreads. *Ashen* describes the pallor of someone caught in the act. When people who believe in ghosts think they are seeing one, their faces turn *ashen.* People's faces turn *ashen* at the hearing of bad news. Sir Walter Scott (1771-1832) wrote of "the *ashen* hue of age." The word is sometimes used for other things—Edgar Allan Poe (1809-1849) began his poem "Ulalume," "The skies they were *ashen* and sober . . ."—but the description *ashen* is ordinarily confined to human faces.

aspect (as′ pekt) *n.* In its most common use, *aspect* refers to the way in which something may be viewed or regarded. It is important to consider every *aspect* of a situation before coming to a conclusion. A politician looks at the political *aspect* of a crisis, the economist and the sociologist at the *aspects* that most concern them. A painter is interested mainly in the physical *aspect* of the countryside, while a farmer is concerned primarily with its agricultural *aspect.* Aspect can mean "appearance" also: One person may present an *aspect* of sadness or gloom, another an *aspect* of joyous expectancy. Dictators like to affect a stern and warlike *aspect,* heads of democratic states a congenial and conciliatory *aspect.* In Shakespeare's famous "Once more unto the breach, dear friends, once more . . ." speech of Henry V, in the play of that name (Act III, Scene 1), Henry exhorts his soldiers to be fierce, and "lend the eye a terrible *aspect.*" In *The Merchant of Venice* (Act I, Scene 1), Salarino uses the phrase "vinegar *aspect*" as the equivalent of our modern colloquialism *sourpuss.* Lord Byron (1788-1824) in his well-known "She walks in beauty . . ." writes the lines: " . . . and all that's best of dark and bright/Meet in her *aspect* and her eyes. . . ." The "visage" or "countenance" or "appearance" *aspect* of *aspect* is best left to poets; we practitioners of prose had better stick to the "phase" *aspect* of *aspect.*

aspire (ə spire′) *vb.* When you *aspire* to something, you seek it eagerly. The word implies that your goal is a high one, that you seek something of important and lasting value. *Aspire* is usually followed by the prepositions *to* or *after,* or by a verb. Scientists *aspire* to a breakthrough in their fields. Explorers *aspire* to the great discovery that will give them immortality. Columbus *aspired* to find a new route to India. The goal itself is the *aspiration* (as pə ray′ shən). It was the *aspiration* of romantic young knights to rescue a damsel in distress. The poet Sir Philip Sidney (1554-1586) wrote: "Leave me, O love, which reacheth but to dust;/And thou, my mind, *aspire* to higher things. . . ." In *Henry VI, Part 3* (Act I, Scene 1), Shakespeare has King Henry point to Richard, Duke of York, sitting on the throne, and say to the assembled lords: "My lords, look where the sturdy rebel sits!/. . . belike he means . . . / To *aspire* unto the crown and reign as King." It is our high *aspirations* that lead us to study, to toil, to sacrifice pleasure to attainment. The term *aspiring* is often applied to young people who are trying earnestly to get ahead in the world: an *aspiring* young architect; an *aspiring* new lawyer in town. This book *aspires* to enrich your life by enriching your vocabulary.

assail (ə sale´) *vb.* When you are *assailed,* you are being set upon, attacked, assaulted, if the word is being used literally, and the attacker is your *assailant* (ə sale´ ənt); but the word can be used figuratively when you are *assailed* by criticism, abuse, objections, arguments of one sort or another, ridicule, or slander, or when your ears are *assailed* by harsh noises, or your eyes by blinding light. *Assail* is a versatile and useful word: Armed forces *assail* the enemy with weapons; debaters *assail* one another with arguments, lawyers with objections. John Milton (1608–1674), in *Comus,* wrote of *assailing* abstract things rather than people or places: "Virtue may be *assailed,* but never hurt. . . ." Shakespeare was fond of the word, using it both literally and figuratively. In *Henry VI, Part 2* (Act IV, Scene 2), William Stafford, speaking of traitors, says: "Well, seeing gentle words will not prevail / *Assail* them with the army of the king." Cloten, in *Cymbeline* (Act II, Scene 3), says of stern Imogene: "I have *assail'd* her with music, but she vouchsafes no notice." (I shall not *assail* you with further examples.)

assent (ə sent´) *n., vb.* To *assent* is to agree or concur, and an *assent* is an agreement, concurrence, or acquiescence. If you state an opinion, and I share it, I *assent* to it. In a negotiation, if one side makes a demand or a proposal, the other side may reject it or *assent* to it. If it *assents,* it gives its *assent.* In Shakespeare's *Henry VIII* (Act III, Scene 2), the Earl of Surrey accuses Cardinal Wolsey of having "wrought to be a legate" (contrived to be a representative of the Pope) "without the king's *assent* or knowledge." The philosopher David Hume (1711–1776), in his *Essay on Miracles,* discussing Christian faith, wrote that "whoever is moved by faith to *assent* to it" must believe in miracles. *Assent* is a bit weaker than *consent.* According to *Webster,* "A lady may *assent* to a gentleman's opening the window, but if he makes a proposal of marriage, he must await her *consent.*" Do not confuse *assent* with *ascent.* If you are brave (or foolhardy) enough to accept an invitation to go up in a balloon, you will *assent* to the ascent.

assess (ə ses´) *vb.* Apart from tax usage, to *assess* is to evaluate, to judge the value, nature, or character of someone or something. The manager of a firm will *assess* the character and ability of a new member of the staff on the basis of past performance. A suitor will *assess* his chances with his new love by reading her responses to his advances. When presented with a problem in life, one must consider all the angles and *assess* the situation. The result will be one's *assessment* (evaluation) of the situation. We are all too familiar with the other kind of *assessment* in the technical sense, whether it be in the form of valuation for tax purposes, or the official determination of tax due, or the amount fixed as a fine or damages, or one's contribution to the club picnic. Nobody loves the tax *assessor* (ə ses´ ər).

astound (ə stound´) *vb.* To *astound* is to amaze, to strike with surprise and wonder, to astonish (a synonym that comes from the same root). John Milton (1608–1674), in *Comus,* distinguished between *startle* and *astound* in stating that if one's conscience is clear, ". . . Calling shapes and beckoning shadows dire [things that, as it were, go bump in the night]/ . . . may startle well, but not *astound*/The virtuous mind. . . ." An *astounding* statement is one that overwhelms you with surprise and amazement. The freeing of the hostages at Entebbe was an outstanding achievement; the news of it was *astounding.* "*Astounding!*" is an appropriate one-word reaction under certain circumstances. "Our men have landed on the moon!" "*Astounding!*" A student who gets 100 percent on all his examinations has done *astoundingly* well. So will you have done, if you can master one-half of the entries in this book.

astute (ə stoot´, -styoot´—*oo* as in *boot*) *adj. Astute* means "shrewd." An *astute* person is perceptive, has keen judgment, is clever in sizing up a situation and knowing what to do about it. The term is generally applied to businessmen and politicians. President Johnson was an *astute* judge of popular opinion until it came to the Vietnam War. Rockefeller, Carnegie, and the other giant robber barons amassed fortunes because of their *astuteness* in business. A new product will prosper as a result of an *astute* merchandising campaign. Bosworth Smith (1839–1908) wrote of "the *astute* fickleness of a barbarian," and Robert Browning (1812–1889) of "one touch of fool in Guido the *astute.*" The adjective *astute* implies that one who merits that description is very keen to look after his own interests and is not often caught napping.

atone (ə tone´) *vb.* When you *atone,* you repent and make amends for something, whether an offense or a failing. The act of atoning is called *atonement.* Both verb and noun are usually followed by the preposition *for:* one *atones for* one's sins, or *for* one's failings or deficiencies. When we were youngsters at school, teacher made us *atone* for our infractions of the rules by standing us in the corner, face to the wall. The holiest day in the Hebrew year is Yom Kippur, called in English the *Day of Atonement,* when religious Jews fast and spend the day in the synagogue reciting prayers of repentance. A popular equivalent of *atone* is to *make up* for having done something we should not have done or for having failed to do something we should have done. In situation comedies, husbands are often shown in circumstances where they are hard pressed to find ways of *atoning* for having forgotten their wedding anniversary or their wife's birthday.

atrocious (ə tro´shəs—*o* as in *note*) *adj.* In its literal and strongest sense, *atrocious* is applied to any act that is brutal and wicked, and such an act is known as an *atrocity* (ə tros´ə tee). Nations at war often accuse each other's armies of *atrocities.* A particularly shocking crime is often described as *atrocious.* In a milder context, *atrocious* can apply colloquially to behavior in terribly bad taste, like wearing a loud plaid suit at a formal wedding or a funeral. In the latter use, *atrocious* is equivalent to strong adjectives like *awful, terrible,* or *dreadful,* which are not meant literally, but only to express a particularly high degree of shockingly bad taste. A person can also be accused of *atrocious* spelling or *atrocious* ignorance, and one may speak of an *atrocious* dress or necktie. Even the noun may be used colloquially that way: "Did you see Brown's get-up at the party? It was an *atrocity*!"

attain (ə tāne′) *vb.* To *attain* a goal or an achievement is to reach it, accomplish it, achieve the result one has been aiming at. The word usually implies that a lot of effort has been spent along the way, and the thing *attained* or achieved is known as an *attainment* (ə tāne′ mənt). One studies hard at school to *attain* success in the exams. One takes great pains in explaining a situation in order to *attain* clarity. Henry Wadsworth Longfellow (1807-1882) wrote, in *The Ladder of Saint Augustine:* "The heights by great men reached and kept/Were not *attained* by sudden flight,/But they, while their companions slept/Were toiling upward in the night." Robert Louis Stevenson (1850-1894), however, on a contrary note, in his *New Arabian Nights,* asked: "Is there anything in life so disenchanting as *attainment*?" (Perhaps the man who wrote that famous ad for the Cunard Line was right: "Getting there is half the fun.")

attest (ə test′) *vb.* When you *attest* something (or *attest* to it), you certify it and bear witness to its truth and correctness. If you support such and such a statement, you are *attesting* (to) its truth. If you have had good experience with your doctor, you can *attest* to his skill and reliability. At the outset of Shakespeare's *Henry V* (Act I, Scene 1), the King calls on his soldiers, fighting the French, to follow the example of their brave fathers: ". . . now *attest*/That those whom you call'd fathers did beget you." The English philosopher David Hume (1711-1776) expressed himself about miracles in these words: "There is not to be found, in all history, any miracle *attested* by a sufficient number of men, of . . . good sense . . . integrity . . . and reputation. . . ." It is unwise and often dangerous to *attest* to anything without making very sure that we know the facts.

attribute (a′ trə byoot—*a* as in *hat, oo* as in *boot*) *n.,* (ə trib′ yoot—*oo* as in *boot*) *vb.* An *attribute* is a characteristic or quality or feature of a person or thing. Ferocity is an *attribute* of wild boars. Longwindedness is an *attribute* of tame bores. Extreme hardness is an *attribute* of diamonds. Delicacy is not one of Idi Amin's *attributes.* To *attribute* a result to something is to consider it as having been caused by that something. You can *attribute* a friend's missing an appointment to his absent-mindedness, inconsiderateness, or illness. The word is often used in the world of arts. An unsigned painting is *attributed* to a particular artist, in the absence of conclusive proof, based on intimate knowledge of that artist's technique; or to a particular period or country, based on expertise in art history. Inventions dating far back in history, like the wheel, are *attributed* to a certain age or culture. Many anonymous witty statements are *attributed* to well-known wits like Dorothy Parker (1893-1967) or Robert Benchley (1889-1945). Sir James Barrie (1860-1937), in *What Every Woman Knows* (Act II), wrote: ". . . the grandest moral *attribute* of a Scotsman . . . [is] that he'll do nothing which might damage his career." The poet Charles Kingsley (1819-1875) wrote of "the cruel crawling foam." The painter and writer John Ruskin (1819-1900) objected: "The foam is not cruel. The state of mind which *attributes* to it these characteristics of a living creature is one in which the reason is unhinged by grief. . . ."

audible (aw' də b'l) *adj.* What is *audible* is, technically speaking, just loud enough to be heard, but the term is often used to mean "actually heard." *Audibly* (aw' də blee) is the adverb. Oliver Goldsmith (1728-1774), in *The Deserted Village* (Sweet Auburn!), wrote in 1770 of "the loud laugh that spoke [revealed] the vacant mind." Lord Chesterfield (1694-1773), in his *Letters*, made an earlier comment on loud laughter (1748): ". . . there is nothing . . . so ill-bred as *audible* laughter." (But writers all the way from the Roman Plautus [254-184 B.C.] and Terence [190-159 B.C.] to Shakespeare, George Kaufman [1889-1961], and Moss Hart [1904-1961] spent a good part of their lives producing plays intended to bring about *audible* laughter!) Thomas Carlyle (1795-1881) used *audible* figuratively: "In books lies the soul of the whole Past Time; the articulate *audible* voice of the Past. . . ." *Audible* can describe any sound, from *clearly heard* to *just able to be heard*, depending on the context. To be specific, it may be advisable to qualify the word: *quite audible*; *barely audible*.

augment (awg ment') *vb.* To *augment* is to increase, enlarge. People in full-time jobs *augment* their income by moonlighting. If you have income-producing capital, its income *augments* your earned income. In Shakespeare's *Henry VI, Part 3* (Act V, Scene 3), the triumphing King Edward IV says to his brothers: "And, as we march our strength will be *augmented*/In every county as we go along./Strike up the drum! Cry 'Courage!' and away." In *Romeo and Juliet* (Act I, Scene 1), Shakespeare uses the word in a more romantic vein: Romeo's mother, Lady Montague, asks her husband and her nephew Benvolio, ". . . Where is Romeo?" Benvolio has seen him, walking alone in the woods. Lord Montague adds: "Many a morning hath he there been seen/With tears *augmenting* the fresh morning's dew. . . ." The Bard was fond of *augmentation* (awg mən tay' shən) by tears: In *As You Like It* (Act II, Scene 1), after the Duke suggests a deer hunt, and then feels sorry for the innocent deer, one of the Lords describes a wounded stag that groaned and wept as it "Stood on the extremest verge of the swift brook/*Augmenting* it with tears." Though tears may literally *augment* dew and brooks, in solid prose it is advisable to confine the use of the word to instances of more substantial increase.

austere (aw steer') *adj. Austere* is generally used to describe a person's severe, stern, forbidding manner or appearance, but the word can also describe a rigorously disciplined way of life. The noun *austerity* (aw sterr' ə tee) is often heard when heads of state, on occasions of economic crisis, warn their people to be prepared to face a "period of *austerity*." One thinks of Dickensian headmasters as severe and *austere*, and of life in a monastery as rigorous and *austere*. *Austere* people are distant and forbidding. An *austere* life is hard and devoid of luxuries and frills. St. Luke (19:22) wrote: "Thou knewest that I was an *austere* man." The English mathematician and philosopher Bertrand Russell (1872-1970) wrote: "Mathematics . . . possesses not only truth, but supreme beauty—a beauty cold and *austere*. . . ." In her poem *Wild Peaches,* Elinor Wylie (1885-1928) wrote: "I love the look, *austere,* immaculate/Of landscapes drawn in pearly monotones." So, faces, manners, ways of life, art forms—all these can be described as *austere,* to portray the idea of severe simplicity, the absence of adornment, and in context, forbidding sternness.

authentic (aw then′ tik—*th* as in *thing*) *adj.* Anything or anyone *authentic* is trustworthy and can be relied on, genuine, supported by the best evidence; the real McCoy, as it were. We know what George Washington looked like because of the various *authentic* portraits of him by Gilbert Stuart (1775-1828). Experts can tell an *authentic* old master from a forgery. Detectives try to distinguish *authentic* evidence from misleading clues and red herrings. Indira and Jawaharlal are *authentic* Indian names, François an *authentic* French name, Kurt an *authentic* German one. The noun is *authenticity* (aw thən tis′ ə tee), meaning "genuineness." To *authenticate* (aw then′ tə kate) something is to establish its genuineness. You must go to an *authentic* gemologist to find out whether a gemstone is *authentic* or imitation, i.e., to determine its *authenticity.* If it is genuine, he will *authenticate* it. Only experts in the field can *authenticate* a real antique, distinguishing it from a clever imitation. Shakespeare, in *Troilus and Cressida* (Act III, Scene 2), has the hero protest his truthfulness by proclaiming himself to be "As truth's *authentic* author to be cited/'As true as Troilus.'. . ." Incidentally, did Shakespeare write all those plays? There are many who contest the *authenticity* of some of them.

autocrat (aw′ tə krat) *n.* Technically, an *autocrat* is an absolute ruler, but the term is commonly used to denote any person who conducts himself in a domineering manner, lording himself over others. The adjective, *autocratic* (aw tə krat′ ik), means "domineering, despotic, tyrannical," and is applicable to persons and their behavior. One can speak of a haughty unapproachable old duchess as *autocratic,* or describe her manner as *autocratic.* Kaiser Wilhelm II of Germany was an *autocrat* in both the technical and figurative senses of the word. Dr. Oliver Wendell Holmes (1809-1894), the famous physician and author, collected a series of his "breakfast-table" contributions to the *Atlantic Monthly* in a book entitled *The Autocrat of the Breakfast Table* (1858)—and well worth reading. *Autocracy* (aw tok′ rə see) is the word for the absolute powers of a despot or despotic government; it is also the name of a state ruled over by such a government. Happily, *autocracies* are thinning out nowadays, though a few still exist.

aver (ə ver′—*e* as in *her*) *vb.* To *aver* something is to state it confidently, in a positive way, without reservation. The term is commonly used in legal circles; it is a handy word in ordinary speech or writing in that it contains, in one short word, the concept of confidence and positiveness in what is said or written. The *-ver* part of *aver* is from the Latin word *verus,* meaning "true," the same word that gave us *verify, veritable, verity,* and other words concerned with truth. When you *aver* something, you really mean every word of what you say; you are *verifying* its *verity.*

averse (ə vurs´) *adj.* When you are *averse* to something, you find it distasteful and have a strong feeling of dislike toward it. Some people love the outdoor life; others are *averse* to it. The English poet Thomas Gray (1716-1771), in *Ode on the Death of a Favorite Cat*, asked: "What female heart can gold despise?/What cat's *averse* to fish?" *Averse* is sometimes a handy word to use in the negative, in a semijocular way, to describe an amiable weakness: Jones is a sensible fellow, but he is not *averse* to a bit of flattery now and then. The feeling of being *averse* to something is *aversion* (ə vur´ zhən), indicating real antipathy, strong distaste, repugnance. *Aversion*, like *averse*, is followed by *to*, rather than *from* (like, for example, *hostile*). Robert Louis Stevenson (1850-1894) has a character in *The Rajah's Diamond* say: "I regard you with an indifference closely bordering on *aversion*." (How much more elegantly can an insult be phrased?) The Latin word *(aversus)* from which we get *averse* means "turned off," which is a good way to describe *averse* in slang. Do not confuse *averse* with **adverse**.

aversion (ə vur´ zhən) *n.* See **averse**.

avert (ə vurt´—*u* as in *fur*) *vb.* To *avert* something is to turn it away, in the literal sense; figuratively, to prevent it or ward it off. A common use, in the literal sense, is to *avert one's eyes*. When someone is making an embarrassing spectacle of himself at a party, or when one comes upon the wreckage, including the victims, of an appalling accident, sensitive souls tend to *avert* their eyes. One tries to *avert* a calamity by warning those concerned. In a very high wind, it is often advisable to reef your sails in order to *avert* the danger of capsizing.

avid (av´ əd) *adj.* When one is *avid* for something, he wants it keenly, even greedily. A glutton is *avid* for food. A miser is *avid* for money. Dictators are *avid* for power. *Avid*, in this sense of greedy craving, is sometimes followed by *of* rather than *for*. The poet Robert Southey (1774-1843) wrote of one who was "*Avid* of gold, yet greedier of renown." But *avid* has a softer side: It can mean simply "enthusiastic." Some people are *avid* concertgoers; others are *avid* football fans. In this use, *avid* is synonymous with *ardent*. The American novelist Dorothy Canfield (1879-1958) described a character as showing "all the strength of his passion in that *avid* gaze."

avocation (av ə kay´ shən) *n.* See **vocation**.

avow (ə vow´—*ow* as in *wow*) *vb.* To *avow* something is to declare it openly, to own up to it, acknowledge it. When you *avow* your principles, you are willing to stand up and be counted. The word is commonly found in the adjectival form *avowed*, meaning "declared." An *avowed* communist (in a democratic society) is one who acknowledges his unpopular political beliefs. The act of *avowing* is an *avowal* (ə vow´ əl). George Canning (1770-1827), the English statesman (Prime Minister for a few months in 1827) and occasional poet, wrote:

Give me the *avowed,* erect and manly foe;
Firm I can meet, perhaps return the blow;
But of all plagues, good Heaven, thy wrath can send,
Save me, oh, save me from the candid friend.

In Shakespeare's *Henry VIII* (Act IV, Scene 2), the King's cast-off wife, Catherine of Aragon, begs the King to "have some pity upon" her women attendants, "Of which there is not one, I dare *avow!* . . . but will deserve . . ./A right good husband, let him be a noble. . . ." When you *disavow* something, you repudiate it. A politician will often *disavow* a previous statement or point of view when it no longer serves his purposes. Ex-communists who see the light loudly *disavow* their former beliefs. When you *disavow* a person, you disclaim any further connection with him, repudiating any previous agreement with or sponsorship of him and dissociating yourself from his present behavior or viewpoint.

aware (ə ware´) *adj.* To be *aware* of something is to have knowledge or consciousness of it. To be *aware* of a person is to know that he or she exists. You can be *aware* of danger, *aware* of someone's presence, *aware* of the work done in your field by a colleague. *Aware* can be used by itself to mean "informed, knowledgeable." The English poet Rupert Brooke (1887-1915), in his touching poem *The Soldier* ("If I should die . . ."), talked of his body as "A dust whom England bore, shaped, made *aware.*" *Aware* people get ahead in the world a lot faster than oblivious people. When the Macedonian general Antigonus (382-301 B.C.) was described as "Son of the Sun," he responded: "My valet is not *aware* of this." The French essayist Montaigne (1533-1592) echoed this observation in these terms: "Few men have been admired by their own households." Mme. Cornuel (1605-1694) came closer to Antigonus when she uttered the immortal words: "No man is a hero to his valet." Antigonus said it best, with his arch use of *aware.*

awkward (awk´ wərd) *adj.* An *awkward* person is clumsy and inept; an *awkward* manner or movement is ungraceful; an *awkward* situation is a tough one, hard to manage; an *awkward* moment is an embarrassing one. Adolescence is known as "the *awkward* age." A swan is one of the most graceful of birds in the water; on land it is one of the most *awkward.* Every actor who plays the title role in *The Hunchback of Notre-Dame* or Caliban in Shakespeare's *Tempest* has to be a master of *awkwardness.* In his last letter, John Keats (1795-1821) wrote a friend: "I can scarcely bid you good-bye, even in a letter. I always made an *awkward* bow. . . ." The word is applicable to many things, all the way from the ungainly movements of people to difficult situations. The British use *awkward* of people the way Americans use it of situations, meaning "difficult," in the sense of "troublesome, hard to deal with." This is a vivid description of that sort of person, and worth adopting.

badger (baj´ ər) *vb*. It is inconsiderate to *badger* anyone, for to *badger* someone is to harass him by keeping after him persistently and mercilessly, to pester and to bait him. (In fact, the verb is based on the sport of baiting the burrowing animals known as *badgers*.) In many Middle Eastern and Asian countries, travelers are usually *badgered* by beggars and street vendors ("Him fake; me real antique!"). Unfortunately, one of the most frequent uses of *badger* is in the negative imperative: "For heaven's sake, stop *badgering* me!"

baffle (baf´ l) *vb*. When you are *baffled*, you are stumped, perplexed, puzzled, defeated, and stopped by confusion. Those "simple, easy instructions" that come with kits (especially from the Mysterious East) are usually couched in *baffling* language. Most people are hopelessly *baffled* by any attempt to explain the Theory of Relativity. When Rudolf Hess dropped into Scotland by parachute in 1941, Winston Churchill (1874–1965) commented in the House of Commons: "This is one of those cases in which the imagination is *baffled* by the facts." Many are those who understand facts but are *baffled* by ideas. Most Americans who do well with crossword puzzles in American newspapers are completely *baffled* by those in English newspapers. This verb is most often found in the passive: *I was baffled by* . . . is much more common than *such-and-such baffled me*.

balk (bawk) *vb*. One can *balk* at something, or *be balked* by something. Even when the facts against him have been proved, an accused will *balk* at making a confession. Little children often *balk* at washing behind the ears. The hopes of rescuing our hostages in Iran were *balked* by the mechanical failure of helicopters. A related adjective is *balky*, meaning "obstinate, stubborn." *Balky* can be applied to human beings who resist attempts to persuade them to do something (most little children are *balky* about kissing Great-Aunt Emilia), but the term is more often applied to animals, especially those managed by man, like donkeys and horses.

balm (bahm) *n*. *Balm* is, literally, a fragrant resin, often of medicinal value. Gilead, a district of ancient Palestine (now Jordan), was known for its *balm*. Hence the fiery prophet's question, berating the children of Israel (Jeremiah 8:22): "Is there no *balm* in Gilead?" Meaning "Is there no remedy, no consolation" for those who have forsaken the laws of God? *Balm* can also denote the fragrance itself: One can speak of the *balm* of fruit blossoms. But the commonest use of the word is in its figurative sense: anything which is a healing, soothing agent, whether the pain be physical or spiritual. One can apply a *balm* or an ointment to an ailing body or ailing spirits. *Baume Bengué* is the original trademark of an ointment to apply to aching muscles; *baume* is French for *balm*. One can use the word in a loftier sense: What is so helpful as the *balm* of understanding in times of trouble? In Shakespeare's *Macbeth* (Act II, Scene 2), the agonized Macbeth longs for sleep, the "*balm* of hurt minds." The related adjective *balmy* usually means either "fragrant" or "soft and soothing," depending on the context. *Balmy* weather is mild and enjoyable. On the other hand, a *balmy* person is slightly demented. This usage seems hardly related to any of the meanings of *balm*; it would appear to be a corruption or variant of the British word *barmy*, meaning "silly," and based on the word *barm*, the name for the froth on fementing malt liquor. *Frothy* is not too far from *balmy* or *silly*.

banish (ban´əsh) *vb*. Literally, *banish* and the noun *banishment* are the terms used when a government officially condemns a person to exile. In Shakespeare's *Romeo and Juliet* (Act III, Scene 2), the Nurse announces to Juliet, "Tybalt is gone, and Romeo *banished;* Romeo, that kill'd him, he is *banished*." And later in the scene, Juliet repeats: " 'Tybalt is dead, and Romeo *banished*!'/That '*banished*,' that one word, '*banished*,'/Hath slain ten thousand Tybalts." (The *e* in *banished* has to be pronounced to keep the rhythm right.) Today, *banishment* to Siberia seems to be a favorite Soviet punishment for dissidents. These are literal *banishments*. The word is used figuratively to mean "drive away" in expressions like *banish sorrow* or *banish care*. Thomas Heywood (1574-1641) wrote: "Pack clouds away, and welcome day,/With night we *banish* sorrow." In *The Miner's Dream of Home* by William Godwin (1756-1836), we read:

> There is a land of pure delight,
> Where saints immortal reign;
> Infinite day excludes the night,
> And pleasures *banish* pain.

banter (ban´tər) *n., vb*. When you *banter* with someone, you indulge in an exchange of light-hearted, playful conversation and good-natured, well-meant teasing. The noun for that kind of playful exchange is likewise *banter*. Viscount Bolingbroke (1678-1751) used *banter* in the sense of "tease" in a letter written in 1714: "What a world this is, and how does fortune *banter* us." The word is met most commonly as a noun: "How did you spend your day?" "Mostly in idle *banter*." *Banter* suggests the kind of exchange that typifies conversational openings at parties or in singles bars. (Later, things may become more serious.)

barb (barb) *n*. A *barb*, literally, is a point projecting backward like that on the end of a fishhook. It is the small bits of wire twisted around the main wire that gives its name to *barbwire*. An arrowhead is also a *barb*. Olive Schreiner (1855-1920) thought of that when she wrote, in *The Story of an African Farm*: "The *barb* in the arrow of childhood suffering is this: its intense loneliness. . . ." Figuratively, the word is commonly used to denote an unpleasantly sharp remark, the kind that is intended to leave a sting. A verbal *barb* sticks in, like a fishhook or an arrowhead; it is intentional and malicious. Dorothy Parker (1893-1967) was given to the making of witty barbs, especially as a drama critic. She described the acting of a young actress in these terms: "[She] runs the gamut of emotions from A to B"; and she commented on a theatrical production in these words: "*The House Beautiful* is the play lousy." (Some critics are often happy to damn a play with a *barb*.) Alexander Woollcott (1887-1943) was another expert in the well-aimed *barb*. In *The Actor and the Streetwalker*, he took a shot at amateur theatricals: "The two oldest professions in the world—ruined by amateurs."

barbarous (bahr´ bə rəs) *adj*. This word should be considered along with two others from the same Greco-Latin root: *barbarian* (bar bair´ ee ən) and *barbaric* (bar bar´ ik—second *a* as in *hat*). *Barbarous* is used most often in a way that implies a degree of contempt: One accuses people of *barbarous* cruelty, *barbarous* ignorance, *barbarous* manners, *barbarous* treatment. *Barbarian* is a noun as well as an adjective, and is used in a more literal sense than *barbarous*: There are *barbarian* people, really uncivilized; but the word can be used figuratively in a phrase like *barbarian courage*, the *barbarian* (uneducated) world. *Barbaric* does not imply contempt, but rather refers to the primitive, simple, uncultured ways of *barbarian* people, in phrases like *barbaric* taste, *barbaric* jewelry or ornaments, *barbaric* simplicity. There might be a hint of wonderment, perhaps admiration, in *barbaric*, when it is used to describe, for example, an African chief resplendent in his *barbaric* finery, or the *barbaric* rhythms of some passages in Stravinsky. It is best, then, to confine *barbarous* to uses that are derogatory, in which we look down on the things and activities so described. We condemn the *barbarous* conduct of hoodlums at rock concerts. We despise the *barbarous* ignorance even of college people who cannot spell, who know no history or literature. We deplore the *barbarous* treatment of political prisoners in dictatorships, and, most of all, look back with disgust at the *barbarous* holocaust set in motion by the Nazis.

barren (bar´ ən—*a* as in *hat*) *adj*. This word has a variety of uses. Applied to land, it means "unproductive," like the Sahara Desert. A *barren* woman is incapable of having children. In Shakespeare's *Julius Caesar* (Act I, Scene 2), Caesar reminds Antony to touch Caesar's *barren* wife Calpurnia while taking part in the race run at the festival known as the *Lupercalia*: "Forget not, in your speed, Antonius,/To touch Calpurnia; for our elders say,/The *barren*, touched in this holy chase,/Shake off their sterile curse." One can speak of a *barren attempt* or *effort*—one that produces no results. Certain periods in the history of a country are described as *barren*, when nothing of cultural or historical interest has occurred. This versatile adjective, then, can apply in any situation where the basic concept is that of unproductiveness and sterility, whether it apply to agriculture, people, or a passage in history. Exercise your mentality; a *barren* mind produces no ideas.

barrier (bar´ ee ər—*a* as in *hat*) *n*. A *barrier*, as the name implies, is something that *bars* your way. The word can be used literally, to describe a gate or a mountain. Steep mountains are a *barrier* against easy passage, as in Tibet or Switzerland. The British call the gate that leads onto a train platform a *barrier*, where you must show your ticket on entering, and surrender it on leaving. In the figurative sense, *barrier* is used to describe anything that obstructs activity or progress. Ignorance of another country's language is a *barrier* to better relations among nations. High import duties are a trade *barrier*. The caste system is a *barrier* to social progress in India. Helen Keller (1880-1968), who was deaf, dumb, and blind, said: "Literature is my Utopia. . . . No *barrier* of the senses shuts me out from . . . books. . . ." The French statesman and author Alexis de Tocqueville (1805-1859), in *The Discovery of America*, wrote: "The power vested in the American courts . . . to declare a statute to be unconstitutional forms one of the most powerful *barriers* that have ever been devised against the tyranny of political assemblies." William Wordsworth (1770-1850) used the word more poetically when he called sleep "Blessed *barrier* between day and day." Did you know that the great English poet John Keats (1795-1821) was a sexual chauvinist? He wrote: "The opinion I have of the generality of women . . . forms a *barrier* against matrimony which I rejoice in."

barter (bahr′ tər) *n., vb.* To *barter* is to exchange goods for goods, without the use of money. *Barter* is also the noun for this process. In primitive cultures, *barter* is the common means of trade, in the absence of the concept of money. With the invention of money, *barter* decreased, but it still persists in periods of economic depression. The term *barter*, especially in the phrase *barter away*, is used figuratively in the sense of bargaining something away foolishly—selling your birthright, as it were, for a mess of pottage. There are legends about the simple soul who starts out from home to sell his cow at the market, and *barters* it for something of less value which he *barters* for something of still less value and keeps *bartering* until he has nothing of value left. People without principle will *barter away* their honor for material advancement. Services as well as merchandise can be *bartered*, like legal advice, in return for medical help, or five haircuts for servicing the barber's jalopy.

bawdy (baw′ dee) *adj.* Anything *bawdy* is obscene and lewd. Some people delight in telling *bawdy* stories, commonly known as dirty jokes. The word comes from *bawd*, the word for a *madam*, a keeper of a brothel, which is also known as a *bawdyhouse*. (*Whorehouse* is the commoner term.) In Shakespeare's *Henry IV, Part 1* (Act III, Scene 3), Falstaff, feeling out of sorts and sorry for himself, says to his pal Bardolph: " . . . come, sing me a *bawdy* song; make me merry." He had not been to a *"bawdyhouse"* more than "once in a quarter—of an hour"! In the prologue to *Henry VIII*, the speaker announces to the audience that this is a serious play: " . . . they/That come to hear a merry, *bawdy* play/ . . . Will be deceived."

bearing (bair′ ing) *n.* This word has, among others, two distinct uses: a person's *bearing* is the way he outwardly shows the world his personality—the kind of person he is, his character, as far as outward appearance and particularly posture can indicate it. One can exhibit a slovenly *bearing* or a dignified *bearing*. One thinks of those Victorian and Edwardian forefathers as men and women of dignified and somewhat forbidding *bearing*. We associate hippies with sloppy *bearing*, and gangsters with frightening *bearing*. An entirely different meaning of *bearing*, usually followed by the preposition *on*, is "relation." The phases of the moon have a decisive *bearing* on the tides. The way a case is presented in court may have a decisive *bearing* on the outcome. The Greek philosopher Aristotle (384–322 B.C.) wrote: "To enjoy the things we ought and to hate the things we ought has the greatest *bearing* on excellence of character." These uses of *bearing* are so different that the meaning will easily be made clear by the context.

beckon (bek′ ən) *vb*. To *beckon* someone is to give him a signal by a gesture, usually of the head or hand. Thomas Tickell (1686–1740), the English poet, wrote:

> I hear a voice you cannot hear,
>   Which says I must not stay;
> I see a hand you cannot see,
>   Which *beckons* me away.

In Shakespeare's *Hamlet* (Act I, Scene 4), the stage direction is: "The Ghost *beckons* Hamlet," and Horatio says to Hamlet: "It *beckons* you to go away with it. . . ." In *Henry VI, Part 1* (Act I, Scene 4), Lord Talbot, coming upon the dying Earl of Salisbury, says: "He *beckons* with his hand and smiles on me. . . ." The usual purpose of *beckoning* is to give a silent signal, but *beckon* can sometimes have the implication of enticement or invitation: in eighteenth-century novels, women of free manners were often depicted as *beckoning* a man with their eyes or a shrug or a toss of the head. Margery Allingham (1904–1966), the English detective-story writer, made much of the silent signal in her chilling whodunit called *The Beckoning Lady*.

bedevil (bih dev′ əl) *vb*. A person *bedeviled* is one tormented or beset or plagued by problems or worries or doubts and indecision. A nation is sometimes *bedeviled* by economic woes, a company by strikes, an apartment or office building by power failures. A.E. Housman (1859–1936) cried out against *bedevilment* (bih dev′ əl mənt) in one of his *Last Poems*:

> . . . let God and man decree
> Laws for themselves and not for me.
> . . . how am I to face the odds
> Of man's *bedevilment* and God's?

The general idea of *bedevilment* is torment, which, after all, is the special function of those awful creatures in hell, with their forked tails and pitchforks.

befall (bih fol′) *vb*. *Befall* is another way of saying *happen* or *occur*, with the implication, usually, that what happened was something grave and fated. It was said by Marcus Aurelius, philosopher and Emperor of Rome (121–180), "Whatever happens at all happens as it should . . . whatever may *befall* you, it was preordained from everlasting." In the Apocrypha we read: " . . . bear with good courage that which hath *befallen* thee." In Shakespeare's *Henry VI, Part 3* (Act III, Scene 1), a hunter, to pass the time of day, says to another: "I'll tell thee what *befell* me on a day/In this self [same] place. . . . " It may seem, from the sources of these quotations, that *befall* is a word reserved for philosophers and writers. It isn't; there is no reason why, as you return home you cannot say to your family, "Let me tell you what *befell* me on my way home just now. . . ."

beguile (bih gīle´—*g* as in *good*) *vb*. Despite this word's being based on the noun *guile,* meaning "deception, cunning," the common meaning of *beguile* is to "charm," not necessarily with *guile* or any intention to lead one down the garden path. An innocent maid may be quite *beguiling* to men; an attractive resort may quite legitimately *beguile* tourists to stay and enjoy its charms. The word is versatile, however, and can be used to express intentional misleading. In Genesis 3:13, Eve explains to God: "The serpent *beguiled* me, and I ate." (In the *New English Bible,* the verb is *tricked.*) The context will determine whether or not the *beguiling* is innocent. *Beguiling,* as an adjective, is perhaps the most common form of *beguile,* in the same way that *charming* comes from the verb *to charm. Beguiling* (in its innocent sense) means simply "charming," or "bewitching."

behalf (bih haf´—*a* as in *hat* or *hand*) *n*. This word is not used alone, but in the following ways: If I act *on your behalf,* I am acting either as your representative, or in your interest, depending on the context. When someone opens his remarks at a meeting by saying: "I speak to you this evening *on behalf of* all the members of my union," he means that he is representing them in expressing the point of view of the membership. In other words, he has their proxy. Sometimes, a person will say, "I am speaking only *on my own behalf"* in order to make it clear that he is not representing anyone else. But when I come to you and ask you for a loan *on behalf* (or *in behalf*) of my friend Jones, the phrase means that I am acting not so much as his representative as in his interest, to help him. The circumstances should make it clear whether you are speaking as someone's representative, with his authority, or in his interest with or without his authority. "On whose *behalf* are you here?" is a proper question for a chairman or moderator to put to a person rising to speak at a meeting. In that case, the question means "Whom are you representing?"

belated (bə lay´ təd) *adj*. Anyone or anything that arrives or happens behind schedule may be described as *belated.* If you forget to congratulate a friend who has achieved a success, and then suddenly remember, you can send your "*belated* congratulations." Unless too much time has elapsed since Aunt Agatha's eightieth birthday, you can always send (and so describe) a *belated* gift, together with whatever explanation and excuse you can dream up. *Belated* best wishes are better than none.

belittle (bə lit´l) *vb*. To *belittle* someone or something is to disparage it, i.e. to talk about a person or thing in unflattering terms, to describe him or it as unimpressive, or, as the word itself implies, to make him or it "little." Damning with faint praise is a favorite form of *belittling*. "What did you think of the Taj Mahal?" "Oh, it's quite nice in its way." "How did you like *Romeo and Juliet?*" "I've had more exciting evenings." To *belittle,* then, is to minimize, run down, pooh-pooh. The implication in *belittle* is that the *belittler* is attempting to enlarge his own importance by assigning less value to what he is *belittling* than it really deserves.

benevolent (bə nev′ ə lənt) *adj.* *Benevolent* describes those who aim to do good. *Malevolent* (mə lev′ ə lənt) is its opposite. People always ready to offer their services in a crisis are *benevolent* members of society. Their attitude is called *benevolence* (bə nev′ ə ləns), goodwill, the desire to benefit their fellow men. Robert Burns (1759-1796) wrote, in *A Winter Night:* "The heart *benevolent* and kind/The most resembles God." But Walter Bagehot, the English economist (1826-1877), expressed a less glowing view of *benevolence*: "The most melancholy of human reflections, perhaps, is that on the whole it is a question whether the *benevolence* of mankind does most harm or good." Not only people may be described as *benevolent*: One may speak of someone's having a *benevolent* attitude toward his neighbors, or as always ready with a *benevolent* smile.

benign (bih nine′) *adj.* This word should be discussed with *benignant* (bə nig′ nənt), *malign* (mə line′), and *malignant* (mə lig′ nənt). A *benign* person is kindly disposed towards his fellow man; a *benignant* person is kind, especially with the implication that he is kind to those inferior to him in social rank, like a *benignant* ruler, and exerts a good influence. A *malign* person has an evil disposition and an evil effect on people; a *malignant* person not only exhibits ill will but is out to cause harm deliberately. These distinctions are not always observed, and it might be safer to stick to *benign* and *malign*: one is attracted to a person with a *benign* smile, and repelled by one with a *malign* look. *Benign* and *malign* can both be applied to things as well as people. William Wordsworth (1770-1850) wrote that when we are tired of the ". . . hurrying world . . . ,/How gracious, how *benign* is Solitude." And Bishop William Stubbs (1825-1901), decrying the feud between the historian James Froude (1818-1894) and the Rev. Charles Kingsley (1819-1875), poet and novelist, wrote: "What cause for judgments so *malign?*" Remember that *malign* is also a verb, meaning "slander, defame," whereas *benign* is only an adjective; and that a harmless growth or tumor is *benign,* while a cancerous one is not *malign,* but *malignant.*

bent (bent) *n.* One's *bent* is one's leaning or inclination, what one is interested in. Some people have a *bent* for music, others are tone-deaf. Accountants have a *bent* for figures. Unless you have a *bent* for a particular profession, better not pursue it. Plato (428-348 B.C.) advised: "Let early education be a sort of amusement; you will then be better able to find out . . . [your] natural *bent.*" Charles Sanders Peirce (1839-1914), the American philosopher, wrote: "Unless a man have a natural *bent* in accordance with nature's, he has no chance of understanding nature at all." Rudyard Kipling (1865-1936) told us, ". . . a fool must follow his natural *bent*/(Even as you and I!). . . ." Apparently, *bent* is most commonly found in the phrase *natural bent,* which sounds, in a way, like a bit of tautology (needless repetition), since the word *bent* would seem to have "natural" built into it.

berate (bih rāte´) *vb.* This is a very strong word; when you *berate* someone, you scold and upbraid him in the harshest terms. If children misbehave in public, it is proper for parents to chide or rebuke, but not to *berate* them; rather, take them to task in private, and explain the nature of their misdeed. When Oliver Twist, poor boy, outraged the school authorities by asking for an additional helping of porridge, he was answered with an outraged "More?" and soundly *berated* for his impudence. *Berating* is much more than simple rebuke; it contains the elements of harshness and violence. Disapproval, criticism, chiding, rebuke, and scolding are involved; upbraiding is close; *berating* is extreme, and involves vilification and harsh abuse. Scold if you must, but save *berating* for situations where you really want to throw the book at somebody. See also **upbraid.**

bereave (bih reev´) *vb. Bereave* has the general meaning of "deprive," cruelly and by force; but the common form of its use is *bereaved,* as an adjective with *spouse, child, parent,* or other relative, to describe the recent and desolating loss of a loved one, as in a phrase like *the weeping face of the bereaved widow.* One reads of the anguish of the recently *bereaved* mother in times of war. There is another form, *bereft,* used in somewhat different contexts, especially in the phrase *bereft of one's senses.* One might describe a person whose home has been emptied by burglars or destroyed by fire as *bereft* of his possessions, but this is a rather literary usage and in most quarters would probably be considered high-flown in everyday speech. The noun is *bereavement* (bə reev´ mənt). After many years of happy marriage, one may suffer acutely at one's *bereavement* on the death of beloved spouse. *Bereavement* conveys a sense of painful loss, of recent vintage.

beset (bih set´) *vb.* To *beset* is to attack, especially in the sense of *trouble,* or *harass.* The word is almost always met with in its figurative rather than its literal military use: One is *beset* by problems, difficulties, fears, worries, temptations. St. Paul, in his *Epistle to the Hebrews,* wrote of "sin which doth so easily *beset* us," and Elinor Wylie (1885-1928) wrote: "I am, being woman, hard *beset* . . ." without specifying any cause except the lot of women in general. In Shakespeare's *The Merchant of Venice* (Act I, Scene 1), Bassanio explains to Portia that he sent her ring to the lawyer who had defended Antonio (Portia herself, in disguise) because, having refused to give it at first, he was later "*beset* with shame." The physician and philosopher Peter Latham (1789-1875), discussing research, wrote: "It is no easy task to pick one's way from truth to truth through *besetting* errors."

betray (bih tray´) *vb. Betray* can be used in a variety of ways. One can *betray* a person, as Judas *betrayed* Jesus. In such a usage, to *betray* is not only to be disloyal, but to turn someone over to the enemy. *Betray* is used more abstractly in situations where one *betrays* a trust, a confidence, or a secret. A guardian who uses his ward's money for his own purposes *betrays* a trust. When one fails to keep to himself something told in confidence, he *betrays* that confidence. When you reveal something involuntarily that you would rather have kept concealed, like showing that you're nervous by trembling, your manner *betrays* your nervousness. Bad manners may *betray* a poor upbringing. In these cases, to *betray* means to "expose unconsciously." The noun is *betrayal* (bih tray' əl).

bewitch (bih wich') *vb.* Literally, to *bewitch* someone is to cast a spell over him, as witches were supposed to be able to do; but the word as used today is simply a figurative intensification of the verbs to *charm, fascinate,* or *enchant. Charms* and *enchantments* were once actually used as well, in the days when people took magic and witchcraft seriously. *Bewitching* is a complimentary adjective, applied usually to lovely young women who steal men's hearts away, and is equivalent to *enchanting* and *captivating.* Lorenz Hart (1895-1943) wrote the lyrics for a song about falling in love, for the 1940 musical *Pal Joey,* entitled "*Bewitched,* Bothered and Bewildered." In Shakespeare's *Henry IV, Part 1* (Act II, Scene 2), Falstaff exclaims about Poins, whose company he has tried to give up for twenty-two years: ". . . yet I am *bewitched* with the rogue's company." *Bewitching* is a lovely way to describe a fascinating woman, but it can apply to a place (a *bewitching* little village, a *bewitching* solitary forest) or to a work of art (a *bewitching* melody, a *bewitching* portrait or piece of verse).

bicker (bik' ər) *vb. Bickering* is the unpleasant act of wrangling, engaging in ill-humored argument and peevish quarreling. Some married couples seem to *bicker* continually as a way of life. The French essayist Michel de Montaigne (1533-1592) wrote: "The same reason that makes us *bicker* with a neighbor creates a war between [nations]." John Milton (1608-1674), in *The History of England,* impatient with detailed accounts of England's quarrels, wrote: "Such *bickerings* to recount, met often in these our writers, what more worth is it than to chronicle the wars of kites or crows flocking and fighting in the air?" In Shakespeare's *Henry VI, Part 2* (Act I, Scene 1), the Duke of Gloucester says to the Bishop of Winchester, his political foe: ". . . 'tis my presence that doth trouble ye./"Rancour will out . . ./ . . . If I longer stay/We shall begin our ancient *bickerings.*" To characterize a dispute as *bickering* is to condemn it as petty, irritating to witness, and worthy only of contemptuous disregard.

bilingual (by ling' gwəl) *adj.* A *bilingual* person is as fluent in a second language as in his native tongue. A *bilingual* notice is written or a *bilingual* address is given in two different languages. It will come as no surprise, then, to learn that the adjective *trilingual* is concerned with three languages, *quadrilingual* four, and so on and so on, having in mind the Tower of Babel. *Multilingual* applies to any number over two. A *multilingual* secretary is much in demand in these days of multinational companies. The electronic system at the United Nations makes possible *multilingual* simultaneous translation via earphones.

biped (by' ped) *n., adj.* This term applies to any two-footed animal, all the way from the lowly chicken to that noblest work of nature, man. Plato (428-348 B.C.) wrote: "Seeing that the human race falls into the same classification as the feathered creatures, we must divide the *biped* class into featherless and feathered." According to the Greek philosopher Diogenes the Cynic (400-325 B.C.)—the one who carried a lighted lamp in daylight, searching for an honest man—"Plato having defined man to be a two-legged animal without feathers, Diogenes plucked a cock and . . . said, 'This is Plato's man.' " An echo of Plato's definition is heard in a poem by John Dryden (1631-1700): "And all to leave what with his toil he won/To that unfeathered two-legged thing, a son." There would appear to be no *tripeds* (though we all know about *tripods*) and we must skip to *quadrupeds* (any four-footed animal), *octopods* (eight-footed creatures), and eventually *centipedes* (which include insects with anything from 30 to 346 legs).

bizarre (bih zahr´) *adj.* Anyone or anything *bizarre* is strange, odd, eccentric in appearance or character. A person can appear *bizarre* because of weird clothing, makeup, mannerisms, or general behavior. *Bizarre* can be applied not only to persons but to things: dress or conduct, a building, a ship, a language, anything. *Bizarre* attire or manners mark eccentric people, who either want to call attention to themselves or don't know any better. The multicolored costumes of gypsies are *bizarre*. When a fire is blazing in the fireplace, it often casts *bizarre* shadows on the walls. Impressionist paintings, now sought after at incredible prices, were originally spurned as *bizarre*. Surrealist painters like Dali achieve *bizarreness* by putting together improbable combinations of things in one composition. Contemporary composers achieve *bizarre* results through clashing notes and chords and the absence of melody or key.

bland (bland) *adj.* The principal meaning of *bland* is "gentle, smooth, tranquil, soothing." All the idols of Buddha show him in contemplation, with a *bland*, imperturbable face. William Ernest Henley (1849-1903) described his hospital surgeon as *"Bland* as a Jesuit, sober as a hymn." Matthew Arnold (1832-1904) wrote about the Roman Emperor Tiberius in these words:

> Cruel, but composed and *bland,*
> Dumb, inscrutable and grand,
> So Tiberius might have sat,
> Had Tiberius been a cat.

Oliver Goldsmith (1728-1774) remembered the painter Joshua Reynolds (1723-1792) in lovely lines: "His pencil was striking, resistless, and grand;/His manners were gentle, complying, and *bland*. . . ." Bret Harte (1839-1902) wrote of a "smile that was childlike and *bland.*" This word, usually complimentary, has been used unflatteringly as well, to describe dull or even insipid people, *too bland,* as it were, lacking in personality. *Bland* can mean "unemotional, casual," in expressions like *a bland admission of guilt* or *the bland acceptance of one's fate*. Finally, we are familiar with the use of the word as it refers to *bland,* tasteless food or to the *bland* diet prescribed for people with ulcers.

blasphemy (blas´ fə mee) *n.* This is the name given to words or actions that show disrespect for God or anything sacred. Such words or acts are *blasphemous* (blas´

fə məs), and to utter or commit them is to *blaspheme* (blas feem'). In Matthew 12:31 we read: "The *blasphemy* against the Holy Ghost shall not be forgiven unto men." *The Book of Common Prayer* condemns "*blasphemous* fables, and dangerous deceits." But George Bernard Shaw (1856-1950), using the word more generally to include defiance of accepted beliefs, religious or other, wrote: "All great truths begin as *blasphemies*." In a similar vein, the French philosopher Blaise Pascal (1623-1662) said: "Men *blaspheme* what they do not know." Here, as in Shaw's usage, *blaspheme* does not imply behavior against God or sacred things, but rather condemnation of current, accepted thinking.

bleak (bleek) *adj.* The literal meaning of *bleak* is "desolate, bare," as in the description of a *bleak*, barren, windswept wasteland, or a *bleak*, dreary, gloomy house. *Bleak* is used figuratively to mean "hopeless, dreary," as a description of a person's prospects and outlook. Edgar Allan Poe (1809-1849) set an ominous note early in his poem "The Raven" with the words: "Ah, distinctly I remember it was in the *bleak* December. . . ." Winter is indeed the *bleak* season. Christina Rossetti (1830-84) starts her poem "Mid-Winter": "In the *bleak* midwinter/Frosty wind made moan. . . ." Charles Dickens (1812-1870) wrote a novel entitled *Bleak House*. *Bleak* is a forceful descriptive word in its figurative sense as well: "How do things look?" "*Bleak*!" Things were *bleak* indeed in the Great Depression (October 1929 through the 1930s), when unemployment was rife and the soup kitchens and breadlines were filled with hopeless men and women.

bliss (blis) *n.* Bliss is the highest happiness, utter joy and contentment, and such a condition, or anything that produces it, is *blissful*. Marriage has been called "wedded *bliss*" (*single blessedness* is the reverse of the coin). The German poet and dramatist Friedrich von Schiller (1759-1805) wrote of "The golden time of first love" when "The heart is intoxicated with *bliss*. . . ." The English poets William Wordsworth (1770-1850) wrote of ". . . the *bliss* of solitude," and George Cooper (1838-1927) of "The *blissful* dreams of long ago." Thomas Gray (1716-1771) coined an immortal phrase when he wrote: "Where ignorance is *bliss*/'Tis folly to be wise."

bluff (bluf—*u* as in *but*) *adj.* Applied to people or their manners, *bluff* means "frank, abrupt, outspoken" in a hearty well-meant way. A *bluff* response or statement, though brief and to the point, is good-natured in a rough way, with no trace of malice. *Bluff* people are hale and hearty; one thinks of them as big, burly, and generous. Henry VIII of England (1491-1547) was known as *Bluff* Harry or *Bluff* King Hal from his portly stance and the lighter side of his nature. A kind answer turneth away wrath, but you never can tell with a *bluff* one, especially when dealing with sensitive souls.

blunt (blunt) *adj.* A *blunt* person is abrupt in manner, particularly in speech, and lacking polish and sensibility. *Blunt* can be applied as well to statements, remarks, and replies. Unlike a soft answer, which turneth away wrath, a *blunt* answer sometimes turneth away friends. *Blunt*, whether applied to people or their manners or speech, implies a lack of consideration for the feelings of others, as opposed to **bluff**, which has in it the element of good nature. In Shakespeare's *Julius Caesar* (Act III, Scene 2), Antony, toward the end of the funeral oration, tells his audience: "I am no orator, as Brutus is;/But, as you know me all, a plain *blunt* man. . . ." Earlier in the play (Act I, Scene 2), Brutus characterizes the plain-spoken Casca in these terms: "What a *blunt* fellow is this grown to be!" *Blunt* people come to the point without worrying too much about the other fellow's feelings, and sometimes attempt to soften the blow by introducing what is to come with "Well, to be *blunt* about it. . . ."

bluster (blus′ tər) *n., vb. Bluster* describes any noisy and violent talk, especially the threatening or boastful kind. Bullies are full of bluff and *bluster*. To *bluster* is to utter loud, boastful threats. *Blustering,* as an adjective, can be applied not only to noisy, threatening bullies, but to the weather as well: One can describe a stormy, windy day as *blustering*. In *Henry IV, Part 1* (Act V, Scene 1), Prince Henry comments on the weather: "The southern wind/ . . . by his hollow whistling in the leaves/Foretells a tempest and a *blustering* day." *Bluster,* whether noun or verb, and *blustering,* as adjective, evoke unpleasant images, whether they apply to boisterous, swaggering people, or windy, stormy weather.

boisterous (boy′ stər əs, boy′ strəs) *adj. Boisterous* people are noisy, rough, and rowdy. The word can describe manners as well as people. The *boisterous* behavior of one guest can upset an entire dinner party. As a festive evening wears on, with the help of wine the mirth and spirits of the guests become more and more *boisterous*. *Boisterous,* like *blustering,* can apply to weather as well as to people and their manners. Applied to wind and sea and weather generally, *boisterous* describes rough, stormy conditions, but its main use is to describe the manners of people. Children at school, the moment the teacher leaves the room, tend to become *boisterous* and unruly. *Boisterousness* often marks the conduct of crowds at hotly contested sporting events, or the carryings-on of old-timers at a reunion.

bombastic (bom bas′ tik) *adj. Bombastic* speech or writing is high-sounding, pretentious, and pompous, meant to impress with high-flown words and phrases, often covering a lack or poverty of content. *Bombast* (bom′ bast) is the noun for high-sounding words, language too elaborate for the occasion. The first-century Roman writer Longinus criticizes the Roman poet Lucan (39–65) in these terms: "It frequently happens that where the second line is sublime, the third, in which he meant to rise still higher, is perfect *bombast*." In the play *The Frogs,* the Greek writer of comedies Aristophanes (450–385 B.C.) invented a word from a combination of *bombastic* and *eloquent* to describe the Greek dramatist Aeschylus (525–456 B.C.), calling him "Uncurbed, unfettered, uncontrolled of speech/ . . . *bombastiloquent*." One must, in speech and writing, draw the line between eloquence and *bombast*. *Bombastic* excess has been referred to as "purple prose."

boon (boon—*oo* as in *boot*) *n*. A *boon* is a benefit, anything to be enjoyed and grateful for, an advantage, a blessing. Robert Browning (1812–1889) wrote of "the *boon* of life," and picking up on that, W.S. Gilbert (the Gilbert of Gilbert & Sullivan—1836–1911) wrote these lyrics in *The Yeoman of the Guard* (Act I):

> Is life a *boon*?
> If so, it must befall
> That Death, whene'er he call,
> Must call too soon.

The invention of the automobile was a *boon* to travel, and, like many such *boons*, brought with it the horrors of pollution and traffic jams. The discovery of penicillin was a *boon* to all mankind. The *boon* in *boon companion*, rarely used except in that expression, means "jovial, convivial," is an adjective, and comes from a different root.

braggart (brag′ ərt) *n*. A *braggart* is a person who *brags* or boasts, and is given to recounting—and often exaggerating—his own virtues and accomplishments. According to Mercutio, in Shakespeare's *Romeo and Juliet* (Act III, Scene 1), Tybalt, who has just mortally wounded him in a duel, was "a dog, a rat, a mouse, a cat . . . a *braggart*, a rogue, a villain." A *braggart* is conceited, full of himself, and the very opposite of modest, shy, or retiring. In Shakespeare's *Timon of Athens* (Act IV, Scene 3), Timon curses "the unscarr'd *braggarts* of the war," i.e., those who escaped being wounded, presumably by playing it safe, but who are just the ones to *brag* about their exploits and bravery. The *-art* ending tacked on to *brag* is a variant of the more familiar *-ard*, seen in *coward, drunkard*, etc.

brash (brash) *adj*. A *brash* person or act is hasty and rough, impetuous, rash, totally lacking in finesse. This adjective was described as obsolete in England by the year 1888 by the *Oxford English Dictionary*, but stayed on in the U.S., first as a colloquialism, then as good, standard English. Sir Ernest Gowers (1880–1966), the reviser of the work of H.W. Fowler (1858–1933), comments in *Modern English Usage* on the use of *brash* by various English journalists showing that *brash* was eventually revived in Great Britain, as in "the United States' *brash* and clumsy political warfare . . . in S.E. Asia." "Bagehot [Walter Bagehot (1826–1877), the English political journalist] . . . equated [democracy] with the *brash* and vulgar American republic." The British are very orderly as they stand in taxi, bus, and other queues; the French and Germans are *brash* in their zeal to get there first. The adopted waif Heathcliff, in *Wuthering Heights*, by Emily Brontë (1818–1848), is the prototype of a *brash* country lad.

bridle (brī′d'l) *vb*. To *bridle* is to show resentment or scorn, especially by drawing up the head and drawing in the chin, thus taking on a lofty pose and assuming a disdainful manner. One *bridles at* the appearance of the disdained person or the speaking of the resented words. Until Pope John II visited Great Britain in 1982 and charmed millions all over the world by his winning ways, good Protestants used to *bridle* at the very mention of the Pope. Those trained in the proper use of English *bridle* at "between you and I" or "he played good" or "do it like I do." When someone asked Princess Margaret of England at a party, "How's your sister?" she *bridled* and came back, "Are you referring to Her Majesty, the Queen?" Cats are especially good at *bridling,* when, for example, a strange cat strolls into their territory.

broach (broch—*o* as in *go*) *vb.* Usually found in the expression *broach the subject, broach* means to "mention" or "bring up" for the first time. One can *broach* a subject or a new idea, i.e., suggest it or bring it up for discussion and consideration, or introduce it as a topic of conversation. In all these contexts, the word often contains the implication that the person *broaching* the subject or topic or idea is being somewhat tentative and perhaps a little concerned about how it is going to be received by the rest of those present.

brusque (brusk—*u* as in *but*) *adj.* A *brusque* manner is abrupt, sharp, short, curt, rough, and blunt. It is a manner characteristic of people who have little time for the amenities and civilities of life. *Brusqueness* of manner may not be intended as rude, but it is certainly unceremonious and can at times seem quite harsh. A *brusque* approach in a doctor, for instance, might be said to be the very opposite of a charming bedside manner. When spoken by an Englishman, the word is apt to be pronounced *broosk—oo* as in *book.* Cf. **bluff** and **blunt**.

bulwark (bool' wərk—*oo* as in *book*) *n.* A *bulwark,* literally, is any solid wall built for defense, especially in military action. Its figurative use is to describe anything that provides protection and support in a dangerous situation. It is often used as a synonym for *safeguard.* A dam is a *bulwark* against flood. In the lives of most people, religious faith is a *bulwark* against despair in dark moments. Using *bulwark* in its literal sense, Thomas Campbell (1777–1844), in his poem *Ye Mariners of England,* wrote:

> Britannia needs no *bulwarks,*
> No towers along the steep;
> Her march is o'er the mountain waves,
> Her home is on the deep.

Sir William Blackstone (1723–1780) had previously written: "The royal navy of England hath ever been . . . the floating *bulwark* of the island." Those sentiments were expressed some time before the events at Kitty Hawk. *Bulwark,* used figuratively, is a favorite word of statesmen. Abraham Lincoln said that "the *bulwark* of our own liberty and independence" was the "love of liberty which God has planted in us." Franklin D. Roosevelt said: "The only sure *bulwark* of continuing liberty is a government strong enough to protect the interests of the people, and a people strong enough . . . to maintain its sovereign control of the government."

buttress (bu' trəs—*u* as in *but*) *n., vb.* In architecture, a *buttress* is an external prop to support and give stability to a building or wall. Used figuratively, a *buttress* is anything that serves to support or strengthen a person, a cause, or a movement. Thus, the free flow of information to the people is a *buttress* of liberty. Anything that lends support is said to *buttress* the thing it supports. Education *buttresses* the cause of freedom; ignorance *buttresses* despotism. William Lamb (1779-1848) wittily utilized both the literal and figurative senses of *buttress* when he wrote: "While I cannot be regarded as a pillar, I must be regarded as a *buttress* of the church, because I support it from the outside."

cache (kash) *n.* A *cache* is a hiding place. Lots of people have a *cache* in the cellar or the attic or in some unlikely spot in the house where they store their valuables while away on a trip. The word can also be used to denote the thing which is hidden, like a *cache* of gin or whiskey stored by a secret drinker, or a *cache* of food hidden away by one who is being unfaithful to his reducing diet. A *cache*, then, is either the place where something is hidden, or the hidden object itself. This word is also a verb, meaning "hide, secrete, stow out of sight," but its use as a verb is rare.

calculate (kal′ kyə late) *vb.* To *calculate*, literally, is to compute. One *calculates* the distance to one's destination, or the cost of a proposed venture; but beyond mathematical *calculation* (kal kyə lay′ shən), the word is used like *determine* or *figure out*, the way one *calculates* a risk, or the chance of success, or the outcome of an attempt. General George Patton (1885-1945) advised: "Take *calculated* risks. That is quite different from being rash." *Calculated* and *calculating* are forms used in various different ways. When something is *calculated* to produce a certain effect, *calculated* means "intended." A military leader's aggressive look and stance are *calculated* to inspire courage and confidence. When something is likely, whether intended or not, to produce a certain result, *calculated* means "likely." Reckless speeding is *calculated* to produce road accidents. Lack of discipline and undue permissiveness in bringing up children are *calculated* to breed personality problems in their adult life. *Calculating* is something else again: A *calculating* person is not only cautious but also shrewd; the word usually implies cold and selfish scheming. A *calculating* merchant is out to get the best of you. A *calculating* person is coldly looking out for his own advantage, regardless of the interests of others. *Cold and calculating* is a common expression, describing the kind of person you'd better be wary of.

callous (kal′ əs) *adj.* A *callous* person is hardened, insensitive, indifferent to the emotions or difficulties or sufferings of others. Hospital personnel sometimes become *callous* after years of exposure to the sufferings of patients. Professional soldiers become *callous* about seeing death all around them on the battlefield. The word is related to the noun *callous*, for a thickened, hardened section of skin. Hence *callous* people are often called "thick-skinned." *Unfeeling* is another synonym for *callous*. *Callousness* is an unpleasant quality in a person. *Callous* people are not neighborly or helpful; they walk away from a scene of distress, wishing to remain uninvolved.

candid (kan′ dəd) *adj*. A *candid* person is sincere, outspoken, frank, without subterfuge. A *candid* opinion or reply is honest, straightforward, and frank. "In my *candid* opinion" is a phrase that precedes many a painful utterance. See the use of *candid* in the quotation from George Canning under *avow*. We are all familiar with the *candid* photo, which is allegedly unposed. *Candidness* is a proper form of the noun, but *candor* (kan′ dər) is the usual one. *Candor* inspires confidence in the speaker's words and impresses listeners. Alexander Pope (1688–1744) enjoined us to "Laugh where we must, be *candid* if we can." In establishing the Monroe Doctrine, President James Monroe (1758–1831), in his First Inaugural Address, declared: "We owe it . . . to *candor*, to declare that we should consider any attempt [by European powers] . . . to extend their system to any portion of this hemisphere as dangerous to our peace and safety." (Monroe must be turning over in his grave at the thought of the developments in Cuba and elsewhere.)

canny (kan′ ee) *adj*. A *canny* person is cautious, wary, prudent, and shrewd. A *canny* statement or response is careful, prudent, astute, and safe to make. *Canny* people don't take chances. A *canny* businessman knows what he's about, and gives his business a great deal of careful thought; he is the opposite of *rash*. *Canny* is an adjective applied to Scotsmen in popular lore and legend. When the Scot who woke up the village druggist in the middle of the night to ask for tuppence worth of sodium bicarbonate was angrily told to go away, and anybody should know that a gulp of hot water would be just as good for indigestion, the *canny* Scot, without apologizing, thanked the hapless druggist for saving him the tuppence. *Canny* indicates careful self-interest and shrewd dealing. *Canniness* may not be an endearing trait, but would be a virtue in legal practice and diplomacy.

capable (kay′ pə b'l) *adj*. A *capable* individual is one who has demonstrated that he is competent, has ability, is efficient, and has sufficient skill for whatever job is involved. A *capable* teacher knows how to handle a class and impart knowledge. A *capable* military leader can be trusted to manage his men, see to their safety, and do his all to beat the foe. *Capability* (kay pə bil′ ə tee) is the noun, describing a quality much to be desired in people, regardless of station in life. One's *capabilities* constitute one's potential. The plural noun can be used of things as well: A derelict cottage or a dilapidated antique may have great *capabilities*, i.e., is *capable* of being improved and restored. When a person is said to be *capable of* something, he possesses the ability to do that thing (e.g., a man *capable* of lifting a great weight, or *capable of* evaluating works of art). When a person or thing is *capable of* improvement, or enlightenment, he has the capacity to better himself or acquire knowledge. *Capable of* relates to a particular ability or quality; *capable*, by itself, denotes ability generally, and particularly in the field in which the person is involved at the moment.

capacious (kə pay′ shəs) *adj.* A *capacious* space is a very large one, capable of containing a great deal of whatever the space is suited for. A *capacious* stadium holds a very large number of spectators; a *capacious* room can hold a great many people; a *capacious* bin can store a large quantity of wheat, rice, etc. One can speak of a *capacious* mind, one storing a great deal of knowledge. *Capacious* can be used humorously in phrases like a *capacious stomach* or a *capacious chin*. John Gay (1685-1732) wrote: "Bring me an hundred reeds of decent growth/To make a pipe for my *capacious* mouth. . . ." The English novelist and poet Robert Louis Stevenson (1850-1894) wrote a great deal more than *Treasure Island*; in "To a Gardner," he wrote:

> Let first the onion flourish there,
> Rose among roots, the maiden-fair
> Wine-scented and poetic soul
> Of the *capacious* salad bowl.

Stevenson was not the only poet to praise the noble onion. Sidney Smith (1771-1845), in *Recipe for Salad,* enjoined: "Let onion atoms lurk within the bowl/and scarce suspected, animate the whole."

caper (kay′ pər) *n., vb.* A *caper,* literally a playful leap (from the Latin noun *caper,* meaning "he-goat"), is used figuratively to describe a prank, an escapade, any frivolous act; the adjective *capricious* (kə prish′ əs) is from the same root. As a verb, *caper* means "leap about friskily, gambol" like a newborn goat (or lamb). Some people, when they get good news, show their euphoria by *capering* around for a brief moment. After the French generals met with the Germans in a railway car at Compiègne to sign an armistice, Hitler went outside and *cut a caper* to show his delight. The most frequent use of *caper,* as a noun, is to denote any strange or outlandish act: "That was quite a *caper* of Jones's, to run off with his psychiatrist's wife." But the word can be used colloquially to indicate notable achievement: "Some *caper,* to walk on the moon!" A slang use of *caper* is to describe a criminal act, like robbery, unlawful entry, etc.

capitalize (kap′ ih tə lize) *vb.* When you *capitalize on* something, you turn it to your immediate advantage, you take quick advantage of it. Opportunity knocks but once; you must recognize and *capitalize* on it. A prizefighter tries to *capitalize* on his opponent's letting down his guard for the briefest moment. A speculator, whether bull or bear, tries to *capitalize* on the state of the market. Chess games are often won by *capitalizing* on the opponent's mistake. Burglars *capitalize* on homeowners' carelessness.

capitulate (kə pich′ ə late) *vb.* When one side, whether nation, army, group, or individual, *capitulates,* it surrenders, either unconditionally or upon agreed terms. France *capitulated* to Hitler's Germany in 1940; in 1945, it was Germany's turn to *capitulate* to the Allies, and Japan *capitulated* promptly after the dropping of the atom bomb. War is not necessarily involved; an individual can *capitulate* to difficult circumstances; in so doing, he simply *gives up.* Samuel Johnson

(1709–1784), beset by difficulties most of his life, wrote in a letter: "I will be conquered: I will not *capitulate.*" The noun is *capitulation* (kə pich ə lay´ shən). Robert Louis Stevenson (1850–1894), in *A Christmas Sermon,* wrote: "To be honest, to be kind . . . to renounce when that shall be necessary and not be embittered, to keep a few friends, but these without *capitulation* [i.e., without giving up one's principles] . . . here is a task for all that a man has of fortitude and delicacy." *Capitulate* can have a figurative romantic twist, as when the lady finally *capitulates* and gives her heart to the suitor.

careen (kə reen´) *vb.*, **career** (kə reer´) *vb.* We take these verbs together because they are so often confused. To *careen* a boat is to turn it over on its side, to clean it or work on its bottom. A boat that heels is said to *careen*; the same goes for a car or any other vehicle that sways and lurches while moving. If you're driving too fast, you'll *careen* around a corner. To *career* is to travel at full speed. Obviously, it is possible (and dangerous!) to *careen* and *career* at the same time. Bernard De Voto (1897–1955), the American critic and novelist, may well have used the wrong one of these two similar words when, in a 1932 article in *Harper's* about New England, he wrote: ". . . the American empire *careens* onward towards its unpredicted end. . . ." It is difficult to visualize America *careening* (swaying to and fro); he must have meant *careering* (going full speed ahead). We should hate to see America *careening*; *careering* is just fine.

careworn (kair´ worn) *adj.* A *careworn* person shows the ravages of care and worry, and is obviously exhausted by anxiety and woe. People who have been awake all night during a crisis like a fire or a flood show *careworn* faces in the morning. Old people who have suffered want for years look *careworn* and haggard. The faces of delegates from labor and management as they emerge after one of those nonstop negotiating sessions look gray and *careworn*. A momentary crisis will cause a puckered brow and startled eyes, which return to normal once the situation clears up. It is after a prolonged period of anxiety that the *careworn* look appears, whether it is the rigors of a sleepless night or the ravages of many years that have brought it about.

carnage (kar´ nij) *n. Carnage* is butchery, great destruction of life, bloodshed, massacre as in battle. The American poet Walt Whitman (1819–1892), in his poem *Reconciliation* celebrating the end of the American Civil War, wrote: "[It is] Beautiful that war and all its deeds of *carnage* must in time be utterly lost. . . ." Lord Byron (1788–1824) called the battle of Waterloo "the crowning *carnage.*" What would he have thought of the battles of the Marne and Verdun in World War I, where the *carnage* involved not thousands but millions, or the *carnage* at Hiroshima and Nagasaki, where many thousands died in one blinding moment?

cashier (ka sheer´—*a* as in *hat*) *vb.* When a person is *cashiered,* he is dismissed or discharged. The word usually implies that the dismissal is from a position of command, or one of trust, and that the dismissal is with disgrace or ignominy.

Iago, in Shakespeare's *Othello* (Act I, Scene 1), bypassed by Othello in the latter's selection of a lieutenant, speaks scathingly of the servile follower who ". . . wears out his time . . . /For nought but provender [nothing but fodder], and when he's old, *cashier'd*. . . ." The most common use of the verb *cashier* is in the context of military disgrace, complete with the ripping off of buttons and stripes, but the word can and should be used in any situation involving a curt dismissal, with a degree of disgrace, especially from a position of trust. New Jersey Senator Harrison Williams resigned from the Senate rather than be *cashiered* after his Abscam conviction. The verb *cashier* has nothing to do with the noun *cashier*. They come from entirely different roots; but that is not to say that a cashier cannot be *cashiered*.

casual (kaz´ yoo əl) *adj.* A *casual* encounter is one that happens by chance, without previous arrangement. A *casual* acquaintance or visitor is someone you see only now and then. A *casual* remark is an offhand remark, unplanned and not to be taken too seriously. A *casual* air or attitude is the nonchalant look of a person who seems to be unconcerned and indifferent to his surroundings. *Casual* clothes are informal attire, to be worn at home or on occasions involving no formality. *Casual*, then, is a versatile word, and its precise effect depends upon the context. Margaret Mead (1901-1978), the American anthropologist, used *casual* in the sense of "nonchalant, unconcerned," when she wrote in *Coming of Age in Samoa*: "In this *casual* attitude towards life, in this avoidance of conflict, of poignant situations, Samoa contrasts strongly not only with America but also with most primitive civilizations." Matthew Arnold (1822-1888) used it in the sense of "offhand, unserious," in writing of ". . . light half-believers of our *casual* creeds/Who never deeply felt . . . ," and Wallace Stevens (1875-1955) used it to mean "chance, spur-of-the-moment" in describing the freedom and randomness of life and nature when he wrote about the "spontaneous cries" of the quail and the "*casual* flocks of pigeons [making]/ Ambiguous undulations as they sink/Downward to darkness, on extended wings." The adverb *casually* has all the nuances of the adjective. Its commonest use is to denote offhandedness. People who see a lot of each other tend to greet each other *casually*. *Casually* has the implication of taking something for granted. People can become friends *casually*, i.e., in an unplanned sort of way. Things that "just happen" can be said to have happened *casually*.

category (kat´ ə gor ee—*o* as in *old* or *on*) *n.* A *category* is a class or general classification of people or things having certain characteristics in common. Diamonds, emeralds, and rubies all belong in the *category* of precious stones. The army, the navy, the air force, and the marines are in the military *category*. The navy, for example, belongs in that *category* as distinguished from the merchant marine. *Categorize* (kat´ ə gə rize) can mean "arrange in *categories*," i.e., "classify," but its common meaning is "characterize" or "label." If I *categorize* you as learned or well educated, I am labeling you as such and putting you in that *category*. The adjective *categorical* (kat ə gawr´ ih kəl) is something else again, meaning "unqualified, absolute, and without reservation." It is commonly met with in the expression *categorical denial*, and politicians charged with corruption usually deny the accusation *categorically*.

cater (kay´ tər) *vb*. Literally, to *cater* is to supply food, as *catering* services or *caterers* do for large dinners, banquets, and social events of all kinds. The word is used figuratively in a derogatory sense: to satisfy the demands of others for things of inferior worth, in the way that television programs *cater* to the alleged low taste of the public in its demand for violence, the sensational, or the sentimental. Hangers-on and lackeys *cater* to the whims of their supposed superiors, like rock and movie stars and victorious prizefighters. In this sense, *cater* is almost synonymous with *pander*, which is a somewhat stronger word, implying that the tastes involved are morbid or degraded.

causal (kaw´ zəl) *adj*. This word is usually found in the term *causal relationship*, and is not to be confused with *casual*, its anagram. A *causal* relationship between two things is one in which one of the things *causes* the other. There is a *causal* relationship, according to the health authorities, between smoking and lung cancer, and between overeating and overweight. On a cheerier note, there is a *causal* relationship between hard work and success. The adjective *causal* describes anything that is the *cause* of a given result; it is the word that involves the relationship of cause and effect.

caustic (kaw´ stik) *adj*. Anything *caustic*, in the literal sense of the word, has the capacity of burning or destroying animal tissue. *Caustic* is commonly applied in a figurative sense to describe biting criticism or comment or any remark that is extremely sarcastic or critical. The American writer and critic Dorothy Parker (1893-1967) was an expert at *caustic* comment. She said about one actress: "She runs the gamut of emotions from A to B." She called the comedy *The House Beautiful* "the play lousy." John Mason Brown (1900-1969), the drama critic, said of a production of Shakespeare's *Antony and Cleopatra*: "Tallulah Bankhead barged down the Nile last night as Cleopatra—and sank." Legend has it that when playwright Moss Hart (1904-1961) pointed out the vast changes he had made in the landscape of his newly acquired home in Bucks County, Pennsylvania, a guest remarked: "Just shows what God could do if He had the money." When the American dancer Isadora Duncan (1878-1927) suggested to the Irish playwright Bernard Shaw (1856-1950) that they produce a wonderful child with her beauty and his brains, he countered with: "But what if he had my beauty and your brains?" A friend of the author remarked about his wife's family: "I cross the street when I think of them." So much for *causticity* (kaw stis´ ih tee).

cavort (kə vort´) *vb*. One who *cavorts* prances and capers about gleefully and elaborately, the way nymphs and satyrs are so often depicted, with more than a hint of sexual frivolity. Children at play *cavort* in high spirits, without rhyme or reason. Square dancers *cavort*, in accordance with strict specifications, but the term usually applies to people jumping around for sheer joy, without a set pattern. *Cavorting* is generally applied to frivolous frisking about, but is sometimes used figuratively, in a rather derogatory way, usually in the expression *cavorting around*, to characterize the philandering of naughty husbands: "She stays home and mends his socks while he's out *cavorting around*."

cease (sees—both *s*'s as in *see*) *vb.* To *cease* is to stop, to terminate, to come to an end, and the act of *ceasing* is *cessation* (seh say´ shən). When a war *ceases*, we speak of the *cessation* of hostilities. *Cease* can be used by itself, or we can say that such-and-such a thing *ceased to happen* or *ceased happening*: Despite the advances of science, superstition has not *ceased* muddying (or *ceased* to muddy) people's beliefs. *Cease* can take an object: *Cease* that noise immediately! *Cease fire* is a familiar expression. *Cease and desist* is used in legal circles, where a demand or order is made to enjoin damaging activity. H.W. Fowler (1858-1933), in his *Modern English Usage,* says that *cease* "is now poetic, rhetorical, formal or old-fashioned" and "should be allowed to go into honorable retirement," but for once (and it is a rare and possibly presumptious occasion), the author dares to disagree.

celestial (sə les´chəl) *adj. Celestial,* in its figurative sense, is equivalent to *heavenly* or *divine* in their figurative senses. One may speak of enjoying *celestial* comfort or *celestial* bliss. In Shakespeare's *Henry VI, Part 1* (Act V, Scene 5), the Earl of Suffolk discourses on marriage for love rather than money:

> For what is wedlock forced, but a hell,
> An age of discord and continual strife?
> Whereas the contrary bringeth bliss,
> And is a pattern of *celestial* peace.

The American patriot and writer Thomas Paine (1737-1809) wrote, in 1776: "Heaven knows how to put a proper price upon its goods; and it would be strange, indeed, if so *celestial* an article as *Freedom* should not be highly rated." The former Chinese Empire was known as the *Celestial Empire,* and its citizens were called *celestials,* so it was appropriate that aliens were referred to as "foreign devils." *Celestial* is a fairly elegant synonym for *heavenly* or *divine,* but it makes a nice change from those overworked adjectives and might make your hostess happy if you applied that term to her soup.

cement (sə ment´) *vb.* To *cement* is to unite, bond, to join together firmly. Our common language *cements* the bond between England and America. Increasing American tourism is doing much to *cement* relations with China. It is a self-evident truth that time *cements* friendship. The origin of this verb is obvious; the noun, too, has been used figuratively for centuries. The poet Robert Herrick (1591-1674) wrote: "What is a kiss? . . ./The sure, sweet *cement,* glue and lime of love." And Shakespeare used it that way, in *Antony and Cleopatra* (Act III, Scene 2), where Octavius speaks to Antony of "the *cement* of our love." Earlier (Act II, Scene 1), Pompey expresses his worry that although Octavius and Antony have had serious enough differences to make them enemies, ". . . the fear of us [Pompey's forces]/May *cement* their divisions and bind up/the petty difference." The pastoral visits of the Pope are aimed not only at strengthening Catholicism, but also at *cementing* friendship and good relations among nations.

censure (sen´ shər) *n., vb.* A *censure* is a particularly stern expression of condemnation for unacceptable conduct, a vehement statement of total disapproval.

The term is often used in Congressional matters. The Senate *censure* of Senator Joe McCarthy (1909-1957) marked the downfall of his career. To *censure* is to give expression to a *censure*, i.e., to reprimand and condemn harshly. The American public were almost unanimous in *censuring* the unlawful acts of President Nixon. The Greek philosopher Plato (428-348 B.C.) wrote: "Men *censure* injustice fearing that they may be the victims of it, and not because they shrink from committing it." The English physician and author Sir Thomas Browne (1605-1682) expressed this lofty sentiment: "No man can justly *censure* or condemn another, because indeed no man truly knows another." In the famous speech of Polonius to his departing son Laertes in Shakespeare's *Hamlet* (Act I, Scene 3), father gives son (among many other gems) this advice: "Take each man's *censure*, but reserve thy judgment." Here, *censure* is used in the now obsolete sense of "opinion."

cerebral (serr′ ə brəl, sə ree′ brəl) *adj.* This word means, literally, "pertaining to the brain" (*cerebrum* is Latin for "brain"). Figuratively, and more commonly, *cerebral* describes any activity that is intellectual rather than emotional or intuitive. Most contemporary forms of art, whether music, poetry, drama, painting, or sculpture, are *cerebral* and tend to leave many of us cold. The "thinking man" is *cerebral*: his speech and actions betray brainwork rather than feeling. There are the related words *cerebrate* (serr′ ə brate), meaning "use the mind, engage in thinking," and *cerebration* (serr ə bray′ shən), the act of *cerebrating*, brainwork. The American historian James Harvey Robinson (1863-1936) wrote: "Political campaigns are designedly made into emotional orgies . . . and . . . paralyze what slight powers of *cerebration* man can normally muster." *Cerebrate* and *cerebration* are hardly everyday words, but *cerebral*, however you choose to pronounce it, is a very handy word when you want to describe people whose brains, rather than their hearts and instincts, control their lives and their activities.

chaff (chaff) *n., vb.* When you *chaff* someone, you are teasing or making fun of him in a playful, good-natured way, and the teasing itself is called *chaff*. There is no hint of malice or ill will in *chaff*. *Chaff*, literally the grain husks separated by threshing, came to mean, in the figurative sense, anything light and worthless; its use in the sense of teasing or bantering and jesting, without much substance, probably derived from the original meaning, and the verb was based on the noun used that way. It is customary for a prospective bridegroom's friends to *chaff* him at the bachelor party. Some people, especially if they are themselves overweight, find it enjoyable (perhaps in self-defense) to *chaff* those who turn down a second helping in order to preserve their figures. Less diligent children often *chaff* their more studious classmates for their interest in learning and good grades. *Chaffing* is defined as "light-hearted mockery" but on occasion there is envy behind it.

challenge (chal′ inj) *n., vb.* A *challenge* is an invitation to join in a test of strength or skill. *Challenge* can also be used to describe the thing that does the challenging: Mt. Everest stands as a *challenge* to daring and endurance. The democratic way of life is a *challenge* to communism and fascism. Quiz shows are a *challenge* to people's education and ingenuity. President Lyndon B. Johnson, in a 1964 address, said: "The *challenge* of the next half century is whether we have the wisdom . . . to advance the quality of American civilization." A *challenge* can be a call for an explanation: Corporate comptrollers sometimes *challenge* expense-account items. The verb *to challenge* covers all these aspects of the noun. One form of it, *challenging,* has the broader, figurative meaning of "thought-provoking." When someone comes up with a *challenging* idea, he stimulates people's thinking. Putting men on the moon was a *challenging* program, and it put lots of brains to work toward an astounding result. Any idea, thought, or suggestion that stimulates interest may be described as *challenging.*

chameleon (kə mee´ lee ən, -meel´ yən) *n.* This is the name of a species of small lizard that can change the color of its skin at will to match its surroundings, for camouflage purposes. Because of that characteristic, the word *chameleon* has gained a figurative use, to denote a fickle, inconstant, changeable person, especially one who assumes different personalities according to the circumstances or company he finds himself in. When people discuss someone and find that they all have very different notions of the absent one's personality, one might exclaim, "Why, he's a *chameleon!* He changes his character and manners to suit whomever he's with." *Chameleons* are unreliable; you never know where you stand with them.

channel (chan´ l) *vb.* To *channel* something is to direct it toward a particular goal or purpose. *Channel* is often found in the expression *to channel one's energies.* Some students *channel* their energies toward getting good grades, others toward sports, others toward broadening their experience. It is best to *channel* your efforts toward one particular goal, rather than disperse them in all directions. One can also *channel* information: It is important to *channel* information directly to its intended destination, rather than run the risk of having it garbled by an intermediary.

chaos (kay´ os) *n. Chaos* is the state of total confusion, utter disorder, complete disorganization. Traffic in most big cities has reached the point of nothing less than *chaos.* General George Marshall (1880–1959), introducing the Marshall Plan at Harvard for the recovery of Europe, stated: "Our policy is directed . . . against hunger, poverty, desperation and *chaos.*" The Chinese philosopher Chuang-tzu (369–286 B.C.) wrote: "All men strive to grasp what they do not know . . . and . . . to discredit what they do not excel in. This is why there is *chaos.*" (What, way back then, too?) The adjective from *chaos* is *chaotic* (kay ot´ ik), meaning "totally confused, utterly disordered." There are people who simply cannot think in an orderly fashion; their minds are *chaotic.* Children can turn an orderly dining room into a *chaotic* mess in a surprisingly short time. Some lawyers keep their desks littered with a *chaotic* pile of files and papers, either because they are naturally untidy, or because they want to look busy. When events happen without rhyme or reason, they can be said to occur *chaotically* (kay ot´ ə kə lee).

characteristic (kar ik tə ris´ tik—*a* as in *hat*) *n., adj.* A person's *characteristics* are his distinguishing qualities or traits. Kindness will be one person's *characteristic,* cruelty another's. In his play *The Knights,* Aristophanes (450–385 B.C.), the Greek writer of comedies, has this to say: "You have all the *characteristics* of a popular politician: a horrible voice, bad breeding, and a vulgar manner." *Characteristic* is also an adjective meaning "typical, distinctive." Haughtiness, unfortunately, is *characteristic* of many very rich people. Purple was the color *characteristic* of the clothes of the nobility in ancient Rome. A related verb is *characterize* (kar´ ik tə rize—*a* as in *hat*), which can be used in two ways: Distinctive qualities or traits *characterize* people, and a person *characterizes* another person when he describes his character or personality. Kindness and sensitivity *characterized* Abraham Lincoln. The tapes *characterized* Nixon as untruthful and obstructive of justice. When the *characterization* (kar ik tər ə zay´ shən) is as unfavorable as that, *characterize* is synonymous with *brand.*

characterize (kar´ ik tə rize), *vb.* See **characteristic**.

chaste (chayst) *adj. Chaste,* literally and specifically, applies to a person (usually to a woman, even in these supposedly single-standard days) who has never engaged in sexual intercourse except in marriage. Its more general meaning is "stainless, pure." Thus, a moral, virtuous person can be described as "chaste," and so can one's manners, particularly conversation, and in this use it means "refined, free from vulgarity." It can also be used to mean "simple," in describing a style, whether of dress or in the arts, as opposed to *ornate* or *florid.* Edward Gibbon (1737–1794), the historian, wrote: "My English text is *chaste* and all licentious passages are left in the decent obscurity of a learned language [Latin]." Modest dress can be referred to as *chaste attire.* Architectural style may be described as *chaste.* The noun *chastity* (chas´ tə tee—*a* as in *hat*) can refer to any of the fields covered by the adjective *chaste,* but its use is almost always confined to the sexual sense (for example, in the term *chastity belt*). *Chastity* is often used as a synonym for *virginity.*

chasten (chay´ sən) *vb.* To *chasten* is to discipline, to correct by means of punishment, or through suffering, to punish for the purpose of improvement. *Chasten* can also mean "subdue," in the way that growing old might *chasten* a person's temper. *Chasten* is different from *chastise* (chas tize´—*a* as in *hat*), in that *chastise* implies punishment for wrongdoing for the sake of punishment, but not necessarily for the sake of improvement, and often connotes physical punishment, as opposed to, for instance, a thorough talking to. "Whom the Lord loveth, he *chasteneth,*" we read in Hebrews 12:6, whereas in I Kings 12:11 we read: "My father hath *chastised* you with whips, but I will *chastise* you with scorpions." (However, Proverbs 13:24 tells us, "He that spareth his rod hateth his son; but he that loveth him *chasteneth* him betimes," so that, at least in that sentence, *chasten* does imply physical punishment.) Experience has a *chastening* effect, in that many of us do improve through suffering. Abraham Lincoln, referring to the sentence that an Oriental monarch always kept in view, "And this, too, shall pass away," exclaimed, "How *chastening* in the hour of pride!" The main idea in *chasten* is the effect of experience, especially of suffering, in softening the soul, subduing egotism and superiority, and humanizing people.

cheerless (cheer´ ləs) *adj.* Anything *cheerless* is gloomy, black, drab. People are depressed by *cheerless* surroundings. *Cheerless,* as you might expect, is the opposite of *cheerful.* The American poet John Greenleaf Whittier (1807-1892), in his poem "Snowbound," wrote:

> The sun, that brief December day
> Rose *cheerless* over hills of gray,
> And, darkly circled, gave at noon
> A sadder light than waning moon.

Those lines do present a bleak and gloomy picture! Toward the end of Shakespeare's *King Lear* (Act V, Scene 3), the faithful Earl of Kent says to the maddened King: " . . . all's *cheerless,* dark and deadly/Your eldest daughters . . . / . . . desperately are dead." Most of that play is pretty *cheerless,* and the final scene practically sets a record for *cheerlessness.* While we are on the subject of *cheer,* the English lexicographer H.W. Fowler (1858-1933), as great a student of human nature as a writer of dictionaries, has some interesting things to say about *cheerful* and *cheery.* "[*Cheery*] has reference chiefly to externals—voice, appearance, manner, etc. . . . a person may be *cheerful* without being *cheery.* . . . The *cheerful* feels and perhaps shows contentment, the *cheery* shows and probably feels it."

cherish (cherr´ ish) *vb.* To *cherish* someone or something is to hold the person or thing dear the way one *cherishes* (or should *cherish*) one's spouse, one's children, one's tried and true friends, one's native land and flag. One can *cherish* abstract things, like freedom and security. *Cherish* can also be used in the sense of "cling to." Despite setbacks, optimists *cherish* the hope of ultimate success. In *The Book of Common Prayer* we find, in the marriage ceremony, the words "to love and to *cherish,* till death us do part," and later on, "to love, *cherish* and obey," though the "obey" is often omitted these days. On the Fourth of July, 1845, at Faneuil Hall in Boston, the American statesman Robert Winthrop (1809-1894) made a toast to "Our Country . . . to be *cherished* in all our hearts, to be defended by all our hands." We *cherish* (cling to) the recollection of happy hours, or to the memory of loved ones who are no longer with us. Abraham Lincoln, in his letter to Mrs. Bixby, who had lost her sons in the Civil War, prayed the Heavenly Father to leave her "the *cherished* memory of the loved and lost."

chic (sheek) *n., adj.* To have *chic* is to have elegant style, especially in dress; to be *chic* is to be stylish, smart, fashionable. Ladies' magazines, like *Harper's Bazaar* and *Vogue,* are particularly devoted to the presentation of *chic* in dress and make-up, while publications like *House & Garden* specialize in *chic* in matters of décor and gracious living. Although *chic,* as both noun and adjective, is most frequently applied to matters of dress, makeup, and personal appearance generally, it can refer as well to matters of life-style. The "beautiful people" devote a great deal of energy to qualifying for the label *chic.* The French designer Gabrielle Chanel (1892–1971) grew to personify *chic.* The racing at Ascot in England and Longchamps in France is secondary to the study in *chic* presented by the fashionable ladies.

chichi (shee′ shee) *n., adj.* While what is *chic* is genuinely elegant and stylish, what is *chichi* is pretentiously and self-consciously so, affected and precious. Much of the contemporary painting, sculpture, and décor that adorns the homes of the "beautiful people" is nothing more than *chichi,* and is there not so much because the owners like it but because they think it's the thing to do. Salvador Dali is *chic*; Andy Warhol is *chichi.* Hiring a horse and carriage in New York is on the *chichi* side. Behavior, as well as dress and décor, can be described as *chichi* when it is particularly fussy and affected and indulged in to call attention to oneself. This might apply not only to dress and makeup, for instance, in the style of the 1920s, but to acting in the manner that was modish in that period. *Chichi* can be amusing, but a little goes a long way. For heaven's sake, do not confuse *chichi* with *chic*!

chide (chyde) *vb.* To *chide* is to scold, to find fault with someone and express it in no uncertain terms, but less forcefully than what is expressed by the verb *rebuke,* and both are much milder than *berate. Chiding* is for children who are on the whole well behaved, but go off momentarily on a naughty tack; *chiding* is for minor faults. Eliza Cook (1818–1889) wrote:

> I love it, I love it, and who shall dare
> To *chide* me for loving that old armchair?

In Shakespeare's *Merry Wives of Windsor* (Act V, Scene 3), Mistress Page gives the advice: " . . . better a little *chiding* than a great deal of heartbreak." Isaac Watts (1674–1748) wrote, in *Love Between Brothers and Sisters*:

> Birds in their little nest agree.
> And 'tis a shameful sight,
> When children of one family
> Fall out, and *chide,* and fight.

(Isaac Watts was the poet who glorified " . . . the little busy bee / [who] Improve[d] each shining hour.")

chintzy (chin′ tsee) *adj.* Anything so described is cheap, gaudy, of inferior quality, or, when the word is applied to a person, mean-spirited and stingy. A poorly made dress, especially one in a loud and flashy pattern, or the second-rate furnishings of a house may be described as *chintzy.* A mean little tip, far below the usual percentage, left for a waiter, for instance, may be called *chintzy,* and one might rebuke the stingy person by telling him that that was rather *chintzy* of him. Authorities disagree on whether this adjective is standard or colloquial; whichever it is, it is derogatory. Avoid *chintzy* articles and *chintzy* people.

chronic (kron' ik) *adj.* Anything *chronic* is constant, long-lasting, as opposed to *acute*. *Chronic* can be applied to conditions or situations, like a *chronic* state of unrest in a nation, or a *chronic* state of war like that in the Middle East. The adjective can describe an illness, like *chronic* heart trouble, as distinct from an *acute* attack, or *chronic* emphysema. One can also thus describe a person with a long-standing illness, habit, defect, weakness, etc.: a *chronic* invalid, a *chronic* heavy smoker, a *chronic* liar. In that usage, *chronic* is synonymous with *inveterate*. The American naturalist and writer John Burroughs (1837–1921) wrote in an essay entitled "Is It Going to Rain?": "I was born with a *chronic* anxiety about the weather." The English novelist and poet Thomas Hardy (1840–1928), in *Tess of the D'Urbervilles*, wrote of "the *chronic* melancholy which is taking hold of the civilized races with the decline of belief in a beneficent power." Edward Lucas (1868–1938), the English satirical essayist, expressed himself this way: "People in hotels strike no roots. The French phrase for *chronic* hotel guests even says so: they are called dwellers *sur la branche*." (In French, to be "like a bird on the branch" is to be *unsettled*.)

clamor (klam' ər) *n., vb. Clamor*, whether noun or verb, has to do with noise. A *clamor* is any loud, continued noise, particularly an uproar, a shouting, an outcry. People living close to a main road are disturbed by the *clamor* of traffic. At the zoo, visitors are deafened by the *clamor* in the birdhouse. If you don't drink at a cocktail party, you are disturbed by the increasing *clamor* of the guests who do. Speakers in the British House of Commons are drowned out by the *clamor* of opposing members. Citizens often indicate their unhappiness by a *clamor* directed at the lawmakers. To *clamor* for something is to demand it, often by shouting, as at a public meeting, or by angry letters of protest. In the latter case, the "noise" is purely figurative, as in the expression *to make a noise* about something, meaning "to protest." In a speech in the Senate in 1838, Daniel Webster (1782–1852) complained about the "persons who constantly *clamor*" (those who complain about everything). In Shakespeare's *Taming of the Shrew* (Act IV, Scene 1), Petruchio has some advice about how to tame a wife by keeping her awake: "And if she chance to nod I'll rail and brawl/ and with the *clamour* keep her still awake...." (Grounds for divorce?)

clique (kleek) *n.* A *clique* is a smallish, rather exclusive group of people, a set, united in pursuing a common interest, or favoring and abetting the interests of a public figure. The word is usually used in a derogatory way, to express disapproval (sometimes by those left out of the *clique*). *Clique* is synonymous with *coterie*, or *circle*, or *crowd* in the sense of one's special group or set. Every new fad seems to develop a *clique*. Most celebrities are surrounded by a *clique* that wants to share the limelight. George Bernard Shaw (1856–1950), in *Back to Methuselah*, says (referring to the fawning sycophant): "The worst *cliques* are those which consist of one man."

cloistered (kloy' stərd) *adj.* To be *cloistered*, or lead a *cloistered* life, is to be secluded, withdrawn from the outside world, confined; sometimes, in context, the sense of the word is "sheltered." Most monasteries had a covered walk known as a "cloister," which usually ran around the three sides of an open court or quadrangle. *Cloister* came to describe any secluded religious institution, like a monastery or convent, but the word was eventually applied to any quiet, secluded place. From this came the adjective *cloistered,* meaning "secluded," but having little or nothing to do with religion or religious institutions. Hermits lead *cloistered* lives, whether in caves or palaces. *The cloistered life* is an expression descriptive of the existence of a loner. *Cloistered* is the opposite of *gregarious, sociable,* and *convivial.*

coherent (ko heer´ ənt) *adj.*, **incoherent** (in ko heer´ ənt) *adj.* A *coherent* argument or speech is consistent and logical. *Coherent* may be applied to people as well: one may speak of a *coherent* speaker. To *cohere* is to *stick together,* in the way that bits of wet plaster *cohere* to form a lump or mass. When an argument or any presentation is *coherent,* the parts "stick together," i.e., are consistent and logical. *Incoherent* (literally the opposite of *coherent*) means "rambling, disjointed, confused, disordered." One may describe an argument or a speech as *incoherent,* or apply the term to a person who becomes *incoherent* because of terror or rage. When Hitler got disagreeable news, he became *incoherent* with rage, and (so they say) chewed the rug. Thus, *coherent* and *incoherent* (in figurative use) are not the opposite of each other. *Coherent* people speak with consistency, order, and logic; *incoherent* people rave and rant and often can hardly speak at all.

coincide (koe in side´) *vb.* This word has two main uses: When things happen at the same time, or in the same place, or both, they are said to *coincide;* when two or more people come to the same conclusion, their ideas can be said to *coincide.* If your vacation plans and mine involve the same place and period, our vacations *coincide.* If, after scanning the list of candidates for a position, we decide on the same person, our choices are said to *coincide.* The Cuban patriot and writer José Martí (1853–1895) said, "Men are products, expressions, reflections; they live to the extent that they *coincide* with their epoch, or to the extent that they differ markedly from it." The noun is *coincidence* (koe in´ sih dəns); the adjective is *coincidental* (koe in sih den´ təl). When two things occur at the same time or place purely by chance, in a striking manner, the event is called a *coincidence,* the happenings are *coincidental,* and they are said to happen *coincidentally* (koe in sih den´ tə lee). Plans or ideas or choices can *coincide* by accident or by arrangement. The main aspect of *coincidence,* however, is pure chance or accident, the absence of prearrangement. When prearrangement is denied, people often ascribe the things to *coincidence.* Lord Byron (1788–1824), in *Don Juan,* popularized the phrase "strange *coincidence,*" as a cynical expression of disbelief of a denial of prearrangement.

colleague (kol´ eeg) *n.* A *colleague* is a co-worker, an associate, a person in one's profession, office, line of endeavor, a member of the team. The members of the physics department of a university, for example, are *colleagues.* Doctors, lawyers, architects, etc., in the same office refer to one another as *colleagues.* The word is related to the noun *league*, in its sense of "association" of persons united by a common goal. Lawyers fighting each other tooth and nail in court sometimes refer to each other as "my learned *colleague*," meaning, of course, that the "*colleague*" in question is an unlearned ignoramus. When a senior member of a professional group wants to turn a client over to a junior member or a mere employee, he might refer to his successor by the high-sounding title of *colleague* in order not to ruffle the client's feathers.

commanding (kə man' ding) *adj.* We are familiar with the verb *command* (kə mand') in the sense of "order," perhaps somewhat less so in the sense of "dominate," in the way a hill *commands* a view. *Commanding*, as an adjective, has a number of meanings. A man of *commanding* appearance is imposing, and *commands* attention. Shakespeare used it that way in *Henry VI, Part 1*, where (Act IV, Scene 7) Joan of Arc refers to Sir William Lucy as speaking "with . . . a proud *commanding* spirit." In military matters, a higher elevation is a *commanding* position, in that it *dominates* the situation. In sports, the player or side that holds a *commanding* lead or position is the one that is far ahead, in a winning position. The general idea behind *commanding* has nothing to do with *ordering*; the theme is one of *domination*, whether in war, sports, or, for that matter, business or even, as between competing suitors, affairs of the heart. Whatever the sphere of activity, it is a fine thing to be in a *commanding* lead.

commemorate (kə mem' ə rate) *vb.* When you *commemorate* a person or a deed, you honor his or its memory in some way. A statue at the famous bridge in Concord, Mass., *commemorates* the second battle of the American Revolution fought by the Minutemen on April 19, 1776 (the "shot heard round the world"). The placing of flowers on the graves of soldiers on Veterans Day *commemorates* those fallen in the service of their country. Class reunions *commemorate* graduations of years gone by. One often sees a plaque affixed to a building *commemorating* a famous person born there, or, particularly in the case of George Washington, who slept there.

commend (kə mend') *vb.* To *commend* someone is to state your approval of him, to praise him. Usually, the *commending* is for a particular act. Heroes are *commended* for bravery. A laywer who wins a difficult case or a doctor who pulls a patient through a dangerous illness or any individual who keeps his head in a crisis and leads others to safety should be *commended* for a job well done. From *commend* we get the adjective *commendable* (kə mend' ə b'l), meaning "praiseworthy." Shakespeare uses *commend* in the famous "Who is Sylvia" song in *The Two Gentlemen of Verona* (Act IV, Scene 2):

> Who is Sylvia, what is she
>   That all our swains *commend* her?
> Holy, fair and wise is she.
>   The heaven such grace did lend her,
>   That she might admired be.

Samuel Pepys (1633–1703), the English diarist, recorded in detail his impressions of life in London from 1660 to 1669. On May 1, 1663, he "Went to hear Mrs. Turner's daughter . . . play on the harpsichord; but Lord! it was enough to make any man sick to hear her; yet I was forced to *commend* her highly." The noun is *commendation* (kom ən day′ shən), meaning "praise" generally, often used in conjunction with the bestowing of military honors for bravery. Your choice of this book is highly *commendable*.

commensurate (kə men′ sər it, -shər it) *adj.* Anything *commensurate* with something else is of a size that properly corresponds to that other thing. When it is said that the laborer is worthy of his hire, it means that his pay should be *commensurate* with his work and accomplishments, i.e., in proper proportion to his services. Let it take years and years to produce a great novel: The result is *commensurate* with the effort. When you hear what rock stars earn you might get the notion that the talent that went into those concerts and recording sessions was hardly *commensurate* with the incredible financial rewards. Mozart and Schubert died poor. The immeasurable effort, sacrifice, and money expended on D-Day were *commensurate* only with the result achieved in the extermination of the Nazi menace.

comment (kom′ ent) *n., vb.* A *comment* is a remark or an observation. A *comment* may be oral or written, and may be made about anything: the weather, a book, a person, an event. In England, even strangers passing each other on the street can hardly refrain from making a *comment* about the weather. ("Cooler today, isn't it?") "Where did you get that hat?" can be a *comment* expressing admiration or derision, depending on the tone of the speaker. *Comment* is also a verb: To *comment* on or about something or someone is to make a remark or express an opinion on the subject. When you go backstage to greet a friend in the cast, it is customary to *comment* favorably or even enthusiastically, regardless of your private feelings. (A safe *comment* was Judy Garland's "Darling, only you could have played it that way.") Sometimes *comment* takes a different twist, in that a play or novel can be said to be, for example, a *comment* on conditions in the world today, or a *comment* on the folly of ruthless ambition. Here, *comment* takes on the shade of meaning of an indirect or suggestive observation or interpretation.

commiserate (kə miz′ ə rate) *vb.* When you *commiserate* (note two *m*'s and one *s*) with someone, you feel sympathy for him. The *commiseration* (kə miz ə ray′ shən) may be silent, but the word usually implies that you express your feeling to the person with whom you are *commiserating*. To *commiserate* is to condole with someone. You *commiserate* with a friend when you hear bad news about him—an illness, the loss of a relative, a business setback. In Shakespeare's *Merchant of Venice* (Act IV, Scene 1), the Duke of Venice speaks to Shylock of the heavy losses (supposedly) suffered by Antonio and describes them as enough to " . . . pluck *commiseration* . . . /From . . . hearts of flint." To *commiserate* is more than merely to express sorrow and sympathy with another person's misfortune; when you *commiserate,* you really feel for the grieving person and tell him so.

commodity (kə mod´ ih tee) *n*. A *commodity* is an article of trade, as opposed to a service; a product having value. A *commodity* can be a product of manufacture, of agriculture, of mining. The term is sometimes applied to anything that is the subject matter of business. Thus, there are those in the banking business who "sell" the use of money (i.e., lend it) and speak of money as a *commodity*, the availability of which fluctuates like that of sugar or cocoa or wheat or automobiles. Some even speak of land as a *commodity*. On that score, the conservationist Aldo Leopold (1886-1948), in *A Sand County Almanac*, wrote: "We abuse land because we treat it as a *commodity* belonging to us. When we see land as a community to which we belong, we may begin to use it with love and respect." Properly speaking, money and land are not *commodities*, and the term should be reserved for products as explained above.

commonplace (kom´ ən plase) *adj*. What is *commonplace* is ordinary, undistinguished, dull, and uninteresting. *Commonplace* may describe a person, a building, a place, a play, novel, painting or any work of "art," a report, a comment. When Dr. Watson, in *A Study in Scarlet* by Conan Doyle (1859-1930), entranced by a deduction of Sherlock Holmes, exclaimed, "Wonderful!" Holmes replied *"Commonplace."* Doyle used the word again in the *Boscombe Valley Mystery*, where Holmes talks of "those simple cases which are so extremely difficult. . . . The more . . . *commonplace* a crime is, the more difficult it is to bring it home." The American writer Jack Kerouac (1922-1969), the prophet of the "beat generation," wrote, in *On the Road:* ". . . the only people for me are the mad ones . . . the ones who never yawn or say a *commonplace* thing. . . . " It is impossible to be brilliant and original with every breath we draw, but silence is usually preferable to a string of *commonplace* utterances.

comparable (kom´ pər ə b'l) *adj*. Note accent on first syllable; never on second. This word can be used in several distinct ways, although the concept of *comparing* is behind all of them; it can mean "alike" or "similar" enough to be worthy of comparison, when we describe two things, for example, the spread of Roman influence in ancient times and the development of the British Empire, as *comparable*. It can mean "as good as," when we speak of sculpture *comparable* to that of classical Greece. Finally, *comparable* is sometimes used to mean "equivalent," as when we say that we have no *comparable* sources of information or no *comparable* data on a certain subject, such as Chinese steel production or weather conditions on another planet. To sum up: Things that are somewhat alike, things that are equally good, things that are equivalent or near enough to be considered, can all be described as *comparable*. *Incomparable* (in kom´ pə rə b'l) has a different twist: Its commonest meaning is "unequaled" or "matchless," as when we speak of a person or a work of art or a landscape as being of *incomparable* beauty.

comparative (kəm par´ ə tiv—*a* as in *hat*) *adj*. The common use of this word is to express something less than absolute, i.e., something relative. For instance, a freshman congressman would be considered a *comparative* newcomer in politics;

a person living on a meager income—not destitute, but unable to afford anything more than the merest necessities of life—might be said to be living in *comparative* poverty. The idea behind *comparative* is that what is being described is "not completely so" when *compared* with an absolute. The adverb, *comparatively* (kəm par´ ə tiv lee), is based on the same idea, and means about the same thing as "relatively." How was the weather in Spain? "*Comparatively* warm." (Compared to the North Pole?) "How was So-and-so in *Othello*?" "*Comparatively* good." (Compared to Olivier?) *Comparatively* is one of those "safe" words: you can always remain vague about your standard of comparison.

compassionate (kəm pash´ ə nit) *adj.* A *compassionate* person or a *compassionate* view or statement or letter is one that expresses heartfelt sympathy and sorrow for another person. *Compassion* (kəm pash´ ən) is the noun, and implies a desire to do something about the other fellow's misfortune, to help him out of it. Hubert Humphrey (1911-1978) said, "*Compassion* is not weakness, and concern for the unfortunate is not socialism." E. B. White (born 1899), the writer of *New Yorker* fame, wrote, "As long as there is one upright man, as long as there is one *compassionate* woman, the contagion may spread and the scene is not desolate. Hope is the thing that is left us in a bad time." In Shakespeare's poem "The Rape of Lucrece," the heroine pleads in vain with the lustful Tarquin not to rape her: "O! if no harder than a stone thou art,/Melt at my tears and be *compassionate*. . . . " Tarquin wasn't.

compelling (kəm pel´ ing) *adj. Compel* (kəm pel´) is a common verb, meaning to "force." The form *compelling* is used as an adjective, and can be used in two distinct ways. When you follow a course of action for *compelling* reasons, you have no alternative; *compelling* reasons are those that *force* you to take that road. But *compelling* takes on a different meaning in phrases like *a leader of compelling power, a woman of compelling beauty, a play of compelling significance*. Here, *compelling* describes things that command great admiration or respect, that are worthy of close attention. There are other verbs whose *-ing* forms become adjectives with a twist that departs in varying degrees from the literal meaning of the verb: Examples, among others, are *alluring, bewitching, challenging, commanding, daring, fleeting, telling, trifling*.

competent (kom´ pə tənt) *adj.* A person *competent* to carry out a particular task or fill a certain job is one with sufficient skill and experience for the purpose. It is not easy to find *competent* people, whether you are looking for a secretary or a President of the United States. Machines can be described as *competent*: a light truck may not be *competent* for a given task. The English poet William Wordsworth (1770-1850) used *competent* in a dramatic way: " 'Tis . . . the most difficult of tasks to keep/Heights which the soul is *competent* to gain." The noun is *competence* (kom´ pə təns), sometimes *competency* (kom´ pə tən see). People are hired because of their *competence* to fill a specific job, for instance, *competence* as a secretary, *competence* as a research assistant. *Competent* can sometimes have a somewhat derogatory shade of meaning, like *adequate*. In the proper context, it implies that the person is not exceptional or outstanding. "What did you think of Jones's Hamlet?" "*Competent*." *Competent* and *competence* have special meanings in law, dealing with legal qualifications, e.g., to testify, to enter into contracts, to make a will, etc.

comply (kəm plyˊ) *vb.* When you *comply,* you act in accordance with someone's wish or demand, or with legal requirements, or with conditions laid down by the circumstances. If the policeman tells you to show him your driver's license and car registration, it is wise to *comply*. *Comply* is often followed by *with*: One must *comply* with the entrance requirements of a university in order to matriculate. Sometimes one *complies,* but silently disagrees. The English poet Samuel Butler (1612–1680) wrote:

> He that *complies* against his will
> Is of his own opinion still.

The related adjective *compliant* (kəm plyˊ ənt) can describe any agreeable person who doesn't make a fuss, but the implication is often that of a timid, yielding, submissive soul, whose motto is "Peace at any price," or "If you can't fight 'em, join 'em."

composed (kəm pozdˊ—*o* as in *note*) *adj.* The verb *compose* has a good many meanings, one of the least used of which is to "calm" or "quiet" someone. The form *composed* is commonly used as an adjective meaning "calm." A *composed* person is tranquil, relaxed, serene, the opposite of nervous or jumpy. There is nothing in the world more *composed* than the face and attitude of Buddha as they appear in countless sculptures and paintings all over India. The English poet Matthew Arnold (1832–1904) wrote these lines:

> Cruel, but *composed* and bland,
> Dumb, inscrutable and grand,
> So Tiberius might have sat,
> Had Tiberius been a cat.

How true: is there anything calmer, more tranquil, more serene, more *composed,* than the household cat sitting on a chair, quite convinced that he or she is the most important member of the family?

comprehend (kom prih hendˊ) *vb.* To *comprehend* something is to understand it fully, to grasp its meaning; in slang, to "get" it; in Black English, to "dig" it. Is it possible that Nixon did not *comprehend* the nature of his acts during Watergate? The American poet Henry Wadsworth Longfellow (1807–1882), in *The Secret of the Sea,* wrote:

> Only those who brave its dangers
> *Comprehend* its mystery!

When people use language loosely, without sufficient attention to the exact meanings of words, it is often difficult to *comprehend* what they are trying to say. *Comprehension* (kom prih hen' shən) is the noun, meaning "understanding, grasp." It is dangerous to underestimate young children's *comprehension* of what is going on around them. (Little pitchers have big ears.) *Comprehend* has another meaning, not in common use: to "include, embrace," in the way that a general science course may *comprehend* both chemistry and physics. Reflecting this meaning, we get the adjective *comprehensive* (kom prih hen' siv), meaning "broad," having a wide scope, covering a lot of territory. A *comprehensive* course or book or study covers a wide range of its subject. The great U.S. Supreme Court Judge Louis D. Brandeis (1856-1941) wrote that "the right to be let alone [is] the most *comprehensive* of rights and the right most valued by civilized men."

comprehensive (kom prih hen' siv) *adj*. See **comprehend**.

concede (kən seed') *vb*. To *concede* is to admit, to yield, to acknowledge. If you and I have been having an argument and you finally convince me, I will *concede* that you are right. As the election returns come in and virtually establish that Jones can't win, he will normally *concede* defeat, i.e., admit it, or *concede* the election, i.e., yield it to his opponent. The noun *concession* (kən sesh' ən) is used in a number of ways. *Concession* is the act of *conceding*. Late at night, as the disappointing returns come in, or at the end of a long but fruitless labor negotiation, *concession* may be the best way out. But *concession* can also be used to signify the point *conceded*, as when a labor union wins enough *concessions* to call off the strike. The great abolitionist Frederick Douglass (1817-1895) declared: "The whole history of the progress of human liberty shows that all *concessions* yet made . . . have been born of earnest struggle." Douglass was speaking of *concessions* won by the underprivileged. The Irish statesman and orator Edmund Burke (1729-1797), championing the struggle of the colonies, spoke of those made by the weaker side. In his great speech to Parliament in 1775 on conciliation with America, he said: "The *concessions* of the weak are the *concessions* of fear." When we speak of the checkroom *concession* in a nightclub or the peanut *concession* at a ball game, all we mean is a commercial privilege granted for a special service in a public space. This is a special business usage.

concession (kən sesh' ən) *n*. See **concede**.

concise (kən sise') *adj*. A *concise* statement or report in one that is succinct, brief, and to the point, while covering the subject adequately for the purpose. When an explanation is demanded in any situation, the more *concise* it is, the better. The American grammarian William Strunk, Jr. (1869-1946), author of a definitive work entitled *The Elements of Style*, wrote: "Omit the needless words. Vigorous writing is *concise*. A sentence should contain no unnecessary words, a paragraph no unnecessary sentences." Good advice, but beware: Samuel Johnson (the great Dr. Johnson—1709-1784, the English dictionary writer, poet, critic, and conversationalist) warned: "In all pointed sentences, some degree of accuracy must be sacrificed to *conciseness.*" How to find your way between the two—that is the art of writing.

conclude (kən klood´—*oo* as in *boot*) *vb. Conclude* has, among others, two common meanings which are quite distinct. When you *conclude* something, like a speech or a letter, you end it, bring it to a close. Politicians like to *conclude* speeches with a quotation from Abraham Lincoln or Franklin D. Roosevelt, or better still, by invoking God. Long-winded people find it hard to *conclude* any sentence. Teachers usually *conclude* their lectures by announcing the next reading assignment. But *conclude* has another meaning, quite different from "terminate." When, after considering the weather and all other circumstances, you *conclude* that the best course of action is to postpone a trip, you are *determining* something by reasoning. To *conclude* something, in this sense, is to decide it after thinking things over. An expert examining a painting will consider all the elements and may or may not *conclude* that it is an authentic old master. After hearing all the witnesses, the jury will *conclude* the guilt or innocence of the accused. The noun *conclusion* (kən kloo´ zhən—*oo* as in *boot*) partakes of both meanings: the *conclusion* of a scene, act, play, book, voyage is its *end*; the *conclusion* of the jury is its *determination*. The English poet and novelist Rudyard Kipling (1865-1936) used the now familiar phrase "ultimate conclusion" in *The Female of the Species*: ". . . Man accepts the compromise./Very rarely will he squarely push the logic of a fact/To its ultimate conclusion. . . ." Shakespeare coined the even more familiar expression "foregone conclusion" in *Othello* (Act III, Scene 3), when, after Iago invents a lie about Cassio's talking in his sleep of his "affair" with Desdemona, Othello exclaims that "this denoted a foregone conclusion" (i.e., that his wife was an adulteress). Shakespeare used the phrase in the sense of "a previous experience," but it has now acquired the meaning of "an inevitable outcome or inference, a sure result." We take these timeworn phrases for granted. It is sometimes difficult to realize that they (like the four-note opening of Beethoven's Fifth) had to be invented.

concoct (kən kokt´) *vb.* When you put together a bit of this and a bit of that and come up with a tasty dish, you have *concocted* it, put it together. To *concoct* a dish is to contrive it by combining ingredients. Food items are not the only thing that people *concoct*: one can *concoct* a scheme, for instance, or an excuse. To *concoct* a scheme or a plan is to devise it; when you *concoct* an excuse, there is the implication that you've had to stretch a bit to invent one that isn't wholly sincere. There is something hit-or-miss and often a bit fishy about *concocting.*

concur (kən kur´—*u* as in *burn*) *vb.* To *concur* is to agree, to share an opinion or a plan of action. If you make a statement and I agree with it, *I concur*; if I don't, I dissent. If you get a second medical opinion and the second doctor doesn't *concur* with the first man's diagnosis, do you get a third man to arbitrate? (This could be expensive.) The noun is *concurrence* (kən kur´ əns—*u* as in *burn* or *but*). A chairman of the board likes to have the unanimous *concurrence* of the directors. *Concur* has another less common meaning: to "coincide." One's wedding anniversary may *concur* with one's birthday, for instance. In this case, *concur* expresses the idea of *happening together,* or at the same time. That shade of meaning is reflected in the adjective *concurrent* (kən kur´ ənt—*u* as in *burn* or *but*). Things are *concurrent* when they occur at the same time, like *concurrent* attacks by land and sea or *concurrent* experiments at several laboratories, or when they exist side by side, like the *concurrent* authority of a number of officials, the *concurrent* jurisdiction of two courts, or *concurrent* (rather than consecutive) sentences imposed by a judge. It often happens in our language that a noun or adjective related to a verb reflects principally only one meaning of the verb, often a less common meaning.

confront (kən frunt´) *vb.* To *confront* someone is to "face" him, not in the passive way in which one building faces another, but actively, sometimes with the implication of presenting evidence of a misdeed that has to be admitted or explained away. A man *confronted* with a bloody knife bearing his fingerprints had better come along quietly. One can speak of two armies *confronting* each other, or labor *confronting* management. In the war between England and France portrayed in Shakespeare's *King John,* the armies (Act II, Scene 1) *confront* each other at Angiers. A messenger announces England's victory; a neutral citizen remarks: "Blood hath bought blood, and blows have answer'd blows;/Strength match'd with strength, and power *confronted* power." In this sense, *confront* denotes meeting in opposition. There was always trouble on the streets of Verona when, in Shakespeare's *Romeo and Juliet,* members of the feuding Montagues and Capulets *confronted* one another. The noun is *confrontation* (kon frən tay´ shən); it partakes of the various meanings of the verb. *Confrontation* usually implies that the parties are in opposition, whether it be *confrontation* of an individual by the police, *confrontation* between congressmen and senators trying to work out a compromise bill, or *confrontation* between armies.

congenial (kən jeen´ yəl) *adj. Congenial* people are agreeable, pleasant to be with, friendly. A *congenial* couple are suited to each other; a *congenial* group of people get along well. In *The Deserted Village,* the English poet Oliver Goldsmith (1728-1774) lists the many things about "Sweet Auburn! loveliest village of the plain" that are so endearing, including "To me more dear, *congenial* to my heart/One native charm, than all the gloss of art." The noun *congeniality* (kən jee nee al´ ih tee—*a* as in *hat*) describes the sort of personality that is warm and outgoing, agreeable, and sociable, easy to get to know and get along with—the very opposite of standoffish.

connoisseur *(kon* ə sur´—*u* as in *hurt*) *n.* This word, borrowed from the French, applies to a person who is knowing and competent judge of what is best in his field, especially in the arts and matters of taste, though it can apply to other fields as well, like dress, food and drink, cars, interior decoration, or social behavior. *Connoisseurs* must be qualified not only to pick and choose, but to issue critical judgments for the guidance of ordinary mortals. Bernard Berenson (1865-1959) was the leading fine-arts *connoisseur* of his generation. Based on its literal meaning, a *connoisseur* is "one who knows," as opposed to a dilettante, who only thinks he knows. Sometimes, in the opinions of some, *connoisseurs* go too far. So thought the Rev. Richard Harris Barham (1788-1845) in his amusing work *The Ingoldsby Legends* (a *connoisseur* of poetry might call it *doggerel*):

> Though port should have age,
> Yet I don't think it sage
> To entomb it as some of your *connoisseurs* do,
> Till it's losing its flavour, and body, and hue;
> —I question if keeping it does it much good
> After ten years in bottle and three in the wood.

The Connoisseur is the name of a magazine devoted to antiques and interior decoration, and the word is a favorite name for shops in that field.

connotation (kon ə tay′ shən) *n.* Words not only have their basic, explicit, primary meanings, but also suggest secondary meanings associated with them, so that a certain additional image is created. These associated meanings are called *connotations,* and the word in question is said to *connote* (kə note′) the secondary meaning or image. The word *flag,* for instance, describes a material object, but *connotes* love of country and patriotism. "Hearth" *connotes* cozy family life; "home" *connotes* a center of comfort and family affection. People's names can have *connotations* as well. "Hitler" *connotes* evil, "Churchill," courage, "Hamlet," indecision ("To be, or not to be . . ."). These associated meanings are *connotations.*

consequence (kon′ sə kwens, -kwəns) *n.* The *consequence* of something is its result or outcome. Poverty is the usual *consequence* of reckless extravagance. A good scholastic record is the *consequence* of efficient study habits. *In consequence* is a phrase meaning "as a result." It is said that many people refrain from crime not because of innate goodness but because of what they fear may happen *in consequence.* The plural is often used to mean "the result": If you act recklessly, you'll have to take *the consequences. Consequence* means "importance" or "significance" in the phrase *of consequence,* as when someone or something is described as *of consequence,* or *of no consequence* or *of little consequence.* The Rev. Richard Harris Barham (1788-1845), in *The Ingoldsby Legends,* gives this good advice: "A servant's too often a negligent elf;/—If it's business *of consequence,* do it yourself!" The related adverb *consequently* means "therefore," or "as a result." Ronald Reagan stressed Jimmy Carter's lack of achievement and *consequently* won the election with ease.

consistent (kən sis′ tənt) *adj.* When you say something which is in agreement with your previous statement, or act in the same manner as you have previously done, your statement or your act is *consistent* with what you previously said or did, and you yourself can be described as *consistent.* The English writer H. G. Wells

(1866–1946) said that no human being "is altogether noble nor altogether trustworthy nor altogether *consistent*, and not one is altogether vile. . . ." *Inconsistent* (in kən sis' tənt) is the opposite: self-contradictory. *Consistency* (kən sis' tən see) in the noun from *consistent*, and is an admirable quality, especially when you are arguing a point. But the American poet and essayist Ralph Waldo Emerson (1803–1882) issued this famous warning: "A foolish *consistency* is the hobgoblin of little minds . . . with *consistency* a great soul has simply nothing to do . . . speak what you think today . . . and tomorrow speak what tomorrow thinks . . . though it contradict everything you said today." The point may be obvious: Literal *consistency* for *consistency's* sake, regardless of changing circumstance, may be nonsense. "Circumstances alter cases," wrote the Canadian jurist and author Thomas Haliburton (1796–1865). Also, on the subject of *consistency*, who was it who first endorsed a lady's privilege to change her mind? *Consistency* has another, altogether distinct meaning: the degree of firmness of a substance, as in the *consistency* of cement or whipped cream.

construe (kən stroo') *vb.* To *construe* is to interpret or explain, to infer or deduce. From someone's expression, you can usually *construe* his mood. When you enter a room and people stop talking and look at one another silently, you might *construe* the situation as a meeting in which you were the subject of discussion. Shakespeare used *construe* in *Julius Caesar* (Act I, Scene 3) in the sense of "interpret," when Cicero says: "Men may *construe* things after their fashion,/Clean from the purpose of the things themselves." In other words, people may *construe* or interpret events in their own way, which may be wholly different from what the events really meant. Again, in *The Two Gentlemen of Verona* (Act I, Scene 2), Julia tells her maid Lucetta, " . . . maids, in modesty, say 'No' to that/Which they would have the profferer [suitor] *construe* 'Ay.' " (They say "No" but want the gentleman to *construe* "No" as "Yes.") This brings to mind the old saw: When a lady says "No," she means "Maybe"; when a lady says "Maybe," she means "Yes"; and when a lady says "Yes," she's no lady. Shakespeare skipped the "Maybe."

conventional (kən ven' shə nəl) *adj. Conventional* behavior or dress or taste is that which is accepted as in line with normal standards. A three-piece pin-striped suit is *conventional* attire for professional and business people; a smock is *conventional* for artists and sculptors. The adjective is based upon the noun *convention* in the sense of "generally accepted practice," endorsed by usage and custom. *The conventions* are the rules of behavior looked upon by society as normal and acceptable. They vary from place to place and from period to period. There is quite a gulf between *the conventions* of New York and those of the Fiji Islands, and between those of the Victorian age and what is acceptable today. *Unconventional* (un kən ven' shə nəl) is the opposite, describing things or manners that do not conform to the usual. The English librarian, writer, and essayist Richard Garnett (1835–1906) gave this advice: "Ascend above the restrictions and *conventions* of the world, but not so high as to lose sight of them." Betty Friedan (born 1921), an American leader in the struggle for women's rights, wrote, in *The Feminine*

Mystique: "When she [woman] stopped conforming to the *conventional* picture of femininity, she finally began to enjoy being a woman."

conversant (kən vur´ sənt—*u* as in *fur*) *adj.* To be *conversant* with something is to be familiar with it, as a result of experience or study. If you live in a country long enough, you become *conversant* with its language, customs, people, and geography. A regular reader of the daily newspapers will be *conversant* with the events of the day. People who are out in the world and rub shoulders with their fellow men are *conversant* with life in a way that cannot be acquired by sitting at home and reading about it. *Conversant* suggests familiarity and acquaintance, rather than deep, definitive knowledge. A person with a good ear, living in France for a while, would be *conversant* with the French language, knowledgeable and able to handle it. But one would not say that the head of the French Department at Harvard or Oxford was *conversant* with French; he would be expert on the subject.

converse (kən vurs´—*u* as in *fur*) *vb.*, (kon´ vurs—*u* as in *fur*) *n.* *Converse* is a familiar verb, meaning to "talk informally" with someone, discussing events, views, ideas, etc. Accented differently, on the first syllable, it is a noun describing something that is the opposite or reverse of something else. The weather in Australia is the *converse* of that in the northern United States: warm in winter, cold in summer. "A rainy day and a clear night" is the *converse* of "a clear day and a rainy night." Two couples may be the *converse* of each other: an attractive woman and an unattractive man meet an attractive man and an unattractive woman. (This may lead to complications.) Which do you think is safer, a stable ship skippered by an unstable captain, or its *converse,* an unstable ship with a stable skipper? (I'll take *terra firma.*)

convey (kən vay´) *vb.* When you *convey* an object from one place to another, you carry it or transport it. But not only tangible objects can be *conveyed*: You can *convey* a thought, an idea, a plan, any item of knowledge to another person. In this sense, to *convey* is to transmit, communicate, impart something, to share it with another person, to make it known to him. It is the duty of Intelligence in every nation to collect information about hostile countries and *convey* it to the proper authorities. The noun is *conveyance* (kən vay´ əns), which, quite apart from its meaning of "vehicle," is equivalent to *transmission* or *communication.* The prompt *conveyance* of information is essential in every military, diplomatic, or business activity.

cope (cope) *vb.* To *cope* is to struggle and strive, with the implication that the struggle meets with success. The verb is usually followed by *with*: one *copes with* whatever problem or situation presents itself. Sailors have to *cope* with weather, tides, and currents. Scientists *cope* with failure after failure in the laboratory. One must admire the physically handicapped for *coping* with all the special problems that arise from their disabilities. Husbands and wives used to have different things to *cope* with—he with the pressures of the office, she with those at home; in these days of working mothers, both spouses tend to *cope* with both types. Every advance in technology seems to bring more problems to *cope* with: The automobile brought pollution and traffic jams, the splitting of the atom, fear of the end of life on our planet.

copious (koe′ pee əs) *adj.* What is *copious* is plentiful, abundant, in great supply. How painful to see starvation in so many parts of the world, while we in the West are surrounded by *copious* supplies of food. Weather is the chief factor in determining whether there will be a meager or a *copious* harvest. People in the theater hope and pray for *copious* audiences. *Copious* is a very positive word, and in connection with material things, like food or money, suggests the image of the horn of plenty, known in classical times as *cornucopia* (in Latin, *cornu* means "horn" and *copia* means "plenty").

correspond (kor ih spond′) *vb.* When one thing conforms to another, it *corresponds* with it. Here, *correspond* denotes that the two things are in harmony or agreement. A report should always *correspond* with the facts. Actions do not always *correspond* with promises. *Correspond* can be used in another way, in pointing out an analogy or similarity. In this usage, *correspond* is followed by *to* rather than *with*. The Prime Minister of England *corresponds* to the President of the United States; each is the head of government. The wing of a bird or the flipper of a seal *corresponds* to the human arm. These usages are distinct from each other, and neither has anything to do with the use of *correspond* to describe communication between persons by exchange of letters.

corrupt (kə rupt′—*u* as in *but*) *adj., vb.* A *corrupt* person is dishonest, guilty of crooked activities and practices. A *corrupt* society is base, evil, depraved. In *The Human Factor*, a novel by the English writer Graham Greene (born 1904), we read: "Our worst enemies . . . are not the ignorant and the simple, however cruel; our worst enemies are the simple and *corrupt*." Adlai Stevenson (1900–1965) said in a campaign speech: "Government . . . must be . . . the effective agent of a responsible citizenry, not the shelter of the incompetent and the *corrupt*." *Corrupt* is also a verb: To *corrupt* is to destroy someone's honesty and integrity, by persuasion, often by bribery. Lord Acton (1834–1900) wrote, in his famous letter to Bishop Creighton: "Power tends to *corrupt* and absolute power *corrupts* absolutely," echoing the English statesman William Pitt (1708–1778), who said: "Unlimited power is apt to *corrupt* the minds of those who possess it . . . ," and the poet Shelley (1792–1822), who wrote: "Power . . . /Pollutes what e'er it touches. . . ." The ancient Greek philosopher Socrates (469–399 B.C.), who introduced new ideas among his young disciples in Athens, was condemned to death by the authorities on the charge of "*corrupting* the youth." *Corruption* (kə rup′ shən) is the noun, and can denote either the act of *corrupting* or its result. In his novels *I, Claudius* and *Claudius the God*, the English poet and novelist Robert Graves (born 1895) painted a vivid picture of the *corruption* of ancient Roman society.

cosmic (koz´mik) *adj.* The *cosmos* is the universe. Its adjective, *cosmic*, apart from its literal meaning, "pertaining to the cosmos," is used figuratively in the sense of "vast, limitless, immeasurably far-reaching." *Cosmic* events are world-shaking; they affect all people and all places. *Cosmic* is sometimes used in the sense of "universal, all-encompassing." In her diary, the American writer Anaïs Nin (1903-1977) wrote: "There is not one big *cosmic* meaning for all; there is only the meaning we each give to our life." *Cosmic* is too often used about things that are not of universal importance, especially in the exaggerated language of promoters. The music of the Beatles, innovative as it was, did not really measure up to its description by one disc jockey as a *"cosmic* breakthrough." *Cosmic* should be saved for events or phenomena that really affect the world, like the discovery of oil, or the landing on the moon.

cosmopolitan (koz mə pol´ ə t'n) *adj.* A *cosmopolis* (koz mop´ə lis) is a city, like New York, Paris, or London, inhabited by people from countries all over the world. Such a place can be described as *cosmopolitan*. A *cosmopolitan* person is one who, having traveled and read widely, feels at home all over the world. *Cosmopolitan* is used to describe people who are the opposite of provincial, people who are without narrow views. A person of that sort can be described as a *cosmopolite* (koz mop´ ə lite). Henry Kissinger is a familiar example. The British poet Alfred, Lord Tennyson (1809-1892) had this to say about such people: "That man's the best *Cosmopolite*/who loves his native country best." This feeling was echoed by his contemporary the British statesman and writer Benjamin Disraeli (1804-1881), who spoke of "*cosmopolitan* critics, men who are the friends of every country save their own." It would appear that these patriotic Englishmen (Tennyson, a Poet Laureate, and Disraeli, a Prime Minister) were somewhat suspicious of *cosmopolites*. Yet it is *cosmopolitan* people, with world outlooks based on *cosmopolitan* living and attitudes, who would seem to be best suited to lead their countries.

couch (kouch—*ou* as in *house*) *vb.* To *couch* a thought or a feeling is to put it into words, to frame it, to express it. When you want someone to do you a favor, you should *couch* your request in modest, rather than demanding, language. If you feel strongly about an abuse, you can *couch* your emotions in forceful language without being abusive yourself. Poets *couch* their thoughts in imaginative, expressive language. In *Troilus and Cressida* (Act I, Scene 1), Troilus, a Trojan prince hopelessly in love with Cressida, daughter of a priest who has gone over to the Greek side in the war, is trying to put on a brave face, and speaks of "sorrow that is *couch'd* in seeming gladness" (tears behind the outward smile). Try to *couch* your thoughts carefully and clearly, and use *couch* occasionally as a variation on *frame* or *express*.

counsel (coun´səl—*ou* as in *hound*) *n., vb. Counsel* is advice, and to *counsel* is to advise. "Who cannot give good *counsel?*" asked the English churchman and writer Robert Burton (1577-1640), "'Tis cheap, it costs them nothing." This cynical truth has come down to us in the shortened version: "Advice is cheap." The Bible (Ecclesiastes 37:13) tells us: "Let the *counsel* of thine own heart stand." In other words, follow the *counsel* or advice of your own heart. Good *counsel* is rare, and often hard to follow. Wise leaders *counsel* calm in emergencies. An honest man will *counsel* objectively, regardless of his own interests. One who *counsels* is a *counselor*, an adviser. *Counselor* has special uses, as in *camp counselor, school counselor*, or *counselor* as a synonym for *lawyer*. Do not confuse *counsel* with *council* (an *assembly*, especially one appointed by a governing official to act in an advisory capacity) or *consul* (an official appointed by a government to protect its citizens and interests in another country). *Consul* is often mispronounced *counsel*.

countenance (koun' t'n əns—*ou* as in *loud*) *n., vb.* A *countenance* is a face, especially its expression, as in a *happy countenance* or a *frightened countenance*. In Shakespeare's *Hamlet* (Act I, Scene 2), Horatio describes to Hamlet the expression on the face of his father's ghost in the famous line: "A *countenance* more in sorrow than in anger." *Countenance* has an entirely different meaning as a verb: to *countenance* something is to tolerate it, to stand for it. If the Western democracies had not *countenanced* Hitler's early aggressions, there might never have been a World War II. Parents who *countenance* bad behavior in little children will have trouble with them as adults. *Countenance*, as a verb, usually appears in the negative: "I will not *countenance* such behavior!" *Countenance* is not always synonymous with *permit* or *allow*; often it has the flavor of *approve* or *endorse*. There are times when we do not have the power to prevent something from happening, but are very much against it. In such a case, to refuse to *countenance* it is to state one's disapproval of it, to withhold one's endorsement, without the ability or authority to stop it.

covert (kuv' ərt—*u* as in *but,* koe' vərt) *adj.* See **overt**.

covet (kuv' it—*u* as in *but*) *vb.* To *covet* something is to desire it eagerly, usually with the implication that the desire is for something belonging to someone else and therefore wrongful. The best-known use of *covet* is the last Commandment (Exodus 20:17): "Thou shalt not *covet* thy neighbor's house . . . thy neighbor's wife . . . nor any thing that is thy neighbor's." The English poet Arthur Clough (1819-1861) wrote a satirical poem, "The Latest Decalogue" (*Decalogue* means "Ten Commandments") in which we read: "Thou shalt not *covet*; but tradition/approves all forms of competition." Inscribed on a marker near his grave in Indiana is the creed of Wendell Willkie (1892-1944): "I believe in America because . . . we hate no people and *covet* no people's lands. . . ." The adjective *covetous* (kuv' ə təs—*u* as in *but*) stresses the wrongful aspect. A *covetous* person is one who is jealous of what others have and spends much energy in envy. *Coveted* (kuv' ə təd) is often used as an adjective in a phrase like the *coveted Nobel Prize*, the *coveted Medal of Honor*, in which *coveted* means only "highly desirable" or "eagerly sought after," with no implication of wrongful craving.

crevice (krev´ is) *n.* A *crevice* is a narrow opening resulting from a crack. The *crevice* can occur in the surface of the earth, a road, the ice, massed snow, walls and floors of buildings, etc. After an earthquake, there are usually wide *crevices* in roads and building walls. The detestable Aaron, in Shakespeare's *Titus Andronicus* (Act V, Scene 1), reciting his bloodthirsty exploits, says, "I pry'd me through the *crevice* of a wall. . . ." That would have had to be a rather large opening.

cringe (krinj) *vb.* To *cringe* is to shrink or crouch out of servility, or to cower in fear or horror. Uriah Heap, the villainous servile clerk in *David Copperfield*, by Charles Dickens (1812-1870), is always pictured as fawning and *cringing*. A self-abasing toady will often *cringe*, to make the object of his flattery feel superior. Another type of *cringing*, having nothing to do with fawning or servility, is *cringing* out of fear. A little boy, or an animal being whipped, will *cringe*. People will *cringe* involuntarily out of fear on hearing a terrific bang, as from an explosion, or out of horror at the sight of a terrible accident or its result.

criterion (kry teer´ ee ən) *n.* A *criterion* is a basic rule for testing something, a principle or standard on the basis of which judgments are made. The English lexicographer Henry Fowler (1858-1933) gives this illustration of the use of *criterion*: "Success is no *criterion* of ability," echoing the Irish statesman and orator Edmund Burke (1729-1827), who wrote these words: "The only infallible *criterion* of wisdom [according] to vulgar judgments—success." A *criterion* of courage is behavior under fire. The basic *criterion* for admission to a first-class college is one's record in secondary school. The plural of this word, taken over intact from classical Greek, is *criteria* (kry teer´ ee ə). *Criteria* may be unvarying in any one person, but differ among people: One man's meat is another man's poison. When one reads the differing reviews of critics, one realizes how subjective *criteria* can be, particularly in matters of taste. Note the plural form *criteria*. Like *phenomenon* and other words from the Greek ending in *-on*, the last syllable becomes *-a* in the plural.

crucial (kroo´ shəl—*oo* as in *boot*) *adj.* Anything *crucial* is critical, decisive, urgent. In its literal sense, *crucial* describes something in the nature of a supreme, final trial, or a final decision or ultimate choice. Imminent danger to others presents a *crucial* test of a person's courage and selflessness. The Civil War was a *crucial* period in American history. Torn between love and duty, man is faced with a *crucial* choice. *Crucial* economic and social difficulties face country after country in these troubled times. What is *crucial* is severe, trying, and supremely critical. The word is too strong to be used as a synonym of merely *important*; it should be reserved for situations far more intense than that.

culprit (kul´ prit—*u* as in *but*) *n.* Technically, this term describes a person charged with a crime, but it is widely used for "the guilty party," any person guilty of an offense or fault. It can be used jocularly, like *villain*, as in "Who is the *culprit* that left the back door open?" In modern usage, you can use the term in a general way: "Robert is a *culprit*. You can't trust him." But it is better to use the term with reference to a particular offense or fault: The lock gate of a dam was left open and the countryside was flooded; a drunken lock keeper turned out to be the *culprit*. Or after a robbery: "Let the *culprit* keep the money. It's my driver's license I want back!"

cumulative (kyoo´ myə lay tiv, -ə tiv—*oo* as in *boot*) *adj.* *Cumulative* describes anything that increases by successive additions. It is often used in the expression *cumulative effect*. The *cumulative effect* of water dripping on a stone is to wear a hole in it. The *cumulative effect* of harsh weather is to erode hills and mountains. Scientific activity builds up a *cumulative* body of knowledge that helps to explain the nature of the world we live in. As witness after witness testifies against an accused, the *cumulative* body of evidence results in a verdict of guilty.

curious (kyoor´ ee əs—*oo* as in *book*) *adj.* This word has two distinct meanings, which have to be understood from context. *Curious* can mean "inquisitive," describing a person eager to learn or find out about something. Thus: "I am *curious* about the origin of that fire." People who come across unexpected objects are *curious* to know how they got there. One feels *curious* about people who dress or act oddly. The other meaning is "queer, odd, strange," applied to anything or anybody that arouses our attention because the person or thing is highly unusual or his or its action is hard to explain. One sees a mongrel dog, the result of an unusual mixture. "There's a *curious* animal for you!" The poor dog isn't *curious* in the other sense (he's not looking about to discover anything); he's just *curious*, odd, strange. An unexplained event, like a loud bang in the middle of the night, may be described as *curious*. The usual form of the comparative of *curious* is *more curious*, even though Lewis Carroll (1832-1898) caused Alice to exclaim "*Curiouser and curiouser!*" as she was exposed to the wonders of Wonderland. *Curiosity* (kyoor ee os´ ih tee—*oo* as in *book*) can apply in either sense. *Curiosity* is inquisitiveness, the desire to learn and find out about something. (*Curiosity* killed a cat.) The English historian G.M. Trevelyan (1876-1960) said: "Disinterested intellectual *curiosity* is the lifeblood of real civilization." Anatole France (1844-1924) wrote: "The whole art of teaching is only the art of awakening the natural *curiosity* of young minds." A *curiosity* (note the article) is anything strange or rare or unusual. *The Old Curiosity Shop* is the title of a novel by Charles Dickens (1812-1870). *Curio* is a shortened form.

current (kur´ ənt—*u* as in *fur* or *but*) *adj.* Anything *current* exists or is happening at the present time. (The phrase *then current* would refer to an earlier time.) *Current* can be applied to opinion, rumor, practice, or fashion, the plays or movies now running. The *current* issue of a newspaper or magazine is the latest one. In medicine, the *current* practice is to call in a specialist if the G.P. has the slightest doubt. The *current* budget deficit is staggering. The *current* state of anything, like a war or a political campaign, refers to what is going on now. The *current* usage in America is to address a letter to *Mr.* So-and-So, whereas the *current* British practice is to address it to So-and-So, *Esq.* The adverg *currently* means "now, at the present time." I am *currently* (Winter 1982–1983) engaged in the writing of this book. *Currently* there is unrest in many parts of the world, alas.

curry (cur´ ee—*u* as in *fur* or *but*) *vb.* Apart from the use of this word in the grooming of horses and the flavoring of food, *curry* often occurs in the expression to *curry favor.* When someone *curries favor* with the boss, he is trying to ingratiate himself and better his position by playing up to him through flattery and servile attentions. "Teacher's pets" incur the contempt and anger of their schoolmates by *currying favor* with the teacher. *Currying favor* is the main activity of toadies who appeal to the ego of those in superior positions by "buttering them up." (There exists, of course, the inevitable wordplay about the Indian people's *favoring curry.*)

cursory (kur´ sə ree—*u* as in *fur*) *adj.* When you give someone a *cursory* glance, you are only looking at him hastily and superficially, without paying any attention to details. A *cursory* look is the opposite of a thorough inspection. In a *cursory* reading of a letter, details or subtleties may escape you, because anything *cursory* is in its nature hurried and hits only the high spots. Some communications require careful, thorough reading and thought; others (like those "Letters We've Never Finished Reading" appearing in *The New Yorker*) deserve nothing more than a *cursory* glance on their way to the wastebasket. (The first sentence usually gives you your cue.) Correspondence from the Internal Revenue Service and other bill collectors is too important to be treated in a *cursory* manner. The material in this book may amuse you, but won't teach you much if it is treated *cursorily* (kur´ sə rih lee).

curt (kurt—*u* as in *fur*) *adj. Curt* is a short, crisp word for *short,* usually found in phrases like *a curt reply* or *a curt dismissal.* The use of *curt* implies a degree of rude abruptness. *Curtness* in speech is unfriendly and can be disconcerting. *Curt* manners are characteristic of people who want to be left to themselves and discourage conversation. Top sergeants are usually depicted as issuing *curt* commands to trembling raw recruits. *Curt* speech may offer the advantage of conciseness, but it contains, at the same time, the defect of bluntness, and invokes the image of a nastily curling lower lip.

curtail (kur tale´—*u* as in *fur*) *vb.* To *curtail* something is to cut it short, to reduce it, to cut out part of it. People who eventually get to the point where they have to say, "Well, to make a long story short" should learn the art of *curtailing* their narratives. An abridged dictionary is a *curtailed* edition of an unabridged one. *The Reader's Digest* consists mainly of *curtailed* versions of articles that have appeared in full elsewhere. *Curtail* can be applied whenever the concept is one of cutting short or lessening, as well as abridging. Inflation has *curtailed* luxury spending; people have had to *curtail* their vacations because of rising costs. Bad weather *curtails* many activities, like picnics and outdoor sports.

customary (kus´ tə merr ee) *adj.* What is *customary* is usual or habitual, established by *custom* or habit, expectable. Churchill almost always appeared with his *customary* cigar, Roosevelt with the *customary* cigarette holder. In Shakespeare's *Hamlet* (Act I, Scene 2), Hamlet refers to his "*customary* suits of solemn black." It is *customary* for the host to taste the wine before filling the guests' glasses. People are quick to condemn anything that is not *customary*. It is *customary* to tip waiters, taxi drivers, and barbers. The announcement of each guest at a Rotary Club meeting is met by the *customary* smattering of applause. What is *customary* depends on the circumstances: long hair among the youth, shorter hair on older heads. It is *customary* for natives to go barefoot in Africa; not so in Manhattan.

cynic (sin´ ik) *n.* A *cynic* believes that the only thing that motivates people is self-interest, that nobody is ever altruistic. The American writer and journalist Ambrose Bierce (1842–1914?) defined a *cynic* as "a blackguard whose faulty vision sees things as they are, not as they ought to be." This definition is from his *Devil's Dictionary,* originally published under the title *The Cynic's Word Book.* Oscar Wilde (1854–1900) wrote these lines (*Lady Windermere's Fan*): "What is a *cynic*? A man who knows the price of everything and the value of nothing." Bierce thought a *cynic* was a realist, despite his jaundiced view of the world; Wilde felt that a *cynic* had a wrong set of values. The adjective *cynical* (sin´ ih kəl) describes people who mistrust everybody's motives. *Cynical* people, believing that nobody is honest, often act dishonestly themselves and exploit really honest people. To take a *cynical* view of people and their actions is to think the worst of them. *Cynicism* (sin´ ih siz əm) is the belief of *cynics*. People who practice *cynicism* don't believe that there is such a thing as goodness or nobility. Such people are said to have a *cynical* disposition, and are much given to making *cynical* remarks about human nature.

dabble (dab´ əl) *vb.* To *dabble* in something is to engage in it in a superficial way. When you *dabble* in an activity, you involve yourself in it in a small way; the thing you *dabble* in is a hobby rather than a career. There are those who *dabble* in politics, others who *dabble* in carpentry. Winston Churchill *dabbled* in landscape painting and bricklaying; Harry Truman *dabbled* in piano playing. *Dabbling* has the implication that one's efforts are incidental and that the results don't count for much. In context, the term is sometimes used in a derogatory way, as though to dismiss the activity as of no account or as presumptuous, as when one is commenting on someone's ineffectual efforts to break into a theatrical career by volunteering for work in amateur productions ("He's not really acting; he's just *dabbling.*"); but *dabble* can be used to describe a perfectly harmless activity in which someone chooses to pass his spare time.

dank (dank) *adj.* This word is used to describe a damp, moist, humid place that has a disagreeable atmosphere. Dungeons are almost always described as *dank*; cellars are often *dank*. A *dank* place is usually cold, in an unwholesome way. Caves, especially long ones, are usually *dank*. *Dank* can be used to describe a deep, dark forest where the sunlight never penetrates. Jungles are *dank*. It is unpleasant to be in a place that is *dank*; the word brings up the image of gloomy, unhealthy surroundings.

dapper (dap' ər) *adj.* A dapper person is trim, neat, and well groomed in appearance. The term is usually applied to small people, and more often to men than to women. It somehow implies that the person described took greater pains than were really necessary to improve his appearance; he fussed too much. Not that the term is derogatory: being *dapper* is preferable to being sloppy. A well-pressed new suit, with shirt, tie, and socks all fitting into a carefully chosen color ensemble, makes a man *dapper*. It doesn't necessarily make him chic—or interesting.

dawdle (daw' d'l) *vb.* To *dawdle* is to hang around doing nothing, loitering, wasting time, taking forever to get started on something. "Stop *dawdling!*" cries Mother. "Help me with the dishes, or get your homework done; stop *dawdling*, do something!" Sometimes followed by *away*: People can *dawdle away* years jumping from one project to another, without ever getting down to anything. One can *dawdle* one's life *away*, daydreaming, never getting down to real work. To *dawdle away* an afternoon waiting for something to happen is to fritter it away. *Dawdlers* get nowhere.

debatable (dih bay' tə b'l) *adj.* To *debate* is to argue, and to *debate* a question or an issue is to discuss various aspects of it in order to come to a decision. *Debatable*, apart from its literal use, means "open to question, doubtful." Whether or not our country should have interfered in Vietnam is *debatable*. It is a *debatable* question whether homicide is grounds for capital punishment. Some paintings presented as old masters and a few plays attributed to Shakespeare are of *debatable* authenticity.

debilitate (dih bil' ih tate) *vb.* To *debilitate* a person is to weaken him, to set him back. A long siege of illness will *debilitate* even the strongest person. *Debilitating* means "weakening" or "tending to weaken." The heat and humidity of tropical countries create a *debilitating* climate. A series of misfortunes can have a *debilitating* effect on anyone's spirit. One financial setback after another will *debilitate* a company's prospects. Fever *debilitates* both mind and body.

debonair (deb ə nare'—*a* as in *dare*) *adj.* A *debonair* person is charming, gracious, lighthearted, bright, cheerful, and of elegant and courteous manners. The English poet William Cowper (1731–1800) described Frenchmen as "easy, *debonair*, and brisk . . . always happy." *Debonair* stresses the aspect of elegance in dress, manners, and general attitude. Maurice Chevalier and Fred Astaire personify the *debonair* approach to life. The white carnation in the buttonhole, the jaunty stride, and the genial smile all typify the *debonair*.

debris (də breeʹ, day-) *n.* This noun is applied to the scattered remains and ruins of something destroyed, the leftover rubbish. Unhappily, we are all too familiar with television pictures of people searching for bodies among the *debris* after an air raid or artillery barrage. *Debris* can denote an accumulation of rubbish generally, like the *debris* littering unswept streets and vacant lots in depressed sections of a city, as well as the *debris* of an ancient civilization being carefully examined by archaeologists. The British accent the first syllable (dehʹ bree), as they almost always do in the case of two-syllable words taken over from the French.

deceive (dih seevʹ) *vb.* This is a familiar word, describing the act of making someone believe something that isn't so, misleading him. It gives rise to two useful adjectives: *deceitful* (dih seetʹ fəl) and *deceiving* (dih seeʹ ving). A *deceitful* person is one who habitually *deceives* people. You can't trust a *deceitful* individual. One can also speak of a *deceitful* manner, *deceitful* language, *deceitful* actions—all intentionally misleading. The Bible warns us (Proverbs 27:5-6) that "the kisses of an enemy are *deceitful*." *Deceiving* is different, in that intention is missing. A mirage in the desert is *deceiving*: it looks like something that it isn't. A quiet man may have a *deceiving* manner; he may have a lot to say when he gets around to saying it. Aesop (lived around 550 B.C.), the author of the fables, reminded us that "appearances are often *deceiving*."

decipher (dih syʹ fər) *vb.* To *decipher* something is to make out its meaning. One has a hard time *deciphering* some people's handwriting. Old manuscripts are often hard to *decipher*. One of the meanings of the noun *cipher* is "secret code." To understand something transmitted in *cipher*, it has to be *deciphered*. This literal meaning of *decipher* was broadened to include the interpretation of anything obscure or difficult to understand, whether the difficulty arises from the words themselves, the handwriting or printing, or the deterioration of a manuscript, an engraving on an ancient monument, etc. The American poet T.S. Eliot (1888-1965) wrote of "old stones that cannot be *deciphered*."

decisive (dih syʹ siv) *adj.* This word can be used in two ways. It describes any event that determines a result and puts an end to arguments. Waterloo was the *decisive* battle of the war between Napoleon and the English. Fossils are the *decisive* proof of the theory of evolution. The tapes were *decisive* in proving Nixon's involvement in the Watergate cover-up. A second use of *decisive* is to describe a person or an act or an attitude that is firm, resolute, determined, and authoritative. Franklin Roosevelt acted in a *decisive* manner as soon as he became President. General George Patton (1885-1945) was known for his *decisive* character and way of commanding the troops. *Decisive* people are those who *decide* and act firmly upon their *decisions*.

decline (dih klīne') *n., vb. Decline* has a number of meanings. As a verb, to *decline* something is to refuse it. If you don't want to go to a party, you *decline* the invitation, or simply *decline*. If you are busy, you *decline* to give a television interview. In a wholly different usage, to *decline* is to decrease, weaken, go lower. Sales *decline* in a recession. Strength *declines* with age. A nation can *decline* in importance. As a noun, a *decline* is a loss of strength. We usually see a sharp *decline* in the stock market after bad news. People tend to go into a *decline* after a serious illness, or other misfortune. The English historian Edward Gibbon (1737-1794) wrote *The Decline and Fall of the Roman Empire*. The English novelist Thomas Hardy (1840-1928) blamed the "melancholy . . . of the civilized races [on] the *decline* of belief in a beneficent power."

decrepit (dih krep'it) *adj. Decrepit* means "feeble, worn-out, dilapidated," with the implication that the condition described is the result of old age or hard use. One is always saddened by the sight of a *decrepit* old horse that can barely walk. Abandoned houses in ghost towns become *decrepit* through age, weather, and neglect. Shakespeare wrote (Sonnet XXXVII) of the " . . . *decrepit* father [who] takes delight/To see his active child do deeds of youth." In his *Henry VI, Part 1* (Act V, Scene 4), Joan of Arc denies that an old shepherd is her father and when he appears, calls him a "*Decrepit* miser! base ignoble wretch!" *Decrepit* is the apt description of those unfortunate alcoholics one sees on the streets, prematurely aged by drink and neglect.

defame (dih fāme') *vb.* To *defame* someone is to attack his good name and character by maliciously or falsely saying or publishing bad things about him, and in that way to injure his reputation. To *defame* orally is to *slander*; to *defame* in writing is to *libel*. These are legal distinctions; *defame* is the general term covering both *slander* and *libel*. Iago *defamed* Desdemona by telling Othello lies about her, accusing her of adultery. The French army *defamed* Alfred Dreyfus (1859-1935) by falsely accusing him of treason. Material which *defames* is *defamatory* (dih fam' ə tor ee), and the utterance or publication of the *defamatory* material is *defamation* (def ə may'shən). The comedian Carol Burnett was awarded a large sum as damages for *defamation* by a periodical. In 1895 Oscar Wilde (1854-1900) ill-advisedly brought suit against the Marquess of Queensberry for *defamation*. (He dropped his suit, but was jailed for immoral conduct on the basis of facts established in the lawsuit.)

defer (dih fur'—*u* as in *fur*) *vb. Defer* has two different meanings. To *defer* an appointment is to postpone it, to put it off for a while. If you're in doubt about what to do, it is usually a good idea to *defer* coming to a decision. When bad weather threatens, people *defer* plans for a picnic. In this sense, the noun is *deferment* (dih fur'mənt), meaning "postponement." The other meaning has to do with yielding and showing respect. It is usually wise to *defer* to the opinions of those with more experience than you. In a proper family, young people *defer* to their elders. In this usage, the noun is *deference* (def´ ər əns), which reflects both the yielding and the respect. *Deference* can describe yielding to the wishes or opinions of others, and also conveys the sense of "respect." We should treat our elders with *deference*. When an important person enters the room, we show *deference* to him by rising. We observe a moment of silence on Veterans Day in *deference* to the memory of fallen soldiers. The adjective is *deferential* (def ə ren´shəl). Lawyers maintain a *deferential* attitude toward judges. Most people act *deferentially* in the presence of celebrities.

deficient (dih fish´ ənt) *adj. Deficient,* usually followed by *in,* means "lacking." A person *deficient* in knowledge is lacking in it; a building *deficient* in space has not enough room for the particular purpose in question. A program for action lacking in detail would be *deficient* in detail. Mentally subnormal people are described as *mentally deficient.* The noun is *deficiency* (dih fish´ ən see). There is a *deficiency* when a person is short of what he needs. A *deficiency* of vitamins may cause illness. A *deficiency* of effort often causes failure. *Deficiency,* in context, can also mean the amount by which something is insufficient or inadequate. If a ticket costs $3, and you have only $2, there is a *deficiency* of $1.

deft (deft) *adj. Deft* means "nimble, skillful." A *deft* person is quick and clever at whatever he puts his hand to. The word is most often used to describe quick, skillful action with one's fingers. A good potter or weaver must be *deft*; so must a good sportsman, mechanic, or waiter. People who use their hands well, for instance, in taking care of repairs around the house, are called "handy." *Deft* would suit the picture just as well.

deign (dane) *vb.* To *deign* is to condescend. When you *deign* to do something, you believe it to be barely within your dignity to do so. It is most often used in the negative. Snobs walk right by common people without *deigning* to look at them. When a stupid remark is aimed at a sensible person, he won't *deign* to respond. In other words, he won't stoop to reply. In Shakespeare's *Taming of the Shrew* (Act V, Scene 2), the reformed shrew, Katharina, compares an angry woman to a muddy fountain, from which there is " . . . none so dry or thirsty/[As] will *deign* to sip or touch one drop of it."

demagogue (dem´ ə gog) *n.* A *demagogue* is a political leader who seeks to gain or retain power by arousing the populace through appeals to their emotions rather than their reason. The noun for this practice is *demagoguery* (dem ə gog´ ə ree). Hitler and Mussolini are examples of a rise to power through *demagoguery.* When Marc Antony, after the assassination of Julius Caesar in Shakespeare's play of that name (Act III, Scene 2), made his famous funeral oration ("Friends, Romans, countrymen, lend me your ears . . . ") he was acting the part of a typical *demagogue.* The Senator from Louisiana Huey Long (1893-1935) was a spellbinding *demagogue. Demagogues* may rise quickly to giddy heights of power, but their fall is even more rapid. Joseph McCarthy, the Senator from Wisconsin (1909-1957), was a skillful *demagogue* for a while, but quickly fell into disrepute and disgrace.

demeanor (dih meen′ ər) *n*. *Demeanor* is a person's way of behaving. People are admired for their gentle *demeanor*, despised for their cruel *demeanor*. People of haughty *demeanor* are generally disliked. The use of *demeanor* often implies that it is behavior toward another person that is being discussed. Someone is in a room, quite passive; on another person's entrance, the first one's *demeanor* changes, based on their relationship, the circumstances, the timing. When, in Shakespeare's *Comedy of Errors* (Act II, Scene 2), Antipholus of Syracuse tells his servant Dromio to "fashion your *demeanor* to my looks," he is telling his servant to take his cue from the way his master looks and behave accordingly. It is quite usual for people's *demeanor* to change according to who's there and what's happening.

demur (dih mur′—*u* as in *hurt*) *vb*. When you *demur* to or at something, you raise an objection to it, take exception to it. *Demur* often implies that the objection is based on scruples or principles. If a decent person is offered a promotion in the company over the head of senior members of the staff, he may well *demur* at accepting it. On the other hand, if given an unfair work load, he may *demur* at the extra responsibility. *Demur* can be used by itself, without taking an object. When the citizens of Rome, a republic, wanted to make Julius Caesar emperor and offered him a crown, he *demurred*. If one is offered an honor or a position he feels he is not entitled to accept, he should *demur*.

denote (dih note′) *vb*. To *denote* is to be a sign of something, to signify or indicate it, or simply to mean it. The hands of a clock *denote* the hour. The thing that *denotes* can be a mark, like the apostrophe in *don't*, which *denotes* the omission of the *o* in *not*, or an *x* in mathematics, *denoting* an unknown quantity. A skin rash can *denote* an insect bite, contact with poison ivy, or an allergic reaction. A guilty look on a child's face *denotes* that he has done something he'd rather you didn't know about.

denounce (dih nouns′—*ou* as in *noun*) *n*. To *denounce* somebody is to speak against him or condemn him publicly. The radio newscaster Edward R. Murrow (1908-1965) *denounced* Senator Joseph McCarthy (1909-1957) in such forceful terms that McCarthy's career went sharply downhill. McCarthy himself had been America's chief *denouncer* for years, ruining innocent people's careers. One can *denounce* a belief or action as well as a person. Churchill *denounced* Nazism; Hitler *denounced* communism; Stalin *denounced* capitalism. *Denounce* can be used to express the idea of making a formal charge against a person for a specific offense, in a court, or to the police in the way a person may be *denounced* as a spy. *Denunciation* (dih nun see ay′ shən) is the noun. Whittaker Chambers' *denunciation* of Alger Hiss as a courier of government documents to the communists led to Hiss's downfall. The *denunciation* of Julius and Ethel Rosenberg for feeding atomic secrets to Russia led to their execution as traitors. The American author and critic H. L. Mencken (1880–1956) wrote: "... newspapers never defend anyone or anything if they can help it; if the job is forced upon them, they tackle it by *denouncing* someone or something else." The American judge Learned Hand (1872–1961) condemned any society "where *denunciation*, without specification or backing, takes the place of evidence."

depict (dih pikt´) *vb.* To *depict* something is to describe it in words or pictures, to present a picture of it, to portray it. We are all familiar with scenes from the Bible *depicted* in stained-glass windows. There is an implication in the verb *depict* that the portrayal of description is vivid and faithful in detail to the original scene. There are huge tapestries that *depict* great occasions in history, like naval battles or royal gatherings. One can *depict* in words as well as pictures. In *Brideshead Revisited*, Evelyn Waugh (1903–1966) *depicted* the breakup of an aristocratic family. *The Divine Comedy* of Dante (1265–1321) *depicts* the tortures of hell and purgatory and the delights of heaven.

deplete (dih pleet´) *vb.* When something is *depleted*, it is used up, consumed, or exhausted until nothing or almost nothing remains. *Depletion* (dih plee´shən) of something implies such a serious decrease as to threaten its continued existence. Pollution has *depleted* marine life in many parts of the world. Waste and carelessness have *depleted* our natural resources. The *depletion* of the water supply in parts of Africa has caused widespread famine and disease.

derive (dih rive´) *vb.* To *derive* something is to get it from a certain source. People *derive* strength from a period of rest and recreation. You *derive* encouragement from the approval of your friends. Students *derive* great benefit from serious attention to their studies. *Derive* has a special meaning in connection with language, in tracing the origin of words. A great many English words are *derived* from Latin. The word *derive* itself is *derived* from the Latin word *derivare*.

desirous (dih zy´ rəs) *adj.* To be *desirous* of something is to have a strong *desire* for it. Some people are *desirous* of wealth, others of power, others simply of peace and quiet. In Shakespeare's *Henry VI, Part 3* (Act IV, Scene 8), the King, worried about the loyalty of the nobles, protests: "I have not been *desirous* of their wealth." *Desirous* should not be used merely to express a passing wish. To *desire* something is to want it; to be *desirous* of something is to want it badly, to *covet* it, to have a powerful longing for it.

desolate (des´ ə lət) *adj.*, (des´ ə late) *vb.* A *desolate* place is neglected, barren, unlived in, gloomy, lonely, and forbidding. One thinks of the wild windswept country around Wuthering Heights in the novel of that name by Emily Brontë (1818–1848), as *desolate*. A battlefield, after a devastating conflict, is *desolate*. Beirut today is a *desolate* city. The noun is *desolation* (des ə lay´ shən); it describes dreariness, devastation, and barrenness when applied to a place, and loneliness and woe when describing a person. War causes *desolation* of both places and people. A *desolate* person is sad, lonely, forlorn, hopeless, with a feeling of friendlessness and abandonment. Exiles feel *desolate* in foreign countries. One sees tens of thousands of *desolate-looking* refugees on television screens, leading *desolate* lives, or mere existences. The verb (note different pronunciation) *desolate* means "lay waste, ravage," and is usually found in descriptions of the effects of war, famine, and plagues. The ten plagues described in the Bible *desolated* the land of Egypt.

despot (des′ pət, -pot) *n*. A *despot* is a tyrant, a ruler with absolute power; the adjective is *despotic* (des pot′ ik). *Despotism* (des′ pət iz əm) describes the manner in which a *despot* rules, equivalent to *tyranny*, and can also apply to a country ruled by a *despot*. The English writer and lexicographer Samuel Johnson (the great "Dr. Johnson," 1709-1784) said: "A country ruled by a *despot* is an inverted cone." Abraham Lincoln, speaking of "the spirit which prizes liberty," said: "Destroy this spirit and you have planted the seeds of *despotism* at your own doors." France, until the death of Louis XVI in the French Revolution, was a *despotism*. The Russian czars were *despots*. *Despot* and its related words apply technically to nations, but they can apply figuratively to any person who rules with an iron hand, like the leader of a gang, a political boss, an office manager, or the top man in a company.

detect (dih tekt′) *vb*. To *detect* something is to become aware of its existence. A trained diagnostician will *detect* an internal condition from external symptoms. Carbon monoxide is especially dangerous because you cannot *detect* its presence by odor or color. *Detection* (dih tek′ shən) is the act of *detecting*. A *detective* (dih tek′ tiv) is engaged in *detecting* crime and criminals. People try to escape *detection* by wearing disguises. Conan Doyle (1859-1930) put these words into the mouth of Sherlock Holmes: "*Detection* is, or ought to be, an exact science. . . . " The American jurist Learned Hand (1872-1961) said: "I had rather take my chance that some traitors will escape *detection* than spread abroad a spirit of general suspicion and distrust. . . ."

deter (dih tur′—*u* as in *fur*) *vb*. To *deter* is to restrain or discourage somebody from doing something. When you want to discourage people from walking on your lawn, you attempt to *deter* them by putting up a sign. (*Beware of the Dog* is more effective than *Keep Off the Grass*.) *Deter* can mean "stop" in the sense of *check* or *arrest*: There are paints that *deter* metals from rusting. The noun *deterrent* (dih tur′ ənt—*u* as in *fur* or *but*; —terr—) is applied to anything that tends to *deter*. People have been arguing for many years about whether the death sentence is a *deterrent* to murder. Nowadays, the word *deterrent*, all by itself, is used in discussions about the pros and cons of great stockpiles of nuclear arms: will they act as *deterrents*—i.e., will they *deter* nations from starting wars?

detest (dih test′) *vb*. When you *detest* something, you dislike it intensely, you find it hateful, you can't stand it, you simply loathe it. Some people adore cats;

others *detest* them. Lazy people *detest* having to get up early to go to work. You can *detest* people as well as things: one *detests* hypocrites as well as hypocrisy. Decent people *detest* road hogs. Everybody *detests* traffic jams. Lord Byron (1788-1824), in *Don Juan*, wrote: "Men love in haste, but they *detest* at leisure." The adjective is *detestable* (dih test´ ə b'l), meaning "hateful, abominable." Is there any crime more *detestable* than child abuse, or the mugging of poor, defenseless old women?

deviate (dee´ vee ate) *vb.*, (dee´ vee it) *n.* To *deviate* from something is to turn away from it, to leave it, with the implication that you are turning away from what is usual or normal. If you travel the same route day after day, and one day turn off to go a different way, you are said to *deviate* from the normal road; or if you act a certain way, and suddenly act differently, you have *deviated* from your customary behavior. To *deviate* from the truth is to lie. An unexpected change of course or habit is a *deviation* (dee vee ay´ shən). A *deviate* (note the difference in pronunciation of the noun) usually refers to any person who departs radically from normal standards of behavior, as encountered in the term *sexual deviate*.

devious (dee´ vee əs) *adj.* A *devious* person is shifty, tricky, deceitful. *Devious* can be applied to crooked plans like those get-rich-quick schemes that fleece naive people of their life savings. *Devious* people or schemes are cunning and underhand, anything but straightforward and honest. Door-to-door salesmen are often *devious* in their approach to the gullible prospect. *Devious* methods are all too common in business and politics. Read the fine print carefully; those "conditions" are sometimes couched in *devious* language.

deviltry (dev´ əl tree) *n.* *Deviltry* is mischief, recklessly uninhibited mischievous behavior. After little Junior has pulled down the tablecloth, pushed over the flower vase, and pulled all the books out of the bookcase, Mother cries, "What *deviltry* will you be up to next?" *Up to some deviltry or other* is a common phrase to express one's feeling about a youngster who's out too late, or a friend who is famous for reckless exploits. *Deviltry* doesn't usually imply wickedness, but rather, well-meant, yet possibly dangerous mischief. The forms *devilry* and *devilment* exist but are relatively uncommon. *Deviltry* is occasionally used in the sense of "high spirits, hilarity," but it usually describes devil-may-care conduct ascribable to high spirits (or simply alcoholic spirits).

devote (dih vote´) *vb.* To *devote* oneself or one's time or energy is to concentrate on a particular cause or activity. Missionaries *devote* themselves to spreading Christianity among pagan natives in faraway places. Albert Schweitzer (1875-1965), the Alsatian doctor, writer, and musician, *devoted* much of his life to the care of lepers in Africa. The form *devoted* (dih voe´ tid) means "loyal, loving." It is well to be surrounded by *devoted* friends. Queen Elizabeth II, of the United Kingdom, takes great pleasure in the love of her *devoted* subjects. *Devotion* (dih voe´ shən) is strong love and deep attachment. The Bible tells us of Ruth's *devotion* to her mother-in-law Naomi (Ruth: 16): "Wither thou goest, I will go. . . . " There are many famous paintings showing a mother's *devotion* to her children. *Devotion* can also mean "dedication," as when a soldier is cited for *devotion* to duty, or a life is spent in *devotion* to science or education. A *devotee* (dev ə tee´) is a fan, an enthusiastic supporter. A rock fan is a *devotee* of rock music; a sports fan is a *devotee* of sports.

devoted (dih voe´ tid) *adj.* See **devote**.

devotee (dev ə tee´) *n.* See **devote**.

diction (dik´ shən) *n.* This word is generally used to mean a person's manner of speaking. *Diction* is usually discussed in terms of *clear diction* or *unclear diction*, especially with respect to actors, singers, and public speakers. Laurence Olivier (born 1907) is famous for the clarity and elegance of his *diction*. Legend has it that the Greek orator Demosthenes (384–322 B.C.) overcame a speech impediment by practicing oratory with a pebble in his mouth, and thus acquired remarkable *diction*. The problem with most singers is that although their notes may be excellent, their *diction* is unintelligible. The word *diction* technically includes choice of words and manner of writing as well as speaking, but its use is almost always confined to matters of clarity of speech.

differentiate (dif ə ren´ shee ate) *vb.* To *differentiate* between two things is to be aware of the *difference* between them, to distinguish them from each other, and generally, to treat them as *different*. In handling people, it is important to *differentiate* between those quick to get the point and those who require patient explanation. When you tackle a situation, you have to *differentiate* the various sides of the problem from one another. It is wrong to *differentiate* between applicants for a job on the basis of the color of their skin. The act of *differentiating* between things or people is called *differentiation* (dif ə ren shee ay´ shən). Women's Lib rightly argues against *differentiation* between men and women in the pay scale. Cf. **discriminate**.

dilapidated (dih lap´ ih day tid) *adj.* Anything described as *dilapidated* is falling to pieces, in a state of decay or ruin, as a result of age, neglect, abuse, etc. After the Civil War, the great plantation homes that weren't burned to the ground became *dilapidated*. Jalopies are *dilapidated* old automobiles. During the 1849 gold rush, prospectors lived in *dilapidated* cabins or tents. *Dilapidation* (dih lap ih day´ shən) describes the state of being or getting to be *dilapidated*. After all those terrific bombings and battles, the once beautiful city of Beirut fell into a state of *dilapidation*. The *dilapidation* of our urban slums is a stain on modern society.

diligent (dil´ ih jənt) *adj.* A *diligent* person is one who pursues his aims with great care and effort, who is hardworking and persevering in his attempts to accomplish his aims. Efforts can be described as *diligent* as well as people. A *diligent* student will make *diligent* efforts to master his subject. *Diligence* (dil´ ih jəns), the noun, describes constant and steady effort in a person's activities. The Bible says (Proverbs 22:29): "Seest thou a man *diligent* in his business? He shall stand before kings." In *Don Quixote*, the great novel by Miguel de Cervantes (1547-1616), we read, "*Diligence* is the mother of good fortune, and idleness, its opposite, never brought a man to the goal of any of his best wishes."

dilute (dy loot´, dih loot´—*oo* as in *boot*) *vb., adj.* To *dilute* something is to make it weaker, by adding something to it, the way one *dilutes* wine with water. *Dilute* can be used in a figurative sense, as when the force or effect of one's efforts is *diluted* by inattention or distraction. (Don't mix business and pleasure!) The noun is *dilution* (dy loo´ shən, dih loo´ shən—*oo* as in *boot*). The degree of *dilution* of whiskey with water determines the "proof," i.e., the alcoholic content. Mixing untrained workers with skilled labor results in *dilution* of efficiency.

diminish (dih min´ ish) *vb.* To *diminish* something is to lessen or reduce it. To *diminish* is to become less. If you turn the faucet down, you *diminish* the flow of water. The supply of water can be said to *diminish*. The enormous expenditures of war cause tremendous borrowing, which *diminishes* the wealth of a nation. Its currency *diminishes* in value. The English poet Robert Browning (1812-1889) asked: "Do your joys with age *diminish?*" The German physicist Herman von Helmholtz (1821-1894) wrote: "Nature . . . possesses a store of force which cannot in any way be either increased or *diminished* . . . " The Roman poet Lucretius (99-55 B.C.) wrote: "Some nations increase, others *diminish* . . . " *Diminishing returns* is a term that describes any situation where added investment or effort fails to produce proportionately increased benefits: you put in 50 percent more effort or money and get back only 25 percent better results. The "returns" are proportionately *diminished*.

diminutive (dih min´ yə tiv) *adj.* Anything or anyone little or tiny may be described as *diminutive*. The use of *diminutive* suggests that the person or thing so described is unusually small. A model railway, especially the tiniest type, consists of *diminutive* cars, locomotives, etc. Midgets are *diminutive* people. In Shakespeare's *Macbeth* (Act IV, Scene 2), Lady Macduff, accusing her husband of cowardice in fleeing from his home, wife, and family, cries: "[even] . . . the poor wren,/The most *diminutive* of birds, will fight—/Her young ones in her nest—/Against the owl." Young married couples often live in apartments so *diminutive* that they can hardly accommodate a single guest. The term *diminutive*, as a noun, is a grammatical term applied to words formed by adding a suffix indicating smallness, like *droplet* (from *drop*), *streamlet* (from *stream*), *lambkin* (from *lamb*), *kitchenette* (from *kitchen*).

disarming (dis ar´ ming) *adj.* A *disarming* smile or look or gesture is one that instantly removes any feeling of suspicion or hostility on the part of the other person. A *disarming* smile makes the people around you friendly. Literally, to *disarm* someone is to deprive him of his weapons, the way prisoners of war have their *arms* taken away. *Disarming* is a figurative use of the word, involving charm that wipes away unfriendly feelings. This usage was undoubtedly brought about by the fact that most people are at least a bit suspicious and worried about the other fellow (if not downright paranoid); though they don't carry actual *arms*, they often have to be *disarmed* of their unfriendly attitude— hence, the *disarming* smile.

disavow (dis ə vow´—*ow* as in *wow*) *vb.* See avow.

discern (dih surn´, -zurn´—*ur* as in *fur*) *vb.* To *discern* is to see clearly, to perceive, either actually (with one's eyes) or intellectually (with one's mind). The use of *discern* often implies that the seeing or perceiving was done with some effort. Through thick smoke, firemen try to *discern* the figures of any people trapped in a burning building. Experienced sailors can *discern* ships at great distances. Moral people know how to *discern* right from wrong. It is sometimes hard to *discern* the truth. *Discernment* (dih surn´ mənt, -zurn´-, *ur* as in *fur*) is the ability to judge and to discriminate; to see what's what; to distinguish fact from fiction. A person of *discernment* in one field, like music or drama, may lack *discernment* when it comes to judging character. A *discerning* person is one who shows good judgment and clear understanding, one who sees clearly. To be a good judge, one must be a *discerning* student of human nature. It is usually safe to buy theater tickets on the basis of the judgment of a *discerning* drama critic.

disclose (dih skloze´) *vb.* When you *disclose* something, you reveal it, make it known. A prisoner of war cannot legally be forced to *disclose* anything more than his rank and serial number. There are those who protest that they can keep a secret, but the people they *disclose* it to can't. The noun *disclosure* (dih skloe´ zhər) can describe either the act of *disclosing* (the *disclosure* of the sailing date resulted in the ship's being torpedoed) or the thing *disclosed* (the sailing date was a tragic *disclosure*). *Disclosure* in the second sense usually refers to something previously kept secret. In Shakespeare's *Julius Caesar* (Act II, Scene 1), Portia, knowing that her husband Brutus is deeply worried about something, but unable to induce him to confide in her, asks him to tell her what's going on: "Tell me your counsels [plans], I will not *disclose* 'em."

disconcert (dis kən surt´—*ur* as in *fur*) *vb.* When you *disconcert* someone, you upset him, ruffle him, disturb his calm and self-possession. A person can be *disconcerted* by realizing that he has gone to the wrong address and is half an hour late for an important appointment. It is *disconcerting* to hear a bad weather report for the day when you are planning a picnic. Heckling is *disconcerting* to a public speaker. It is quite *disconcerting* to discover, when you are out for the evening, that you have left the key to the house at home.

disconsolate (dis kon´ sə lət) *adj.* To *console* (kən sole´) an unhappy person is to offer him sympathy and comfort. *Consolation* (kon sə lay´ shən) is the act of *consoling*, or the thing that *consoles*: a wide circle of well-wishing friends can be a *consolation* during illness. One who is beyond *consolation* is *inconsolable* (in kən soe la b'l), usually at the loss of something or somebody. People become *disconsolate* at the loss of a loved one, or of their youth, their beauty, their health, or their wealth. In Shakespeare's *Julius Caesar* (Act V, Scene 3), Titinius tells Messala that he left Cassius, whose forces had just been overthrown by Marc Antony's, "All *disconsolate* . . . on this hill"; when they look further, they find Cassius's body.

discord (dis' kord) *n*. *Discord* is disagreement; when it becomes active, it amounts to quarreling. *Discord* between husband and wife can lead to divorce. All too often, when a parent dies, there is *discord* in the family about the division of the estate. *Discord* between your ideas and mine is merely a difference of opinion, and should be ironed out without strife. In music, *discord* is a harsh and unpleasant combination of tones. *Discord* is common in contemporary musical composition. The adjective is *discordant* (dis kor' dənt). When you and I don't agree on a subject, our opinions are *discordant*. When music is *discordant*, it grates on the ears. In *The Song of Hiawatha* by the American poet Henry Wadsworth Longfellow (1807-1882), this advice is given to warring factions:

> All your strength is in your union.
> All your danger is in *discord*;
> Therefore be at peace henceforward,
> And as brothers live together.

He echoed Aesop (c.550 B.C.), the writer of fables, who said, in "The Bundle of Sticks": "Union is strength." And remember: "*E pluribus unum*," to say nothing of "Divide and conquer!"

discourse (dis' kors—*o* as in *core*) *n.*, (dis kors'—*o* as in *core*) *vb*. A *discourse* is a formal discussion, whether written or oral, like a speech, a lecture, or a treatise. A sermon is a *discourse* delivered by a religious official in a place of worship. Lectures at school are specialized *discourses*. To *discourse* (note difference in accent) upon a subject is to discuss it formally, in speech or writing, to lecture on it, with the strong implication that the talking or writing is done at length. Some teachers *discourse* upon a subject at such length that boredom sets in and nothing is remembered. Sir William Gilbert (1836-1911), of Gilbert and Sullivan, has the poseur poet in *Patience* (Act I) sing:

> You must lie upon the daisies
> and *discourse* in novel
> phrases of your complicated
> state of mind,
> The meaning doesn't matter if
> it's only idle chatter. . . .

Here, Gilbert uses *discourse* intentionally to indicate tiresome bombast.

discreet (dih skreet') *adj*. A *discreet* person is tactful, careful, and prudent in what he says or does; a *discreet* person maintains a *discreet* silence about things of a delicate nature when he judges that the situation requires it. The English poet Alexander Pope (1688-1744) wrote: "Satire's my weapon, but I'm too *discreet!* To run amuck, and tilt at all I meet." One should be *discreet* about passing confidential information on to friends. *Discretion* (dih skresh' ən) has two distinct meanings: "*discreetness*" and "freedom of choice or action." It is important to use *discretion* (i.e., to be *discreet*) in choosing your friends or partners. The "age of *discretion*" is the age at which one is deemed capable of making one's own decisions. *Discretion* (we all know) is the better part of valor; in other words, don't stick your neck out unnecessarily. The Greek writer of comedies Menander (342-291 B.C.) gave this advice: "The man who runs may fight again," echoed later by the Carthaginian Tertullian (160-230): "He who flees will fight again," and still later in the jingle "He who fights and runs away/ Will live to fight another day." However, the same Menander also wrote: "At times *discretion* should be thrown aside and with the foolish we should play the fool." In the other sense, freedom of choice, to *use your own discretion* is to do whatever you think best. When you are given *full discretion* or *discretionary* (dih skresh' ə nerr ee) *powers* in a situation, you have full freedom to make decisions and act as you judge to be for the best.

discretion (dih skresh' ən) *n*. See **discreet**.

discriminate (dih skrim' ə nate) *vb*. *Discriminate* may be used in two quite different ways. To *discriminate between* two things, or *discriminate* one thing *from* another, is to see the difference between them. Only an art expert can *discriminate* between an original and a copy. One must be careful to *discriminate* a sincere compliment from mere flattery. In quite another sense of the word, to *discriminate in favor of* or *against* someone is to make a choice on the basis of something other than true worth or merit. One should treat all people the same way, and not *discriminate* against anyone because of race, color, creed, or sex. One should not *discriminate* against foreigners. It is unfair to *discriminate* in favor of a particular job applicant just because he is a neighbor's son. *Discriminating* (dih skrim' ə nay ting) is quite another story: it is used as an adjective describing those who have developed sensitive tastes and opinions that enable them to distinguish between superior and inferior people or things like works of art, food, etc. *Discriminating* people are connoisseurs. It is wise to follow the advice of a *discriminating* drama critic in choosing the plays you want to see, or to choose your restaurants on the basis of the suggestions of *discriminating* friends. Cf. **differentiate**.

dishearten (dis har' t'n) *vb*. Anything that *disheartens* a person causes him to lose hope or confidence or courage; it depresses his spirits and discourages him. If at first you don't succeed . . . don't be *disheartened*; try again. It is *disheartening* for a writer to receive one rejection slip after another. *Hearten* (har' t'n) is the opposite of *dishearten*: To *hearten* someone is to give him courage, to cheer him. When a friend is in the hospital, we wait and hope for *heartening* news. There were too many *heartening* reports about light at the end of the tunnel, during the Vietnam War, that turned out to be false. The discovery of the truth was quite *disheartening*.

disinterested (dis in′ tə res tid, -trih stid) *adj. Disinterested* and *uninterested* (un in′ tə res tid, -trih stid) *adj.* should not be considered synonymous. A *disinterested* person or decision is one free from personal bias or prejudice, uninfluenced by any selfish motives or considerations. A judge hearing a case must be entirely *disinterested* in the outcome, though deeply *interested* in the proceedings. An *uninterested* person is indifferent; his attention is elsewhere. Even though some dictionaries treat the two words as synonyms, keep *disinterested* to express freedom from personal bias or prejudice, and *uninterested* to express indifference and lack of attention. Sir Ernest Gowers (1880–1966), the reviser of the English lexicographer H. W. Fowler (1858–1933), in *Modern English Usage,* had this to say, after giving examples of the use of *disinterested* where *uninterested* should have been used: "A valuable differentiation is . . . in need of rescue, if it is not too late." It is not too late: Do not let this "valuable differentiation" disappear!

dismay (dis may′) *n., vb. Dismay* is a feeling of fear, surprise and discouragement, disheartenment, deep disturbance and agitation. To *dismay* is to cause any of those feelings. Sudden bad news fills people with *dismay.* The news of the failure of the American attempt to rescue the hostages in Iran struck the entire country with *dismay.* One is always *dismayed* to find out about the disloyalty of a supposed friend. News that poses a threat to the economy *dismays* both management and the working force. At Christmas we hear the carolers sing: "God rest you merry gentlemen,/Let nothing you *dismay.*"

dispatch (dih spach′) *n., vb.* A *dispatch* is a report. Leading newspapers receive *dispatches* from news agencies or reporters all over the world. *Dispatch* can be used in an entirely different way: to *act with dispatch* is to act promptly and efficiently. When the boss gives you an assignment, act with *dispatch* if you want to get ahead in the firm. As a verb, to *dispatch* is to send off with speed, the way you *dispatch* a messenger. If a letter is too slow, *dispatch* a telegram. When Argentina invaded the Falklands, England *dispatched* a great many ships and troops to drive the invaders off. The main idea behind *dispatch,* as a verb, is promptness in sending something or somebody off on a journey to a specific destination.

dispel (dih spel′) *vb.* To *dispel* is to drive off, disperse, scatter to the four winds. A good strong breeze will *dispel* even a heavy fog in a matter of minutes. *Dispel* can be used in the figurative sense. In *The Beggar's Opera* (Act I, Scene 3) by John Gay (1685–1732), we hear these nice words sung: "If the heart of a man is deprest [depressed] with cares/The mist is dispell'd [*dispelled*] when a woman appears." Strong action on the part of the newly elected President Franklin D. Roosevelt in the financial crisis helped to *dispel* the fears of the people. A little experience in the big city, alas, often *dispels* the illusions of young people who have gone there to seek quick fame and fortune.

disperse (dih spurs′—*u* as in *fur*) *vb. Disperse* is very close to *dispel,* and emphasizes the idea of not merely removing or sending away, but actually scattering, sending things off in various directions. A loud noise will quickly *disperse* a flock of birds. The sound of gunfire will cause a crowd to *disperse* in a hurry. One can *disperse* things other than animals and people. It is of the utmost importance, in the developing countries, to *disperse* knowledge in the field of hygiene. A prism *disperses* light into its primary components. Soluble solid chemical compounds are *dispersed* when dropped into the appropriate liquid. *Dispersal* (dih spur′ səl—*u* as in *fur*) is the noun. The *dispersal* of information is vital in the life of a democracy.

dispute (dih spyoot′—*oo* as in *boot*) *n., vb.* A *dispute* is a quarrel, an argument, or a controversy. It is best to settle a *dispute* by reason, not force. When a land title is said to be *in dispute*, there is a question as to who the legal owner is. Anything *beyond dispute* is unquestionable; the phrase is often used adverbially: Shakespeare is *beyond dispute* the world's greatest playwright. Another way of expressing the certainty of something is to use the expression *without dispute*. One can say *without dispute* that there is no sign of life on the moon. To *dispute* is to quarrel or wrangle. There are people who like to *dispute* with anybody about anything. The verb *dispute* is often used to express the idea of questioning the truth or validity of something: Lawyers will *dispute* the testimony of opposing witnesses. There are still those who *dispute* Darwin's theory of evolution. When a will is *disputed* there is a legal contest as to its validity.

disrupt (dis rupt′) *vb.* To *disrupt* something is to throw it into disorder and confusion. Hecklers *disrupt* meetings or conferences by shouting and other antics. Continual disagreement among factions can *disrupt* a coalition government or a labor union. *Disrupt* can express the idea of temporarily breaking something off. Trees blown down by the gale fall on telephone lines and *disrupt* service. The noun is *disruption* (dis rup′shən). As a result of the war between Israel and the PLO, Lebanon has degenerated into a state of *disruption*. Anything causing *disruption* is *disruptive* (dis rup′ tiv). Wildcat strikes have a *disruptive* effect on production. At a court trial, persistent objections by counsel are *disruptive* and delay the proceedings.

dissipate (dis′ ə pate) *vb.* Literally, *dissipate* is synonymous with *dispel* and *disperse* in the sense of "scatter," but its principal use is to express the idea of wasteful and extravagant squandering. People who have no sense of values sometimes *dissipate* a sudden inheritance. Undisciplined people too often *dissipate* their energies by undertaking too many activities at the same time. The noun *dissipation* (dis ə pay′shən) can refer to squandering, when someone speaks of a person's *dissipation* of his fortune, but *dissipation* has come to express the concept of riotous living, especially of heavy drinking and womanizing. The English historian Edward Gibbon (1737–1794) expressed his distaste for the London of those days in these words: "Crowds without company, and *dissipation* without pleasure." The form *dissipated* (dis′ ə pay tid) is used as an adjective to describe people who give themselves up to foolish pleasures, especially wine, women, and song. *Dissipated* people waste their health and money in excessive devotion to the pleasures of the flesh, and, at least in Victorian literature, always come to a sad end. Today, if they have any money left, they sometimes seek help in psychoanalysis.

distasteful (dis tāste´ fəl) *adj. Distaste* (dis tāste´) is dislike; *distasteful* is anything that causes *distaste*, that is unpleasant or offensive or disagreeable. *Distasteful* can describe a nasty medicine, which has a most disagreeable *taste*, but it usually applies to a state of mind. Hard work is *distasteful* to lazy people. The hard facts are often *distasteful* to dreamers. It is *distasteful* to have to face a deluded friend with the unpleasant truth. The English poet Robert Browning (1812–1889) wrote:

> Have you found your life *distasteful?*
> My life did, and does, smack sweet. . . .
> Was your youth of pleasure wasteful?
> Mine I saved and hold complete.

(Lucky Robert!)

distort (dih stort´) *vb.* When you *distort* something you twist it out of shape. When you look into a curved mirror, you see a *distorted* image. Grief can *distort* a person's face. *Distort*, when applied to reporting or narrating, describes twisting the meaning, giving a false account. The communiqués we received from Vietnam *distorted* the facts. Newspaper accounts are sometimes *distorted* because of the reporter's bias. The noun *distortion* (dih stor´ shən—*o* as in *for*) can be applied to the act of *distorting* (the *distortion* of the facts by a reporter) or to the result of *distorting* something (what you see in the curved mirror, or read in a false report). A false bulletin is a *distortion* of the events. Whether one is dealing with a face *distorted* by pain or sorrow, an image *distorted* by a flaw in a mirror, or a report *distorted* by a bias, in every case there is an element of *twisting* (the features, the image, the facts), and that is the literal meaning of *distort*.

diversify (dih vur´ sə fy, dy-, *u* as in *fur*) *vb.* To *diversify* something is to give variety to it. It is wise to *diversify* one's investments, rather than put all one's eggs in one basket. People who *diversify* their activities lead more interesting lives than those who stick to the same routine day after day. Wise farmers *diversify* their crops in accordance with the changing seasons. A landscape *diversified* by streams and rolling hills is much more attractive than a dull, flat plain. The adjective *diverse* (dih vurs´, dy-, *u* as in *fur*) means "of different kinds." Wild flowers in some countries are extremely *diverse*. Versatile people engage in *diverse* activities. From *diverse*, we get the noun *diversity* (dih vur´ sih tee, die-, *u* as in *fur*), meaning "variety". The *diversity* of wild life in Africa induces adventurous people to undergo the discomforts of safari. Restless people seek hobbies to bring *diversity* into their everyday lives.

diversity (dih vur´ sih tee, die-, *u* as in *fur*) *n.* See **diversify**.

divert (dih vurt´, dy-, *u* as in *fur*) *vb. Divert* has two distinct meanings. To *divert* something is to turn it off its course, in another direction, to deflect it. It is sometimes necessary, for building purposes or for irrigation of fields, to *divert* a stream from its natural course. *Divert* can also mean "entertain" or "amuse." Since one's attention from serious activities may be *diverted* by entertainment, *divert* acquired the sense of "amuse." Most people are *diverted* by light comedy on the stage. The noun *diversion* (dih vur´ zhən, dy-, *u* as in *fur*) reflects both meanings. *Diversion* can be used in the sense of turning something off course, as in the *diversion* of traffic, or in the sense of "pastime," such as a hobby like model trains, a sport, or a game like bridge or chess. In addition, *diversion* has a special meaning in military usage: a maneuver that draws the enemy's attention away from the point of the main attack. This procedure is called "creating a *diversion*."

divest (dih vest´, dy-) *vb.* To *divest* someone of something is to take it away from him, to strip or deprive him of it. The word is commonly used in connection with stripping an official, or an official body, of power or authority. Dictators *divest* parliaments or legislatures of their authority. In a successful coup, the rebels *divest* the reigning head of state of his power. A change in the law may *divest* people of the right to travel in certain areas, or *divest* companies of the right to trade with certain countries. One can *divest* oneself of power and authority by resigning from office. People often try to *divest* themselves of responsibility by passing the buck. It is sometimes difficult to *divest* oneself of a nagging idea or worry. Whereas to *divest* someone else of something is to take it away from him, to *divest* yourself of something is to get rid of it. In Shakespeare's *King Lear* (Act I, Scene 1), the aged King unfortunately announces his intention to abdicate in favor of his three daughters in these words, using the royal "we": " . . . now we will *divest* us both of rule/ . . . territory, cares of state . . . " (It turned out to be a foolhardy thing to do.)

divisive (dih vie´ siv) *adj.* Anything *divisive* creates disagreement and discord; it puts an end to harmony. When a parent dies, the problem of distributing the physical assets among the heirs can be a *divisive* factor, causing discord and dissension. Friends can become estranged because of political differences that become *divisive*. The religious question in Northern Ireland has created a tragically *divisive* atmosphere. Smooth relations between management and labor can be affected by the *divisive* tactics of leaders on both sides. *Divisive* has an unpleasant flavor; anything *divisive* always means trouble.

docile (dos´ əl) *adj. Docile* people or animals are easily controlled or managed. It is much more relaxing to ride a *docile* horse than a skittish one. It is easy to bring up a child who is *docile* without being dull, but *docile* and its noun *docility* (doh sil´ ə tee) produce an atmosphere of meekness and timidity when applied to grownups. A husband or wife described as *docile* comes off as being without spirit or sparkle. All the action in Shakespeare's *Taming of the Shrew* is concerned with the husband Petruchio's efforts to turn his shrewish wife Katharina into a manageable, *docile* wife, and live happily ever after. (This was some time before Women's Lib.)

doddering (dod´ ər ing) *adj.* To *dodder* (dod´ ər) is to tremble or quiver from weakness or old age, to struggle along in a shaky, trembling way, to totter. *Dodder,* *totter, teeter,* and *dither* are all related in sound and meaning. The commonest form of *dodder* is *doddering*, usually coupled with *old*, used as an adjective to describe a trembling, tottering person. The phase *doddering old man* brings up the picture of a weak and trembling aged person, shuffling along with short, uncertain steps. An unfortunate sight on our streets is that of a *doddering* alcoholic, an old soak with watery eyes, barely conscious of the world around him.

dominate (dom´ə nate) *vb.* One who *dominates* has control and authority over others. Great men *dominate* through the force of their character and their energy. Strong nations *dominate* over neighboring weak ones. In a message to Congress, President Truman said: "The responsibility of the great states is to serve and not *dominate* the world." The noun is *domination* (dom ə nay´ shən). Theodore Roosevelt (1858-1919) warned that "If we seek merely . . . ease . . . [and] shrink from the hard contests . . . bolder and stronger peoples . . . will win for themselves the *domination* of the world." Apart from its meaning as applied to strong people and nations, *dominate* can be used figuratively to describe a landscape, where a mountain *dominates* a plain or valley, an enormous fir *dominates* the countryside, or a skyscraper *dominates* the skyline. The adjective *dominant* (dom´ə nənt) can describe people, nations, mountain peaks, tall trees, or, in the sense of "ruling, predominating," abstract things: greed is unfortunately a *dominant* motive in human affairs. Wouldn't it be a lovely world if neighborly love were the *dominant* attitude among people?

dowdy (dow´ dee—*ow* as in *down*) *adj.* *Dowdy* clothes are the opposite of chic—they are unfashionably out of style, on the stuffy side. A woman, as well as clothes, can be called *dowdy*; it means that she is dressed in *dowdy* clothes. The term seems never to be applied to men, though there would seem to be no reason why it should not be. The term can also be used of the furnishings of a house or an apartment. *Dowdy* clothes or furnishings are usually messy and shabby as well as out of fashion. People dressed in *dowdy* clothes often acquire their attire at the Goodwill outlets, or seem to have done so.

drastic (dras´ tik) *adj.* The term *drastic* is applied to any act or method or remedy that has a very strong effect. A *drastic* action is severe, often violent. In times of panic, the government has to take *drastic* measures to restore calm. Electric shock is a *drastic* remedy to cure certain emotional or mental illnesses. There is a serious question whether *drastic* punishment or enlightened rehabilitation is the more effective method of curbing crime.

dubious (doo´ bee əs, dyoo´-, *oo* as in *boot*) *adj.* This word can be used in a variety of ways, all of which, in one way or another, involve an underlying element of *doubt.* When one is *dubious* about something, he feels doubtful about it. Some people look so shady that you become immediately *dubious* about their honesty. *Dubious* can mean "questionable" as well. When you feel doubtful or suspicious about someone, or think he is unreliable, you can call him a *dubious character.*

When something is of doubtful quality or effect, it can be called *dubious*. If someone says you're better-looking than a rather ugly person, that's a *dubious compliment*. Triplets might be called a *dubious blessing*. When the outcome of a situation is in doubt, you can refer to it as *dubious*. If a jury stays out day after day, it is obvious that the outcome is *dubious*. As the lead in a game goes back and forth between the rivals, you can describe the teams as engaged in a *dubious* contest. However you use this versatile word, the underlying idea is always that of *doubt*.

dynamic (dy nam' ik) *adj*. *Dynamic* people are energetic, forceful, vigorous, extremely active. A *dynamic* person has great force of character. The word comes from *dynamo*, an electric generator that develops power. A *dynamic* person is sometimes colloquially described as a "dynamo," who is forceful and full of energy. General George Patton (1885–1945) typified the *dynamic* military leader, always on the go, straining at the leash. Franklin D. Roosevelt acted *dynamically* (dy nam' i kəl ee) in his handling of the banking crisis right after he took office. *Dyna-* at the beginning of a word indicates power; *dynamic* people are sometimes colloquially described as *dynamite*.

earmark (eer' mark) *n., vb*. An *earmark*, literally, is a distinguishing mark made on an animal's ear to identify ownership. *Earmark* is commonly used in the figurative sense of a characteristic, a feature that stamps or identifies a person or thing in a special way. The speeches of Senator Joe McCarthy (1909–1957), the father of "McCarthyism," had all the *earmarks* of hypocrisy and demagoguery. A dilapidated house will usually have the *earmark* of poverty and neglect. As a verb, to *earmark* has a quite different use. To *earmark* something is to set it apart for a specific use. Certain funds of a corporation may be *earmarked* for research. A university will *earmark* a specific sum as a scholarship fund. A new shop may *earmark* various types of merchandise as loss leaders. In all these uses, to *earmark* something is to set it aside and devote it to a specific purpose.

earthy (ur' thee—*ur* as in *fur, th* as in *thing*) *adj*. An *earthy* person is down-to-earth, practical, realistic, sensible, unaffected, someone who goes straight to the point. Those legendary Maine farmers, short on speech but long on common sense, are *earthy* fellows. *Earthy* has about it a sense of robustness. One thinks of an *earthy* woman as wearing sensible shoes and wasting no time on the shy and retiring approach. Realists have an *earthy* attitude toward problems, brushing aside those delicate manners that often get in the way of a practical solution. One of the great *earthy* characters in drama is Juliet's nurse, in Shakespeare's *Romeo and Juliet*. In the phrase *earthy humor*, *earthy* takes on the sense of "coarse" or "spicy." Traveling salesmen's jokes have the reputation of *earthiness*. In the old days, women retired to the drawing room after dinner while the men stayed behind at table and indulged in *earthy* conversation, including spicy stories unfit for ladies' ears.

eccentric (ek sen′ trik) *n., adj.* An *eccentric* person or *eccentric* behavior is odd, peculiar, not normal. An *eccentric* is (simply) an *eccentric* person. *Eccentricity* (ek sen tris′ ə tee) is abnormal conduct; *eccentricities* are odd habits. *Eccentrics* are often marked by their strange clothes. It is an *eccentricity* of one person (known to the author) to walk up the stairs backward, for fear of falling down. *Eccentric* conduct is often whimsical, like wearing Edwardian clothes in these modern times. Creative people often behave in an *eccentric* manner, believing themselves to be a cut above the run of the mill. Some men and women, however, are known for nothing but their *eccentricities*, which are all they have to offer. *Eccentricity* is often, like beauty, in the eye of the beholder; what seems *eccentric* to you may seem entirely normal to someone else.

echo (ek′ o—*o* as in *go*) *vb.* We all know what an *echo* is. *Echo* is also a verb, and can be used in two distinct ways. When the audience approves of actors or speakers, the theater or the hall *echoes* with applause. In a figurative sense, to *echo* someone is to repeat or imitate his words or sayings or sentiments. One can speak of *echoing* a person, or *echoing* his sayings or sentiments. Minor officials are fond of *echoing* the words of their leader, whether in government or business. Writers will often *echo* the sayings or sentiments or attitudes of the originators who have gone before. In Shakespeare's *Othello* (Act III, Scene 3), Othello is cross-examining Iago, who keeps stalling by repeating Othello's words. Othello asks, "What dost thou think?" Iago replies, "Think, my lord?" Othello bursts out: "Think, my lord?/By heaven he *echoes* me. . . ." Children are prone to *echo* their elders; take care!

ecstasy (ek′ stə see) *n. Ecstasy* is overpowering, rapturous delight, a feeling of intense joy and emotional uplift. On receiving especially good news, emotional people are thrown into an *ecstasy* of delight. *Ecstasy* is sometimes used to describe the joy and frenzy of artistic inspiration. It was so used in the title of the biography of Michelangelo by the American writer Irving Stone (born 1903), *The Agony and the Ecstasy*. The word is sometimes used in the plural: After an agony of waiting for news about their son reported missing at the front, he is reported alive and well and the family goes into *ecstasies* over the news. In Shakespeare's *Hamlet* (Act II, Scene 1), Ophelia's father, Polonius, ascribes Hamlet's strange conduct to "the very *ecstasy* of love." A person in a state of *ecstasy* is said to be *ecstatic* (ek sta′ tik—*a* as in *hat*). Good news makes sensitive people *ecstatic*. The American poet Emily Dickinson (1830–1886) was wary of *ecstasy*:

> For each *ecstatic* moment
> We must an anguish pay
> In keen and quivering ratio
> To the *ecstasy*.

Ecstatic is often used by gushy people to mean simply "happy" or "delighted," the way "Terrific!" is used when "Great!" or even "Good!" would be enough.

efface (ih fayse´) *vb*. To *efface* something is to wipe it out, obliterate it, remove every trace of it. *Efface* can be used of tangible or abstract things: Time and weather *efface* inscriptions on gravestones. Time alone *effaces* unhappy memories. *Efface* is used figuratively in another way: to *efface* oneself is to keep in the background, to withdraw out of modesty or shyness, to make oneself as inconspicuous as possible. Humble people who do this regularly are said to be *self-effacing*; they want to be lost in the crowd. *Self-effacing* is the opposite of *pushy*, but one must be wary of some *self-effacing* people, who keep a very low profile while waiting to pounce.

effect (ih fekt´) *vb*. We know the meaning of *effect* when it is used as a noun in a sentence like "Rain has a good *effect* on the crops." As a verb, to *effect* something is to bring it about, to accomplish it, to make it happen. The election of a new President or Prime Minister usually *effects* a change in the life of a country. Great care in preparation (and the help of Lady Luck!) *effect* victory in war, debates, or lawsuits. One must work hard to *effect* one's purpose. The right medicine will *effect* a cure. As a result of the efficiency and modern outlook of the new president of the company, the installation of new machinery was *effected* in a short time. Beware of confusing the verb *effect* with *affect*, which means to "act on, produce a change in or an impression on," to "*have an effect* on." It is this last meaning that causes the confusion.

effortless (ef´ ərt lis) *adj*. *Effort* is the use of one's energy to accomplish something. When you *make an effort* to do something you put yourself into it, you make a strenuous attempt to get it done. *Effortless*, as you might expect, means "without effort," and is a meaningful synonym, if used correctly, for "easy." An *effortless* job is an easy one, requiring no or little *effort*. A common phrase is *effortless skill*: a great virtuoso performs with seemingly *effortless* skill (though you can be sure a tremendous amount of *effort* went into study and practicing). *Effortlessly* (ef´ ərt lis lee) is the adverb, and is a good synonym for *easily*, especially when you want to indicate a smooth performance, one that shows no strain. When an athlete or a musician or an actor performs without apparent strain, you say that he did it *effortlessly*. When people perform *effortlessly*, they make it look easy.

egoist (ee´ go ist, eh´-) *n.*, **egotist** (ee´ go tist, eh-) *n*. Though these words (both based on *ego*, Latin for *I*) are often used interchangeably, there is a real difference between their true meanings. An *egoist* is a person who is always selfish, thinking only of his own interests. Such a person can also be described as *egocentric* or *self-centered*. The word *egotist* applies to a vain, conceited, boastful person, self-important, much given to talking about himself. The *egotist* is objectionably full of himself and hogs the conversation with glowing accounts of his achievements. An *egotist* need not be an *egoist*: If you let an *egotist* have his own way and don't interfere with his excessive boastfulness and smug vainglory, he may turn out, in the long run, to be a generous fellow. An *egoist* is the opposite of an altruist; an *egotist* is not necessarily so. *Egoism* (ee´ go izm) and *egoistic* (ee go is´ tik) apply to *egoists*; *egotism* (ee´ go tizm) and *egotistic* (ee go tis´ tik) apply to *egotists*. The difference was well understood by General de Gaulle (1890-1970), who said: "Every man of action has a strong dose of *egotism* . . . [and] pride. . . ."

eke (eek) *vb. Eke* is always used in the phrase *eke* out, usually in the expression *eke out a living*, describing a strenuous effort to support one's existence, by one laborious means or another. A good many people *eke out a living* nowadays by moonlighting at a second or even a third job. Underpaid employees find that the only way they can *eke out* a livelihood is by taking on additional work.

elaborate (ih lab′ ə rate) *vb.*, (ih lab′ ə rət) *adj.* The verb is usually followed by *on* or *upon*: to *elaborate* on a subject, an idea, a theme, a topic, or a proposal is to expand on it, to give it fuller treatment by going into more detail. An author proposes a new book to a publisher; the latter may ask him to *elaborate* on the theme. A job applicant may be asked to *elaborate* on a résumé that is interesting but too sketchy. The adjective (note difference in pronunciation) describes anything worked out with great care and attention to detail. An *elaborate* design is one worked out with minute detail. An *elaborate* proposal will leave little to the imagination. An *elaborate* meal will consist of a number of carefully prepared courses. A person eager to make a point will often indulge in an *elaborate* explanation. Someone truly sorry for a misdeed may enter into an *elaborate* apology. Dangerous journeys of exploration should be undertaken only after *elaborate* preparations. (There is no need to *elaborate* on that subject!)

elite (ih leet′, ay-) *n.*, *adj.* As a noun, *elite* is often used as a plural. *The elite* are the chosen few, the choice group. Speaking of an intellectual conference or a society party, a reporter might say that only the *elite* were present. The *elite* of society are "the 400." The *elite* in any art form are the few at the top; in any audience, the *elite* are the real connoisseurs. The *elite* among the people are the flower of society. The word can also be used as an adjective: "The writers' conference was attended by an *elite* group." There is often the implication, in the use of *elite*, whether as noun or adjective, that the group so described are quite aware of their superiority over the common herd and rather relish it. The Spanish philosopher and critic José Ortega y Gasset (1883-1955) said: "A society without an aristocracy, an *elite* minority, is not a society."

eloquent (el′ ə kwənt) *adj. Eloquent* language is expressive and forceful in its appeal, skillfully aimed at the feelings of those to whom it is addressed. Not only speech or language, but also a speaker or orator skilled in the use of words may be described as *eloquent*. Sometimes a great deal can be expressed by an *eloquent* silence. The German poet Christoph Wieland (1733-1813) said: "To be not so *eloquent* would be *more eloquent*." A look, as well as speech or silence, can be *eloquent* (if looks could kill!). The noun is *eloquence* (el′ ə kwəns), which can apply either to the skill of a speaker or to the forcefulness of the language used. When the English writer and politician Edward Bulwer-Lytton (1803-1873) said, "The pen is mightier than the sword," he used *pen* as a symbol of *eloquence*. Later on, the American essayist and poet Ralph Waldo Emerson (1803-1882) was somewhat more literal: "*Eloquence* a hundred times has turned the scale of war and peace at will."

elude (ee lood´) *vb*. To *elude* is to escape, the way a clever, speedy prisoner *eludes* his captors, or a nimble fox *eludes* the hounds. To *elude* is also to avoid, to steer clear of, the way, by hiding carefully, a person avoids observation or detection, or a bore at a party, or in times of stress, a bill collector. To *elude*, finally, can also mean "evade," in the sense of "slip away from," the way the solution of a puzzle can *elude* you. The noun is *elusion* (ee loo´ zhən)—not to be confused with **illusion**—and covers all the senses of *elude*: escape, avoidance, and evasion. *Elusive* (ee loo´ siv), the adjective, is commonly used to describe an idea or concept that is hard to grasp, like the theory of finite space; but it can also be used of a person or animal that is hard to catch. The slippery eel is a good example of an *elusive* fish. The hard-to-catch Scarlet Pimpernel in the novel of that name by the English novelist Baroness Orczy (1865-1947) was the very model of *elusion*:

> We seek him here, we seek him there,
> Those Frenchies seek him everywhere.
> Is he in heaven?—Is he in hell?
> That damned *elusive* Pimpernel?

emanate (em´ ə nate) *vb*. To *emanate* is to flow out of or arise from or originate in a certain source. A bad odor *emanates* from uncollected garbage. Trouble *emanates* from the discontent of the populace. But good things can *emanate* as well: wonderful poetry *emanated* from the pen of William Shakespeare. The *emanation* (em ə nay´ shən) can be of something physical, like steam out of a boiler, or spiritual, like the music out of the soul of Beethoven, or intellectual, like the Theory of Relativity from the brain of Albert Einstein. The main concept in *emanate* and *emanation* is the flowing of something out of a particular source.

embody (em bod´ ee) *vb*. When someone or something is typical of a quality, like kindness or cruelty or brilliance or stupidity, the person or thing is said to *embody* that quality, to express it, to be a symbol of it. The English nurse Florence Nightingale ("the Lady with the Lamp"—1820-1910) *embodied* courage and merciful kindness. Some public buildings *embody* the spirit of their age. The English poet Rudyard Kipling (1865-1936) *embodied* British imperialism. The noun, *embodiment* (em bod´ ee mənt), is synonymous with *personification*. Hitler was the *embodiment* of evil. Romeo and Juliet are the *embodiments* of young love. The statue of Venus de Milo is the *embodiment* of womanly grace. Cf. **personify.**

embrace (em brase´) *vb*. Apart from its literal use to describe the taking of a person into one's arms as a sign of affection, the verb *embrace* can be used in a number of ways. When an opportunity arises, you will *embrace* it (avail yourself of it) if you are alert. If someone gives you a good idea, you should *embrace* it (accept it willingly). Some people, seeking new experience, *embrace* a new religion (adopt it) or a new career (enter into it). *Embrace* has another distinct meaning, to "include": A comprehensive study of a subject should *embrace* all its aspects. *Embrace* is a useful word for a number of things beyond the *fond embrace*. A stirring example of the versatility of this word is shown in the following bit of repartee between the fourth Earl of Sandwich (1718-1792), inventor of the sandwich, and John Wilkes (1727-1797), the English politician and journalist: *Sandwich*: "'Pon my honor, Wilkes, I don't know whether you'll die on the gallows or of the pox [syphilis]." *Wilkes*: "That must depend, my lord, upon whether I first *embrace* your lordship's principles, or your lordship's mistresses." (This conversation is often attributed to the English Prime Minister William Gladstone [1809-1898] and Benjamin Disraeli [1804-1881].)

eminent (em´ ə nənt) *adj. Eminent* means "distinguished," and describes people of high rank or reputation. We are all familiar with the words and deeds of the *eminent* American President Abraham Lincoln. Marie Curie (1867-1935) and her husband Pierre (1859-1906), the discoverers of radium, were *eminent* as physicists and chemists. Michelangelo (1475-1564) was *eminent* for his sculpture, painting, architecture, and poetry. The noun is *eminence* (em´ ə nəns), meaning "high position or reputation." A person of *eminence* is one of high rank or status, or one who has earned fame for his services or accomplishments. Franklin D. Roosevelt and Winston Churchill were men *of eminence*. Those who win the Nobel Prize are people *of eminence*. Do not confuse *eminent* with **imminent**, or *eminence* with *imminence*.

empathy (em´ pə thee—*th* as in *thing*) *n. Empathy* is the identification of yourself, emotionally or intellectually, with the feelings or attitudes of another person, so that you fully understand what's going on in his mind. When you *empathize* (em´ pə thize—*th* as in *thing*) with someone, you identify with him to the extent of vicariously experiencing his thoughts or feelings. Sometimes, you can *empathize* with someone without necessarily agreeing with him: "I know how you feel and why you feel that way, though I don't agree with you."

emphasize (em´ fə size) *vb*. To *emphasize* something is to make it stand out in a special way by giving it special importance, or, figuratively speaking, underlining it. *Emphasis* (em´ fə sis) is the attachment of special importance to something so as to bring it to someone's attention. In writing, *emphasis* is given by underlining; in printing, by italics. In speech, you *emphasize* words or phrases by your tone of voice. President Reagan's speech about a Middle East settlement *emphasized* the need for a complete solution to the troubles in that area. Parents should *emphasize* the importance of regular study habits in training their children. It is up to a painter to decide whether to *emphasize* the figures or the background.

encumber (en kum´ bər) *vb*. To be *encumbered* is to be burdened and weighed down, with the implication that the burdens are hampering you, getting in your way. Life is made difficult if you are *encumbered* with debts. It is best, when traveling, not to be *encumbered* with too much luggage. Action is often *encumbered* by bureaucratic red tape. Anything that *encumbers* is an *encumbrance* (en kum´ brəns). An *encumbrance* is a burden, often a hindrance. A large family may turn out to be a blessing or an *encumbrance*, depending on the circumstances. In law, any lien or mortgage on property is known as an *encumbrance* (it "burdens" the property, as it were). The English lexicographer and writer Dr. Samuel Johnson (1709-1784) used *encumber* forcefully and dramatically in his famous letter to Lord Chesterfield (1694-1773), who had ignored Johnson in the early days and then wanted to climb on his bandwagon after he had established himself; he described Chesterfield as "one who looks with unconcern on a man struggling for life in the water, and, when he has reached ground, *encumbers* him with help." Even well-meaning "help" can *encumber* an effort.

endearing (en deer´ ing) *adj*. *Endearing* applies to anything that makes someone *dear* to someone else. A person will *endear* himself to others by a pleasant manner and helpful ways. Cheerful smiles, spreading happiness, and thoughtful gestures, showing consideration and concern for others, are *endearing* traits. The best-known use of this word occurs in the poem by the Irish poet Thomas Moore (1779-1852) that starts: "Believe me, if all those *endearing* young charms . . . ," later set to music and sung the world over by Irish tenors. The English poet Alfred, Lord Tennyson (1809-1892) wrote of the

> . . . blessings on the falling out
> That all the more *endears*,
> When we fall out with those we love
> And kiss again with tears!

An *endearment* (en deer´ mənt) is an act or expression of affection. Romeo and Juliet showered each other with *endearments*. Words of *endearment*, like "darling" and "sweetheart," are much appreciated by a spouse, but should be reserved for proper occasions and not become automatic and mechanical.

endow (en dow´—*ow* as in *now*) *vb*. *Endow* is used literally to describe the giving of funds to a public institution like a college or a hospital in order to provide it with a permanent source of income. One can *endow* a bed at a hospital, or a chair (professorship) at a university. There is a quite distinct figurative use having nothing to do with money. When we say that nature has *endowed* a woman with great beauty, or an artist with a magnificent voice, we mean that nature provided those assets. To *be endowed* with great athletic skill or great leadership ability is to have been born with them, to have those qualities naturally. When people say that geniuses are born, not made, they are referring to a natural *endowment* (en dow´ mənt—*ow* as in *now*). *Endowment*, in that context, means "natural ability, inborn quality," but the word also covers the literal meaning of *endow* and applies to a fund given to a public institution.

endure (en door´, -dyoor´—*oo* as in *look*) *vb*. *Endure* can be used in a variety of ways. By itself, it means to "last, go on, continue to exist." Some ancient monuments have *endured* for thousands of years. When they say that Shakespeare's plays have *endured* for centuries, they mean that his plays have stood the test of time, and will continue to gain recognition for their greatness. To *endure* pain or hunger is to bear or undergo or suffer it, often with the implication of holding out against it, without yielding to it or caving in. Travelers in the desert often *endure* thirst; soldiers *endure* shellfire. *Can't endure* means "can't stand" or "can't tolerate": "I simply can't *endure* that person; he drives me crazy." Or, "I cannot *endure* to hear that woman sing." *Endurance* (en door´ ǝns, -dyoor´-, *oo* as in *look*) is the ability to *endure*. Long-distance runners have amazing *endurance*. *Endurable* (en door´ ǝ b'l, -dyoor-, *oo* as in *look*) applies to anything that can be *endured*, whether pain, abuse, or punishment. *Unendurable* is the adjective for what cannot be *endured*, and is usually used in a figurative sense: "That child's practicing the trumpet next door is *unendurable*." The smugness or haughtiness of some people is *unendurable*. (They may have to be *endured*, but, figuratively speaking, they're *unendurable*, in the same way that a good many "intolerable" things in life nonetheless have to be tolerated.)

engulf (en gulf´) *vb.* To *engulf* is to swallow up, in the literal sense (as in a *gulf*). Floods can *engulf* villages along the banks of the river. A tidal wave can *engulf* a whole city. High waves in a storm at sea will sometimes *engulf* a boat. In a figurative sense, when a person is said to be *engulfed* in his work, it means that he is completely absorbed in it, "swallowed up" by it, as it were. Scientists become *engulfed* in their research. In this sense, *engulfed* can be replaced by *immersed* or *absorbed*, both of which are associated, in their literal sense, with liquid.

enhance (en hans´) *vb.* When something is *enhanced*, it is intensified, added to, made greater. The proper use of makeup and lighting *enhances* a woman's beauty. Rarity *enhances* the value of a collector's item. Wit *enhances* conversation. The noun is *enhancement* (en hans´ mǝnt). *Enhancement* is the increasing of the value or attractiveness of something or the increasing of someone's power. Boldness and eloquence lead to the *enhancement* of a statesman's power. Expert direction lends *enhancement* to the actors' skill. Study of this book will *enhance* your conversational and writing ability.

enlighten (en ly´ tǝn) *vb.* To *enlighten* someone is to impart knowledge or understanding to him, to free him from misunderstanding or ignorance, to shed *light* upon him on one subject or another. When you *enlighten* someone on computer technology, for instance, you help him to understand it. Missionaries seek to *enlighten* pagans as to the "true religion." *Enlightened* (en ly´ tǝnd) is used as an adjective to express freedom from ignorance, false beliefs, superstitions, and prejudices. It is difficult, in this *enlightened* age, to comprehend the barbarous goings-on in Iran. *Enlightenment* (en ly´ tǝn mǝnt) is the act of *enlightening*, or the result: the state of being *enlightened*, freedom from ignorance and erroneous beliefs. Serious educators devote their lives to the *enlightenment* of mankind. In every age, politicians like to refer to "these *enlightened* times." Thomas Jefferson (1743–1826) said these stirring words: "*Enlighten* the people generally, and tyranny and oppression of body and mind will vanish like evil spirits at the dawn of day."

The Chinese philosopher Lao-tzu (604-531 B.C.) said: "He who knows others is wise. He who knows himself is *enlightened*." (The Delphic Oracle, in ancient times, exhibited the inscription: "Know thyself." The English poet Alexander Pope [1688-1744] wrote: "Know then thyself . . . /The proper study of mankind is man.")

ensue (en soo´—*oo* as in *boot*) *vb*. Anything that *ensues* happens as a result of something else. Divorce sometimes *ensues* from mere misunderstanding. Wars can *ensue* from a failure of diplomacy. The use of *ensue* generally implies that the thing that *ensues* happens as the consequence of something that occurred previously. However, the form *ensuing* is used as an adjective meaning simply "following": Two people marry, and a child is born in the *ensuing* year. A great and joyous Christmas feast may be followed by lots of tummyaches in the *ensuing* hours.

ensure (en shoor´—*oo* as in *book*) *vb*. To *ensure* is to make sure, to guarantee. Diligent study will *ensure* success in your examinations. Figure out how long it will take you to get to your destination, then leave a little earlier to *ensure* that you'll arrive on time. These lines of the English poet A.E. Housman (1859-1936) are inscribed on his tombstone in Shropshire:

> Good night. *Ensured* release,
> Imperishable peace,
> Have these for yours.

Learning the proper use of the words in this book will *ensure* a considerable increase in your vocabulary.

entertain (en tər tane´) *vb*. One *entertains* by giving cocktail and dinner parties. Actors *entertain* audiences. *Entertainers* work on the stage and in night clubs. *Entertaining* means "amusing, enjoyable." The English playwright and novelist Somerset Maugham (1874-1965) said that timetables and catalogues were "much more *entertaining* than half the novels that are written." *Entertainment* is amusement, something you enjoy hearing or watching. But *entertain* has two additional distinct uses. To *entertain* a proposition or a proposal or a suggestion is to be willing to consider it. To *entertain* a doubt or an idea is to harbor it or to have it in one's mind. If the seller asks $1,000 and you offer him $700 and he says he will think about it or think it over, he is *entertaining* your offer. If he tells you it is a genuine antique and you don't like the newish look of the handles, you are *entertaining* a doubt about its authenticity. In these usages, to *entertain* is to consider (a proposal) or to harbor (a doubt), depending on the context.

enthrall (en throll´) *vb*. To *enthrall* is to charm, fascinate, captivate. An *enthralling* play is one that holds your complete attention. An *enthralling* novel is one that you can't put down. An audience will be *enthralled* by a great actor or singer. A good storyteller can *enthrall* a large group of children. History and fiction are full of situations where a man is *enthralled* by a woman's beauty (and all kinds of trouble ensue).

entice (en tīse´) *vb*. To *entice* is to tempt, to persuade by exciting someone's desires or hopes, to inveigle. Many country people are *enticed* away from their homes into the big city by dreams of fame and riches. In Victorian melodrama, villains were routinely pictured as *enticing* innocent young maidens into a life of shame, and foolish men were *enticed* away from home and duty by designing women. Bad companions can *entice* weak people away from fulfilling their obligations. Whatever it is that does the *enticing* is called the *enticement* (en tīse´ mənt). The *enticement* of a girl's flirtatious ways is often hard to resist. The hope of easy money is an *enticement* to crime. Dreams of power are an *enticement* to politics. *Enticing* (en tī´ sing) means "tempting": a get-rich-quick scheme is an *enticing* prospect. The word *entice* somehow implies unworthy goals and the raising of false hopes.

entreat (en trēet´) *vb*. To *entreat* is to beg, implore, beseech. At the end of a trial, the lawyer for a convicted criminal sometimes *entreats* the judge for leniency. In stories of olden times, kings were always being *entreated* to show mercy. "Please! I *entreat* you!" is a strong way of asking someone for something, like help badly needed. The plea is known as an *entreaty* (en trēe´ tee). When someone remains deaf to your *entreaties*, there is not much use in going on. *Entreat* and *entreaty* are strong words; to *entreat* is more than simply to ask; an *entreaty* is more than a simple request. In Shakespeare's *Winter's Tale* (Act I, Scene 2), King Polixenes of Bohemia, a visitor at the court of King Leontes of Sicilia, after begging off because of urgent business at home, changes his mind and prolongs his visit. "How came't, Camillo [a lord], that he did stay?" asks Leontes. "At the good queen's *entreaty*," answers Camillo. This arouses the furious jealousy of King Leontes and starts the whole tragedy on its way. It is her *entreaty* that infuriated the King.

environment (en vy´ rən mənt) *n*. The *environment* is the surrounding conditions, influences, and circumstances that have an effect on people. A person's *environment* plays a very large part in shaping his character and career. There has always been disagreement among students of social problems about the degree to which *environment*, as opposed to heredity, determines a person's character and tendencies. The American sociologist Franz Boas (1858–1942) wrote: "The behavior of an individual is determined not by his racial affiliation, but by the character of his ancestry and his cultural *environment*." The American engineer and designer Buckminster Fuller (1895–1983) said: "Change the *environment*; do not try to change man." The English anthropologist Jacob Bronowski (1908–1974), in *The Ascent of Man*, wrote: "Nature . . . has not fitted man to any specific *environment*. . . . Man is the only one who is not locked into his *environment*. . . . Man from age to age has remade his *environment*. . . . " An *environmentalist* (en vy rən men´ tə list) is a person who is active in opposition to anything that upsets the *environment* or the ecology, like the destruction of trees or wetlands, the dumping of nuclear waste, etc. Do not confuse *environment* with *environs* (en vy´ rəns), a plural noun which describes the outskirts or suburbs of a town or city.

environs (en vy´ rəns) *n., pl*. See **environment**.

equivalent (ih kwiv´ ə lent) *n., adj.* Things that are *equivalent* are equal in some respect: in value, meaning, importance, effect, or some other way. At the present time (July, 1983), the British pound is *equivalent* to about $1.53 in American money. Under the American political system, we have no *equivalent* to the British Queen. Silence can sometimes be taken as *equivalent* to agreement. There are words in some languages that have no exact *equivalent* in any other language. The Greek poet Hesiod (c.700 B.C.) gave this sound advice: "Do not seek evil gains; evil gains are the *equivalent* of disaster."

eradicate (ih rad´ ə kate) *vb.* To *eradicate* something is to destroy it utterly, to remove any trace of it. Through the worldwide efforts of medical authorities, smallpox has now been *eradicated*. All kinds of methods have been suggested to *eradicate* crime in our urban centers. The English poet Oliver Goldsmith (1728–1774), in *The Good-Natured Man*, wrote: "We must touch his weaknesses with a delicate hand. There are some faults so nearly allied to excellence, that we can scarce weed out the fault without *eradicating* the virtue." The American naturalist and writer Henry David Thoreau (1817–1862) tells us: "The savage in man is never quite *eradicated*."

ergo (ur´ go—*u* as in *fur,* err-) *adv., conj. Ergo* is Latin for *therefore*. Shakespeare used it frequently, always facetiously, as a mock-educated way of saying "therefore." It is now certainly obsolete, or at least archaic, as a serious substitute for *therefore*, but can be used in fun to point up an illogical argument. The English lexicographer H. W. Fowler (1858–1933), in *Modern English Usage*, includes *ergo* in his list of words under the heading *Pedantic Humour*, and gives this example of its use: "He says it is too hot for anything; *ergo*, a bottle of Bass." One shouldn't make a habit of *ergo*, but its occasional use (in Fowler's words) "to draw attention facetiously to the illogical nature of a conclusion" is pardonable, if not overdone.

erotic (ih rot´ ik) *adj.* Anything described as *erotic* has to do with love and sexual desire. An *erotic* poem, passage in a book, picture, or sculpture involves love and sex. A work of art can be *erotic* without being pornographic; fine examples are The Song of Solomon in the Bible, and the luscious ladies painted by the Flemish painter Rubens (1577–1640). The Swiss psychiatrist Carl Jung (1875–1961) said: "The *erotic* instinct in man. . . belongs, on the one hand, to the original nature of man. . . . On the other hand, it is connected with the highest forms of the spirit." *Eroticism* (ih rot´ ə sizm) can apply either to the *erotic* quality of something (e.g., the *erotic* nature of a poem or a painting), or to the use of sexually arousing elements in a work of art (e.g., scanty clothing on the female form divine), or to sexual desire itself. *Erotica* (ih rot´ ih kə) is the collective name given to works of art or literature dealing with the subject of sexual love and desire. Do not confuse *erotic* with **erratic** (though *erotic* conduct can be *erratic* at the same time).

erratic (ih rat´ ik) *adj.* When *erratic* is applied to people, it means that they are unpredictable, capable of irregular behavior. It is hard to deal with *erratic* people;

you never know which way they are going to jump. *Erratic* people behave inconsistently; they sometimes do the opposite of what you would expect; they are changeable and undependable. *Erratic* conduct is the hallmark of certain nervous or mental diseases. *Erratic* can be used of things as well as people. We have all had trouble with *erratic* clocks or watches; they seem unrepairable, with a will of their own. Changeable winds are *erratic*, and can confuse a sailor. Do not confuse *erratic* with **erotic.**

erroneous (ih roe′ nee əs, eh-) *adj*. *Erroneous* (based on the noun *error*) means "incorrect, mistaken." If you jump to conclusions, you may well come up with an *erroneous* one. Shy people often create an *erroneous* impression of unsociability. The American scientist and educator James B. Conant (1893–1976), in *Science and Common Sense*, wrote of "the stumbling way in which even the ablest of the scientists in every generation have had to fight their way through thickets of *erroneous* observations." The English philosopher Herbert Spencer (1820–1903) said: "We too often forget that not only is there 'a soul of goodness in things evil' [quoting King Henry V's speech at the opening of Act IV, Scene 1 in Shakespeare's *Henry V*], but very generally a soul of truth in things *erroneous*."

espouse (eh spouz′—*ou* as in *house*) *vb*. To *espouse* a cause, a theory, a principle, a proposal, is to come out in support of it. As might be guessed from the second syllable, *espouse* means, literally, to "marry, take in marriage," but that use is hardly ever met with nowadays. However, it explains why the word means to "support," because when you support a cause or a principle you "make it your own" and you're "married to it." Abraham Lincoln, early in life, *espoused* the cause of abolition of slavery. Franklin D. Roosevelt *espoused* the Four Freedoms. When you agree with a principle or a cause with sufficient sincerity and force to adopt it and support it, you are *espousing* it. All right-thinking people *espouse* the principle of religious freedom.

esteem (eh steem′) *n., vb*. *Esteem* is high opinion, great respect or regard; to *esteem* someone is to have a high opinion of him. By continual good work at the office, you win the boss's *esteem*. He will hold you in high *esteem*. Be careful not to let him down and lower yourself in his *esteem*. The Chinese and Japanese peoples *esteem* their ancestors to the point of actual ancestor worship. The whole world *esteems* Abraham Lincoln for his rugged honesty and forthrightness. Lindbergh was greatly *esteemed* for his courage and accomplishment. The French writer of comedies Molière (1622–1673) says, in *Le Misanthrope* (Act I, Scene 1): "*Esteem* is based on some sort of preference; to *esteem* everything is to *esteem* nothing." To *esteem* can mean merely to "consider, regard." Some *esteem* it a great privilege to be seen in the company of a celebrity. The French writer François Rabelais (1495–1553) wrote: "A man is worth as much as he *esteems* himself." (This was said, of course, tongue in cheek, else every man would be priceless.)

estimation (es tə may′ shən) *n*. *Estimation* is most often used as the equivalent of *judgment* or *opinion*. In the *estimation* of most people, Shakespeare was the world's greatest dramatist and poet. The phrase *in my estimation* often precedes an expression of opinion: "*In my estimation*, the market is heading for a boom." *Estimation* can be applied as well to the act of *estimating*, as when an appraiser is engaged in the *estimation* of the value of property. *Estimation* is sometimes used as a synonym for *esteem*, when people say, for instance, that they hold so-and-so "in high *estimation*," but *esteem* is preferable in this connection. *Estimation* is also used occasionally to mean "estimate" (the noun, pronounced es′ tə mət), as in *a rough estimation* of the cost, but *estimate* is a better choice in this context.

ethnic (eth′ nik—*th* as in *thing*) *adj. Ethnic* applies to anything that has to do with a race or cultural group, any group characterized by common background, customs, or other factors. When people immigrate to another country but cling, as a group, to their native customs, they are often referred to as an "*ethnic* group or unit." Many restaurants in cities like New York and London serve *ethnic* foods; one goes to recitals of *ethnic* songs or *ethnic* dances. People too often look down on *ethnic* ways and customs, instead of studying and appreciating them for making the world a more interesting place. The expression *ethnic minority* has become associated with racial disturbances in urban centers, particularly New York and London.

eventful (ih vent′ fəl) *adj.* An *eventful* period is one marked by important or notable *events*. The periods 1914–1918 and 1939–1945 were *eventful* because of world conflict. The stock-market crash of 1929 made that an *eventful* year. A period does not have to be *full* of events in order to be known as *eventful*; one notable event is enough. Columbus discovered America in the *eventful* year 1492. In the expression *an eventful life*, *eventful* indicates a *series* of striking happenings. Winston Churchill led an *eventful* life. The Roosevelt years were an *eventful* period of American history. *Eventful*, applied to a time or period, implies that the things that happened had far-reaching consequences, and in this context, *eventful* means about the same thing as *momentous*. Jaques, in Shakespeare's famous speech about the seven ages of man (*As You Like It*, Act II, Scene 7), ends with: "Last scene of all,/That ends this strange *eventful* history,/Is second childishness [childhood]. . . ."

eventual (ih ven′ choo əl—*oo* as in *boot*) *adj. Eventual* applies to something that finally happens after a series of *events*, or as the result of an earlier happening. Constant change in a company's management may result in confusion and *eventual* bankruptcy. The publication of work after work of extensive research may lead to one's *eventual* acceptance as an authority on the subject. An employee's continual lateness in getting to work will lead to his *eventual* dismissal. *Eventually* (ih ven′ choo ə lee—*oo* as in *boot*) means "finally, in the long run, some time in the future." Crime does not pay; the police will *eventually* get you. We must all die *eventually*. If you keep gazing into that shop window long enough, you will *eventually* yield to temptation and buy something you can't afford. If I keep plugging away at this job, I'll finish it *eventually*. Do not confuse *eventual* with **eventful**. A well-known household product was advertised under the self-assured slogan "*Eventually*; why not now?" An *eventuality* (ih ven choo al′ ih tee—*oo* as in *boot*, *a* as in *hat*) is a possible event. In planning an outdoor event, always remember that bad weather is an *eventuality*.

eventuate (ih ven' choo ate—*oo* as in *boot*) *vb*. To *eventuate* is to finally come about, to turn out as a result of something. After a long period of trial and error, a sound management policy may *eventuate*. Luckily, many of the dire consequences we worry about never *eventuate*. Do not use *eventuate* as a synonym for *happen* or *occur*. When something *eventuates*, it does not merely happen; it happens *in the long run*, or *as the result of* something that went before. Following the crash of 1929, a long period of severe economic depression *eventuated*. An artist's success usually *eventuates* after a great deal of hard work rather than as the result of a burst of inspiration.

evocative (ih vok' ə tiv) *adj*. See **evoke**.

evoke (ih voke') *vb*. To *evoke* memories of the past, or a smile or sympathy, or admiration or gratitude or emotional reactions or feelings generally, is to produce them or call them up. Old photographs *evoke* memories of the past. A dramatic plea for mercy by the defense attorney may *evoke* the sympathy of a judge. Tactless comments often *evoke* anger or disgust. Powerful writing can *evoke* a vivid picture of the people, places, and happenings that figure in the novel. Things that tend to *evoke* memories, feelings, etc., are *evocative* (ih vok' ə tiv). An odor can be *evocative*, calling up memories of associated past happenings. *Evocative* words produce images over and above their everyday meanings: a word like *grandeur* may *evoke* images of royal processions or magnificent temples. *Evocation* (eh və kay' shən) is the act of *evoking*, as in the *evocation* of joy or sadness or laughter. Looking at old love letters results in the *evocation* of memories of years gone by.

evolve (ih volv') *vb*. To *evolve* is to develop gradually. One can *evolve* a system; a system can *evolve* on its own. Einstein *evolved* the Theory of Relativity. Committees often keep busy *evolving* plans that don't work out. The Founding Fathers of America *evolved* a constitution; the British constitution *evolved* with the passage of time. A new invention may *evolve* from a spark of inspiration. Charles Darwin (1809–1892), in his great work on *evolution*, *The Origin of Species*, wrote: "From so simple a beginning endless forms most beautiful and most wonderful have been and are being *evolved*." It is easy to see the connection between the verb *evolve* and the noun *evolution*. According to Darwin's doctrine of *evolution*, all plants and animals, including man, *evolved*, over millions of years, from a primal one-celled organism.

exasperate (ig zas' pə rate) *vb*. When a person is *exasperated*, he is irritated, angered, and annoyed to an extreme degree. It is easy to become *exasperated* at someone's stubbornness. Prosecutors are *exasperated* by witnesses' evasions or nonresponsiveness, especially when they take the Fifth Amendment. It is exasperating to miss your plane because of delays in traffic. *Exasperation* (ig zas pə ray' shən) is extreme annoyance, the state of being *exasperated*. "Turn off that radio!" the neighbors cry *in exasperation* on a summer's night when windows are left open. It is difficult for a speaker to conquer his *exasperation* at the continual interruptions of hecklers.

exceedingly (ik see′ ding lee) *adj.* To *exceed* (ik seed′) something is to surpass it, to go beyond it in degree, rate, quantity, or size, to be greater than it. This gives us *exceedingly*, which means "extremely, to an unusual degree." Inflation is *exceedingly* difficult to control. Ballet is an *exceedingly* demanding discipline. *Exceedingly* is much stronger than *very*, and on a par with *extremely* or *exceptionally*. It must be carefully distinguished from *excessively* (ik ses′ iv lee), which means "to too great a degree, to an unreasonable extent, disproportionately."

excel (ik sel′) *vb.* To *excel* in something is to be very good at it. People *excel* in different things: Some *excel* in the arts, others *excel* in the professions or in business. It is important for a secretary to *excel* in both accuracy and speed. The Chinese philosopher Chuang-tzu (369-286 B.C.) wrote: "All strive to discredit what they do not *excel* in." The English poet John Sheffield, Duke of Buckingham (1648-1721), wrote: "Of all those arts in which the wise *excel*,/Nature's chief masterpiece is writing well." When you *excel* others, you surpass them, outdo them. Shakespeare *excels* all other poets. Sir Isaac Newton (1642-1727), the discoverer of the theory of gravitation, so far *excelled* his classmates at Oxford that in the list of honors, his name came first, then a line was drawn, and under that the other winners were listed. From *excel* we get the familiar adjective *excellent*.

excerpt (ek′ surpt—*u* as in *fur*) *n.*, (ek surpt′—*u* as in *fur*) *vb.* An *excerpt* is a passage, a section, or an extract from a book, speech, document, motion picture, or the like. The verb *to excerpt* (note difference in accent) describes the taking of a passage out of a book, etc. An *excerpt* can be misleading if, removed from its background, it is taken out of context. Dictionaries of quotations contain *excerpts* from the writings and saying of famous people. Do not confuse *excerpt* with *condensation*, of the *Reader's Digest* variety: An *excerpt* must be an exact quotation. Selections from great literature, in schoolbook form, consist of *excerpts*.

excessive (ik ses′ iv) *adj. Excessive* describes anything that is too much or too great, that *exceeds* the proper degree. An *excessive* price is one that is too high. Hotels and restaurants are making *excessive* charges nowadays. *Excessive* permissiveness is bad for children. *Excessive* speed will get you a traffic ticket. Do not confuse the adverb *excessively* (ik ses′ iv lee) with **exceedingly** (under which *excessively* is discussed).

exclude (ik sklood′—*oo* as in *boot*) *vb.* To *exclude* is to keep out or shut out. Through the blackballing process, clubs try to *exclude* undesirable applicants from membership. Immigration laws *exclude* certain people from entry into the country. Certain words are *excluded* from conversation in mixed company. We all attempt to *exclude* unpleasant memories from our thoughts. Thorough consideration of a question will *exclude* certain solutions. A moment's thought about a puzzling situation may *exclude* certain possible explanations. *Exclusion* (ik skloo′ zhən—*oo* as in *boot*) is the act of *excluding* or the state of being *excluded*. The *exclusion* of known criminals from a neighborhood will make the residents feel much more secure. From *exclude* we get the adjective *exclusive* (ik skloo′ siv), which has a number of uses. It can apply to prices: Dinner costs $10, *exclusive* of tips and taxes. Teachers want pupils to give their *exclusive* attention to their studies. An *exclusive right*, e.g., to dramatize a novel, to interview a celebrity, or to act as agent, is one reserved to one party. A common use of *exclusive* is to describe a club, group, school, etc. that maintains very strict rules of admission. (Groucho Marx said he wouldn't join any club that would admit him. It wouldn't be *exclusive* enough.)

exclusive (ik skloo′ siv—*oo* as in *boot*) *adj.* See **exclude**.

excruciating (ik skroo′ shee ate ing—*oo* as in *boot*) *adj.* This word, based on *crux* (krooks), the Latin word for *cross*, applies to anything that causes severe, acute physical pain or mental anguish. *Excruciating* is the equivalent of *tormenting*, and *excruciating pain* is sometimes described as *racking pain*. (The rack, like the cross, was an instrument of torture.) *Excruciating* pain is strongly associated with the dentist's office. Suspense can at times be more *excruciating* than bad news itself. A poor result of an examination or an audition can be *excruciatingly* disappointing.

exert (ig zurt′—*u* as in *fur*) *vb.* To *exert* power, effort, influence, pressure, strength, etc., is to put it forth, apply it, exercise it, put it to vigorous use. A good friend will *exert* every effort to help you in time of trouble. The British *exerted* tremendous strength in the Battle of Britain. The American economy *exerts* great influence on that of the rest of the world. Russia *exerts* not only pressure but power over its satellite states. To *exert oneself* is to make an effort. If you have a lot of work to do, you must *exert* yourself to get up early. My good friend will *exert* himself on my behalf. *Exertion* (ig zur′ shən—*u* as in *fur*) is the act of *exerting*, and also describes any vigorous activity. The *exertion* of authority is sometimes less effective than the use of persuasion. Excellence at sports requires mental as well as physical *exertion*. The *exertion* of commuting leads many people to retire sooner than they otherwise would. *Exertion* often appears in the plural, meaning "vigorous efforts": Despite all our *exertions*, we sometimes find ourselves unequal to certain tasks.

exhaustive (ig zost′ iv) *adj.* To *exhaust* oneself is to wear oneself out, as a result of which one feels *exhausted*. To *exhaust* a supply of anything is to use it all up, to consume it. To *exhaust* a subject is to deal with it thoroughly, by drawing out of it everything that is necessary for its complete understanding. *Exhaust* gives us the adjective *exhaustive*, which is used in the related but separate sense of "thorough, complete." An *exhaustive study* or *treatment* of a subject is one that goes into the matter thoroughly, dealing with all its aspects. An *exhaustive search* is one that leaves no stone unturned. We often read about the *exhaustive inquiries* gone into by the police after a much-publicized crime. The list of words dealt with in this book is representative, rather than *exhaustive*.

exhilarate (ig zil′ ə rate) *vb.* Anything that *exhilarates* you makes you joyful and merry, fills you with high spirits. The English poet William Cowper (1731–1800) loved the countryside:

> Nor rural sights alone, but rural sounds,
> *Exhilarate* the spirit, and restore
> The languid tone of Nature.

The commonest form of the word is *exhilarating*: Good news is *exhilarating*. *Exhilarating* may take on the meaning of "invigorating": Sparkling, cold weather is *exhilarating* to a group of hikers. What is more *exhilarating* than a merry party with good friends and a plentiful supply of witty conversation? Winston Churchill had the answer: "Nothing in life is so *exhilarating* as to be shot at without result."

expedient (ik spee′ dee ənt) *n., adj.* An *expedient* is a means to an end, an advantageous method or plan of action for accomplishing a purpose, especially in a crisis or emergency. Sleeping pills are an *expedient* for overcoming insomnia. Espionage is employed by most countries as an *expedient* for safeguarding their own interests. *Expedient* usually has in it the implication that the end justifies the means: an *expedient* is a way of doing what needs to be done in a given situation, even if it violates one's normal way of conducting one's affairs. An *expedient* "gets you there"; principles be damned! The British statesman Benjamin Disraeli (1804–1881) said: "Free trade is not a principle, it is an *expedient*." The adjective *expedient* applies to any action that serves your purpose, to the method that is most likely to get results, proper under the circumstances, even though it may be against your principles generally. It is sometimes *expedient* to use threats even though you don't intend to carry them out. *Expediency* (ik spee′ dee ən see) is advisability, suitability for a purpose. Sometimes one is told to stop discussing right and wrong and do what he considers *expedient*. But Theodore Roosevelt (1858–1919) said: "No man is justified in doing evil on the ground of *expediency*." All too often, people try to justify wrongful acts on the ground of *expediency*. Do not confuse *expedient* with *expeditious*, which is discussed under the next entry.

expedite (ek′ spə dite) *vb.* To *expedite* something is to speed it up, to hasten its progress or accomplishment. Automation *expedites* production, but causes unemployment. Proper communication facilities *expedite* the management of large companies. Be grateful for anything that *expedites* your work, whatever it may be. Serious writing or thinking is *expedited* by freedom from interruption. *Expedite* gives us the adjective *expeditious* (ek spə dish′ əs), which means "prompt, quick, and efficient." Serious crime requires *expeditious* inquiry. *Expeditious* management and attention to the needs of customers are the hallmarks of successful companies. There is no more *expeditious* road to learning than hard and persistent study. Do not confuse *expeditious* with **expedient**.

explicit (ik splis′ it) *adj.* To be *explicit* about something, to make an *explicit* statement on a subject, is to leave nothing in doubt, to be absolutely clear and definite about it. *Explicit* instructions are clearly and fully expressed, with nothing vague about them. When you are *explicit* about a matter, you leave no doubt what is meant. *Explicit* is the opposite of *indefinite, unclear,* or *ambiguous. Explicitness* (ex plis' it nəss) is of great value in speech and writing, especially when instructions are involved, or a clear and definite picture of a situation is required.

extant (ek' stənt, ik stant') *adj.* Anything *extant* is still in existence, not destroyed or lost. Only a few copies of Shakespeare's First Folio (the first printed collection of his plays) are *extant*. The few *extant* copies of the Gutenberg Bible are each worth a considerable amount of money. The early *extant* fragments of the skeletons of primitive man tell us a great deal about the evolution of the human race.

extract (ek' strakt) *n.*, (ek strakt') *vb.* Apart from its meaning as a concentrate of something *extracted* from a plant or an animal, like vanilla *extract* or beef *extract*, *extract* describes something *extracted* from a book or a speech, and in that sense is synonymous with *passage, quotation,* or *excerpt.* An *extract* taken out of context can be misleading. Many *extracts* from Shakespeare have become so familiar as to seem trite. The English essayist and philosopher Francis Bacon (1561-1626) said: "Some books are to be tasted, others to be swallowed, and some few to be chewed and digested. . . . Some books may be read by deputy, and *extracts* made of them by others." (In view of Bacon's dates, this was quite an early anticipation of the various "digests" offered to the reading public.)

extraordinary (ek strawr' d'neer ee) *adj.* This word covers anything that is not run-of-the-mill, or beyond what is usual or ordinary, like the *extraordinary* powers given to an American President in time of war, but its more common use is to describe people or things that are remarkable, exceptional, noteworthy. Men like Shakespeare and Beethoven were endowed with *extraordinary* gifts. The first ascent of Mt. Everest was an *extraordinary* achievement. Some years are memorable for *extraordinary* weather. Winston Churchill was an *extraordinary* leader. As the word implies, people and things that are *extraordinary* are *out of the ordinary.*

extricate (ek' strə kate) *vb.* To *extricate* someone is to free or release him from something. A friend in need will do everything possible to *extricate* you from a difficult situation. In old movies, the U.S. Cavalry rode up in strength to *extricate* the good guys from all kinds of danger. Quick wits are necessary to *extricate* oneself from an embarrassing situation. *Extrication* (ek strə kay' shən) is the act of *extricating*, or the result of being *extricated.* Your *extrication* of a friend from a perilous position results in his *extrication*. If a person can be *extricated*, he is *extricable* (ek' strə kə bəl); if he can't, he is *inextricable* (in ek' strə kə bəl).

façade (fə sahd'—*a* as in *arm*) *n.* This word is taken intact from the French. Note the little mark, called a "cedilla" (sih dil' ə), under the *c*; it gives the *c* an *s* sound. Façade is a technical term in architecture for the front of a building, particularly an imposing one. Figuratively, a *façade* is a false or superficial appearance, a show of something. People who live beyond their means put on a *façade* of wealth. A buyer who doesn't want to appear too eager may put on a *façade* of indifference. Large cities sometimes exhibit a *façade* of glamour behind which poverty and sadness lurk.

factual (fak' choo əl—*oo* as in *boot*) *adj.* A *factual* statement is one based on *fact*, not supposition or guesswork. Good reporting should be *factual*, and stick strictly to the *facts*, without slant or bias. Good raconteurs often let their imagination take over and find it hard to keep their stories *factual*. *Factualness* (fak' choo əl nes) eliminates all elements of supposition and unsupported conclusions.

faculty (fak' əl tee) *n.* This word has two distinct meanings. The *faculty* of a school or university is its teaching staff. A person's *faculties* are the powers of his mind, such as reason, memory, or speech. The human race is differentiated from other animals by the *faculty* of speech. We sometimes speak of a person who, though very old, is *in possession of all his faculties. Faculty* can also mean "aptitude." Some people have a *faculty* for making friends easily. There are those who have a *faculty* for leadership, or management, or invention, or language.

fallible (fal' ə b'l) *adj.* A *fallible* person is one who is capable of error, who may be wrong. The possibility of being wrong, of committing error, is called *fallibility* (fal ə bil' ə tee). "Nobody's perfect" is another way of saying "Everybody's *fallible.*" Thomas Jefferson (1743-1826) wrote, on the question of freedom of opinion, "Subject opinion to coercion: whom will you make your inquisitors? *Fallible* men, men governed by bad passions, by private as well as public reasons." The English writer and sociologist Mary Wollstonecraft Godwin (1759-1797), on the subject of women's rights, declared, "If women be educated for dependence; that is, to act according to the will of another *fallible* being, and submit, right or wrong, to power, where are we to stop?" *Infallible* is the opposite: never liable to error, incapable of making mistakes. No human being is *infallible*. The term can be applied to things as well as persons: Certain antibiotics are *infallible* remedies for various illnesses. Multiple-choice tests are not *infallible* tests of intelligence. The Pope, when formally expressing an opinion on a matter of morals or faith, is considered *infallible* according to the doctrine of the Roman Catholic Church.

famously (fay' məs lee) *adv.* We know that *famous* means "widely known" and that *infamous* (in' fə məs) means "wicked, shameful." *Famously*, the adverb from *famous*, has a distinct meaning, having nothing to do with either fame or wickedness. People who get along *famously* are getting along excellently; their relationship is first-rate. To do *famously* in an exam is to do extremely well in it, to get a top grade. A person who gets over injuries from an accident quickly and completely has recovered *famously*.

fanciful (fan' sih fəl) *adj.* What is *fanciful* is imagined or imaginary, induced or suggested by imagination rather than reason or actual experience. People who haven't traveled dream of *fanciful*, romantic places. Those with vivid imaginations jump to conclusions with all sorts of *fanciful* ideas. Some modern painters fill their canvases with *fanciful* figures and unlikely combinations of objects. Practical people feel that all knowledge must come through action and trial, not *fanciful* theories and tests.

fashion (fash′ ən) *n., vb.* The noun *fashion* has two distinct main uses: as a synonym of *manner* or *way* (He walks in a peculiar *fashion*), and to indicate the current style of dress (She dresses in the latest *fashion*; hats for men are mostly out of *fashion*). Less well known, but quite useful, is *fashion* as a verb. To *fashion* something is to mold it, to give it a particular form or shape. The Indians *fashioned* their canoes out of tree trunks. Whittlers can *fashion* almost anything out of a piece of wood. It is amazing that statues like Michelangelo's *Pietà* and Rodin's *Thinker* were *fashioned* out of mere blocks of marble. To *fashion*, then, is to make, but always with the implication of creativity.

fastidious (fa stid′ ee əs—*a* as in *hat*) *adj.* A *fastidious* person is very "choosy," very careful and particular in selecting what is good and rejecting what is not; hard to please and easily disgusted or "turned off"; extremely sensitive, meticulous in matters of taste. *Fastidious* people are often hard to be with, they are so demanding in their taste and choice. A *fastidious* diner will engage in a detailed discussion with a waiter and will send back anything not cooked and served to perfection. A person *fastidiously* dressed is extremely careful about color combinations. *Fastidious* attention to detail may bring a venture to success, but when excessive, may result in failure. *Fastidiousness* may be a good or a bad quality, depending on its degree under the circumstances.

fatalist (fate′ ə list) *n.* A *fatalist* is one who accepts his *fate* as inevitable and submits to events without protest. The doctrine to which he subscribes is *fatalism* (fate′ ə lizm); his attitude is described as *fatalistic* (fate ə lis′ tik). A *fatalistic* approach to life is one that accepts one's lot as fated and predetermined; a *fatalistic* attitude is one of calm submission to whatever happens. *Fatalists* follow the belief expressed by King Edward IV in Shakespeare's *Henry VI* (Act IV, Scene 3): "What *fates* impose, that men must needs abide;/It boots not to resist both wind and tide."

fateful (fate′ fəl) *adj.* A *fateful* event is one that involves **momentous** consequences; it is not only important, but decisive. In these troubled times, heads of state are called on to make one *fateful* decision after another. November 22, 1963, the day that President Kennedy was shot, was one of the most *fateful* days in recent history. The *fateful* meeting between Franklin D. Roosevelt and Winston Churchill at sea on August 14, 1941, resulted in the Atlantic Charter. The most *fateful* words ever spoken were: "Let there be light."

fauna (faw′ nə) *n.*; **flora** (floe′ rə, flaw′ rə) *n. Fauna* is the term describing all the animals peculiar to a given region or era, taken as a whole; *flora* covers all the plants of a given region or era, taken as a whole. Naturalists devote their lives to the study of the *fauna* and *flora* of specific places and times. Charles Darwin (1809-1892), the father of the theory of evolution, made an intensive study of the unique *fauna* and *flora* of the Galapagos Islands. In addition to their common household names, the classified *fauna* and *flora* of the world have been assigned technical Latin names by zoologists and botanists.

fawn (fawn) *vb.* To *fawn* on someone is to try to win his favor by flattery and servile behavior. In olden times, courtiers *fawned* upon kings and queens. The English historian Thomas Macaulay (1800-1859) wrote of "courtiers who *fawn* upon their master while they betray him." Greedy people *fawn* on rich relatives, jostling for a place in their wills. It is common to see a rock star or ring champion surrounded by a group of *fawning* hangers-on. Headwaiters often *fawn* on known big spenders as they enter a restaurant; they bow and scrape and address them by name as they show them to the best table.

fervid (fur′ vid—*u* as in *fur*) *adj.* A *fervid* person is ardent, impassioned, spirited, enthusiastic, one who shows earnest feeling. Romeo and Juliet were *fervid* lovers, as were Antony and Cleopatra. We are all swayed by *fervid* oratory. Experienced trial lawyers sum up with *fervid* appeals to the jury. *Fervid* people exhibit *fervor* (fur′ vər—*u* as in *fur*), which is warmth of feeling and earnestness. People who are *fervid* in a cause will plead their beliefs with great *fervor*. A related adjective is *fervent* (fur′ vənt—*u* as in *fur*), which has much the same effect as fervid. Hatred, as well as love, can be *fervent* or *fervid*. *Fervent* oratory can sway masses. A *fervid* or *fervent* plea for mercy or leniency may result in a reduced sentence. Cyrano, in the play *Cyrano de Bergerac* by Edmond Rostand (1868-1918), played the role of a *fervent* suitor, on someone else's behalf.

fetter (fet′ ər) *n., vb.* A *fetter*, literally, is an ankle chain or shackle for the restraint of a prisoner or a horse. It is used figuratively, in the plural, to describe anything that hinders progress or limits freedom. Increasing traffic in urban centers puts *fetters* on movement. Dictatorship imposes *fetters* upon freedom of speech. Timidity places *fetters* upon action. To *fetter* is to put a *fetter* or *fetters* on a person or animal, and figuratively, to hinder or restrain. Subservience to popular taste will never *fetter* a serious writer or artist. All over the world, there are regimes that seek to *fetter* freedom of expression.

figurative (fig′ yər ə tiv) *adj.* The *figurative* use of a word or phrase is its use, not in its literal, usual sense, but in an imaginative way, as a *figure of speech*. When a man is described as having a heart of stone, the use of *stone* is *figurative*; his heart does not, of course, really consist of stone. When someone is described as having a fiery temperament, nothing is literally on fire; *fiery* is used to indicate that such a person is passionate and quick to anger. *Stone* and *fiery* are being used *figuratively*. *Heart of stone* and *fiery temperament* are *figures of speech*. If you speak of an Australian aborigine's throwing a boomerang, you are using *boomerang* in its literal, physical, everyday sense. When you say that the candidate's indiscreet youthful statements acted as a boomerang in his campaign, i.e., that something he said years ago has come back to hurt him, you are using *boomerang* in its *figurative* sense. A man who doesn't see what's going on right around him "has blinders on." He isn't really wearing blinders. *Blinders* is being used *figuratively*.

filial (fil′ ee əl) *adj*. A *filial* relationship is that of a child to its parent. *Filial* conduct is that which befits a son or daughter in relation to a parent. *Filial* respect is owing to a parent (Honor thy father and thy mother). A child has certain *filial* duties to its parents. *Filial* obedience is expected of children. Confucius (551–479 B.C.) said: "A youth, when at home, should be *filial*, and, abroad, respectful of his elders." Thomas Jefferson (1743–1826) wrote: "A lively and lasting sense of *filial* duty is more effectually impressed on the mind of a son or daughter by reading *King Lear*, than by all the dry volumes of ethics . . . that were ever written." "Quotations," wrote the American poetess Louise Imogen Quincy (1861–1920), ". . . from the great old authors are an act of *filial* reverence on the part of the quoter. . . ."

finesse (fih nes′) *n., vb*. *Finesse* is skill and delicacy, particularly in handling a tricky, difficult, sensitive situation. It takes a lot of *finesse* to handle a nervous horse. Great chess players must use extreme *finesse* in anticipating the opponent's strategy. *Finesse* implies subtlety and delicate maneuvering, whether in business, politics, sports, or games. The word, especially when used as a verb, can express the idea of cunning and a certain degree of trickery, as when a politician *finesses* his opponent into making a telling error. *Finesse* has the force of *maneuver*, when the heroes of movie thrillers, like Agent 007 (alias James Bond), keep *finessing* their way through one tight spot after another without batting an eyelash.

flagrant (flay′ grənt) *adj*. A *flagrant* crime is a scandalous one, openly, shamelessly committed. A *flagrant* criminal or offender is one who openly defies the law and isn't the least bit bothered about the harm done to his victim. *Flagrant* is applied to wrongdoing that is so conspicuously and outrageously bad that it cannot remain unnoticed. *Flagrant* criminals flaunt their crimes, not caring one bit about public reaction. The building of the Berlin Wall was a *flagrant* act of defiance on the part of East Germany. A *flagrant* error is a glaring one, an error that is immediately obvious to the naked eye. The Argentinians committed a *flagrant* error in invading the Falklands. That famous headline in the *New York Daily News*, "DEWEY ELECTED," is about as good an example of a *flagrant* error as one can find in newspaper history. Harry Truman enjoyed it immensely.

flair (flare—*a* as in *dare*) *n*. A *flair* is a knack, a natural ability to do something well. Some people have a *flair* for languages, and can pick them up in no time. Others have a *flair* for finding bargains, seeming able to find them instinctively. A *flair* for hospitality and entertaining can make a woman a social leader. *Flair* can be used in a general way, by itself, as the equivalent of chic, smartness of style.

People with *flair* get a lot of attention. When you walk into a home or a shop that has *flair,* you know that someone with discrimination and taste is at the bottom of it.

flaunt (flawnt) *vb.* To *flaunt* something is to show it off, to parade it before people's eyes, to display it conspicuously in a colorful way. The newly rich too often *flaunt* their newly acquired finery. "If you've got it, *flaunt* it" was the slogan of an airline that painted its planes in vivid colors (but succumbed to the vivid red in its balance sheet). Boasters *flaunt* their achievements; modest people let their achievements speak for themselves. Do not confuse *flaunt* and *flout,* which is quite a different story; to *flout* is to scorn, scoff at, mock, to violate (a rule, law, principle, etc.).

flawless (flaw' lis) *adj.* A *flaw* is an imperfection, a defect, a blemish. It follows that *flawless* means "perfect." Helen of Troy was a woman of *flawless* beauty. Great actors speak their lines with *flawless* diction. When a man conducts himself perfectly in any situation, he can be said to have behaved *flawlessly.* The success of the Israeli raid that freed the hostages at Entebbe was the result of *flawless* planning and execution. Tremendous preparation goes into the *flawless* performance of great musicians. Practice makes *flawless.*

fleece (flees) *vb.* To *fleece* someone is to swindle them out of money or property. *Fleece* does not contain any implication of violence. The old joke about selling Brooklyn Bridge to the hayseed is an imaginary example of *fleecing.* Confidence men *fleece* their innocent victims by one trick or another. We know that sheep are covered with *fleece,* and to *fleece* a sheep is to remove its covering. To *fleece,* in the sense of "swindle," is a good example of how an originally figurative use of a word can eventually give it an additional literal meaning. See **figurative,** for a discussion of the figurative uses of words and phrases.

flex (flex) *vb.* To *flex* a part of one's body is to bend it. People *flex* their arms in order to show off their muscles. One can also speak of "*flexing* one's muscles," a phrase often used figuratively to mean "make a show of strength," as when one seeks to intimidate a foe. *Flex* gives us the adjective *flexible* (flek' sə b'l). Anything *flexible,* like a slim willow branch, can be easily bent. *Flexible* is used figuratively to describe persons or things that are adaptable, like a *flexible* individual or a *flexible* system of operations, or a *flexible* work program or schedule. A *flexible* personality is one that is pliable, willing to yield to the needs of the moment. From *flexible* we get the noun *flexibility* (flek sə bil' ih tee), which also has both literal and figurative uses. One can describe material, like a thin metal sheet, as having *flexibility,* and one can admire the *flexibility* of an open mind.

flimsy (flim' zee) *adj. Flimsy* means "weak," both literally and figuratively. A piece of *flimsy* material is thin and light, without strength or solidity. A *flimsy* box, like one of cardboard, is easily damaged or destroyed. A *flimsy* excuse is an unsatisfactory one; inadequate and unconvincing. A *flimsy* argument is ineffective and not persuasive. When dictators want to invade neighboring territory, they often attempt to justify the invasion by *flimsy* "evidence" that the victimized country was about to violate the border. *Flimsy* security for a loan will usually be rejected as inadequate.

flora (floe′ rə) *n.* See **fauna**.

fluctuate (fluk′ choo ate) *vb.* To *fluctuate* is to keep changing from one position to another, the way stock prices *fluctuate*, or the daily temperature *fluctuates*, or a politician's popularity *fluctuates*. *Fluctuate* is used figuratively to indicate indecision and wavering. There are unstable people who constantly *fluctuate* between hope and despair, or elevation and depression. The noun, *fluctuation* (fluk choo ay′ shən), has both the literal and figurative meanings of the verb. One may speak of the *fluctuations* in stock prices or temperature, or of *fluctuations* of people's emotions. John Adams (1735-1826), the second President of the United States, wrote: "The law, [despite all] *fluctuations* of the passions, . . . will preserve a steady undeviating course."

fluent (floo′ ənt) *adj.* The commonest use of *fluent* is in relation to speech, whether in one's native language or in a foreign tongue. A person with an aptitude for languages, living abroad for some time, can become *fluent* in one or more foreign languages. An American who has lived in Paris for five years may become *fluent* in French. By that time, he should speak *fluent* French (or speak French *fluently*). *Fluent* can apply to one's own language as well: A *fluent* speaker is one who speaks easily, smoothly, and without hesitation. One can describe a speech as graceful and *fluent*. The image evoked by *fluent* is that of a smoothly flowing stream.

flummox (flum′ əks) *vb.* To *flummox* someone is to confuse, bewilder, or disconcert him, or to do all of those things. Lawyers cross-examining witnesses do their best to *flummox* them. Lots of people trying to make sense out of most railroad and plane schedules, or road maps, are often completely *flummoxed*. *Flummox* is an informal or colloquial word, but colorful and useful. The origin of *flummox* is unknown, but the irrepressible Mr. Weller in *The Pickwick Papers*, by Charles Dickens (1812-1870), arbitrarily gave it an Italian derivation: "If your governor [i.e., boss] don't prove a alleybi [alibi], he'll be what the Italians call reg'larly *flummoxed*."

flurry (flur′ ee—*u* as in either *fur* or *hut*) *n.* Literally, a *flurry* is a snow shower. It is commonly used in its figurative sense: a sudden excitement or commotion, a spasmodic agitation or rush or hurry. At even a well-planned reception, there is usually a *flurry* of activity on the arrival of the guest of honor. The sound of a police-car or fire-engine siren causes a *flurry* of alarm among drivers on the highway. Backstage, there is always a *flurry* of excitement on opening night. *Flurry* has a special use as a stock-exchange term: a sudden rush of activity or a sudden and brief jump or decline in prices.

fluster (flus′ tər) *n., vb.* To *fluster* someone is to make him nervous, to put him into a state of nervous confusion, to confuse or muddle him one way or another. Even the most experienced speakers can be *flustered* by constant heckling from the audience. Rude, destructive criticism can *fluster* almost anyone. Witnesses are often *flustered* by aggressive cross-examination, as are unprepared students when called upon to recite. *Fluster* is occasionally used as a noun, to describe a state of nervous excitement. Sudden confrontation with an unexpected problem can put a person into a *fluster*. *All in a fluster* is a vividly descriptive phrase describing a state of agitated confusion.

fob (fob) *vb.* To *fob* something *off* on someone is to palm it off, to trick someone into accepting something inferior or worthless, to cheat him by substituting something inferior for the genuine article. In England, crooks try to *fob off* stolen goods like watches or fur pieces by explaining that they "fell off the back of a lorry [truck]." Fraudulent art dealers have been known to *fob off* copies of old masters as originals, on collectors and even museums.

forbear (for bare′) *vb.* To *forbear* from doing something is to abstain or refrain from doing it. When listening to a long-winded, rambling account, it is difficult to *forbear* from crying, "Get to the point!" After attending a friend's poor performance in a play, it is unfair to *forbear* from criticism if you really want to be helpful. The noun *forebearance* (for bare′ əns) departs from the meaning of the verb somewhat, and means "patience, tolerance, leniency." Do not be quick to anger; show *forbearance* toward the offender; there may be an explanation. It is best to exercise *forbearance* in your dealings with people generally. *Forbearance* and self-control are admirable qualities in an executive, and need not lessen authority.

foremost (for′ most) *adj.* *Foremost* describes whoever or whatever is first in rank, most notable, chief. Shakespeare is the *foremost* dramatist of all time. Beethoven's third symphony, the *Eroica*, is thought by many music lovers to be the *foremost* symphonic work in history. Rembrandt was the *foremost* painter of his era. In Shakespeare's *Julius Caesar* (Act IV, Scene 3), Brutus describes the conspirators who assassinated Caesar as those "that struck the *foremost* man of all the world." Sir Isaac Newton (1642–1727), who first formulated the law of gravitation, was the *foremost* philosopher and mathematician of his time, just as Albert Einstein (1875–1955), who formulated the Theory of Relativity, was the *foremost* physicist of his era.

forerunner (for′ run ər) *n.* Literally, a *forerunner* is a predecessor (someone or something that has gone before), sometimes, more especially, an ancestor; but the word's common, figurative use is to describe an omen of something about to happen. The appearance of swallows is a *forerunner* of spring. Sniffles and a dry throat are a *forerunner* of a head cold. There are a number of economic indicators that are *forerunners* of a change in the economy, for better or worse.

forestall (for stawl´) *vb.* To *forestall* something is to prevent it from happening by acting first. To *forestall* a person is to thwart him by getting in ahead of him. Detention without trial is an attempt to *forestall* crime. It is advisable to install an alarm system in order to *forestall* burglary. Being the first to introduce a new product is the best way to *forestall* the competition. To *forestall* serious complications, it is best to consult the doctor at the first sign of unusual symptoms.

forgo, forego (for go´) *vb.* When you *forgo* something, you do without it, give it up. If you want to lose weight, you have to *forgo* fattening food. To succeed in your studies, you must *forgo* many pleasant activities. If an employee is offered his choice between a raise and a pension, it is usually wise to *forgo* the immediate benefit of the increase in favor of the advantages of long-term security. It is sad, when one moves to a faraway community, to *forgo* the pleasant day-to-day contacts with friends and neighbors. Never *forgo* the opportunity to bring a little happiness into the world.

forlorn (for lorn´) *adj.* A person who is *forlorn* is miserable, despairing; he feels uncared-for, forsaken. *Forlorn* describes someone who is sad and lonely, deserted, abandoned. We are all too familiar with pictures of *forlorn* refugees on our television screens. The *forlorn* alcoholics we see on city streets are the lost souls of society. *Forlorn* is a rather poetic word. In the great sonnet beginning "The world is too much with us . . . " the English poet William Wordsworth (1770–1850) wrote: "I'd rather be/A Pagan [and] . . . /Have glimpses that would make me less *forlorn*." In "A Christmas Mystery," William Morris (1834–1896), the English painter and poet (designer of the Morris chair), describes how, on "the longest day of all the year," he "sat down . . . /And ponder'd sadly, wearied and *forlorn*." The curious phrase *forlorn hope* is not related to the word *forlorn*. It comes from the Dutch *verloren hoop,* signifying the "lost squad," the troop selected for the most dangerous service. (In Dutch, *hoop* is pronounced *hope*.) A *forlorn hope* is a vain hope, a plan or enterprise with practically no chance of success. After days of fruitless searching for the wreckage in terrible weather, the task is given up as a *forlorn hope*.

formative (for´ mə tiv) *adj.* A person's *formative* years are those that mold his character and shape his future. The *formative* period in a company's existence is that which determines its success. *Formative* influences are those that come to bear on a person's development and play a part in molding his character and personality. Sociologists argue the question whether it is a person's genes or the circumstances of his environment during his *formative* period that have the greater influence in determining his character and the course of his life.

forsake (for sake´) *vb.* To *forsake* is to abandon, desert, renounce, break away from. The Family Court is full of cases where a man has *forsaken* his wife and children. All too often, a rich man's friends *forsake* him when he loses his fortune. Unfortunately, it also happens that a poor man *forsakes* his old friends when he becomes rich. Things, as well as people, can be *forsaken*. When an actress marries, she may have to *forsake* the theater in order to raise a family. Some people *forsake* city life in order to enjoy the peace and quiet of the countryside. *Forsook* is the past tense.

forte (fort—*o* as in *old*) *n*. A person's *forte* is his strong point, the quality in which he excels, the thing he is best at. One person's *forte* is cooking, another's playing the flute. Some people excel in verbal studies; with others, the sciences are their *forte*. Aptitude tests are supposed to determine a person's *forte*, so that he will head his career in the right direction. Do not confuse this *forte* with the musical direction *forte* (pronounced for´ tay).

forthright (forth´ rite—*o* as in *hole*, fawrth-) *adj*. A *forthright* person is outspoken, frank; a *forthright* statement is straightforward, goes straight to the point. A *forthright* approach to a problem or a messy situation is one that goes directly to the nub of the matter, without hemming or hawing. It is sometimes difficult to give a friend *forthright* criticism without offending him. A *forthright* method of doing business will attract and keep customers. A soft answer turneth away wrath; a *forthright* answer may turn away friends.

fortunate (for´ chə nit) *adj*. A *fortunate* person is a lucky one, one blessed with good *fortune*. A *fortunate* happening is one that brings good luck. *Fortunate* circumstances are auspicious ones, ones that promise a happy outcome. If a man is happily married, he was obviously *fortunate* in his choice of mate. Some people are *fortunate* enough to have gone through life without a serious problem. Do not confuse *fortunate* with *fortuitous* (for tyoo´ ə təs), which means "accidental" and describes events that happen by chance, and are not necessarily *fortunate*. The English playwright John Webster (1580–1625) wrote:

> And of all axioms this shall win the prize,—
> 'Tis better to be *fortunate* than wise.

fragrant (fray´ grənt) *adj*. *Fragrant* means "sweet-smelling," and the picture evoked by the word is that of *fragrant* flowers. Breezes can be *fragrant*, too. Those odors that waft in from the kitchen, especially when you're hungry, might be described as *fragrant* if you were feeling poetic. Figuratively, *fragrant* can take on the meaning of "pleasant" or "delightful," especially in the phrase *fragrant memories*, like the memories of a happy childhood, or the *fragrant memories* of a first love. The noun is *fragrance* fray´ grəns). The *fragrance* of some flowers is almost overpowering. Perfumes and toilet water are bought for their *fragrance*. The English critic and poet Arthur Symons (1865–1945) wrote: "Without charm there can be no fine literature, as there can be no perfect flower without *fragrance*."

fray (fray) *n*. A *fray* is a battle, a fight, a quarrel, a conflict, a noisy brawl, a contest. Depending on the context, a *fray* can be anything from a historic battle between armies to an angry confrontation between individuals. When in Shakespeare's *Romeo and Juliet* (Act III, Scene 1) the Prince of Verona learns of Romeo's fatal duel with Tybalt, he asks angrily, "Who began this bloody *fray?*" The gangs of youths who roam big-city streets seem eager for the *fray*. Old westerns gloried in bloody saloon *frays*. Election campaigns in the United States amount to interminable *frays* lasting months before election day.

frenetic (frə net' ik) *adj*. *Frenetic* is a synonym for *frantic* (fran' tik) and *frenzied* (fren' zeed), and describes a person, an act, or a scene that is wild with excitement, fear, or panic. The state of mind that makes one *frenetic* is *frenzy* (fren' zee). Whenever the stock market goes up or down sharply, there is a *frenetic* scene on the floor of the stock exchange. In that context, *frenetic* is a strong word for *hectic*. The rush-hour crowds in the New York subways seem to be impelled by a *frenetic* urge to beat deadlines.

frequent (free' kwənt) *adj.*, (frih kwent', free-) *vb*. *Frequent*, the adjective, describes anything that happens often, and *frequently* (free' kwənt lee) means "often." *Frequent* visits from good friends are a source of great pleasure. To *frequent* (note different pronunciation of the verb) is to visit often, to go habitually. People interested in art *frequent* museums and art galleries. Seals *frequent* the northwestern coast of the United States. Religious people *frequent* their churches. People who want to get ahead in politics soon learn to *frequent* their local political clubs.

frugal (froo' gəl)—*oo* as in *boot*) *adj*. A *frugal* person spends as little as possible; he is careful to live economically. Poor people have no choice; they have to be *frugal* at all times. Misers may be very rich and still feel impelled to live as *frugally* (froo' gəl lee) as church mice. *Frugal* can describe things as well as people: A *frugal* meal is a scanty, meager one; a *frugal* way of life is one that involves a minimum outlay of expenses.

fruitful (froot' fəl—*oo* as in *boot*) *adj*. *Fruitful* describes activities that produce results. An effort, an attempt, a search, study, research—any such activity that is profitable and productive and gets results may be called *fruitful*. A good heart-to-heart talk between parent and child may be quite *fruitful*. A successful expedition to raise sunken treasure would certainly be described as *fruitful*. As you might imagine, *fruitless* (froot' lis) describes unproductive activities, those that get nowhere. A session of Congress may turn out to be *fruitful* or *fruitless*. A surgical operation that saves the patient is indeed *fruitful*; one that produces no result is *fruitless*. *Fruitless* can be used in the sense of "vain, useless": It would be *fruitless* to attempt to climb Mt. Everest without the necessary experience and equipment.

function (funk' shən) *n.*, *vb*. As a noun, *function* has two distinct meanings: *function* is the word for anyone's or anything's special purpose or activity (the *function* of a lawyer is to advise a client of his legal right); a *function* is any special public or social or official ceremony or event (there are many *functions* that the chief of state must attend). It is the *function* of the heart to pump blood through the system. It is often the *function* of a public figure to throw out the first ball in a World Series. As a verb, to *function* is to operate or perform properly. When a fuse blows, an electrical circuit stops *functioning*. Any device that doesn't *function* is out of order, inoperative. *Function* can also be used in the sense of serve: An overcoat can *function* as an extra blanket on a cold night. A pencil will *function* as a conductor's baton in case of need.

furbish (fur' bish) *vb.* To *furbish* something is to renovate it, to freshen it up, give it a new look, to revive it, especially something that has been suffering from disuse. *Furbish* is often followed by *up*: Some people like to buy run-down houses and *furbish* them *up*. It makes good sense to hold on to old clothes and *furbish* them *up* when they come back in style. A week in a foreign country will *furbish* your command of its language in which you have become rusty. It takes a lot of effort to *furbish* a skill that you have neglected, like the playing of a musical instrument.

futile (fyoo' t'l, -til—*oo* as in *boot*) *adj.* A *futile* effort is one that cannot succeed, is a waste of time, gets nowhere. Anything *futile* is ineffective, vain, useless, incapable of producing a result. Trying to start a car with a flooded carburetor by stepping hard on the gas pedal is a *futile* effort. It is *futile* to attempt to convince stubborn people of your point of view. *Futility* (fyoo til' ə tee—*oo* as in *boot*) is the noun. An *exercise in futility* is a vain attempt. Whipping and yelling at a determined mule is an *exercise in futility*. *Futility* is uselessness. When the English poet Thomas Gray (1716–1771) wrote, "The paths of glory lead but to the grave," he was speaking of the *futility* of glory, might, and power.

gainsay (gane' say, gane say') *n., vb.* To *gainsay* something is to deny or contradict it. *Gainsay* is often used in the negative: There is *no gainsaying* the honesty of Abraham Lincoln. As a noun, *gainsay* means "denial." Beyond *gainsay*, the *Pietà* is a genuine work of Michelangelo and a masterpiece of sculpture. That jealousy usually accompanies love cannot be *gainsaid* (gaine' sed, gane sed'). When someone speaks the truth, no matter how much it may hurt, you must not *gainsay* him. The *gain-* in *gainsay* is Old English for *against*.

gallant (gal' ənt) *adj.* A *gallant* person is courageous and full of spirit. *Gallant* and its noun, *gallantry* (gal' ən tree), have in them the flavor of "high-spirited, dashing, chivalrous, resolute." *Gallant* evokes the image of the fearless soldier of fortune. There can be no meanness, no pettiness in a *gallant* soul. The charge of the light brigade may have been foolhardy, but it certainly was *gallant*. Those never-say-die people who struggle for life in the face of fatal illness are often said to be making a *gallant* fight for life. L. E. G. Oates, in the Antarctic, became crippled and walked off to certain death in a blizzard (1912) in order not to hinder his companions; they marked his gravestone, "A very *gallant* gentleman." Pronounced gə lant́, *gallant* means "chivalrous, courteous, attentive to women," and can also be used as a noun describing such a man. In *Don Juan,* the English poet Lord Byron (1788-1824) wrote:

> What men call *gallantry,* and gods adultery,
> Is much more common where the climate's sultry.

gallivant (gal ə vant́) *vb.* To *gallivant* is to gad about, full of gaiety and frivolity. When a young son rushes in, grabs a sandwich, and rushes out again, a mother might ask, "Where are you *gallivanting* off to now?" Unfaithful husbands are sometimes described as off *gallivanting* with other women. Aimless, restless people who roam about spend their time *gallivanting* all over the world. *Gallivanting* has in it the quality of flitting about, with no fixed purpose or goal or schedule or itinerary.

gambit (gaḿ bit) *n.* Literally, a *gambit* is a series of opening moves in chess, in which the player gives up a pawn or other piece to obtain an advantage. The figurative use of the word covers any maneuver for the purpose of gaining an advantage, whether in conversation or other action. "Offense is the best defense" describes a *gambit* that people often resort to when they're in the wrong. A useful conversational *gambit* is to change the subject when the argument is going against you.

gamut (gaḿ ət) *n.* The *gamut* is the whole range, extent, scope, or scale of anything. In a single hour, a sensitive person can experience the whole *gamut* of emotion from gaiety to deep despair. A good actor can express whatever in the entire *gamut* of feeling is appropriate to the situation. One who has led a long, active life must have undergone the *gamut* of experience. A detective must consider the whole *gamut* of motivation. A harsh critic once characterized the acting of a noted actress as "running the *gamut* of emotions from A to B."

garish (gaŕ ish—*a* as in *dare* or *hat*) *adj.* Anything *garish* is gaudy, tastelessly and unpleasantly showy, overelaborate, overdecorated, flashy. Tourists in tropical countries have a weakness for *garish* sport shirts. New York subway cars are spray-painted in *garish* colors by young vandals. *Garishness* is always in bad taste, whether in dress, decor, or oratory. Even a perfume can be described as *garish,* if it is excessive and offends the sensibilities.

gauge (gaje) *vb.* To *gauge* something is to appraise it, form a judgment or an opinion of it. It is dangerous to attempt to *gauge* a person's character on brief acquaintance. Before setting out on an enterprise, one should do one's best to *gauge* its pitfalls and the chances of success. On the morning of a picnic, better *gauge* the weather. The purpose of politicians' polls is to *gauge* the reactions of the public and determine which way the wind is blowing.

ghastly (gast´ lee, gahst´-) *adj*. This word describes anything horrible, frightful, terrible. We read in the newspapers about one *ghastly* murder after another. The television news programs are catalogues of *ghastly* events all over the world. *Ghastly* is applied to crimes and accidents that are shocking and unspeakable. Informally, *ghastly* can be used in a semijocular way, to describe something that doesn't shock the senses, but is very, very bad, like a simply awful dinner prepared by an exceedingly inept cook. It would be a *ghastly* mistake to write two confidential letters and put them into the wrong envelopes. Most people hate to face the *ghastly* job of preparing their income-tax returns.

ghoul (gool—*oo* as in *boot*) *n*. Literally, a *ghoul* is a grave robber. In Oriental legend, the name *ghoul* was applied to horrible demons who not only robbed graves but devoured the corpses. Figuratively, a *ghoul* is anyone of gruesome tastes who delights in revolting, unnatural things. *Ghoulish* (gool´ ish) is the adjective. There is so much explicit violence on the television screen these days that much of it seems tailored to *ghoulish* tastes. It must take a *ghoul* to enjoy the act or the exhibition of eating live goldfish and mice. Normal people feel sick about what *ghouls* delight in.

gibberish (jib´ ər ish, gib-) *n*. *Gibberish* is meaningless, unintelligible nonsense speech or writing. To *gibber* (jib´ ər) is to speak fast, making nonsense sounds, especially when one is terrified or in shock. *Gibberish* is used generally to describe talk or writing that may not be literally unintelligible, but adds up to stuff and nonsense. "Stop talking *gibberish*!" is the usual reaction of the listener. An explanation that doesn't hang together or add up to anything sensible can be dismissed as sheer *gibberish*. Arrogant tourists who don't take the trouble to learn a word of the native language impatiently characterize perfectly good Arabic or Chinese (or French or German!) as *gibberish*. To an outsider, the technical language of workers in an alien field, speaking in their own special terms, sounds like *gibberish*. Even to lawyers, the language of some tax statutes or regulations look like *gibberish*.

glean (gleen) *vb*. Technically, *glean* is used to describe the activity of gathering the bits and pieces of grain left by the regular harvesters. Figuratively, *glean* describes the activity of picking up scraps of information, bit by bit, from one source or another. A biographer has to consult hundreds of sources to *glean* what he can about the subject of his book. Lawyers go through every scrap of paper they can lay their hands on to *glean* ammunition for the case. The results of such painful and laborious hours of toil are called *gleanings*. From the *gleanings* of dogged research, biochemists have made many discoveries of great benefit to the human race.

glib (glib) *adj*. *Glib* is far from a complimentary word: A *glib* talker is ready with words, smooth but insincere, or at best superficial. When faced with a difficult question, some people blurt out a *glib* reply that is not really an answer. People with *glib* tongues are always ready with *glib* excuses when criticized. *Glib* answers and excuses are made hastily, without thinking or preparation, and usually fool no one. *Glib* people may be facile in the use of words, but the superficiality, inaccuracy, or downright deceitfulness of their words is usually apparent except to the most naive of persons. A soft answer turneth away wrath; a *glib* answer turneth away confidence.

glimmer (glim' ər) *n., vb.* In the literal sense, a *glimmer* is a weak, unsteady light, and to *glimmer* is to shed such a light, to twinkle. Distant lighthouses *glimmer* in the night; all we see of the stars is their distant *glimmer*. Figuratively, a *glimmer* is an inkling, a faint conception of something, an irreducible minimum. When people try to explain relativity, most listeners haven't the faintest *glimmer* of understanding. In the face of the most desperate situations, most people hold on to a *glimmer* of hope. Greta Garbo's early films gave only a *glimmer* of the potential she later realized.

glimpse (glimps) *n., vb.* A *glimpse* is a brief, passing look. As your train speeds by, you catch a *glimpse* of an occasional house or station. To *glimpse* (at) something or somebody is to catch a *glimpse* of the thing or person. As you look through your morning mail, there are bits of advertising material that you merely *glimpse* at and quickly throw away. On a cloudy, windy night, you may catch *glimpses* of the moon as the clouds scud by. The American poet Robert Frost (1874–1963), in his poem *A Passing Glimpse*, wrote:

> Heaven gives its *glimpses* only to those
> Not in a position to look too close.

The English poet Alfred, Lord Tennyson (1809–1892) wrote of "*glimpses* of forgotten dreams."

glower (glou' ər—*ou* as in *out*) *n., vb.* To *glower* is to scowl, to stare sullenly, angrily; a *glower* is such a look. A schoolteacher, entering her schoolroom that has been vandalized in her absence, will stand and *glower* at the damage. A person who finds one distasteful item after another in the morning newspaper will stare at it *gloweringly* (glou' ər ing lee). When a person has planned a nice outdoor excursion and looks up to see threatening clouds, he may *glower* at the sky. A *glowering* person is a study in sullen, brooding, barely controlled anger.

gobbledegook, gobbledygook (gob' əl dee gook—*oo* as in *look*) *n*. *Gobbledegook* or *gobbledygook* is wordy, bureaucratic jargon, full of pompous words and rather evasive language, inflated, needlessly involved, and obscure to the point of being practically unintelligible; it is sometimes known as "double-talk." The author's professor at Columbia Law School, Roswell Magil, called the then current tax law "a masterpiece of complexity and *gobbledegook*." *Gobbledegook* is also a specialty of many writers of those "simple, easy directions" that accompany do-it-yourself kits. Many of the speeches made at that worthy and noble institution, the United Nations, are pure *gobbledegook*.

gouge (gouj—*ou* as in *out*) *vb.* To *gouge* (often followed by *out*) is to dig out or force out. The commonest use of the verb in its literal sense is in the horrible expression to *gouge out someone's eye* (with a thumb)—a barbaric act which has been known to occur in the history of ancient enmities. Figuratively, to *gouge* is to overcharge, swindle, extort from, the way people are often treated by merchants using "inflation" as an excuse. Ticket scalpers are specialists in *gouging* the public. In purchasing goods or services from people with whom you are dealing for the first time, it is wise to settle the price in advance, in order to prevent being *gouged* when it is too late to bargain.

gracious (gray´ shəs) *adj.* A *gracious* person, or a *gracious* act, is kind and courteous. A *gracious* way of life is a life of ease and good taste. A *gracious* home is a pleasant one, marked by comfort, tranquillity, ease, and taste. *Gracious* living is usually associated with breeding and sensitivity and good taste. Those magnificent plantation homes of a now vanished society were symbols of *graciousness*. *Gracious* sometimes implies the generosity of forgiveness, as in a *gracious* letter accepting an apology. *Gracious* people are always kind and courteous to their subordinates, whether toward domestic servants, public servants like waiters and cab drivers, or office employees. *Gracious!* and *Goodness gracious!* are old-fashioned exclamations expressing surprise.

grandeur (gran´ jər, -joor—*oo* as in *look*) *n.* *Grandeur* is magnificence, splendor, greatness. One can speak of the *grandeur* of the Rocky Mountains, the *grandeur* of the style of the King James Version of the Bible, the *grandeur* of the Cathedral of Notre Dame in Paris or of St. Peter's in Rome, the *grandeur* of the life-style of ancient monarchs. The American poet Edgar Allan Poe (1809-1849) wrote of ". . . the glory that was Greece,/ And the *grandeur* that was Rome." The English biologist and writer Thomas Henry Huxley (1825-1895) wrote: "Size is not *grandeur*, and territory does not make a nation." The English poet Gerard Manley Hopkins (1844-1889) wrote a poem entitled "God's *Grandeur*," which starts, "The world is charged with the *grandeur* of God."

grandiose (gran´ dee ose—*s* as in *see*) *adj.* *Grandiose* applies to anything planned on a large scale and impressive; but in context it can mean "pompous" and describe people or things trying (and failing) to be grand and impressive. The great cathedrals of Europe, like the ancient temples of Egypt, are built on a *grandiose* scale. Great poems like *Paradise Lost* and *The Divine Comedy* are based on *grandiose* conceptions. Egotists have *grandiose* notions of their own importance. Mussolini built *grandiose*, tasteless monuments to celebrate fascism. *Grandiose* plans often fail for lack of attention to details. In the heat of a campaign, candidates put forth *grandiose* programs that have little to do with reality.

graphic (graf´ ik) *adj.* A *graphic* account of a happening is one that gives the listener or reader a vivid and clear picture of what went on. It takes a trained reporter to give the public a *graphic* report of a confused event. Edward R. Murrow (1908-1965), the American news commentator who broadcast regularly from London during World War II, was famous for his *graphic* accounts of the Battle of Britain. Witnesses in court proceedings are usually too frightened to be able to testify *graphically* (graf´ ə kə lee).

grave (grave) *adj.* A *grave* person is serious and solemn. *Grave* thoughts are earnest, dignified, and serious. *Grave* news is serious, and to be seriously considered. A *grave* situation is a serious one, and requires careful consideration. A *grave* mistake can lead to serious consequences. In this context, the noun is *gravity* (grav´ ih tee). The *gravity* of a situation is the degree of its seriousness. A *grave* illness is a serious one, that requires prompt attention. The *gravity* of the illness would be measured by the attending physician.

grievance (gree´ vəns) *n. Grief* (greef) *n.* is sorrow; to *grieve* (greev) *vb.* is to feel sorrow; to *grieve* someone is to make him feel sorrow; the adjective *grievous* (greev´ əs) is discussed under the next heading. *Grievance,* though related in form, takes off in a different direction: A *grievance* is a wrong (whether real or imagined) which one believes to be a ground for complaint. The term is often used in labor-management conflicts and negotiations, when union officials present the workers' *grievances* to management. It was the *grievance* of taxation without representation that led to the Boston Tea Party, and eventually to the American Revolution. The First Amendment to the United States Constitution provides that "Congress shall make no law . . . abridging [curtailing] . . . the right of the people . . . to petition the government for a redress of *grievances* [righting of wrongs].

grievous (greev´ əs) *adj. Grievous* has a number of meanings, depending on the context. *Grievous* applies to anything like news or a report or tale that causes grief or sorrow. The news of the death of an old friend is *grievous* news. In this use, *grievous* is equivalent to *distressing.* Thus, one may speak of a *grievous* loss. *Grievous* can mean "atrocious" when it describes a flagrant offense against morality. Hitler's treatment of the Jews was one of the most *grievous* crimes in history. Here, *grievous* is synonymous with *shameful, outrageous. Grievous* is used in the law in statutes concerning *grievous bodily harm,* where it means "severe, serious." *Grievous* has the sense of "serious" or "grave" in the English translation of the Roman Catholic Missal, where *mea maxima culpa* becomes "my most *grievous* fault." The same is true when Shakespeare (*Julius Caesar,* Act III, Scene 2) has Marc Antony say of Caesar: ". . . The noble Brutus/Hath told you Caesar was ambitious;/If it were so, it was a *grievous* fault;/and *grievously* hath Caesar answered it." Although *grievous* and *grievance* are both based on the word *grief,* they go off in quite different directions. Also, be careful about the pronunciation of *grievous.* Influenced by *previous* and *devious,* people have been known to insert a superfluous *i* before the *-ous.*

grimace (grim´ əs, grih mase´) *n., vb.* A *grimace* is a twisted, ugly facial expression, expressing disapproval, contempt, disgust, pain, or fright. To *grimace* is to make such a face. Sometimes a *grimace* is nothing more than a "funny face," intended to make people laugh, and when that happens, *grimacing* is nothing more than "making faces," a common amusement of children. *Grimaces* caused by pain or fright are involuntary; those caused by contempt or disgust may or may not be, depending on circumstances; *grimaces* to amuse are intentional.

grovel (gruv´ əl, grov-) *vb.* To *grovel* is to cringe, to humble oneself in such a servile way as to show a complete loss of self-respect. *Groveling* is self-abasement, and such a show of servility as to earn the contempt of those before whom one *grovels*. The English novelist William Makepeace Thackeray (1811-1865) wrote of a character in *Vanity Fair* who "whenever he met a great man . . . *groveled* before him." The French playwright Pierre de Beaumarchais (1732-1799), in *The Marriage of Figaro,* expresses this cynical attitude: "If you are mediocre and you *grovel,* you will succeed."

grueling (groo´ ə ling, groo´ ling—*oo* as in *boot*) *adj.* A *grueling* race or trial or experience is one that is exhausting, extremely tiring, taxing, one that knocks you out. Test after test in a laboratory to determine the cause of an illness can be a *grueling* experience. The building of the pyramids must have involved *grueling* labor. Marathons, measuring 26 miles, 385 yards, must be among the most *grueling* tests of human endurance. What can be more *grueling* than the ascent of Mt. Everest?

grudging (gruj´ ing) *adj. Grudging* means "reluctant," and describes any act or feeling marked by unwillingness. After a long campaign and a close contest, the loser will sometimes announce his *grudging* acceptance of the result. Stingy people *grudgingly* pick up the bill in a restaurant. Only after indispensable employees threaten to leave will some employers make a *grudging* agreement to raise salaries. When a jury says, "Not guilty," the prosecutor may give the defense attorney his *grudging* congratulations.

gullible (gul´ ə b´l) *adj.* To *gull* someone (an uncommon word) is to cheat or trick him, to pull the wool over his eyes; hence, a *gullible* person is easily fooled, tricked, cheated; he is unsuspecting, naive, innocent as a newborn babe, "born yesterday," "wet behind the ears," green. There once was a verb to *gull,* meaning "swallow." A *gullible* person will "swallow" anything. It is easy to bamboozle or hoodwink a *gullible* person. Country hicks, just arrived in the big city, are prototypes of *gullibility* (gul ə bil´ ih tee), and are often portrayed as easy to separate from their money. Swindlers prey on *gullible* old ladies and run off with their life savings.

habitual (hə bich´ oo əl) *adj.* What is *habitual* is customary, usual, regular. When one takes his *habitual* place at table, he sits in the seat that he occupies by *habit,* his regular, usual place. When you go to the theater as a matter of routine or *habit,* you are a *habitual* theater-goer. Some people are *habitual* gossips; others are *habitual* liars. Thomas Jefferson (1743-1826) said: "He who permits himself to tell a lie once finds it much easier to do it a second and third time, till at length it becomes *habitual*. . . ." If you go to the theater only once in a while, you are an occasional theater-goer; *occasional* is the opposite of *habitual*. When you do something regularly, as a matter of *habit,* you can be said to do it *habitually* (hə bich' oo ə lee). Some men *habitually* smoke a cigar after dinner. There are people who *habitually* turn on the television the moment they enter a room.

habituate (hə bich' oo ate) *vb*. To *habituate* someone to something is to get him accustomed or used to it; to become *habituated* to something is to get used to it. Many years of scraping by on a pittance will *habituate* a person to counting his pennies. Commuting for a long period *habituates* a person to early rising. Life in the frozen north will *habituate* people to the cold. It is amazing to what extremes of climate or noise or other discomfort man can eventually become *habituated*.

habitué (hə bich' oo ay, hə bich oo ay') *n*. This term applies to a person who regularly frequents a particular place or group. Lonely young people are often *habitués* of singles bars or clubs. Art lovers are *habitués* of art galleries and museums. The rich are *habitués* of expensive vacation spots. There are *habitués* of opera who come to know every aria by heart. *Habitués* of night clubs become *habituated* to the fawning attentions of headwaiters.

hack (hak) *n*. This unflattering word is applied to a person, like a writer or an artist, who uses his talent and training in the production of commonplace, mediocre work for money; or one who accepts dull and boring tasks in the field of politics for money or other rewards. There are writers who could do a lot better than the potboilers they turn out as literary *hacks,* in hopes of a fast buck. One can usually find literary drudges and *hacks* on newspaper staffs who perform the dull routine services assigned by editors. Every political party has its political *hacks* who carry out boring assignments, hoping for eventual reward in the form of promotion to a higher rung of the ladder. A *hack* in the arts may be of limited talent, incapable of producing anything better. He may sometimes do *hack* work far beneath his potential because of greater or more immediate financial reward.

haggard (hag' ərd) *adj*. A *haggard* person has an exhausted, emaciated appearance, the way one looks if beset by anxiety, or after prolonged exertion, lack of sleep, or continued fear or worry. A *haggard* look is a worn look, a gaunt look, a run-down, wearied, drained look, with dark circles under the eyes and pale or colorless cheeks. Long-distance runners often have a *haggard* look toward the end of the race. Grade B movies are fond of showing the *haggard* face of our hero, lost in the trackless Sahara, peering at a mirage. One sees a great many *haggard* students trudging around the campus at exam time.

haggle (hag' l) *vb.* To *haggle* is to bargain, in a petty, quarrelsome way, particularly over the price of something, or to argue, wrangle, nag, and fuss over almost anything. Arab merchants in the bazaars of the East spend endless time *haggling* over prices. Armenian rug dealers are supposed to be famous *hagglers*. Incredible amounts of time are spent by labor and management in *haggling* over every point in a labor negotiation. The English political scientist Harold J. Laski (1893–1950) said: "When it comes to making peace, we must not *haggle* over trifles."

hamper (ham' pər) *vb.* To *hamper* someone is to hinder him, prevent his free movement or activity, hold him back, slow him down, cramp his style. Noise in the next room *hampers* one's concentration and progress in the work at hand. A tight skirt *hampers* a woman's freedom of movement. Lack of funds *hampers* many a benevolent social program. Static *hampers* radio communication. Carrying a tremendous backpack *hampers* a hiker's progress. Old-fashioned ideas can *hamper* forward-looking political programs.

hangdog (hang' dog) *adj.* A *hangdog* look is a browbeaten one, an air of dejection, a defeated, crestfallen appearance. People who go about with a *hangdog* look don't command attention or respect. *Hangdog* people are abject and spineless. *Hangdog* can also describe a shamefaced look of guilt, or a furtive air of embarrassment. People who are down and out for a long time often develop a *hangdog* look. A person caught in the act of doing something shameful, whether stealing or eavesdropping or snooping, may react by putting on a *hangdog* expression. Children or pets sharply reprimanded often go off with a *hangdog* air.

haphazard (hap haz' ərd) *adv.* Anything *haphazard* lacks planning or order, happens by chance; it is aimless, random, accidental, hit-or-miss, and totally unmethodical. Some people plan every moment of their lives; others live a carefree, *haphazard* existence. A *haphazard* collection of furniture indicates a lack of taste or care. Some of our young people affect a *haphazard* way of dress as a badge of rebellion against convention. *Haphazardness* in the approach to any task is the surest road to confusion and failure.

harangue (hə rang') *n., vb.* A *harangue* is a long, loud, emotional talk or speech. To *harangue* is to deliver a *harangue*, to hold forth, to spout forth, to drone on and on, to rant. To *harangue* a person is to direct a *harangue* at him, to lecture him at length and passionately. *Harangue* evokes the image of a soapbox, whether the *haranguer* gets up on one or not. There are all sorts of *harangues*: those of the politician seeking votes or support for a bill, those of the promoter seeking money, the lobbyist representing special interests, the passionate young rebels trying to reform the world. Our legislators never tire of *haranguing* their colleagues (with one eye on the visitors' gallery) whether for support or to denounce the opposition.

harass (har´ əs, hə ras´—*a* as in *hat*) *vb*. In military usage, to *harass* the enemy is to keep troubling him by repeated attacks or raids; in general use, to *harass* someone is to annoy him continually, to pester him, keep after him, "bug" him. A person can be *harassed* by people bothering him with requests or endless complaints, by insects, by circumstances like lack of funds, illness, bad weather, and all kinds of bad luck. The Book of Job is a prime record of the *harassment* (hə ras´ mənt, har´ əs-,—*a* as in *hat*) of an individual by repeated woes. A business can be *harassed* by poor cash flow. In some urban areas, there are repeated instances of *harassment* of teachers by pupils.

harbor (har´ bər—*a* as in *bar*) *vb*. To *harbor* a person is to give him refuge, to shelter him. It is the duty of a secure nation to *harbor* the poor, innocent refugees made homeless by war and violence. To *harbor* a fugitive from justice is to hide him, and can make you an accessory. To *harbor* a thought or an idea or a suspicion is to have it in your mind, to entertain it or believe it. When you really trust someone, you won't *harbor* the thought that he has acted against you or violated your confidence. Some people hold on to grudges for a long time; they seem to enjoy *harboring* resentment.

harry (har´ ee—*a* as in *hat*) *vb*. To *harry* someone is to *harass* him, to be a nuisance to him in one way or another, to badger him, pester and nag him, plague him. Moneylenders often *harry* their clients for repayment of loans. Badly brought-up children too often *harry* their parents for toys or candy. Inconsiderate patients keep *harrying* their doctor with fancied complaints. *Harry* and *harass* are very close in meaning. It may surprise you to know that the two words (like *sorrow* and *sorry*) are from entirely different roots.

hazard (haz´ ərd) *n.*, *vb*. A *hazard* is a danger or risk, or anything that is a source of danger. These days, one is constantly faced with the *hazards* of the highways. The country girl who leaves her home to seek fame and fortune must undergo the *hazards* of the big city. It requires courage to take a job that involves lots of *hazards*. Sailors face the *hazards* of the open sea. To *hazard* a guess is to venture it, to offer it, though the situation is uncertain and your guess may subject you to criticism. To *hazard* a suggestion is to make it for what it is worth. In the case of both guess and suggestion, you are running the *hazard* that you may be wrong. *Hazardous* (haz´ ər dəs) means "dangerous, risky." Shortcuts over rough terrain may be *hazardous*. It is foolish to risk your savings on a *hazardous* venture. Most of us are well aware that cigarette smoking is *hazardous* to our health.

hearten (har´ t'n) *vb*. See **dishearten**.

hector (hek´ tər) *vb*. To *hector* someone is to bully him, intimidate him, browbeat him, "ride" him, give him a hard time. Some foremen think they can get more out of their workers by *hectoring* them. There are domineering husbands and wives who try to *hector* their spouses into submission and acceptance of their selfish ways.

Hectoring is somewhat like *badgering,* but stronger: To *badger* is to pester or bait; to *hector* is to play the bully, to bluster and intimidate. Top sergeants are typical *hectorers*. Schoolmasters in nineteenth-century English novels sometimes seem to enjoy *hectoring* their pupils mercilessly.

heedless (heed´ ləs) *adj.* To *heed* something is to pay careful attention to it, the way one should *heed* a warning from a trustworthy source. *Heedless* (usually followed by *of*) means "unmindful," and describes the state of mind of someone paying no attention. Lifeguards plunge in, *heedless* of raging waters, to rescue a drowning swimmer. Speculators sometimes risk their all, *heedless* of stock-market hazards. A *heedless* person is thoughtless, impulsive, rash, deaf to advice, and blind to warning signals. Franklin D. Roosevelt said, in his second Inaugural Address (1937): "We have always known that *heedless* self-interest was bad morals; we know now that it is bad economics." *Heedlessness* (heed´ ləs nəs) is thoughtlessness, recklessness, rashness.

heighten (hite´ ən) *vb.* When something is *heightened,* it is increased, raised to a higher level; when something *heightens,* it intensifies. An appropriate sound track *heightens* the emotional appeal of a motion picture. Excitement *heightens* a person's blood pressure. Good character description *heightens* the interest of a novel. Clear diction *heightens* one's enjoyment of a play. Good makeup *heightens* a woman's beauty. Interest and excitement *heighten* as a well-told narrative develops. As most people grow older, they make fewer mistakes in selecting friends as their understanding of others *heightens.*

herald (herr´ əld) *vb.* A *herald* is a messenger. To *herald* something is to announce its approach or usher it in. Movie companies spend millions on advertising and publicity campaigns to *herald* a new picture. A shift in the wind usually *heralds* a change in the weather. The introduction of automation has *heralded* new problems in labor-management relations. The development of supersonic air travel *heralded* a new era, not only of travel, but of international relations.

heresy (herr´ ə see) *n. Heresy* is any belief that varies from accepted doctrine. Originally, *heresy* was religious unorthodoxy; any nonbeliever was a *heretic* (herr´ ə tik) and was punished for straying from the true religion. Galileo, the Italian astronomer (1564–1642), on announcing his belief that the earth revolved around the sun rather than vice versa, was accused of *heresy* by the Inquisition and had to renounce his belief at the trial in Rome. (He is said to have murmured, as he left the trial, "But it does. . . .") Nowadays *heresy* and *heretic* apply to any departure from what is commonly accepted in any field. Original thinkers and innovators are often accused of *heresy* and called *heretics.* Beliefs that differ from established doctrine are labeled *heretical* (hə ret´ ih kəl). As our knowledge increases, much that was once considered *heresy* becomes the accepted truth. Charles Darwin (1809–1882), the English naturalist who formulated the theory of evolution, was reviled by many as a *heretic* (and still is in some quarters). There are many modern composers, once accused of *heresy,* whose music is now familiar to our ears and is no longer controversial.

heritage (herr´ ə tij) *n.* Technically, a person's *heritage* is his birthright, that which he has inherited or expects to inherit. Figuratively, the term is used to describe the traditions and values that have been passed on by previous generations. The children of refugees are conditioned by a *heritage* of fear and suffering. Our country has given us a *heritage* of national pride and honor. Abraham Lincoln, in an 1858 speech denouncing slavery, spoke of "the spirit which prized liberty as the *heritage* of all men." In his Inaugural Address, President Kennedy spoke of "a new generation of Americans . . . proud of our ancient *heritage.*"

hibernate (hy´ bər nate) *vb. Hibernate,* technically speaking, is a term applied to certain animals, like bears, that spend the winter sleeping or in a dormant stage, in close quarters. The noun is *hibernation* (hy bər nay´ shən). Both verb and noun are used figuratively in two ways: Many people who live in cold climates like to *hibernate* in Florida and other warm places (i.e., like to winter in a warm climate). *Hibernate* and *hibernation* are also used when people withdraw from active life and retire into seclusion. In this latter use, these terms have nothing to do with climate or the seasons. After an active career in the public eye, Harry Truman chose to *hibernate* and enjoy his later years in quiet retirement.

highfalutin (hy fə loot´ ən—*oo* as in *boot*) *adj.* This adjective, however spelled, is an informal word meaning "pretentious, pompous, high-and-mighty." Some people use *highfalutin* letterheads to impress their correspondents. Sermons in *highfalutin* language leave many people cold (or asleep). Movie stars are all too prone to practice *highfalutin* manners. Too many articles on important subjects are written in a *highfalutin* way. Politicians and lawyers might be more successful in their approach if they used less pompous and *highfalutin* language. Sometimes written *highfalutin', hifalutin, hifalutin', highfaluting.*

hinder (hin´ dər) *vb.* To *hinder* someone is to get in his way, to obstruct, to check or hamper him, to delay his progress, or to go all the way and actually prevent him from doing something. One can *hinder* a person or an act: Confusion about one's ultimate goal can *hinder* one from attaining it, or can *hinder* one's success or progress. There are many distractions that can *hinder* people in their efforts. Traffic can *hinder* prompt arrival. Embarrassment often *hinders* people from answering a searching question. The related noun, *hindrance* (hin´ drəns), can signify the act of *hindering,* or the thing that *hinders.* An older person's *hindrance* of a young person from committing a crime can save him from a lifetime of sorrow. Bad advice can be a *hindrance* to wise action. Submerged wrecks are a *hindrance* to safe navigation.

horde (hord—*o* as in *hole,* hawrd) *n., vb.* A *horde* is a crowd, a large group, a mass, a multitude. A *horde* of admirers often surrounds celebrities like rock stars and famous athletes. The term *horde* is usually applied to an unorganized mass of individuals, and is often used in a contemptuous way. The doors opened and a *horde* of fans swarmed into the hall. *Hordes* of tourists often shatter the peace and quiet of the countryside. *Hordes* of mosquitoes can ruin a picnic. To *horde* or *horde together* is to mass together. Groups of students tend to *horde* in cliques. People in danger tend to *horde* together.

horrendous (haw ren′ dəs) *adj.* Anything *horrendous* is horrifying, horrible, dreadful. After a hurricane, the landscape is strewn with *horrendous* sights. The history of Nazi Germany is one long catalogue of *horrendous* crimes against humanity. Our purchasing power has been drastically lowered by *horrendous* inflation. It is embarrassing to go backstage and have to say something to a friend who has just put on a *horrendously* bad performance. (One might try: "Darling, only *you* could have done it that way!")

hostile (hos′ t'l) *adj.* Literally, *hostile* describes an enemy, anyone or any group or nation that feels or indicates enmity. Apart from its use in such phrases as a *hostile nation* or a *hostile crowd*, *hostile* is used to indicate unfriendliness or opposition to an idea or plan or theory. Obviously, nations at war are *hostile* to each other, and are said to be engaged in *hostilities* (ho stil′ ih teez—*o* as in *hot*). When one is opposed to an idea or plan, one can be described as *hostile* to it. Conservatives are generally *hostile* to reform. Many religious people are still *hostile* to the theory of evolution. Fiscal conservatives are *hostile* to budget deficits. A look can be described as *hostile*. Intruders are usually met by *hostile* glances. The *hostility* of a crowd can be a frightening experience. Daniel Webster (1782-1852), the American statesman and orator, spoke of those who "constantly clamor . . .[and] carry on mad *hostility* against all established institutions."

humanitarian (hyoo man ih tare′ ee ən, yoo-, *oo* as in *boot*, second *a* as in *Mary*) *n., adj.* A *humanitarian* is a person active in promoting human welfare. A *humanitarian* person or act or attitude is one that is concerned about the welfare of mankind and is doing something about the reduction of human suffering. *Humanitarians* work for social reform. There are still serious questions on *humanitarian* grounds whether it was right to drop the atom bomb. Organizations like the Red Cross and the Salvation Army make *humanitarian* appeals for financial support. The Good Samaritan is an early example of *humanitarianism* (hyoo man ih tare′ ee ən izm, yoo-). The *humanitarian* reaction to the sufferings of refugees all over the globe is exhibited in the distribution of food and medical supplies by the developed nations.

humorous (hyoo′ mər əs, yoo-, *oo* as in *boot*) *adj.* A *humorous* person or story or look or act is funny, droll, comic, and tends to make us laugh or smile. Cartoons are *humorous* drawings, especially if the captions point up the *humor*. A *humorous* anecdote at the beginning of a lecture is a good way to get the attention of the audience. Mark Twain (Samuel Langhorne Clemens, 1835-1910) wrote many *humorous* tales. Clowns make *humorous* gestures, and toastmasters tell *humorous* stories. People with a *humorous* twinkle make pleasant companions.

hybrid (hy′ brid) *n., adj.* The term *hybrid* is applied literally to any animal or plant that is the product of the crossbreeding of different species. A mule is a *hybrid* resulting from the mating of a donkey and a horse. *Hybrid* corn is crossbred from different varieties. Mongrel dogs are *hybrids*. Figuratively, *hybrid* is applied to anything made from different elements. There are *hybrid* words, like *television*: *tele-* is derived from Greek, *-vision* from Latin. There are *hybrid* cultures resulting from immigration or invasion. The Vice-Presidency of the United States has been described as a *hybrid* office since the Vice-President is active in both the executive and legislative branches of the government.

hypochondriac (hy pə kon′ dree ak) *n., adj.*; as an *adj.*, also *hypochondriacal* (hy pə kon drý ə kəl). A *hypochondriac* is an imaginary invalid, a person who is abnormally worried and preoccupied with his health and keeps dreaming up one illness after another. The condition is called *hypochondria* (hy pə kon′ dree ə). A *hypochondriac* (or *hypochondriacal*) attitude takes all the fun out of life, and usually irritates and at least bores those who have to listen to the imaginary complaints. *Hypochondriacs* often go from one physician to another to tell about their afflictions, and are unsatisfied with doctors who tell them there's nothing wrong. *Le Malade Imaginaire (The Imaginary Invalid)*, a play by the French writer of comedies Molière (1622–1673), centers on the imagined illness of a *hypochondriac*.

idiosyncrasy (id ee ə sing′ krə see, -sin′-) *n.* An *idiosyncrasy* is a personal mannerism or habit peculiar to an individual, a personal quirk, eccentricity, or peculiarity. It is the *idiosyncrasy* of some people to move their lips when they read, or to talk to themselves while they think or plan. A friend of the author has the *idiosyncrasy* of touching every picket of any picket fence he passes (this slows him up a great deal). Superstitious people display the *idiosyncrasy* of touching wood whenever they relate that "all's well thus far." The English physician and author Sir Thomas Browne (1605–1682) wrote, in *Religio Medici*, a treatise attempting to reconcile science and religion: "I am of a constitution so general . . . I have no . . . *idiosyncrasy*, in diet, humour, air, anything." It is difficult to conceive of a person with no *idiosyncrasy* whatever.

ignoble (ig noe′ b'l) *adj.* An *ignoble* person is one of low moral character, base, vile, lowdown, dishonorable. An *ignoble* act is base, vile, contemptible, a rotten way to behave. Appeasement, betrayal, and treachery are *ignoble* acts. Judas's betrayal of Jesus is the most notorious *ignoble* act of all. The great judge Oliver

Wendell Holmes (1841-1935) wrote in a United States Supreme Court opinion: "... it is a less evil that some criminals should escape than that the government should play an *ignoble* part." Theodore Roosevelt (1858-1919) wrote: "If we seek merely swollen, slothful ease and *ignoble* peace ... bolder and stronger peoples ... will win ... the domination of the world."

illiterate (ih lit' ə rit) *n., adj.* Technically, an *illiterate* person (also called an *illiterate*) is one who cannot read or write. This inability is known as *illiteracy* (ih lit' ə rə see), the opposite of *literacy* (lit' ə rə see). One measure of the level of development of a nation is its *literacy* rate. The American economist John Kenneth Galbraith (born 1908) wrote, "People are the common denominator of progress. ... Conquest of *illiteracy* comes first." There are still tribes in remote parts of the world that have no written language and are therefore wholly *illiterate*. In a more general sense, the term *illiterate* is applied to people who lack education or culture, especially those who are unfamiliar with literature and the proper use of language. In thise sense, *illiterate* is close to "ignorant." A letter full of mistakes in grammar and spelling can be described as an *illiterate* letter. *Illiteracy* can also apply to ignorance in a particular field: people totally unfamiliar with music are called "musically *illiterate*." People inept at politics are sometimes spoken of as "politically *illiterate*." *Illiterate* is often used as a general term of abuse to describe a person whose lack of education or culture or taste makes him uncouth and unpresentable. Much in the news these days is the term *functional illiterate,* describing a person unable to read well enough to fill out a job application or to follow warnings like "Poison!" or "Caution!"

illuminate (ih loo' mə nate—*oo* as in *boot*) *vb.* To *illuminate* a room or a dark corner or a street is to light it up. To *illuminate* a subject is to make it clear, help to explain it, throw light on it, make it understandable. Until the advent of electricity, the streets of big cities were *illuminated* by gaslight. The noun is *illumination* (il loo mə nay' shən—*oo* as in *boot*). Increased *illumination* of streets and alleys is a deterrent to crime. A good teacher will do his best to help students by *illuminating* difficult passages in books assigned for reading.

illusion (ih loo' zhən—*oo* as in *boot*) *n.* An *illusion* is a misapprehension, a false idea or mental image, which may arise from a misconception of something real; or it may be a figment of the imagination, something that a person wrongly believes to exist. Heat waves rising from a road create the *illusion* of pools of water. The American writer Sherwood Anderson (1876-1941) said: "Most modern great men are mere *illusions* sprung out of a national hunger for greatness." People often make mistakes because they are under the *illusion* that things are different from what they really are. Optical *illusions* are the stock in trade of professional magicians. A good painting produces the *illusion* of a third dimension. The American journalist and politician Horace Greeley (1811-1872) said: "The *illusion* that times that were are better than those that are, has probably pervaded all ages." When the American general and novelist Lew Wallace (1827-1905) wrote: "Beauty is . . . in the eye of the beholder," he was speaking of the *illusions* of a person in love. Do not confuse *illusion* with *allusion*. See **allude**.

imaginative (ih maj′ ə nə tiv, -nay-) *adj.* A person who has a vivid *imagination* and uses it can be described as *imaginative*. An *imaginative* person is inventive and creative. An *imaginative* planner thinks of all the possibilities and contingencies. An *imaginative* writer creates intriguing plots and believable characters. An *imaginative* biography is more than a mere record of events and dates; it furnishes background and psychological analysis. *Imaginative* research that considers all the angles is the most successful approach to a problem. It is the *imaginative* passages in poetry that we remember best.

imbue (im byoo′—*oo* as in *boot*) *vb.* To *imbue* a person with certain feelings like unselfishness, patriotism, cunning, fear, or hatred is to inspire or fill him with those feelings, to instill those feelings in him. One can *imbue* another with opinions as well as feelings. Good teachers can *imbue* their students with a thirst for knowledge. Service at the front often *imbues* soldiers with the futility of war. We admire statesmen *imbued* with patriotism and a feeling of national pride, but not those *imbued* with a sense of their own importance.

immaculate (ih mak′ yə lit) *adj.* Anything *immaculate*, in the literal sense, is spotless. Good hotels furnish *immaculate* linen. *Immaculate* can be used figuratively in the sense of "pure, undefiled, stainless," as in the description of a person's soul, motives, or way of life. It is used in the description of the conception of the Virgin Mary in the womb of St. Anne: the "*immaculate* conception." Another sense of *immaculate* is "flawless." A book entirely free of misprints (extremely rare these days) can be described as an *immaculate* book or text. Admirers of the writing of the American novelist Henry James (1843-1916) often speak of his "*immaculate* prose." The American poet Elinor Wylie (1885-1928) wrote: "I love the look, austere, *immaculate*, / Of landscapes drawn in pearly monotones."

immerse (ih murs′)—*u* as in *fur*) *vb.* To *immerse* someone or something is to dip him or it into liquid. There are baptism rituals in which the minister *immerses* a person's entire body in a stream or lake. Blacksmiths get a horseshoe red-hot and then *immerse* it in a tub of water. Figuratively, *immerse* is used in the sense of "involve" or "absorb." Philosophers are supposed to be *immersed* in deep thought. One can become *immersed* in an exciting book. Some people become so *immersed* in their business or profession as to neglect the family. The American historian Samuel Eliot Morison (1887-1976) said: "An historian should . . . become *immersed* in the place and period of his choice. . . ."

imminent (im′ ə nənt) *adj.* Anything likely to happen soon, at any moment, can be described as *imminent*. It became clear, as soon as Germany marched into Poland in 1939, that war was *imminent*. As great black clouds gather and the wind freshens, a storm is obviously *imminent*. When the visitors hear the cry "All ashore that's going ashore!" they bustle off in the face of the ship's *imminent* departure. The noun is *imminence* (im' ə nəns). People flee when the roar of deep explosions warns of the *imminence* of an earthquake. Do not confuse *imminent* with **eminent,** meaning "distinguished," or *immanent,* meaning "inherent."

immoderate (ih mod' ər it) *adj. Moderate* (mod' ər it) describes people, activities, feelings, or things that are kept within reasonable bounds, like *moderate* prices, a *moderate* drinker, a *moderate* appetite, *moderate* demands. *Immoderate* is the opposite, applying to people, activities, etc., that exceed reasonable limits, that are excessive or extreme. Self-indulgent people are often *immoderate* in their eating and drinking habits. The newly rich often spend *immoderate* amounts of money on external show, like fancy estates and big cars. People who want to flatter the boss often laugh *immoderately* at his jokes. The English writer Dr. Samuel Johnson (1709-1784), in *Prayers and Meditations,* wrote: "Preserve me from unseasonable and *immoderate* sleep."

impair (im pare'—*a* as in *dare*) *vb.* To *impair* is to weaken, damage, undermine, spoil. Overwork, worry, and lack of sleep can seriously *impair* one's health. Excessive length of a speech often impairs its effectiveness. Unseasonable frost will *impair* the fruit crop. A lack of adequate rehearsal will *impair* the quality of a dramatic or musical production. Inability to suppress hostile feelings *impairs* the progress of labor negotiations. Smoking *impairs* health. The noun is *impairment* (im pare' mənt—*a* as in *dare*). Nagging and bickering result in the *impairment* of a marriage or a partnership.

impart (im part') *vb.* To *impart* can mean to "give," as when a tan *imparts* a healthy look to a face, or to "tell, reveal, disclose," as when one *imparts* news to a friend. Vigorous exercise *imparts* a glow to a person's body. It is the function of a teacher to *impart* not only knowledge but also a thirst for knowledge to students. "I can keep a secret," says the gossip, "but the people I *impart* it to can't." The ringing of a bell at Lloyd's of London *imparts* the sad news that a ship has gone down. The dreaded "pink slip" *imparts* the news that your services are no longer required.

impasse (im' pas, im pas') *n.* An *impasse* is a deadlock, a situation that permits of no progress, no way out—a blind alley, a stalemate, a standstill, a catch-22: It is a predicament from which, no matter which way you turn, there is no escape. When, during the course of a negotiation, both sides refuse to give an inch, the parties have arrived at an *impasse.* Mr. and Mrs. Jack Spratt, on the other hand, dovetailed their demands beautifully; had they not, and had both of them wanted all the fat or all the lean, they too would have reached an *impasse.*

impeccable (im pek' ə b'l) *adj. Impeccable* is one of those words that are negative in form (*im-*), but positive in meaning. To be *impeccable* is to be faultless, flawless (both also negative in form), in other words, perfect. The adverb *impeccably* (im pek´ ə blee) is often used in the phrase *impeccably dressed,* describing the splendid attire of a dandy. The American writer Truman Capote (born 1924) described a character as "an *impeccable* figure in trim dinner jacket and starched shirt." It is a fine accomplishment to practice a profession with a lifelong *impecable* record. Our elected officials should be men and women of *impeccable* character. It is to be hoped that this little dictionary is of *impeccable* correctness and clarity.

impediment (im ped´ ə mənt) *n.* To *impede* (im peed´) is to hinder. An *impediment* is a hindrance or obstacle. A lack of education is an *impediment* to advancement in one's work. In *The Book of Common Prayer,* the marriage banns contain the familiar language: "If any of you know cause, or just *impediment,* why these two persons should not be joined together in holy Matrimony. . . ." *Impediment* has a special meaning with regard to speech: a speech defect or disorder is known as a speech *impediment,* or simply as an *impediment.* The great Greek orator Demosthenes (384-322 B.C.) overcame a speech *impediment* by practicing speaking with his mouth full of pebbles as he walked along the seashore.

impel (im pel´) *vb.* To *impel* is to force, drive, urge by applying pressure. Conscience *impels* us to do the right thing. Curiosity *impels* people to inquire and investigate. Many are *impelled* by deprivation and poverty to commit desperate acts. The desire to get ahead in the world is an *impelling* reason to concentrate on one's studies. The Declaration of Independence states that when one nation feels it necessary to dissolve its political bonds with another, it must "declare the causes which *impel* them to separation." An *impelling* reason is one that you cannot ignore. The preservation of health is an *impelling* reason for exercise and moderate eating habits. *Impelling* can have the meaning of "forceful." Franklin D. Roosevelt had an *impelling* personality.

imperative (im perr´ ə tiv) *adj.* When something is said to be *imperative,* it is urgent, essential, obligatory, something that requires attention and action. These days, the great powers feel that it is *imperative* for them to have bigger and bigger stocks of nuclear weapons. In times of economic recession, our leaders tell us that it is *imperative* that we tighten our belts. In a United States Supreme Court opinion, Chief Justice Charles Evans Hughes (1862-1948) stated: "The greater the importance of safeguarding the community from incitements to the overthrow of our institutions by force and violence, the more *imperative* is the need to preserve . . . the . . . rights of free speech, free press and free assembly. . . ." When you come across an unfamiliar word, it may not be *imperative* to stop and look it up, but it's a very good idea to do so.

imperceptible (im pər sep´ tə b'l) *adj.* Literally, *imperceptible* applies to anything that is not visible, but it is more commonly used in the sense of "very slight" or "gradual," or slight or gradual as to be practically invisible. Plants and animals grow by *imperceptible* stages. Sometimes the differences between political opponents are so slight as to be almost *imperceptible.* The French novelist Marcel Proust

(1871-1922) used the word in the more literal sense when he wrote: ". . . if we turn round to gaze at the remote past, we can barely catch sight of it, so *imperceptible* has it become."

impersonal (im pur' sə n'l—*u* as in *fur*) *adj.* An *impersonal* remark is one made without reference to a particular person, and without the speaker's being influenced by personal feeling. When a speaker says that he is speaking *impersonally*, he means that he is being objective and unbiased, and is not aiming his remarks at anyone present. Doctors making diagnoses or lawyers stating opinions must be entirely *impersonal*, guided only by the truth as they see it. Philosophers and scientists uttering general principles must speak *impersonally*, without emotional bias or reference to any one individual. The noun is *impersonality* (im pur sə nal' ə tee—*u* as in *fur*), the absence of emotional involvement. The French physiologist Claude Bernard (1813-1878) spoke of a "modern poet . . . [who] characterized the *personality* of art and the *impersonality* of science as follows: 'Art is I. Science is We.' " *Impersonality* can also describe indifference to the needs or feelings of individuals, as in the case of some of our public institutions, which depress people in need of comfort and consolation by their *impersonality*.

impertinent (im pur' tə nənt)—*u* as in *fur*) *adj.* When a person is *impertinent*, he is insolent, rude, impudent, saucy, and acts without showing proper respect. *Impertinent* may apply to acts as well as to people. Celebrities are often harassed by *impertinent* reporters asking *impertinent* questions. The noun is *impertinence* (im pur' tə nəns—*u* as in *fur*), which implies offensive concern or unwarranted interference with somebody else's affairs. Hecklers keep busy throwing out *impertinent* remarks. Badly brought-up children say *impertinent* things to their elders. *Pertinent*, often followed by *to*, means "relevant, pertaining": A judge should rule out details not *pertinent* to the case. *Impertinent* can mean "not pertinent," but that is a formal usage heard mainly in legal circles.

impetuous (im pech' oo əs) *adj.* See **impetus.**

impetus (im' pə təs) *n.* *Impetus* is driving force, impulse, momentum, thrust. Ambition to get ahead gives *impetus* to concentration on one's studies. The offering of a reward provides *impetus* to widespread search for lost property. The lowering of import duties will give an *impetus* to better trade relations between nations. Do not confuse *impetus* with the related adjective *impetuous* (im pech' oo əs), which goes off in a different direction, and means "impulsive, rash." An *impetuous* person acts hastily, without sufficient thought; an *impetuous* decision is one arrived at emotionally, without due consideration.

implausible (im plaw' zə b'l) *adj.* *Plausible* describes things like arguments, theories, excuses, or alibis which make sense, are believable, and have the appearance of truth and reasonableness, whether or not they are actually true. *Implausible* means the opposite: "unworthy of belief, lacking in credibility." Truants are notorious for giving the principal *implausible* excuses for absence. (The classical example is "grandmother's funeral.") Novels and plays full of coincidences have *implausible* plots. The accused in murder cases sometimes plead *implausible* motives and invent *implausible* circumstances. The Baron von Münchhausen (1720-1797) was famous for telling tall, *implausible* tales.

implore (im plore', -plawr') *vb.* To *implore* someone is to beg, beseech, or entreat him, to make a most urgent request of him. To *implore* something is to beg for it, request it most urgently. People in trouble *implore* you to come to their aid. Defense lawyers sometimes *implore* the judge to impose a lenient sentence. One can *implore* a wronged friend to forgive, or *implore* the forgiveness of the injured friend. In Shakespeare's *Macbeth* (Act I, Scene 4), Malcolm says to his father, King Duncan, that the traitor Cawdor, before his execution, "*Implor'd* your highness' pardon and set forth/ A deep repentence." A person in difficulties may give you an *imploring* glance, silently begging for help.

imply (im ply') *vb.* To *imply* something is to indicate it without actually saying it. When you *imply* something, you expect the listener to understand it or to infer it. What is *implied* can be "read between the lines." If one says, "I'd rather not do business with that man," one is *implying* that the man in question is dishonest. It is said that silence *implies* consent (the failure to deny can be taken to mean "Yes"). If I tell you something and you look skeptical, your look *implies* that you don't believe I'm telling the truth. An X rating *implies* that a film contains erotic material. When something is *implied* rather than stated, the listener or onlooker *infers* what is *implied*; he "gets the message." Do not confuse *imply* and **infer**. See **infer**.

impregnable (im preg' nə b'l) *adj.* To describe a fort or other military installation as *impregnable* is to assert that it can withstand any attack and cannot be captured. When an argument or any position taken in a discussion is called *impregnable*, it means that no argument can prevail against it; it is irrefutable, undeniable, indisputable, beyond question. An *impregnable* position can refer to a physical position, like the top of a steep hill that cannot be successfully stormed, or to an argumentative position that cannot be challenged. It is comforting to know that people with whom you are doing business are in an *impregnable* financial position, with an *impregnable* reputation for honesty and fair dealing. This adjective has nothing to do with female fertility.

inadequate (in ad' ə kwit) *adj. Inadequate* means, of course, "not adequate, insufficient," but is much used in the general sense of "inept," and applies to people or things found wanting, not up to the job or up to snuff, unsuitable. The American chemist and educator James B. Conant (1893-1978), and incidentally the author's professor of organic chemistry at Harvard) wrote about the "erroneous observations, misleading generalizations, *inadequate* formulations and unconscious prejudice" that beset the path of scientists in every generation. Harry S. Truman, speaking of the needs of the Third World, stated: "Their food is *inadequate.*" The noun is *inadequacy* (in ad´ ə kwə see), meaning "insufficiency." Conservatives find our social services quite *adequate*; liberals complain of their *inadequacy*. See **adequate**.

inadvertent (in əd vur´ t'nt—*u* as in *fur*) *adj.* An *inadvertent* remark or observation or offense is unintentional, unthinking. Slips of the tongue are *inadvertent*. *Inadvertent* violation of the law, like ignorance of it, is no defense; *inadvertent* speeding will still get you a ticket. The Athenian statesman Phocion (402–317 B.C.), when he was applauded by the audience after delivering an opinion, asked cynically, "Have I *inadvertently* said some evil thing?" An *inadvertent* general reference to a fault or defect from which someone present happens to suffer may cut him to the quick.

inane (ih nane´) *adj.* An *inane* person or remark is silly, senseless, asinine, insipid, idiotic. Too much conversation consists of *inane* comments on the weather. Many people find the technical jargon used in the criticism of abstract art *inane*. Often, at public meetings, a person will stand up and make an *inane* suggestion, just to hear himself speak. Children "caught in the act" often offer *inane* excuses. The noun is *inanity* (ih nan´ ə tee), not to be confused (if you happen to run across it) with *inanition* (in ə nish´ ən), which denotes extreme weakness resulting from malnutrition and has nothing to do with senselessness.

inaugurate (in aw´ gyə rate) *vb.* In a narrow sense, this verb is used to describe the installation of a newly appointed or elected public official, or the formal commencement of a new public service. January 20 is the date when a newly elected President of the United States is *inaugurated*. After formal relations were established between the United States and China, regular plane service between the two countries was *inaugurated*. In a more general usage, *inaugurate* means simply "begin" or "initiate." The invention of the airplane *inaugurated* a new era in travel. The nuclear age was *inaugurated* with the dropping of the first atom bomb. The noun is *inauguration* (in aw gyə ray´shən). The *inauguration* of cable TV solved the problem of poor reception by many sets.

incapable (in kay´ pə b'l) *adj.* When someone is *incapable* of performing a certain act, he lacks the ability to do it. George Washington, according to legend, was *incapable* of telling a lie. A truly honest man is *incapable* of deceit. A thing, as well as a person, can be *incapable* of something: A pint bottle is *incapable* of containing a quart of liquid. *Incapable* can be used in a somewhat different way; in this usage, the subject is not *incapable* of doing something, but rather of having something done to it. The English writer and critic George Henry Lewes (1817–1878) wrote: "We must never assume that which is *incapable* of proof." To be *incapable* of proof is to be *incapable* of *being* proved, i.e., not provable. To be *incapable* of measurement is to be *incapable* of being measured, i.e., immeasurable, like the universe.

incapacitate (in kə pas´ ə tate) *vb.* To *incapacitate* someone is to disable him, to make him unfit. A bad cold will *incapacitate* someone for work. A person *incapacitated* is put out of action. We constantly hear of athletes suffering injuries that *incapacitate* them from participating in their usual activities. *Incapacitate* can sometimes be the equivalent of "disqualify." A conflict of interests *incapacitates* a lawyer from taking a case. Close acquaintance with one of the parties *incapacitates* a judge from sitting on a case.

incessant (in ses´ ənt) *adj.* Anything unceasing, continual, going on without interruption, nonstop may be described as *incessant*. There are people addicted to *incessant* chatter who never give you a chance to get a word in edgewise. In *Rain*, the English writer Somerset Maugham (1874-1965) sets the action of the play against a background of *incessant* rain. In *Alice in Wonderland*, Lewis Carroll (1832-1898) gives us these lovely lines:

> "You are old, Father William," the young man said,
> "And your hair has become very white;
> And yet you *incessantly* stand on your head—
> Do you think, at your age, it is right?"

The American poet Edwin Arlington Robinson (1869-1915) wrote a poem about Miniver Cheevy who "wept that he was ever born":

> Miniver loved the Medici,
> Albeit he had never seen one;
> He would have sinned
>   *incessantly*
> Could he have been one.

Have you ever listened to the *incessant* twittering in an aviary?

incite (in site´) *vb.* To *incite* is to rouse, stir up, urge on to action, spur on. It is part of the communist creed to *incite* oppressed people to rebel. When in Shakespeare's *Julius Caesar* (Act III, Scene 2) Marc Antony delivered the famous funeral oration ("Friends, Romans, countrymen, lend me your ears"), his purpose was to *incite* the populace to rise against Caesar's assassins. Mean conduct may *incite* retaliation. Ambition *incites* hard work. The noun is *incitement* (in site´ mənt). Judge Oliver Wendell Holmes (1841-1935) of the United States Supreme Court wrote: "It is said that this manifesto is more than a theory, that it was an *incitement*. Every idea is an *incitement*." It is to be hoped that this book will serve as an *incitement* to expand your vocabulary.

incoherent (in koe heer´ ənt) *adj.* When things *cohere* (koe heer´), they stick together. When, in reasoning, an argument, a thought, or a theory *coheres*, it is consistent and is said to be *coherent*; it "sticks together"; it is clear and easy to follow and understand. An *incoherent* speech or argument is the opposite in that it fails to "stick together" or "hang together." An *incoherent* speaker or speech rambles on in a disjointed way; an *incoherent* argument is illogical and gets nowhere. People can become *incoherent* with fear or rage or grief. It is impossible to reason with an *incoherent* person.

incomparable (in kom′ pər ə b'l, -prə b'l) *adj.* *Incomparable* (except in the technical sense of "not comparable," as in the case of dissimilar things like apples and chairs) is an adjective of praise, the equivalent of "matchless, without equal, beyond compare." Helen of Troy was said to have possessed *incomparable* beauty. Sir Isaac Newton (1642-1727), the English mathematician and philosopher who formulated the law of gravitation, was an *incomparable* scholar at Oxford; his name, separated by a line, came ahead of the list of those who obtained a "first" honors degree. The American writer and critic William Dean Howells (1837-1920), in *My Mark Twain*, wrote: "Clemens [Mark Twain's real name was Samuel Langhorne Clemens] was sole, *incomparable*, the Lincoln of our literature."

inconsistent (in kən sis′ tənt) *adj.* See **consistent**, of which *inconsistent* is the opposite. An *inconsistent* argument or narrative is self-contradictory; its various parts conflict, are at odds with one another. *Inconsistent* statements make a witness's testimony or an accused's alibi worthless. People declare fine principles for human conduct, and then proceed to act in ways quite *inconsistent* with those principles. The noun is *inconsistency* (in kən sis′ tən see). The *inconsistency* between the flat-earth theory and the observable sights (e.g., the ship "sinking" below the horizon as it sailed away, and then reappearing over the horizon as it returned to port) made thinking people realize that the earth was round. The American statesman Daniel Webster (1782-1852) said: "*Inconsistencies* of opinion, arising from changes of circumstances, are often justifiable." (Said the French poet Auguste Marseille Barthélemy [1796-1867]: "The absurd man is he who never changes.")

indelible (in del′ ə b'l) *adj.* An *indelible* pencil is one that cannot be erased. An *indelible* impression is one that cannot be erased. *Indelible* is used in both the concrete and abstract senses. The adverb is *indelibly* (in del′ ə blee). Some scenes are so vivid that they are *indelibly* stamped on one's memory; they are unforgettable, there to stay. All who knew Franklin D. Roosevelt agree that he made an *indelible* impression. Speaking of man's evolutionary descent, the English naturalist Charles Darwin wrote: ". . . man, with all his noble qualities, . . . still bears in his bodily frame the *indelible* stamp of his lowly origin."

indifferent (in diff′ ər ənt, -dif rənt) *adj.* This word, which is *not* the negative of *different*, has two entirely different main uses. It can mean "unconcerned, unfeeling, not caring," as when a person is *indifferent* to the sufferings of the poor and ailing. Mountain climbers appear to be *indifferent* to the dangers and discomforts they undergo. Doctors, after long experience, are sometimes accused of being *indifferent* to the anxieties of their patients. The noun is *indifference* (in dif′ ər əns, -dif rəns). The English statesman and orator Edmund Burke (1729-1799) said: "Nothing is so fatal to religion as *indifference*. . . ." The other meaning is "commonplace, mediocre, passable, not particularly good," as when an actor is said to have given an *indifferent* performance, or a book or play is called an *indifferent* success. People who do *indifferent* work at the office don't usually get ahead. There are reverse snobs at college who believe that any grade better than an *indifferent* C shows that a student belongs to that inferior class—the eggheads.

indisposed (in dih spozd´) *adj.* This word has two separate meanings. Standing alone, *indisposed* means "not feeling well, out of sorts, under the weather." A great many man-hours of work are lost because of employees' feeling *indisposed* (with a cold, a headache, a hangover, etc.). One would not use *indisposed* in cases of severe illness. The noun *indisposition* (in dis pə zish´ən), in this frame of reference, describes merely a slight illness. In the other sense, *indisposed* describes the attitude of a person who is disinclined or unwilling to do something. It is a sad commentary on human relations that so many passersby are *indisposed* to come to the aid of someone who is being harmed by thugs or muggers. In this sense, *indisposed* is simply the opposite of *disposed* (dis pozd´), meaning "inclined" or "willing," as in the description of a good Samaritan as someone *disposed* to help out in any situation.

induce (in doos´, -dyoos´—*oo* as in *boot*) *vb.* When someone *induces* a person to do something, he is persuading or influencing him to do it. It is impossible to *induce* some people to look after their health. The warning on cigarette packages has failed to *induce* millions of people to quit smoking. It is to be hoped that this book will *induce* you to vary your vocabulary. In this sense, the noun is *inducement* (in doos´ mənt, -dyoos´-, *oo* as in *boot*), meaning "incentive." Higher pay is an *inducement* to better work. The offer of a reward for good behavior is a better *inducement* to children than the threat of punishment for bad conduct. *Induce* can be used in another way, to mean "bring about." Sleeping pills *induce* sleep. Overwork *induces* nervousness. Poverty *induces* crime.

industrious (in dus´ tree əs) *adj.* An *industrious* person is hardworking, diligent, devoted to the task at hand. Some animals and insects are *industrious*, like the hardworking beaver building his dam; or the "little busy bee" sung by the English poet Isaac Watts (1674-1748), who doth ". . . improve each shining hour/And gather honey all the day . . ."; or the ant, to whom the frivolous grasshopper is referred: "Go to the ant, thou sluggard; consider her ways and be wise" (Proverbs 6:6). The English novelist Aldous Huxley (1894-1963) wrote: "There are not enough *bon* [sic] *mots* in existence to provide any *industrious* conversationalist with a new stock for every occasion." (Aldous, you left out the *-s* in *bons*!) Whether a candidate wins or loses an election, he winds up his campaign with a speech of heartfelt thanks to his *industrious* campaigners.

inert (in urt´, ih nurt´—*u* as in *fur*) *adj.* As a scientific term, *inert* describes matter that has no power of movement or resistance, or substances without active chemical properties, like *inert* gases (e.g., neon). Figuratively, *inert* describes people who are heavy and sluggish, slow to move or act, lethargic, lackadaisical, lifeless. It is difficult to get the right people elected by a body of politically *inert* voters. Instead of reading, too many people are stuck *inertly* in front of their television sets. It is irritating, when we want action, to be confronted by *inert* bureaucracy. *Inertia* (in ur´ shə, ih nur´ shə—*u* as in *fur*), like *inert,* has two meanings. It is a term in physics, describing the property of matter by which it remains motionless or, if moving, continues along a straight line if not interfered with. Applied to people, *inertia* is synonymous with *inertness* (in urt´ nəs, ih nurt´ nəs—*u* as in *fur*), meaning "sluggishness, inactivity, lethargy." It is difficult to overcome the *inertia* of people when an attempt is made to change their voting habits. *Inertia* stands in the way of progress and the acceptance of new ideas.

inertia (in ur´ shə, ih nur´ shə) *n.* See **inert**.

inevitable (in ev´ ə tə b'l) *adj.* What is *inevitable* is bound to happen, sure to occur, unavoidable. Every journey, it seems, has its *inevitable* delays and complications. Taxes are an *inevitable* aspect of life; death is its *inevitable* end. No matter what misunderstandings, dangers, and horrors beset the hero and heroine of a B movie, their union and a happy ending are *inevitable* (so much for suspense!). *Inevitable* is used informally in a special way, to mean "so familiar as to be expected" or "boringly familiar." When sightseeing, you bump into hordes of tourists, each equipped with the *inevitable* camera. As you come to an intersection in otherwise beautiful country, there is the *inevitable* gas station. At every gala movie opening, here come the *inevitable* mink coats.

inextricable (in eks´ trə kə b'l) *adj.* To *extricate* (eks´ trə kate) someone is to get him out of something, to release him from some kind of entanglement like a difficult situation, or a maze or labyrinth. If someone is in an unsolvable difficulty, his position is said to be *inextricable. Inextricable* describes anything from which one cannot be *extricated.* The Vietnam War was an *inextricable* mess, so bad that Senator Aiken of Vermont (born 1892) suggested that we say we'd won and go home. A crowd leaving after a big sporting event is often involved for a while in almost *inextricable* confusion.

infamous (in´ fə məs) *adj.* Anything described as *infamous* is wicked, shameful, of extremely ill repute (see **famously**). When we hear people or things or events described as *famous,* we think of them as particularly notable (a *famous* writer, or battle, or ship, or building). *Infamous* people and deeds may well be notable, but only because they are particularly shameful: The gangster Al Capone was both *famous* and *infamous. Infamy* (in´ fə mee), the noun, is evil reputation, public condemnation for a shameful act. One of the most *famous infamous* characters in history was Judas, *famed* for his *infamy* in betraying Christ. When the Japanese bombed Pearl Harbor, Franklin D. Roosevelt called December 7, 1941, "a date which will live in *infamy.*"

infer (in fur´—*u* as in *fur*) *vb*. To *infer* is to judge or conclude, to arrive at an opinion by reasoning, to understand what is implied, to surmise, to guess, after considering all the facts. If you hold out your hand and I refuse to take it, you can *infer* that I disapprove of you and don't want your friendship. My refusal to take your hand *implies* as much. If you shake your head while I am talking to you, I must *infer* that you disagree with what I am saying; if you nod, I will *infer* that you agree. *Infer* is often confused with *imply* (see **imply**); even some dictionaries consider them synonymous. But Sir Ernest Gowers (1880-1966), who revised the work of the English lexicographer H. W. Fowler (1858-1933), has this to say, in his *Modern English Usage*: "This misuse of [*infer*] for *imply* is sadly common—so common that some dictionaries give *imply* as one of the definitions without comment. But each word has its own job to do, one at the giving end and the other at the receiving (*What do you imply by that remark? What am I to infer from that remark?*) and should be left to do it without interference."

infernal (in fur´n'l—*u* as in *fur*) *adj*. The literal meaning of *infernal* is "pertaining to hell," and in polite Victorian society, when hell was still a taboo word, it was referred to as "the *infernal* regions." Now *infernal* is used to mean "hellish" in the figurative sense: "devilish, detestable, outrageous." Hitler was guilty of *infernal* cruelty. Anwar Sadat was assassinated in accordance with an *infernal* plot. *Infernal*, like *hellish* or *devilish*, can be used in a much milder, exaggerated sense. In the tropics, mosquitoes are an *infernal* nuisance. Garbage trucks, in the early morning, make an *infernal* racket. It's out of date now, but people used to call a time bomb an "*infernal* machine." Richard Sheridan (1751-1816), the English playwright, has this to say about newspapers in *The Critic*: " . . . they are the most villainous—licentious—abominable—*infernal*—Not that I ever read them. . . ."

infinite (in´ fə nit) *adj*. Literally, *infinite* describes anything that is immeasurable, unlimited, boundless, endless. It is the opposite of *finite,* meaning "limited." There is still a question whether space or time is *finite* or *infinite*. The English philosopher Alfred North Whitehead (1861-1847) wrote: "Our minds are *finite,* and yet . . . we are surrounded by possibilities that are *infinite*." In a figurative sense, *infinite* is used to express vastness. The discovery of electricity had *infinite* consequences. Wars cost *infinite* sums of money. There are people who seem to possess *infinite* wisdom. The rearing of children requires *infinite* patience. We must wonder at the *infinite* ingenuity of man. The adverb *infinitely* (in´ fə nit lee) is used figuratively as well: Would you rather remain here? Oh, *infinitely*! People who fall in love go on *infinitely* singing the praises of the beloved. (And why not?)

infrequent (in free´ kwənt) *adj*. *Infrequent* describes events that happen rarely, only once in a long while. Halley's Comet regularly appears over the earth every seventy-five or seventy-six years; those are, to say the least, *infrequent* appearances. Thanks to medical science, cases of polio are now very *infrequent*. *Infrequent* can apply to people as well as events: One who pays *infrequent* visits is an *infrequent* visitor. *Infrequently* (in free´ kwənt lee) is the adverb. Because of the high cost of tickets, many theater lovers now go to the theater *infrequently*. It happens *infrequently* that friends run into one another in a big city.

ingenious (in jeen′ yəs) *adj.* An *ingenious* person or mind is inventive, one that comes up with clever and original ideas and solutions. A novel machine or tool that shortcuts an operation, or a clever solution of a difficult problem, can be described as *ingenious*. According to Greek legend, anyone who could untie the remarkably *ingenious* knot in the Temple of Zeus at Gordium would become the lord of all Asia. No one succeeded until Alexander the Great came along and, when he couldn't untie it, cut the Gordian knot with his sword—an *ingenious* solution! *Ingenuity* (in jə noo′ ih tee, -nyoo′-, *oo* as in *boot*) is the noun. It took great *ingenuity* to carry out the rescue of the hostages at Entebbe. The *ingenuity* and resourcefulness of a long line of inventors have reduced the size of computers to an amazing degree. The patent office is crammed with examples of the *ingenuity* of man. Do not confuse *ingenious* and *ingenuous,* which means "frank, open, sincere, innocent, straightforward."

ingratiate (in gray′ shee ate) *vb.* To *ingratiate* oneself with someone is to win his favor, to get on his right side, play up to him, especially for the purpose of promoting one's own interests. Professional people trying to gain new clients sometimes give dinner parties and try to *ingratiate* themselves with the guests. A politician running for office will perform all kinds of petty services and even kiss babies in order to *ingratiate* himself with the voters. There are those who constantly wear an *ingratiating* smile in order to be popular. Toadies and flatterers work hard to *ingratiate* themselves with those who they think can do them some good.

ingratitude (in grat′ ih tood, -tyood—*oo* as in *boot*) *n. Ingratitude* is the absence of *gratitude* (grat′ ih tood, -tyood—*oo* as in *boot*), the lack of thanks for kindness received. Shakespeare's *King Lear* is a study in *ingratitude*. The old King disinherits his truly loving daughter, and divides his estate between the other two. They, in return for his generosity, drive him out of their houses, and this eventually leads to his madness. In Act I, Scene 4, the disillusioned King cries: "*Ingratitude,* thou marble-hearted fiend,/More hideous, when thou show'st thee in a child,/Than the sea-monster." The song sung by Amiens in Shakespeare's *As You Like It* (Act II, Scene 7) starts: "Blow, blow, thou winter wind,/Thou art not so unkind/as man's *ingratitude*...." A person exhibiting *ingratitude* is *ungrateful* (un grate′ fəl); he is what we call an *ingrate* (in′ grate).

inherent (in heer′ ənt, -herr′-,) *adj.* When something is *inherent* in something else, it exists as a natural, permanent, inseparable, built-in part or quality of it. Weight is *inherent* in all matter (i.e., there is no such thing as matter without weight). There is tremendous power *inherent* in the Presidency of the United States. Franklin D. Roosevelt's Four Freedoms are *inherent* in a democratic society. Qualities or characteristics can be *inherent* in people or animals as well as things. Some people have an *inherent* interest in the occult. Birds have an *inherent* sense of direction.

Salmon are born with an *inherent* instinct that leads them back to the place where they were spawned.

inhibit (in hib′ it) *vb*. When an impulse or an action is restrained or repressed, it is said to be *inhibited*: the person involved is also described as *inhibited*, and the restraint, as well as the psychological block that does the restraining, is called an *inhibition* (in ih bish′ ən). Our upbringing in a civilized society necessarily *inhibits* many of our natural impulses. Fear of rejection *inhibits* many a male attempt to win a lady's favors. Some *inhibitions* are beneficial, such as those imposed upon children in the normal course of child guidance and education. Other *inhibitions* are neurotic, caused by unfortunate early training, and result in defects like the inability to socialize or make decisions or think clearly and concentrate. *Inhibited* people tend to be timid; *uninhibited* people may be difficult to live with.

initial (ih nish′ əl) *n*., *vb*., *adj*. The adjective *initial* applies to anything at the beginning of something. The *initial* letters of the alphabet are *a, b, c*. The *initial* stages of an undertaking or a conference are often the most important and trying ones. The *initial* moves in chess are standard openings. It is important to consult the doctor on the appearance of the *initial* symptoms of a disease. The *initial* stages of World War II were known as the "phony war" because nothing much seemed to be happening. *Initial*, as a noun, is the label given to the first letter of a proper name, like *G.B.S.* (standing for George Bernard Shaw). To *initial* a document is to sign it with your initials, as a token of agreement or approval, or a sign that you have read it and passed it on.

initiate (ih nish′ ee ate) *vb*. *Initiate* has several meanings. To *initiate* a plan, a scheme, or a movement is to originate it and get it going. Early in his presidency, Franklin D. Roosevelt *initiated* a number of public-works programs. Hitler *initiated* World War II by marching into Poland. The Wright brothers *initiated* the era of flight. In this use, *initiate* is the equivalent of *usher in*. To *initiate* someone into a club is to admit him to membership. To *initiate* someone into a special field of knowledge is to give him *initial* instruction in the field; a course in astronomy will *initiate* students into the mysteries of the universe. The noun, reflecting all these meanings, is *initiation* (ih nish ee ay′ shən). The *initiation* of legislation is an important part of a congressman's or senator's job. *Initiation* into a fraternity can be a trying experience. *Initiation* into the field of psychology can bring about a new understanding of people and their behavior.

innovate (in′ ə vate) *vb*. To *innovate* is to introduce something new, to bring about changes. Pioneers in industry are those who keep *innovating*. To *innovate* something is to introduce it for the first time. Airplane engineers are constantly *innovating* new aircraft designs. A new thing so introduced is called an *innovation* (in ə vay′ shən). The shift from the standard four-year college curriculum to a three-year system was an *innovation* in education. An *innovation* is a change from existing forms to new ones. *Innovations* in the field of electronics keep appearing in dazzling numbers. *Innovation,* as such, denotes the introduction of new methods or inventions. *Innovation* is the springboard of industrial development.

innumerable (ih noo' mər ə b'l, -nyoo-, *oo* as in *boot*) *adj.* This adjective, though negative in form and technically negative in meaning (incapable of being counted), actually expresses a quite positive concept: the quality of being very numerous. *Innumerable people were there* does not mean that they couldn't be counted; all it means is that a very great number of people were there. A good slang equivalent is *umpteen.* When the English poet Alfred, Lord Tennyson (1809–1892) wrote of "Myriads of rivulets hurrying thro' the lawn/ . . . The . . . murmuring of *innumerable* bees," he wasn't worried about not being able to count the bees; all he meant was that there was an awful lot of them. The same goes for the author of Psalms 104:25, who wrote of the ". . . .great and wide sea,/Wherein are things creeping *innumerable."* *Innumerable* is rarely used in its literal sense.

insight (in' site) *n.* This noun varies in meaning depending on whether we are speaking of a particular instance of *insight* or of *insight* generally. *Insight* generally is the ability to see beneath the surface of things with the mind, to get at the true nature of things or the inner character of people. It is important for psychologists and psychiatrists to have well-developed *insight.* A novelist cannot be great unless he has the gift of *insight* into human character. It takes time to gain real *insight* into the life of your community. When *insight* refers to a particular instance, it means a sudden, penetrating glimpse into the true nature of something. One uninhibited act of a person can give you a sudden *insight* into his true character. The discovery of a great truth after long study comes with a flash of *insight.*

insipid (in sip' id) *adj.* An *insipid* person, personality, book, or work of art is one without attractive qualities, dull, uninteresting, unstimulating; an *insipid* conversation is flat, dull, boring, a waste of time, pointless, vapid; *insipid* food or drink is tasteless, totally lacking in flavor, utterly bland. Can you imagine the horror of having an *insipid* conversation with an *insipid* person while sipping an *insipid* drink? The English poet Alfred, Lord Tennyson (1809–1892) hit the exact note when he described someone in these terms: *"Insipid* as the queen upon a [playing] card." Anatole France (1844–1924), the French novelist, said: "A tale without love is like beef without mustard: an *insipid* dish." The noun is *insipidity* (in sə pih' dih tee). The *insipidity* of the remarks of people at a meeting who just want to hear themselves talk can be extremely irritating.

insistent (in sis' tənt) *adj.* To *insist on* something is to declare it emphatically. Guilty people usually *insist on* their innocence. To *insist on* doing something is to be firm about accomplishing it: Despite poor health, he *insists on* working. To *insist that* something is such-and-such is to maintain it firmly. The adjective *insistent* partakes of all these meanings, but is also used in another way to indicate such persistency or urgency as to force something on people's attention. The *insistent* ringing of a doorbell will usually get results. The *insistent* wailing of an air-raid siren sends people scurrying to shelters. The *insistent* demands of children must be dealt with in order to maintain peace and quiet. The *insistent* throb of a steamship engine is characteristic of an ocean voyage.

instigate (in′ stə gate) *vb.* When you *instigate* someone to a particular action, you incite or goad or provoke him into doing it; when you *instigate* the action, you are bringing it about by incitement or urging. Lenin and Trotsky *instigated* the Russian people to revolt; they *instigated* the Russian revolution. Iago, in Shakespeare's *Othello*, did everything he could to *instigate* Othello's jealousy. *Instigate*, as opposed to *initiate*, appears to be used when the *instigation* (in stə gay′ shən) produces unhappy results: revolutions, strikes, quarrels, jealousy, fear, etc. One would not normally speak of *instigating* peace or joy or happiness or satisfaction.

integral (in′ tə grəl) *adj.* When something is *integral to*, or *an integral part of*, something else, it is a necessary part, serving to complete the whole. Without all its *integral* parts, nothing can be complete. Arms and legs are *integral* parts of the human body. All fifty states are *integral* parts of the United States. As an argument progresses, each step is *integral* to the whole. It is said that political and economic power are each *integral* to the other. The American writer T.S. Eliot (1888–1965) pointed out that in great drama, character is always *integral* to plot.

interim (in′ tər im) *n., adj.* An *interim* is the time between two events. *In the interim* means "meanwhile." A soldier goes away to war; he is gone for several years, and *in the interim* his children have grown so that on his return he hardly recognizes them. The *interim* between presidential elections in the United States is four years. As an adjective, *interim* has the force of "provisional" or "temporary." An *interim* report is one that precedes the final report. An *interim* order of a court settles one or more points in advance of the final judgment disposing of the entire case. Until refugees can be finally housed, *interim* arrangements are made concerning their food and shelter. *Interim* arrangements are temporary; they serve for the time being, until final arrangements can be made.

interrogate (in terr′ ə gate) *vb.* To *interrogate* someone is to question him formally and closely. In legal parlance, *interrogate* is synonymous with "examine." Suspects in a roundup are *interrogated* and then held or released. It is the function of trial lawyers to sift the evidence and *interrogate* witnesses. The examination of a witness is an *interrogation* (in terr ə gay′ shən). *Interrogation*, especially on cross-examination, can be a trying experience. *Interrogate* would not be used in informal situations, such as one in which, for example, a tourist who has lost his way is asking directions of a native.

interval (in′ tər vəl) *n. Interval* can relate to time or space. In relation to time, the *interval* is the period between events; in regard to space, the *interval* is the distance between two objects. World Wars I and II were begun at an *interval* of twenty-five years. Church bells usually toll at slow *intervals*. The length of the *inter-*

val between a flash of lightning and the subsequent thunder indicates the distance of the storm from the observer. People of unbalanced minds sometimes enjoy *intervals* of sanity. In the theater, the program tells you the *interval* that has elapsed between scenes or acts. There is an *interval* of ten yards between the lines on a football field. Milestones along a road are set at regular *intervals*.

intervene (in tər veen´) *vb*. This word can be used in two quite different ways. Events that *intervene* come between other events. The Wall Street crash of 1929 and the subsequent depression *intervened* between World Wars I and II. In the second sense, to *intervene* in a dispute or a quarrel is to step in between the parties to help straighten things out. In this use, whatever or whoever *intervenes* has an effect on what was happening, and *intervene* is the equivalent of *interfere*. If you are having a picnic and a thunderstorm *intervenes*, it *interferes* with your completing your picnic. The noun is *intervention* (in tər ven´ shən). *Intervention* is commonly used in international politics, where one country *intervenes* unlawfully in the affairs of another, and is charged with *intervention*. Here, *intervention* means "interference." *Armed intervention,* as in the case of Russia's marching into Afghanistan, is nothing more or less than military invasion and suppression.

intimate (in´ tə mate) *vb.*, (in´ tə mit) *adj.* The adjective, as in *an intimate friend,* means "close, familiar"; in a phrase like *an intimate circle,* it describes a group of closely associated people. *Intimate* knowledge of a subject is great familiarity with it and expertise in it. To know someone *intimately* is to know him extremely well. To know a subject *intimately* is to know it thoroughly. When two people are said to be *intimate,* it can usually be taken to imply that they are lovers. The noun is *intimacy* (in´ tə mə see) and partakes of all the meanings of the adjective. *An intimacy* can usually be understood as a sexual liberty: a woman, unless she wants to invite further steps, will not allow a man the *intimacy* of putting his arm around her waist. The verb (note difference in pronunciation) means to "hint" or "suggest." If you are asked your opinion of a person's honesty and you remain silent, you are *intimating* that you don't believe him trustworthy. You can *intimate* a good deal by a wink or a shrug. Here, the noun is *intimation* (in tə may´ shən), meaning "hint" or "suggestion." *Intimations* sometimes speak more loudly than words.

intimidate (in tim´ ih date) *vb*. To *intimidate* someone is to frighten him, to inspire him with fear. Old-time preachers *intimidated* their parishioners by threatening sinners with hellfire. Lion tamers *intimidate* the animals by brandishing a chair. Witnesses under cross-examination are often *intimidated* by aggressive lawyers. To *intimidate* someone into doing something is to force the action by threatening him. People can be *intimidated* to abstain from action. In dictatorships, voters are often *intimidated* into staying away from the voting booth. Such action is called *intimidation* (in tim ə day´ shən). It is distressing to see a child's *intimidation* by a cruel parent. The American publisher Arthur Hayes Sulzberger (1891–1968) spoke of the "smoke screen of *intimidation* that dims essential thought and essential talk."

intricate (in´ trə kit) *adj.* When something is described as *intricate*, it is complicated, and in context, puzzling, difficult to understand or follow. It is sometimes hard to keep track of a long historical novel with many characters and an *intricate* plot. The larger airplanes get, the more *intricate* the instrument panels become. The cartoons of Rube Goldberg (1883–1970) were sketches of exaggeratedly *intricate* nonsense machinery. The noun is *intricacy* (in´ trə kə see). Rube's English counterpart was Heath Robinson, whose nonsense gadgets rivaled the American's in *intricacy*. The *intricacy* of full-blown legal documents baffles most clients, poor souls!

intriguing (in tree´ ging) *adj.* The verb to *intrigue* (in treeg´) has various shades of meaning. To *intrigue* with one group against another is to conspire, to make and carry out secret plans. The related noun *intrigue* (in treeg´, in´ treeg) means "secret plotting," or in context, "hidden love affair." To *intrigue* has a much less sinister meaning when, in context, it means to "fascinate." In this sense, anything or any person that *intrigues* you arouses your interest and curiosity. *Intriguing* events, situations, or people are beguiling. Many find gossip *intriguing*. Franklin D. Roosevelt found detective stories *intriguing* enough to take his mind off affairs of state. *Intriguing* can take on the connotation of "baffling": The *Mona Lisa* has an *intriguing* smile.

intrinsic (in trin´ sik, -zik) *adj.* The *intrinsic* value of anything is that which belongs to it or is part of it by its very nature. The *intrinsic* value of a coin is its worth purely as metal, not the face value as stamped on the coin. The *intrinsic* value of a $1, $10, or $100 bill, or any bill, is negligible: it is whatever an otherwise useless piece of paper that size is worth. Its *extrinsic* value is its purchasing power, the quality attached to it by law and custom. A man's *intrinsic* worth is his qualities of strength, courage, valor; his *extrinsic* worth is imparted by his family connections, wealth, etc. A person's *intrinsic* nature is what he was born with, his natural, true, real self. Do not confuse *intrinsic* with *extrinsic*.

intuitive (in too´ ih tive, -tyoo´-, *oo* as in *boot*) *adj. Intuition* (in too ish´ ən, -tyoo-) is the immediate and direct understanding of something without reasoning. *Intuitive* describes that process. *Intuitive* knowledge is immediate and spontaneous, and comes without one's having to resort to reasoning or figuring things out. It is said that women are more *intuitive* than men. After years on the bench, most judges develop an *intuitive* feeling about the credibility of witnesses. Sensitive people are *intuitive* about other people's feelings.

invariably (in vare´ ee ə blee—*a* as in *dare*) *adj.*. To *vary* is to change. *Invariable* (in vare´ ee ə b'l) describes things that are unchanging, constant, always the same. *Invariably* means "always, constantly, consistently." If you frequent a restaurant and *invariably* bump into Jones, you *always* find him there. A person who *invariably* gives the right answer on a quiz, *always* gets it right. Someone who *invariably* annoys you *constantly* gets on your nerves. Legend has it that George Washington ("I cannot tell a lie") *invariably* told the truth.

invoke (in voke´) *vb.* To *invoke* God, or justice, or the power of the law is to call upon the Deity, the law, etc., for help or support. When a lawyer *invokes* a particular law, he is resorting to it in support of his legal position. Witnesses who are afraid of self-incrimination *invoke* the Fifth Amendment. Hitler *invoked* phony racist theories to justify his genocide. When there is a flood or other natural disaster, those in trouble *invoke* the help of their neighbors or of the authorities. The noun is *invocation* (in və kay´ shən), which shares all the meanings of the verb. Employers sometimes resort to the *invocation* of economic statistics to justify their refusal to raise salaries.

iota (eye o´ tə—*o* as in *note*) *n.* *Iota* is the ninth and smallest letter of the Greek alphabet, the Greek equivalent of *i*. It is used in English to mean "tiniest part, bit, speck, particle." It often appears in the protest that "there is not an *iota* of truth in that accusation" (i.e., no truth at all). One criticizes a proposal or theory as not having an *iota* of common sense. You can compliment your dentist by telling him that you have not suffered an *iota* of pain. After days of fruitless search for a missing person, the searchers report that they have not had an *iota* of success, or made an *iota* of progress. If you do not take this book seriously, there will not be an *iota* of improvement in your vocabulary. As you can see from these examples, *iota* is invariably coupled with a negative; it is always *not an iota*.

irate (eye´ rate, eye rate´) *adj.* An *irate* person or an *irate* remark or answer is a very angry one. When a person is beside himself with anger, he can be described as *irate*. The noun, *ire*, means "anger, wrath," but is less commonly used than *irate*. An angry look is an *irate* glare. A whole neighborhood can be *irate* and up in arms about vandalism, crime, and police neglect. Teachers grow *irate* when their students become indifferent or disorderly.

irksome (urk´ səm—*u* as in *fur*) *adj.* *Irksome* tasks are annoying, irritating, boring, tiresome. The adjective comes from the verb *irk*, to exasperate or irritate. These days, businessmen waste a lot of time in filling out a great many *irksome* government forms. The automobile was a great invention, but motorists sometimes curse it when caught in *irksome* traffic jams. In Ecclesiastes 27:13 we read: "The discourse of fools is *irksome*." Our second President, John Adams (1735–1826), said: "All great changes are *irksome* to the human mind . . . ."

irony (eye´ rə nee, eye´ ər-) *n.* When you express your thought by saying the direct opposite of what you really mean, you are using *irony*. Examples: It's raining cats and dogs; you say, "Lovely weather we're having, isn't it?" A proof comes back from the printer full of mistakes, and the secretary says, "That'll make a big hit with the boss!" In each case, the statement is to be taken the opposite of literally; the speaker is being *ironic* (eye ron´ ik), is making an *ironic* remark. *Irony* and *ironic* can be used in another way, to describe a situation in which something happens that is desirable in itself, but so ill-timed that it doesn't do any good. Thus it is *ironic* if a person wins the Nobel Prize after a lifetime of hard work, only to die the day before it is awarded. It is a bitter *irony* if a person who has been poor all his life inherits a fortune after he has become too old and ill to enjoy it. Such situations may be characterized as "the *irony* of fate," or "one of life's little *ironies.*" In the latter phrase, the word *little* is itself being used *ironically.*

irrational (ih rash' ə nəl) *adj.* An utterly illogical act may be described as *irrational.* *Irrational* applies to any person or behavior that is *not* **rational** (rash' ə nəl), i.e., the opposite of *reasonable, logical, sensible.* People often become hysterical and *irrational* after an accident. A person suffering from a persecution complex is obsessed with *irrational* suspicions about the motives of the people around him. Even grown-ups suffer from *irrational* fears in the dark. The adverb is *irrationally* (ih rash' ə nə lee). Jealousy caused Othello to act *irrationally.* See **rational.**

irrelevant (ih rel' ə vənt) *adj.* What is *irrelevant* is not to the point and has nothing to do with the subject under discussion. If we were talking about the probable action of the stock market in the next few days and one of us brought up the subject of the weather, that would be *irrelevant.* It would be *irrelevant,* in analyzing the artistic merit of a painting, to mention the number of galleries where it had been shown. The noun is *irrelevancy* (ih rel' ə vən see). *Irrelevancy* can apply to the state of being *irrelevant* (the *irrelevancy* of a remark) or to the *irrelevant* statement itself (don't bring any *irrelevancies* into the discussion). Lawyers often object to the introduction of evidence that is *irrelevant,* like the size of the defendant's bank account in a collision case. The objection is usually made on the ground that the evidence is "*irrelevant,* incompetent, and immaterial." *Immaterial* is a useful synonym for *irrelevant.*

irresistible (ih rih zis' tə b'l) *adj.* This word can describe anything that literally cannot be *resisted,* like a tidal wave or any other great physical force; or an emotional impulse, like the desire to kill or injure. We all remember the old question: "What happens when an *irresistible* force meets an immovable object?" The American poet Robert Frost (1874-1963) said: "Love is an *irresistible* desire to be *irresistibly* desired." *Irresistible* is most commonly used in the figurative sense of "tempting" or "lovable." People on a diet too often find rich desserts *irresistible.* A much too expensive dress can be an *irresistible* temptation. A little child can win your heart with an *irresistible* smile. In this sense, *irresistible* comes close to "enticing" or "alluring" or "enchanting."

irritable (ihr' ih tə b'l) *adj.* An *irritable* person is one who is easily annoyed or provoked, quick to take offense, touchy, peevish, grouchy, grumpy. *Irritable* people are easily exasperated; the least annoyance sets them off. Hot weather, fatigue, sleeplessness, and similar annoyances make most people *irritable.* When the boss walks in looking or sounding *irritable,* better stay out of his way. Top sergeants are traditionally depicted in comedies as *irritable* and snappish. It is best to give *irritable* people a wide berth; when they complain, they don't like to listen to reason.

isolated (eye´ sə lay tid) *adj.* To *isolate* (eye´ sə late) is to set apart, separate. Anyone or any group or anything that has been *isolated* has been set and kept apart from other people or things. People with infectious diseases are usually *isolated.* Towns can be *isolated* by hurricanes or blizzards. When *isolated* is used as an adjective, it means "all alone, solitary, all by oneself or itself." An *isolated* village is a lonely village, without near neighbors. An *isolated* instance of something is a rare occurrence of it. An *isolated* case of polio is a lone one. *Isolation* (eye sə lay´ shən) is the noun, and describes the act of *isolating,* or the quality of being *isolated,* alone, solitary. The *isolation* of life in the country doesn't appeal to hardened city dwellers. *Isolationism* (eye sə lay´ shə nizm) is the label given to a country's foreign policy of nonparticipation in the affairs of other countries and avoidance of foreign entanglements or commitments of any sort.

jaded (jay´ did) *adj.* Referring to persons, *jaded* describes someone who is or looks tired, overworked, played out, done in, "pooped," or "beat." A *jaded* appetite is one that is dulled by overindulgence, satiated, lacking in zest for food or other pleasures of the flesh. It is hard to avoid looking *jaded* after a hard day at the office, let alone a hard night at the disco. Not much is left to stimulate the *jaded* appetites of those "beautiful people" usually referred to in the periodicals as the "jet set," with their jewels, endless wardrobes, fleets of cars, and inexhaustible bank accounts.

jamboree (jam bə ree´) *n.* This term can be applied to the noisy, merry goings-on of a group getting together for fun, especially for a reunion or a celebration of something or other. Any large rally can be called a *jamboree. Jamboree* has a special application to national or international gatherings of Boy Scouts, but it can be used to describe any frolic, like a political rally or an industrial convention, where people meet to celebrate and let themselves go. The very word has a merry sound that evokes the image of a noisy, fun-making crowd.

jar (jar) *vb.* This verb has a number of meanings. When something *jars* on somebody, or *jars* on his nerves or ears, it has a disturbing, unpleasant effect. It *jars* on most people to hear the squeak of chalk on a blackboard. There are certain types of voice or laughter that *jar* on people's ears. One can become accustomed to a good deal of contemporary music, but there is some that keeps *jarring* on one's ears no matter how often it is played. *Jar* can express the effect of things that are out of harmony. It is hard to maintain a friendship with those whose opinions usually *jar* with yours. Colors that *jar,* whether in clothing or interior decoration, should be carefully avoided.

jeopardy (jep' ər dee) *n*. *Jeopardy* is danger or peril. *In jeopardy* is the common phrase. When a person is *in jeopardy*, he is in serious trouble, in great danger. When his life is *in jeopardy*, he is in danger of losing his life. When a project or a business is *in jeopardy*, it is in danger of failing. In law, the term *in jeopardy* is applied to an accused in danger of being convicted and punished. *Double jeopardy* is the term for subjecting an accused to a second trial for an offense for which he has already been tried, and is forbidden by law. The verb is *jeopardize* (jep' ər dize), meaning "endanger" or "imperil." Brave soldiers receive medals for *jeopardizing* their lives in rescuing fallen comrades. We must do everything possible to prevent the passage of laws *jeopardizing* freedom of speech.

jerry-built (jerr' ee bilt) *adj*. A house constructed poorly, of inferior materials, is *jerry-built*. Although the term is most commonly applied to housing, anything sloppily or hastily put together can properly be described as *jerry-built*. The term implies carelessness and a lack of thoroughness. "Quickie" movies can be criticized as *jerry-built*. *Jerry-built* legislation is pushed through hastily without proper thought or consideration, and the resulting laws create uncertainty and confusion. Anything *jerry-built* is unsubstantial. Some people think the word is connected with Jericho, whose walls came tumbling down, but this appears to be a *jerry-built* derivation.

jettison (jet' ih sən, -zan) *vb*. Technically, to *jettison* something, particularly cargo, is to throw it overboard in order to lighten a ship or an airplane in a storm or other emergency; the goods that are *jettisoned* are known as *jetsam* (jet' səm). But the term can apply generally to the discarding or abandoning of anything unwanted. We must *jettison* outworn ideas that obstruct progress. Cruel though it may be, any group, whether in science or teaching or business or sports, must *jettison* its weaklings in order to improve its efficiency. The American scholar and critic John Livingston Lowes (1867-1945) spoke of the *jettisoning* of the obsolete, i.e., discarding what is outworn.

jocund (jok' ənd, joe' kənd) *adj*. A *jocund* person or group is merry and cheerful, joyous, in high spirits, and tends to be playful. The English poet William Wordsworth (1770-1850), in his poem about "a host of golden daffodils," wrote: "A poet could not but be gay,/In such a *jocund* company. . . ." To him, the expanse of flowers "fluttering . . . in the breeze" seemed like a *jocund*, merry, frolicsome group. Another English poet, Edward Fitzgerald (1809-1883), in *Omar Khayyam*, speaking of the delights of wine, advised us to "be *jocund* with the fruitful Grape." *Jocund* is not the special property of English poets. One can just as well speak of a *jocund* group of children at a party, or a *jocund* group of well-wishers at campaign headquarters celebrating the victory of their candidate.

jovial (joe' vee əl) *adj*. A *jovial* person is good-humored and full of fun; a *jovial* mood is mirthful, merry, hearty, and full of life and the spirit of good fellowship. The potbellied, white-whiskered, red-suited Santa Claus, patting his copious belly and going "Ho-ho-ho!" is the best-known *jovial* figure of all time. In Shakespeare's *Macbeth* (Act III, Scene 2) Lady Macbeth tells the worried Macbeth: "Be bright and *jovial* among your guests tonight." *Jove* is another name for the god Jupiter. Astrologers tell us that people born under the planet Jupiter (*Jove*) are naturally happy: hence *jovial*. See the author's 1000 *Most Important Words* (Facts On File, 1984) for the astrological source of *saturnine* ("gloomy").

juncture (jungk′ chər) *n*. A *juncture* is a point of time that becomes important because of the surrounding circumstances or the state of affairs at the moment. The use of *juncture* indicates that the state of affairs has reached the crisis stage. *At this juncture* means more than "at this time"; it means "in this state of affairs," or "in view of the present circumstances." The expression *at this juncture* is misused and weakened if it is used merely as a fancy equivalent of *at this time*. A person relating his mountain-climbing experience, having told about the gathering fog or the dwindling food supply, might say: "*At this juncture,* we had to make up our minds whether to go on." If a nation's borders are violated, the government has arrived at a *juncture* where it must decide between negotiations and war.

junket (jung′ kit) *n*. As a food item, *junket* is curdled milk, often sweetened and flavored. In an entirely dissociated use, a *junket* is a picnic or outing. It is commonly used, however, to characterize a trip by a public body, often a legislative committee, at the taxpayers' expense, for the avowed purpose of securing information, but with more than a hint—in fact, a strong indication—that the real purpose is for the public officials to have some fun. The use of the word *junket* implies that the declared purpose of the trip (e.g., an investigation into the educational system of Lapland, or a study of the water supply of Upper Volta) is only ostensible, to put it charitably. Unnecessary *junkets* by public officials or groups can take a good deal of money out of the pockets of the public.

kaleidoscope (kə ly′ də skope) *n*. This is the name of a tube containing a number of small, loose pieces of variously colored glass and a mirror system, so arranged that when the tube is rotated, constantly changing patterns can be seen through an eyepiece. Figuratively, a *kaleidoscope* is a series of changing patterns. A rippling pond in the sunlight is a *kaleidoscope* of changing colors. The term can be used when no changing colors are concerned: One can speak of a *kaleidoscope* of events or activities; in this sense, a *kaleidoscope* is a rapidly changing pattern or succession. A doctor's or a lawyer's day can be a *kaleidoscope* of experiences. The adjective is *kaleidoscopic* (kə ly də skop′ ik—*o* as in *got*) and means "continually and rapidly shifting." The *kaleidoscopic* events of the twentieth century present an enormous task to historians. It is hard to keep up with the *kaleidoscopic* advances in science. *Kaleidoscopic* may be a mouthful to pronounce, but it is a colorful and useful word to describe the hectic pace of change in today's world.

ken (ken) *n.* *Ken* is knowledge, understanding; one's *ken* is one's range of knowledge or perception. This word is almost always used in the expressions *within one's ken* and *beyond one's ken*. One must instruct children at a pace conforming to their ability to understand; there is no point in discussing things *beyond their ken*. This is the age of specialization; in this rapidly changing world, with new discoveries by the minute, it is impossible for the general practitioner in any profession to have all the answers *within his ken*.

kindred (kin' drid) *n., adj.* A person's *kindred* are his relatives (note plural verb). Mr. Jones stayed in England; practically all of his *kindred* emigrated to Canada or America. It gives one a happy feeling to be surrounded by one's *kindred* on occasions like Thanksgiving or anniversaries. As an adjective, *kindred* means "related" by origin or nature, or "similar" in general attitudes and beliefs. French, Italian, and Spanish, all derived from Latin, are *kindred* languages. Earthquakes and tidal waves are *kindred* phenomena. When people think alike and feel congenial, they are said to be *kindred* spirits. People who react the same way, with similar sets of values, have *kindred* natures. Somehow, amid the throngs, *kindred* souls seek each other out.

knave (nave) *n.* A *knave* is a scoundrel, a rogue, a rascal, a thoroughly dishonest person, without scruples or principles; in cruder terms, a stinker, a louse, a lowlife. Daniel Defoe (1661-1731), English poet and author of *Robinson Crusoe*, expressed a cynical point of view when he said, "Necessity makes an honest man a *knave*." George Berkeley, Bishop of Cloyne (1685-1753), wrote: "He who says there is no such thing as an honest man, you may be sure is himself a *knave*." *Knave* may have an old-fashioned ring, but there seem to be so many rascals about that one more name for the species should be welcomed for variety's sake.

knotty (not' ee) *adj.* We are familiar with the noun *knot*, as it refers to a tie or tangle in a piece of string, rope, or wire; or to the dark, hard, cross-grained areas in a length of lumber. In literal use, the adjective *knotty* refers to a board containing numerous *knots*, generally undesirable except in *knotty pine*, which is much admired in rustic décor. In figurative use, *knotty* describes something difficult to untie or untangle. It applies to problems that are hard to solve, situations that present complications, and that sort of thing. Lawyers deal continually with *knotty* points of law. Life was simpler in the old days; today we are faced with many *knotty* problems that arise in our complex society. In this figurative sense, *knotty* applies to anything that is "tough" to figure out.

labyrinth (lab' ə rinth) *n*. A *labyrinth* is a maze, a complicated network of passages through which it is difficult to find your way around and reach the exit. Many *labyrinths* were intentionally built in ancient times. Figuratively, the word is applied not only to any complicated arrangement of rooms, offices, streets, highways, etc., but to an entangled state of affairs from which it is hard to extricate oneself or a situation which it is hard to understand or follow. It is often difficult to find one's way through the *labyrinths* of political struggle, or of labor negotiations. The adjective, *labyrinthine* (lab ə rin' thin, -theen—*th* as in *thin*), can be used in its figurative sense to describe anything complicated, intricate, hard to follow, bewildering, baffling. There are novels whose *labyrinthine* plots are almost impossible to follow. It is most discouraging for businessmen to have to deal with the *labyrinthine* bureaucracy of contemporary government. *Labyrinthine* may sound like a complicated word, but it is a very useful way of describing anything so intricate and mazelike as to baffle and discourage.

lapse (laps) *n.*, *vb*. *Lapse*, as a noun, has a number of meanings. A *lapse* of good manners or a *lapse* of high principles is a fall in one's standards, usually temporary. A *lapse* of memory is a slip, an occasional failure, not very serious in nature. A *lapse* of time is a passage of time: At a play, the lowering of the curtain can signify a *lapse* of twenty minutes, or two weeks, or whatever the plot requires. The verb to *lapse* means to decline from a standard previously established. Many an idealistic youth has later *lapsed* into greedy business pursuits. Unless a cure is absolutely established, a drug addict may *lapse* into the habit the first time he is faced with a tense situation. A *lapsed* Catholic (or member of any religion or group) is one who has stopped following the established rules of his church or sect.

laughable (laf' ə b'l—*a* is in *hat* or *arm*) *adj*. We all know what *laugh* means, and *laughable* can describe, in its literal sense, anything funny or amusing that makes you laugh. But its common, figurative use is to describe anything that is ridiculous, ludicrous, silly, not to be taken seriously. When James Boswell (1740–1785), the Scottish author famous for his biography of the English writer and lexicographer Samuel Johnson (1709–1784), asked the latter: "So, Sir, you *laugh* at schemes of political improvement?" the answer was: "Why, Sir, most schemes of political improvement are very *laughable* things." One should be charitable enough not to ridicule the local dramatic club's *laughable* attempt to produce *King Lear*. President Nixon's rationalizations about Watergate were *laughable*.

lavish (lav' ish) *vb.*, *adj*. As an adjective, *lavish* applies to people or other sources that give freely and generously, like philanthropists who are *lavish* in the distribution of their wealth, or trees that are *lavish* in their production of fruit. Whatever is *lavishly* given or produced can itself be described as *lavish*, like a *lavish* donation or a *lavish* crop. A *lavish* spender engages in *lavish* expenditures. A *lavish* fig tree produces a *lavish* crop of figs. The verb to *lavish* applies to the act of giving *lavishly*, i.e., liberally. Doting parents *lavish* love on their children. Plant lovers *lavish* care on their plants. Lonely people sometimes *lavish* too much hospitality on their infrequent guests. The aristocrats of bygone times *lavished* untold amounts of money on their sumptuous homes.

lax (lax) *adj. Lax* is the opposite of strict. *Lax* morals characterize people who pay no attention to a decent code of conduct. *Lax* attention to rules can result in confusion and even disaster. A *lax* attitude toward discipline will get you nowhere in the armed forces. *Laxity* (lak´ sih tee) is characteristic of people who are careless, too casual, the kind you would hesitate to rely on. Easygoing people may be pleasant to be with, but their *laxity* can land you in trouble if you count on them to be there when they're needed. *Laxity* in enforcement of the law encourages crime.

lecher (lech´ ər) *n.* A *lecher* is a man who has a strong sexual drive and gives way to it. The adjective describing such a person is *lecherous* (lech´ ər əs). *Lecherous* can also apply to anything that is sexually suggestive, like bodily movements, photographs, or drawings. *Lechery* (lech´ ə ree) is lust, excessive indulgence in sexual activity. Don Juan, who actually existed (he was the scion of a fourteenth-century Seville family), has, in legend, become the supreme *lecher,* the very symbol of *lechery.* In Mozart's opera *Don Giovanni,* the Don has had, according to his valet, 640 mistresses in Italy, 231 in Germany, 100 in France, 91 in Turkey, and 1,003 in Spain (total 2,065!). Another legendary *lecher* was the Italian Casanova (1725–1798), famous for his insatiable sexual appetite. Both names have become synonymous with *lecher.* Without attaining such heroic (or satanic) statistics, any man who gives way to excessive sexual desires is a *lecher;* he is *lecherous* and indulges in *lechery.*

leech (leech) *n. Leech* is a name of a bloodsucking type of worm which doctors in former days applied to a patient's skin for bloodletting purposes. *Leeches* are no longer used in that way (bloodletting, the old-time universal cure, has been out of fashion for many years), but the term is in common figurative use to describe the sort of person who, clinging to someone for personal gain, sucks out his wealth rather than his blood. A *leech,* in this sense, is a parasite, a sponger, a freeloader. Every new boxing champ or rock star seems to attract a set of *leeches. Leech* is used in another figurative way: To *stick like a leech* is to be hard to get rid of. In this usage, a *leech* is a persistent hanger-on who doesn't necessarily want to drain your assets, but does like to bask in your company. When you just can't shake off a hanger-on, you can say, "He sticks like glue" or "He sticks like a *leech.*" Real *leeches* live mostly in fresh water. If you find one sticking to you (ugh!), the remedy is to sprinkle salt on it; it will shrivel up and fall off. Unfortunately, salt doesn't work with human *leeches.*

legend (lej´ ənd) *n.* A *legend* is a tale handed down from the past, usually one of doubtful authenticity. *Legends* often center on real or supposedly real persons, like the *legends* of King Arthur and the Knights of the Round Table. There are many *legends* of buried treasure, like Captain Kidd's. The American poet Henry

Wadsworth Longfellow (1807-1882), in the introduction to his famous *Song of Hiawatha*, writes: "Should you ask me, whence these stories?/Whence these *legends* and traditions?" William Butler Yeats (1856-1939), the Irish poet and dramatist, said: "All the well-known families had their grotesque or tragic or romantic *legends*." George Washington's "I cannot tell a lie" is one of America's best-loved *legends*. *Legend*, as a general term, is the whole body of such *legends*, especially as applied to a particular place or people. Johnny Appleseed has a permanent place in American *legend*. The adjective *legendary* (lej´ ən derr ee) applies to famous persons or feats celebrated in *legend*. The wooden horse brought into Troy is one of the most famous *legendary* ruses of literature. *Legendary* can be used in the sense of "famous" or even "world-famous" about real people and events. What American hasn't heard of the *legendary* John Brown, or Babe Ruth, or Muhammad Ali? Truman's *legendary* defeat of Tom Dewey, against all odds, is part of America's rich political lore.

legible (lej´ ə b'l) *adj. Legible* describes anything in handwriting or print that can be read easily, or at least is capable of being made out. Inscriptions on ancient tombstones are often hardly *legible*. A *legible* handwriting is a blessing to one's correspondents. The noun is *legibility* (lej ə bil´ ə tee). The *legibility* of business signs at night has been enhanced by the use of neon lights (with unhappy effects on the nocturnal urban scene). *Illegible* (ih lej´ ə b'l) is the opposite of *legible*: impossible to read or make out, or at least very hard to decipher. People with *illegible* handwriting should type their letters.

legitimate (lih jit´ ə mət) *adj. Legitimate* is used in a number of ways. Its most common meaning is "lawful": Public funds must be used only for *legitimate* purposes. Only the *legitimate* owner of property can transfer title to it. In context, *legitimate* can mean "reasonable" or "acceptable": One must present a *legitimate* excuse to explain absence from work. The police will listen only to *legitimate* complaints. *Legitimate* applies to children born in wedlock. Those not so born are known as *illegitimate* (il ih jit´ ə mət). The *legitimate* theater or drama applies to professionally produced stage plays, as opposed to movies, television, vaudeville, etc. *Legitimate* stage productions require wholly different techniques from those employed in other forms of entertainment.

leisure (lee´ zhər, lezh´ ər) *n. Leisure* is time free from the demands of work. Those born with a silver spoon in their mouths can enjoy a life of *leisure*. It is pleasant to have the *leisure* to pursue your real interests. To be *at leisure* is to be free, unoccupied. People interested in art visit museums and galleries when they are *at leisure*. The English dramatist William Congreve (1670-1729) wrote the famous line: "Marry'd in haste, we may repent *at leisure*." *At one's leisure* means "when one has some free time, at one's convenience, when one can get to it." If you want a friend to criticize your essay, you ask him to look it over *at his leisure*. One can speak of *leisure time* or *leisure clothes* or *wear*. The adjective *leisurely* (lee´ zhər lee, lezh´ ər-) describes anything done without haste, in a deliberate manner: It is agreeable to take a *leisurely* walk in the woods. *Leisurely* can be used as an adverb as well: Take your time; work *leisurely*. *Leisured* (lee´ zhərd, lezh´ ərd) is an adjective describing people with lots of *leisure* at their command: The *leisured* classes are the rich who are usually the patrons of the arts. A *leisured* person doesn't understand the pressures of competition for jobs during a recession.

lenient (lee´ nee ənt, leen´ yənt) *adj.* A *lenient* person is permissive, tolerant, easygoing, never severe in giving out punishment. A *lenient* punishment is the opposite of a severe one; it is gentle, merciful, and understanding. A *lenient* judge hands down *lenient* sentences. It is possible for parents to be too *lenient* in bringing up their children. *Leniency* (lee´ nee ən see, leen´ yən-) is the noun, the opposite of *strictness* and *severity*. *Leniency*, based on an understanding of human weakness, is a great virtue, but must not itself be mistaken for weakness.

lethal (lee´ thəl—*th* as in *thing*) *adj.* Whatever is *lethal* is deadly, fatal. Any weapon that can cause death, like a gun or a dagger, is a *lethal* weapon. Because of the fatality statistics on our highways, the automobile has been ironically described as a "*lethal* weapon." There are medicines and other substances which, taken in moderation, may be beneficial, but in excess can be *lethal*; the excessive quantity is called a *lethal dose*. Gathering mushrooms, to the unwary, can turn out to be a *lethal* pastime. A leak in the floorboard of a car may result in *lethal* exposure to carbon monoxide. *Lethal* can be used figuratively to mean "devastating." Vicious criticism of a play can have a *lethal* effect. The incriminating picture of Nixon shown by those *lethal* tapes put an end to his political career.

liquid (lik´ wid) *adj.* Apart from its common and familiar meaning as a noun, *liquid* is an adjective used in the description of one's property: *liquid assets* are cash and other property that can be readily sold for cash, and are thus available for the cash needs of the individual or company owner. Real estate is not a *liquid asset*. Stocks and bonds listed on an exchange are *liquid assets*. The state of being so readily available is called *liquidity* (lih kwid´ ə tee). The *liquidity* of a company's assets should be taken into consideration before one invests in it.

literal (lit´ ər əl) *adj.* The *literal* meaning of a word is its usual, obvious, or strict material meaning, rather than its **figurative** sense. When you read of a boomerang thrown by an Australian aborigine, you visualize a bent wooden stick that comes back to the thrower; when you read of a boomerang damaging to a political campaigner, you know that it refers to something he said or some proposal he set forth earlier in his career that has now come back to hurt him. In the case of the aborigine, boomerang was used *literally* (lit´ ər ə lee), i.e., in its *literal* sense; as to the unhappy politician, it was used *figuratively*, i.e., in its *figurative* sense. The same aborigine has nothing to wear because he *literally* goes naked. The impoverished young lady who stays away from a party because she "has nothing to wear" isn't going around nude; she is speaking *figuratively* about her restricted wardrobe. See **figurative**.

literate (lit´ ər it) *adj.* In its technical, literal sense, *literate* means simply "able to read and write." One test of a nation's progress is the percentage of its people who are *literate*. *Literate* is commonly used in the figurative sense of "educated" or "well-read." It is stimulating to be in the company of *literate* individuals. Our educational system today, placing, as it does, so much emphasis on the sciences, is turning out fewer and fewer really *literate* people. See **illiterate** for analogous literal and figurative uses.

livelihood (live´ lee hood— *i* as in *life, oo* as in *good*) *n.* A person's *livelihood* is his means of making a living, of supporting himself (and his family, if he has one). There are countless ways of gaining a *livelihood*. Teaching may pay less than other professions, but it is a satisfying way of earning a *livelihood* because it offers the opportunity of guiding the next generation. Depressions, alas, deprive millions of their *livelihood*. The English writer Somerset Maugham (1874-1965), in *Of Human Bondage*, wrote: "There is nothing so degrading as constant anxiety about one's means of *livelihood*."

livid (liv´ id) *adj.* Technically, *livid* is a color: blue-gray, as from a bruise or blood-vessel congestion. It also describes the ashen, strangulated look of a person shaken by a strong emotion like terror or rage. However, the meaning most frequently met with is simply "furious, enraged." Being stuck in an endless traffic jam makes some people absolutely *livid*. Political speeches promising everything often make voters *livid* rather than happy. The people became *livid* at Nixon's insistence on his innocence when his guilt was so apparent.

loath, loth (loth—*o* as in *go, th* as in *think*) *adj.* To be *loath* to do something is to be reluctant, unwilling, not in the mood to do it. Most children are *loath* to perform household chores. When people are happy in one another's company, they are *loath* to part. After a person has taken a firm position in an argument, he is usually *loath* to change his mind no matter how strong the evidence to the contrary may be. Most people are *loath* to admit mistakes. Do not confuse the adjective *loath* with the verb to **loathe** (loth—*o* as in *go, th* as in *this*), the next entry.

loathe (loth—*o* as in *go, th* as in *this*) *vb.* To *loathe* is to detest, to be disgusted by, to feel intense aversion to. Some people like gossip; sensitive people *loathe* it. Why do small children *loathe* spinach? People of refined tastes *loathe* the violence on television. From *loathe* we get the adjective *loathsome* (loth´ səm—*o* as in *go, th* as in *this* or *thin*) meaning "hateful, disgusting" and the noun *loathing* (lo´ thing—*o* as in *go, th* as in *this*) meaning "disgust." King James I of England (1566-1625) called smoking "a custom *loathsome* to the eye, hateful to the nose, harmful to the brain, dangerous to the lungs . . ." etc., etc. (Pity *he* didn't write the warning note on cigarette packs!) A disease that causes nasty external symptoms is often referred to as "a *loathsome* disease." Treason is a *loathsome* crime. The sight and sound of blatant hypocrisy fill honest people with *loathing*. Any decent person has a *loathing* for child-beating. One can only react with *loathing* to the bloody slaughter of baby seals. Do not confuse *loathe* with **loath**, the previous entry.

lofty (lawf´ tee, lof´-) *adj. Lofty* can be used in several ways. A *lofty* mountain or building is one of great height; in this sense, *lofty* is the equivalent of *towering*. As a ship nears the southeastern coast of England, one sees the impressive, *lofty* White Cliffs of Dover. Describing one's aims, feelings, style, etc., *lofty* can mean "noble, superior." A judge must be a person of unquestioned integrity and *lofty* standards of fairness and justice. In context, *lofty* can mean "haughty." In a class-ridden society, the "upper" classes all too often treat the "lower" ones with *lofty* scorn. In Shakespeare's *Henry VIII* (Act IV, Scene 2), Griffith, an attendant of Queen Catharine, describes Cardinal Wolsey as a man "*lofty* and sour to them that lov'd him not;/But to those men that sought him sweet as summer." The context must indicate whether a person acting in a *lofty* manner is acting nobly or haughtily and scornfully.

lucid (loo´ sid—*oo* as in *boot*) *adj. Lucid* describes a literary style or a way of thinking or speaking that is clear and easy to understand. The American poet Robert Frost (1874-1963) used a *lucid* style; his poetry is simple and direct. Many other poets write in an obscure style that is difficult to follow, sometimes even incomprehensible. A gifted teacher is able to give his pupils *lucid* explanations of the subject matter. *Lucid* has a special meaning in the expression *lucid interval*, describing a period of sanity between periods of insanity; here, *lucid* means "rational." The noun is *lucidity* (loo sid´ ə tee). Abraham Lincoln's Gettysburg Address is a model of *lucidity*. Cf. **luminous**.

ludicrous (loo´ də krəs—*oo* as in *boot*) *adj. Ludicrous* can describe either something funny that provokes laughter, or something ridiculous and laughable, not worthy of serious consideration. A person (especially a dignified one) slipping on the ice or a banana peel, and falling on his derrière, is a *ludicrous* sight. Laurel and Hardy are famous for getting into *ludicrous* situations. Idi Amin's row upon row of medals was a *ludicrous* spectacle. It is annoying when, in a complex situation requiring expert advice, amateurs offer oversimplified and *ludicrous* suggestions. There are still people who share the *ludicrous* belief that the television pictures of men walking on the moon were a hoax.

lull (lull—*u* as in *but*) *n., vb.* A *lull* is a temporary quiet, an interval of stillness or lessened activity. Sometimes there is a *lull* in a storm, when the rain lessens and the wind stops howling. When a performer comes on stage, there is always a sudden *lull* in the hum of audience conversation. As a verb, to *lull* is to quiet, soothe. Mothers look their sweetest while they *lull* their babes to sleep. Babies are *lulled* by *lullabies*. Sedatives *lull* the senses. Good advice can *lull* one's fears. A convincing explanation is required to *lull* a person's suspicions. When danger threatens, be careful not to be *lulled* into a false feeling of security.

luminary (loo′ mə nerr ee—*oo* as in *boot*) *n*. In its literal sense, a *luminary* is any light-giving body in the sky, like the sun or the moon or a star, but its chief use is figurative, to denote a person who is a leading light (here, *light* is used figuratively) in his field, who has attained leadership. Jonas Salk (born 1914), the American bacteriologist, is a *luminary* in medical science. Laurence Olivier is a theatrical *luminary*. The word is often used loosely to describe any celebrity. Whenever there is a well-publicized Broadway opening, crowds gather to catch a glimpse of the *luminaries* who attend.

luminous (loo′ mə nəs—*oo* as in *boot*) *adj*. Anything bright and shining that radiates or reflects light can be described as *luminous*. Road signs are often painted with *luminous* material that shines brightly at night. On some clocks and watches, the numerals and hands are made *luminous* for reading in the dark. *Luminous* is used figuratively to mean "clear, readily understandable," in describing, for instance, a style of writing or speaking. Executives want from their subordinates memoranda that are concise and *luminous*. A *luminous* prose style is a great asset to a writer. A speaker, as well as what he says or the way he says it, can be referred to as *luminous*. A *luminous* speaker or lecturer is the opposite of one who is obscure, complex, and hard to follow. Cf. **lucid.**

lure (loor—*oo* as in *poor*) *n., vb*. A *lure* is anything that attracts, invites, or entices; the word can also refer to the attraction itself. For centuries, men have left home because of the *lure* of the sea. The *lures* used by "vamps" in old movies now look hilariously funny to modern audiences. Money, fame, and power are the *lures* that motivate most people. To *lure* is to tempt, attract, entice. It doesn't take much to *lure* you into a position you really don't like. Advertisements and commercials seem to stop at nothing in the attempt to *lure* you into buying whatever they're touting. The English poet John Masefield (1878-1967) wrote:

> My road calls me, *lures* me
> West, east, south, and north;
> Most roads lead men homewards,
> My road leads me forth.

luster (lus′ tər) *n*. *Luster* is sheen, glitter, brightness, especially of a polished surface. Women adorn themselves in the *luster* of satin. The pinkish *luster* of genuine pearls has made them favorite jewels for centuries. Sir Walter Scott, the English novelist and poet (1771-1832), wrote this lovely couplet:

> The dew that on the violet lies
> Mocks the dark *lustre* of thine eyes.

(Note the British spelling of *luster*. *Mocks* is used in the sense of "imitates," as in *mockingbird*.) Apart from the literal meaning of "brightness" or "glitter," *luster* is used figuratively to mean "distinction" or "glory": Great deeds add *luster* to one's name. The presence of celebrities in an opening-night audience lends *luster* to the occasion.

lusty (lus´ tee) *adj.* We all know what *lust* is—sexual desire, usually with the implication of lecherousness, and figuratively, overwhelming desire generally, as in *lust for power, lust for life. Lust* is also a verb, as used by Jimmy Carter, for instance, in his *Playboy* interview ("I have *lusted* after many women.") The adjective is *lustful,* describing persons having lewd desires or motivated by greed. *Lusty* is quite a different matter. It means "vigorous, robust, sturdy." The BBC, announcing the birth of a son to the Princess of Wales on June 22, 1982, described the newborn baby as a *"lusty* baby boy," and other reports stated that he had "cried *lustily*" on emerging. In Shakespeare's *As You Like It* (Act II, Scene 3), old Adam tells young Orlando: "Though I look old, yet I am strong and *lusty,*" and a moment later: " . . . my age is as a *lusty* winter,/Frosty, but kindly." Sir Thomas Malory (died 1471), in *The Death of Arthur,* wrote of "The month of May . . . when every *lusty* heart beginneth to blossom . . . and flourisheth in *lusty* deeds. For it giveth unto all lovers courage, that *lusty* month of May." Walt Whitman (1819-1892) wrote of "Youth, large, *lusty,* loving." Both adjectives stem from the noun *lust,* but be very careful not to confuse *lusty* with *lustful.*

machination (mak ə nay´ ən) *n.* This word is almost always used in the plural—*machinations*—to mean plots, schemes, intrigues, always with the implication that the scheming is crafty and evil. *Machinations* are the work of conniving people, who, either by tacit consent or active cooperation, carry out maneuvers so sly and so evil of purpose as to qualify as "dirty tricks." In Shakespeare's *King Lear* (Act I, Scene 2), the Earl of Gloucester, describing the troubled condition of the kingdom, speaks of *"machinations,* hollowness, treachery, and all ruinous disorders." The Committee to Re-elect the President (Nixon) organized a network of *machinations* against Democratic candidates that shocked the world. Many people mispronounce *machinations;* be sure to pronounce the *ch* as *k.*

magnitude (mag´ nə tood, -tyood—*oo* as in *boot*) *n.* Literally, *magnitude* is size, extent, dimensions, as in the *magnitude* of an angle, the *magnitude* of the distance that an electric car can travel. It is difficult for a small company to recover from a loss of real *magnitude.* The word is used mainly in the sense of "greatness" or "importance." The *magnitude* of the accomplishment of landing men on the moon was cause for celebration. The *magnitude* of the discovery of penicillin is immeasurable. The United Nations cannot waste its time on petty quarrels; it is designed to deal with affairs of *magnitude. Of the first magnitude* is an expression meaning "of the greatest importance." The election of a President of the United States is a political event *of the first magnitude.*

malice (mal´ iss) *n. Malice* is ill will, the desire to harm someone. To bear *malice* toward a person is to have a deep-seated grudge against him, and to hope that harm befalls him. In *The Book of Common Prayer,* the *Litany* speaks of "Envy, hatred, and *malice,* and all uncharitableness." (Here, *malice* is in good company!)

In Abraham Lincoln's second Inaugural Address we read the immortal words: "With *malice* toward none; with charity for all; with firmness in the right. . . ." The adjective is *malicious* (mə lish′ əs), describing a person, motive, or purpose that is full of *malice*, spite, and the intent to harm. We all know the dangers of *malicious* gossip. *Malice aforethought* is a legal phrase denoting the deliberate intent to kill that is a component of the crime of first-degree murder, as opposed to lesser degrees or manslaughter.

malign (mə līne′) *vb., adj.* To *malign* someone is to speak ill of him, to "bad-mouth" him, to tell lies about him, defame him, "smear" him. To *malign* an innocent person and damage his reputation is one of the most evil acts imaginable. There are many people today who believe that King Richard III was actually a good monarch, but that contemporary historians *maligned* him, and in so doing, misled Shakespeare into portraying him as an evil character. As an adjective, *malign* means "injurious" and describes things or people who have an evil effect on whomever or whatever they influence. President Nixon appeared to exercise a *malign* influence on his subordinates. Gloomy weather or a gloomy house often has a *malign* influence on people's spirit. It has been proved that the company of hardened criminals in prison has a *malign* effect on the characters of young first offenders. The related adjective *malignant* (mə lig′ nənt) applies to people who feel the urge to cause harm, or to the actions of such people (a *malignant* ruler, a *malignant* disposition, a *malignant* glance). The adjective *benignant* (bih nig′ nənt) means "kind" or "gracious." In medicine, a cancerous tumor is labeled *malignant* (not *malign*), while one that is not cancerous or harmful is called *benign* (not *benignant*). Such are the accidents of language.

mannerism (man′ ə riz əm) *n.* Whereas a *manner* is a way in which things are done, a *mannerism* is a peculiarity of behavior, whether of speech, dress, walking, carrying one's body, etc. Every human being has his peculiarities and *mannerisms*: the characteristic way in which he speaks, sits, stands, walks, dresses, eats—you name it. Birds, animals, fish, insects also have their peculiarities. One may be able to recognize the species by watching the *mannerisms* of a single bird. There are *mannerisms* in painting, literary style, composing, etc. One can ascribe a painting to an individual painter or to his school of painting by pointing to the *mannerisms* evident in the work. You would never confuse Bach and Beethoven or George Gershwin and Richard Rodgers because of the distinctive *mannerisms* in each composer's style.

maudlin (mawd′ lin) *adj. Maudlin* conduct is tearfully sentimental and emotional, uncontrolled—sometimes in a self-pitying manner. The flavor of the word may be explained by the fact that it is a corruption of *Magdalene*, the Mary Magdalene who is shown in thousands of paintings as a weeping penitent sinner, with red, swollen eyes. We are all too familiar with the *maudlin* ravings of drunks, especially at parties and class reunions. Victorian music-hall performers specialized in *maudlin* songs and recitations about outraged virginity, fallen women, tiny orphans, and little strayed doggies. "Enough already!" you want to cry, as your companion goes on forever with *maudlin* expressions of regret (he was two hours late) or of praise (he thinks you're simply wonderful).

maverick (mav′ ər ik, mav′ rik) *n.* A *maverick* is a dissenter, an individualist, an unorthodox person whose ideas or acts are different from those of his group or associates. One can be a political *maverick* like former Senator Eugene McCarthy, or an artistic *maverick* like Picasso or Dali, or a scientific *maverick* like Galileo. *Mavericks* refuse to conform; they take independent action, and are often pioneers in their fields. The term originated in the southwestern United States, where a rancher, Samuel Maverick (1803–1870), refused to brand his cattle. Over the years, his name came to be applied to any unbranded cow or steer, and eventually developed its present meaning.

meager (mee′ gər) *adj. Meager* means "scanty, inadequate." It's hard to get along on a *meager* salary. People of wealth don't realize how *meager* meals are on the poverty level. *Meager* attendance at church is most discouraging to a minister. The possibility of a *meager* harvest is always a threat to a poor nation. It is irritating to listen to people discussing subjects of which they have *meager* knowledge. Families of *meager* means have a hard time pulling through in an inflationary economy.

mediocre (mee dee o′ kər—*o* as in *go*) *adj.* Anything *mediocre* is second-rate, neither very good nor very bad, run-of-the-mill, ordinary, fair to middling. It is painful to watch a *mediocre* performance of a great play. Traveling salesmen have to put up with *mediocre* food and *mediocre* hotels. Many of our leading figures got through college with *mediocre* records. The noun *mediocrity* (mee dee ok′ rih tee—*o* as in *got*) can be used in two ways: to express the quality of being *mediocre* (a person of *mediocrity*, the *mediocrity* of one's accomplishments in life) or to denote a person of *mediocre* ability or attainments (President Warren G. Harding went down in history as a *mediocrity*). The Italian criminologist and doctor Cesare Lombroso (1836–1909) said: "The appearance of a single great genius is more than equivalent to the birth of a hundred *mediocrities*."

melancholy (mel′ ən kol ee) *n., adj. Melancholy* is low spirits, a gloomy attitude toward life, a depressed state of mind, despondency. We are all familiar with the *melancholy* of rejected lovers. The English novelist and poet Thomas Hardy (1840–1928), in *Tess of the D'Urbervilles*, wrote of "the chronic *melancholy* which is taking hold of the civilized races with the decline of belief [in God]." Sydney Smith, the English clergyman and writer (1771–1845), cautioned: "Never give way to *melancholy*; resist it steadily, for the habit will encroach." Indeed, the noun *melancholy* suggests not a sudden, short state of sadness or gloom, but rather chronic depression, a habitually gloomy outlook. *Melancholy* is also an adjective. A *melancholy* person can cast a spell of gloom over his companions. One can speak of a *melancholy* attitude or mood. A funeral is a *melancholy* occasion. The American poet and short-story writer Edgar Allan Poe (1809–1849) asked: "Of all *melancholy* topics, what . . . is the most *melancholy*? Death . . . [is] the obvious reply."

A popular song of the 1920s, by George Norton and Ernie Burnett, began, "Come to me, my *melancholy* baby."

memento (mə men' toe) *n.* A *memento* is anything that serves as a reminder, especially of things past. People often keep their deceased parents' wedding rings or Masonic emblems or pocket watches as *mementos*. *Memento* can have the force of *keepsake*, as when, in the old days, a boy gave a girl his fraternity pin. Old snapshots are probably the commonest *mementos* of times long past. People are all too fond of taking away an ashtray as a *memento* of a pleasant stay at a hotel. Do not confuse *memento* with *momentum*, which is an entirely different affair.

memorable (mem' ə rə b'l) *adj.* This adjective can be applied to anything deserving to be remembered, anything notable. One's wedding is always a *memorable* occasion. Lincoln's Gettysburg Address is one of the most *memorable* speeches in history. The victory of William the Conqueror over King Harold at Hastings in 1066 was indeed a *memorable* event: it marked the beginning of the history of modern England. The 1929 Wall Street crash was *memorable*, to put it mildly, in that it led to the worldwide depression of the 1930s.

menial (mee' nee əl, meen' yəl) *adj.* *Menial* applies literally to domestic servants and domestic tasks, but it is used figuratively to mean "degrading." It seems such a waste when an intelligent person has to spend a lot of time on *menial* tasks like washing pots and pans and doing the laundry. Errand boys and shipping clerks are often overqualified for the *menial* services they are called upon to perform. One doesn't see much *menial* staff in these days except in the homes of the very rich. Town life would be a lot more difficult but for those who are willing to fulfill *menial* duties like street cleaning and garbage collection.

merit (merr' it) *n., vb.* *Merit*, as a noun, is excellence, worth, any deserving quality. The *merit* of a good education is the enrichment of life it affords. Nobel Prize winners are persons of great *merit*. A really great novel must have the *merits* of plot, character, and style. The noun is used in the plural to mean the essential issues in legal matters, as opposed to technicalities. A case should be decided on its *merits* alone. To *merit* something is to deserve it, be worthy of it: Hard work *merits* good compensation. Abraham Lincoln *merited* the veneration we pay him. People don't always receive the rewards they *merit*, or *merit* the rewards they receive. In a cynical vein, the English poet Samuel Taylor Coleridge (1772–1834) wrote:

> It sounds like stories from the land of spirits
> If any man obtain that which he *merits*
> Or any *merit* that which he obtains.

meticulous (mə tik' yə ləs) *adj.* A *meticulous* person is extremely attentive to detail, sometimes too attentive, fussy, or finicky. *Meticulous* can be a compliment or the opposite, depending on the context. If a person approves of another's *meticulous* work, he is approving of the care and thoroughness that went into it; in this case, *meticulous* has the force of *conscientious*. However, if the context suggests that time and effort have been wasted, *meticulous* has the effect of *finicky, fussy, picky, overconscientious*. A teacher might commend a student for *meticulous* work on a term paper. A client might condemn a lawyer for sending a very large bill for *meticulous* attention to a comparatively simple matter. On the whole, there are good substitutes for *meticulous* in the complimentary sense (*exact, precise, careful, attentive*), and *meticulous* in the derogatory sense might well be reserved as a good variation on *finicky*. The American poet T.S. Eliot (1888-1965) certainly used it that way in his poem "The Love Song of J. Alfred Prufrock," in which the hero declares himself to be

> Deferential, glad to be of any use,
> Politic, cautious and *meticulous*. . .
> At times, indeed almost ridiculous. . .

metropolis (mə trop' ə lis) *n*. A *metropolis* is a large, busy city, the principal city of a region, but not necessarily the capital of a nation, state, or province. Chicago is the *metropolis* of the Middle West. *Metropolis* may be used to describe the center of any industry: Detroit is the automobile *metropolis* of the United States. The English poet Alfred, Lord Tennyson (1809-1892) called Edinburgh the "gray *metropolis* of the North." William Cobbett, the English political essayist (1763-1835), referred to London as "The monster, called . . . 'the *metropolis* of the empire.'" The adjective is *metropolitan* (meh trə pol' ə t'n), describing anything pertaining to or characteristic of a *metropolis*, its populace, culture, lifestyle, etc. People who cherish peace and quiet prefer rural to *metropolitan* life. Some businessmen aim especially at *metropolitan* markets. *Metropolitan* figures in the names of many public institutions, all the way down from the *Metropolitan Museum of Art* and the *Metropolitan Opera* to the *Metropolitan Transit Authority*—all of New York City.

mettle (met' l) *n*. A person's *mettle*, broadly speaking, is his nature, temperament, or character, but the word is almost always used in the more specific senses of "vigor, spirit, courage, endurance." It is life's hard knocks that try a person's *mettle*. In a phrase like *a man* (or *woman*) *of mettle, mettle* means "courage, guts." You may have heard the expression "Grasp the nettle!" ("Face the situation!") Aaron Hill, the English poet (1685-1750), found a good rhyme for *mettle*:

> Tender-handed stroke a nettle
> And it stings you for your pains;
> Grasp it like a man of *mettle*,
> And it soft as silk remains.

To be *put on your mettle* is to be roused to do your best, your utmost. The lifelong advantage of winning a prize in an international music competition puts all the young musicians *on their mettle*.

minimal (min' ə məl) *adj*. The *minimal* amount of anything is the least possible under the circumstances; in context, *minimal* means merely "small" or "slight."

In order to enforce only *minimal* standards of education and student behavior, a class should not exceed twenty in number. Even the *minimal* defense needs of our country require enormous expenditures. The cost of a work of art, whether painting or sculpture, includes only a *minimal* charge for materials. The adverb *minimally* (min′ ə mə lee) means "to a minimal degree." To make urban residents *minimally* safe on urban streets, we must have good lighting and an adequate police force.

mirror (mir′ ər—*i* as in *hit*) *vb.* We all know what a *mirror* is, but *mirror* is also a verb, meaning to "reflect," "parallel," or "be a close copy of" something. A calm pool *mirrors* the sky and its clouds; a lake may *mirror* the mountains. The mood of the people often *mirrors* the weather. The leading figures of a nation usually *mirror* the era in which they live. If our ideas are similar, they *mirror* each other. The political views of Adlai Stevenson (1900-1965) *mirrored* those of the liberal wing completely.

misfortune (mis for′ chən) *n. Misfortune* is bad luck in general; *a misfortune* is a particular unlucky incident or happening, a stroke of bad luck. It is during *misfortune* that one discovers one's true friends. *Misfortune* is the theme of the *Book of Job. Misfortunes,* they say, never come singly. Some people bear their *misfortunes* bravely. Poland had the *misfortune* in World War II of being situated between the enemy powers Germany and Russia. The American poet James Russell Lowell (1819-1891) said: "Let us be of good cheer . . . remembering that the *misfortunes* hardest to bear are those which never come." Edmund Burke (1729-1797), the Irish statesman and orator, wrote: "I am convinced that we have a degree of delight . . . in the real *misfortunes* and pains of others." The Germans have an adjective for that feeling: *schadenfroh* (shah′ d'n fro), defined in the dictionary as "gloating over other people's *misfortunes.*" How awful!

misgiving (mis giv′ ing) *n. Misgiving* is a feeling of doubt, distrust, suspicion, uncertainty, uneasiness, worry. The American novelist Theodore Dreiser (1871-1945) wrote of "those doubts and *misgivings* which are ever the result of a lack of decision." It is only natural to have *misgivings* when entering upon a new career. Winston Churchill (1874-1965), speaking in 1940 of the growing bond between Britain and the United States, said: "For my own part, looking out upon the future, I do not view the process with any *misgivings.*" There is no such thing in the business world as a "sure thing": prudent people don't make new investments without at least a minimum of *misgiving.*

mishap (mis′ hap) *n.* A *mishap* is an unlucky accident. An *accident* is anything that happens by chance: It may be lucky, as when two old friends meet by *accident*; or unlucky, as when a gun goes off by *accident* and kills someone. *Accident* usually implies misfortune; *mishap* always does. But a *mishap* is a slight misfortune, not serious or fatal, not a calamity or a disaster. Most thrillers put the hero through one *mishap* after another. It is a lucky thing to return home without *mishap* after a long journey. To *suffer* or *meet with a mishap* is to run into a bit of bad luck.

modify (mod´ ə fy) *vb.* To *modify* something is to make a change in it, to alter it somewhat, to vary it. The design of the airplane has been *modified* so many times since the days of Kitty Hawk that the Wright brothers would hardly recognize the Concorde. Students soon learn that they have to *modify* their study habits when they enter graduate school. The American novelist and humorist Mark Twain (Samuel Langhorne Clemens, 1835–1910) wrote: "A round man cannot be expected to fit in a square hole right away. He must have time to *modify* his shape." The noun is *modification* (mod ə fə kay´ shən). No plan should be so rigid as not to permit of *modification*. *Modification* applies not only to change in general, but also to the new form resulting from the change; thus, next year's automobiles will be *modifications* of this year's.

momentous (moe men´ təs) *adj.* What is *momentous* is of great importance and significance, of far-reaching consequence. The splitting of the atom brought about *momentous* changes that have affected the lives of everyone on earth. America's entry into World War I was a *momentous* step that changed the course of history. What is more *momentous* in a man's lifetime than the day he meets the woman he marries? The United States election of 1932, which made Franklin D. Roosevelt President and ushered in the New Deal, was one of the most *momentous* in American history.

monogamy (mə nog´ ə mee) *n.* *Monogamy* is the practice of having only one spouse at a time. There is a series of related words: *polygamy* (pə lig´ ə mee), the practice of having more than one spouse at a time (this term is usually understood to denote the marriage of one man to several women); *polyandry* (pol ee an´ dree), having several husbands at a time; *monandry* (mə nan´ dree), having one husband at a time; and *bigamy* (big´ ə mee), the crime (in Christian societies) of marrying again while one has an undivorced spouse still living. All these words have related adjectives: *monogamous* (mə nog´ ə məs); *polygamous* (pə lig´ ə məs); *polyandrous* (pol ee an´ drəs); *monandrous* (mə nan´ drəs); and *bigamous* (big´ ə məs). Christian societies permit only *monogamous* marriages. Arabic societies allow *polygamous* marriages. There are *polygamous* and *polyandrous* societies among primitive people. For practical purposes, the only words in ordinary use are *monogamy* (*-ous*), *polygamy* (*-ous*) and *bigamy* (*-ous*). So much for anthropology!

monopolize (mə nop´ ə lize) *vb.* To *monopolize* something is to gain control of it to the exclusion of all others; to *monopolize* someone is to occupy all of his time and attention. It is rude and inconsiderate, at a dinner party, to *monopolize* the conversation, not giving anyone else a chance to get a word in edgewise. Celebrities are bored with hangers-on who try to *monopolize* them. *Monopolize* is based on the noun *monopoly* (mə nop´ ə lee), which, in commerce, is the exclusive control of a product or service that gives one company an unfair advantage in the market.

monumental (mon yə men´ t'l) *adj.* Anything that can be described as *monumental* is, literally speaking, huge, massive, big as a *monument*; but the figurative and usual meaning is "imposing, impressive, overwhelming, awe-inspiring." Beethoven's Fifth Symphony is a work of *monumental* proportions. Putting men on the moon was a *monumental* achievement. The discovery of penicillin was a *monumental* step in medical history. When a musical that costs a million dollars closes after the first night, it can be called a *monumental* failure. The sinking of the *Titanic* was a *monumental* disaster. There are those, alas, who drink enough to produce *monumental* hangovers.

morose (mə rōs´—*o* as in *go*, *s* as in *so*) *adj.* A *morose* person or his mood is glum, sullen, moody, ill-humored, gloomily unsociable, depressed, in the dumps, down in the mouth. People in a *morose* mood don't make good company. The Roman poet Martial (40-104), as translated by Dudley Fitts, complained to a friend: "You're obstinate, pliant, merry, *morose*, all at once. For me there's no living with you, or without you." Lord Macaulay, the English historian and statesman (1800-1859), in his *History of England*, wrote: "Those who compare the age in which [they live] . . . with [an imaginary] . . . golden age, may talk of degeneracy . . . , but no man who is correctly informed as to the past will be disposed to take a *morose* . . . view of the present." Some people become merry when they drink; others become tearful, sullen, and *morose*.

morsel (mawr´ səl) *n.* A *morsel* is a tiny bit (especially of food), a mouthful. One can't go working forever without a *morsel* of food! A particularly tasty bit of any dish is often referred to as a *choice morsel*. *Morsel* can refer to things other than food. Some people don't have a *morsel* of common sense. A detective investigating a case is grateful for any *morsel* of information that gives him a lead. The German philosopher Friedrich Nietzsche (1844-1900) said: "A strong . . . man digests his experiences . . . just as he digests his meat, even when he has some tough *morsels* to swallow."

mortal (mawr´ t'l) *adj.* *Mortal* has a number of meanings, all connected, one way or another, with death. When we are told that all men are *mortal*, *mortal* is used as contrasted with *immortal*, and means "incapable of living forever"; in other words, all people must die. A *mortal* wound is one that causes death; here, *mortal* means "fatal." If someone suffers *mortal* injuries in an accident, he will not recover. If you feel *mortal* hatred for someone, you will hate him unto death. *Mortal* combat ends only with the death of one of the combatants. Gladiators in ancient Rome engaged in *mortal* combat. *Mortal* enemies are enemies forever, i.e., right up until death. Informally, *mortal* is used to mean "extreme" in expressions like *mortal fear* or a *mortal hurry*. You don't have much time to make the plane; you pack in a *mortal* (i.e., helluva) hurry. People walk the streets of urban centers at night in *mortal* fear of being mugged. To be *mortally* (mawr´ tə lee) wounded is to suffer a wound that will cause death. Again informally, *mortally* can mean nothing more than "seriously": Sensitive people can feel *mortally* offended by a harmless criticism.

176   1000 MOST PRACTICAL WORDS

multitude (mul′ tə tood, -tyood—*oo* as in *boot*) *n. Multitude* can be used in a variety of ways. It can mean "a great number of, a great many." Sociable people like to have a *multitude* of friends. Politicians and lobbyists develop a *multitude* of contacts. Standing alone, the term *a multitude* means "a throng, a great crowd." As the celebrities arrived for opening night, they were surrounded by a *multitude* on the sidewalk. The term *the multitude,* by itself, means "the masses, the common people." Politicians try to win the favor of *the multitude. The multitude* is fickle, its whims are unpredictable. The English poet John Dryden (1631-1700) wrote: "If by the people you understand *the multitude* . . . , 'tis no matter what they think; they are sometimes in the right, sometimes in the wrong; their judgment is a mere lottery." The English poet and essayist Wentworth Dillon (1633-1685) differed: "*The multitude* is always in the wrong." Hitler and Mussolini appealed to *the multitude.*

naïve, naive (na eev′—*a* as in *arm*) *adj.* A *naïve* person is unsophisticated, natural, artless, innocent, and straightforward as a result of a lack of experience. *Naïve* people believe everything they're told. A *naive* remark indicates a simple, unaffected soul. It would be naïve of you to think that you could go to the big city and make your fortune—just like that! The American cartoonist James Thurber (1894-1961) drew a *New Yorker* cartoon satirizing those intolerably knowledgeable wine experts with this caption: "It's a *naïve* domestic Burgundy without any breeding, but I think you'll be amused by its presumption." The noun is *naïveté, naiveté* (na eev tay′—first *a* as in *arm*), meaning "artlessness, innocent simplicity, unaffected naturalness." The *naiveté* of the country girl unable to resist the wicked designs of the city slicker was a favorite topic of Victorian novels. The *naïveté* of the public is reflected in the level of TV commercials (though occasionally this same public does elect a Truman over a Dewey). People who inherit money are often *naïve* in financial matters and need the advice of an expert.

narrate (nar′ rate, na rate′—first *a* as in *hat*) *vb.* To *narrate* one's experiences or the events of the day is to tell about them, to give an account of them. Children like to listen to Daddy as he *narrates* the adventures of his youth. The act of *narrating* is called *narration* (na ray′ shən—first *a* as in *hat*); the recital of events is called *a narration.* Interesting *narration* is an art in itself. The *narration* of the events in Germany leading up to Hitler and the Nazis warns us that "It can't happen here" ain't necessarily so. The person *narrating* is the *narrator* (nar′ ray tər—first *a* as in *hat*). A *narrative* (nar′ ə tiv—first *a* as in *hat*) is any story or tale, whether a recital of true events or fiction. Historical *narratives,* a mixture of history, legend, and fiction, are not only interesting but instructive as well.

negligible (neg′ lih jə b′l) *adj. Negligible* applies to things so trivial and insignificant that they can be ignored. Compared to the initial price of a Rolls-Royce, the cost of its gas consumption is *negligible*. In cost accounting, an error of one-hundredth of a percent would normally be considered *negligible*. It is frustrating to be a teacher when, despite his strenuous efforts, a pupil makes *negligible* progress. Most of the prospectors in the gold rush of 1849 found only *negligible* quantities of gold dust. The American bacteriologist Hans Zinsser (1878–1940) observed: "The scientist . . . shows his intelligence by discriminating between the important and the *negligible*." In any argument, don't bother with *negligible* side issues and trifling examples; go straight to the point.

nimble (nim′ b′l) *adj.* A *nimble* person moves quickly, lightly, easily, is agile and spry. Ballet dancers must be *nimble* as well as graceful. Rabbits and deer are easily frightened and *nimble*. The *nimble* leaps of a mountain goat are a wonderful sight. The *nimble* fingers of a great pianist are almost impossible to follow. *Nimble* is a favorite word in nursery rhymes: ". . . If your heels are *nimble* and light,/You may get there [to Babylon] by candlelight." "Jack, be *nimble*,/Jack, be quick,/Jack, jump over the candlestick." One may speak of a *nimble* mind, one that is quick to understand, inventive, ingenious. Shakespeare, in Sonnet XLIV, wrote: ". . . *nimble* thought can jump both sea and land." Oscar Wilde (1854–1900) and George Bernard Shaw (1856–1950), the Irish playwrights, are famous for their *nimble* wit and repartee.

noisome (noy′ səm) *adj.* This adjective applies to anything offensive, putrid, or disgusting, like a smell. When sanitation men go on strike, *noisome* heaps of garbage pile up on the streets. Glue factories emit *noisome* odors. In Psalms 91:3 we read: "Surely He shall deliver thee . . . from the *noisome* pestilence." Beatrice says to Benedick, in Shakespeare's *Much Ado About Nothing* (Act V, Scene 2): ". . . foul breath is *noisome*, therefore I will depart unkissed." *Noisome* has nothing to do with noise; the syllable *noi-* comes from the verb *annoy*.

nominal (nom′ ə n′l) *adj.* This word has several quite distinct uses. It describes things that exist in name only, not in fact. In many countries, the office of President is only *nominal*; the real chief of state is the Prime Minister. When property (like stock or real estate) belonging to one person is registered in the name of another, for purposes of convenience or concealment, the latter is a *nominal* owner, i.e., an "owner" in name only. Another use is in expressions like *nominal price* or *cost* or *consideration*, where the amount paid is named as a matter of form only, and is far below the real value. Legal documents often contain the phrase "in consideration of $1." The "$1" is the *nominal* price, not the actual one. There are cases where a tenant pays only a *nominal* rent. There is still a third use. When something is said to be of *nominal* value, *nominal* means "trifling" or "negligible." An original first edition may be of great value; a facsimile is of only *nominal* value.

noncommittal (non kə mit´ əl) *adj.* A *noncommittal* answer or statement is a guarded one that does not *commit* the speaker to a particular position or course of action. "Time will tell" is a good example; or "We shall have to await developments." A *noncommittal* position on a matter is one that permits a person to go in any direction. Politicians in television interviews usually give safe, *noncommittal* answers to pointed questions. Those joint communiqués issued by the parties to international conferences are masterpieces of *noncommittal* language.

nostalgia (nos tal´ jə, nə stal´-) *n.* *Nostalgia* is a wistful, romantic yearning for the past, with recollections of one's old way of life, or as Shakespeare put it (Sonnet XXIX), "remembrance of things past." Homesickness is a form of *nostalgia*. The very phrase *the good old days* was born of *nostalgia*. An odor or a snatch of melody can suddenly summon up recollections of past experience and give rise to a wave of *nostalgia*. The adjective is *nostalgic* (nos tal´ jik—*o* as in *got*, *a* as in *hat*). "Where have all the years gone?" sighs the aging man, suffering a *nostalgic* longing for his lost youth. A sentimental journey to one's birthplace can evoke *nostalgic* recollections.

notable (noe´ tə b'l) *n., adj.* Anything *notable* is remarkable, worthy of notice, outstanding, exceptional, out of the ordinary. The first ascent of Mt. Everest was a *notable* achievement. The discovery of America was one of the most *notable* events in history. Hawaii is *notable* for its wonderful climate. The *notable* increase in crime in recent years is cause for alarm. A *notable* person is distinguished, renowned, prominent, a VIP. Washington, D.C., teems with *notable* personalities. *Notable* scholars make up the faculties of our leading universities. *Notable* is also a noun, and applies to a prominent person, a figure of note. It is one of the functions of the White House to receive and entertain *notables* from all over the world. It is distressing to see how many *notables* have been involved in divorces and scandals.

notorious (noe tore´ ee əs, -tawr´-) *adj.* A *notorious* person or event is widely known, usually with the implication that his reputation is unfavorable. Al Capone was a *notorious* gangster. The Watergate affair was a *notorious* scandal. The *notorious* Stalin purges of the 1930s shocked the world. Although *notorious* can, on rare occasions, mean "widely known" in a *favorable* sense (metals are *notorious* conductors of heat; Sigmund Freud is *notorious* as the father of psychoanalysis), the implication of widespread *unfavorable* publicity has become so strong that it is unsafe to use the word except in its pejorative sense. This is certainly true of the noun *notoriety* (noe tə ry´ ə tee), which always implies scandal and shame, despite what the dictionaries say. Frequent divorces involve Hollywood society in continuous *notoriety*. Great *notoriety* attached to the name of the Irish poet and playwright Oscar Wilde (1854–1900) for sexual practices that are generally condoned these days, at least in the world of the arts.

numerous (noo´ mə rəs, nyoo´-, *oo* as in *boot*) *adj. Numerous* means "very many," or "consisting of many individuals," depending on the context. There are *numer-*

ous tales of buried treasure in all parts of the world. It is difficult to keep up with the *numerous* advances in technology. An apple a day is much less costly than *numerous* visits to the doctor's office. Newspaper proofreading is so poor these days that *numerous* misprints can be found in even the most respected journals. Plays that, despite poor reviews, receive favorable word-of-mouth publicity will gain increasingly *numerous* audiences. *Numerous* armies are sometimes held back by a heroic few. When families are *numerous*, each child inherits less.

objective (əb jek´ tiv) *n., adj.* An *objective* is a goal, a purpose, a target, an end, something at which one's efforts are aimed. The *objective* of hard study is a good report card. The doing of good works among the poor is the *objective* of a charity drive. As an adjective, *objective* has an entirely unrelated meaning. An *objective* view of a situation is one that is based on facts, unbiased, and free of personal prejudice. It is the exact opposite of a *subjective* view, which is personal and individual, and therefore likely to ignore facts and be influenced by the individual's prejudice and bias. A scientist must make an *objective* analysis of the data and reach an *objective* conclusion. An attorney has to disregard all personal bias in order to reach an *objective* evaluation of his client's chance of success. The noun is *objectivity* (ob jek tiv´ ih tee). A judge must always maintain *objectivity* in reaching his opinion. It is only natural for a person to be influenced by past experience and to take a *subjective* view of a situation; that is why witnesses differ. It is said that teachers are naturally *objective* when they mark arithmetic papers, but that they tend to be *subjective* in evaluating students' literary efforts. *Subjectivity* should be avoided as far as possible in selecting staff employees, but it should determine the choice of a spouse. The Scottish philosopher David Hume (1711–1776) wrote, "Beauty in things exists in the mind which contemplates them," a statement that was later compressed by the Irish novelist Margaret Wolfe Hungerford (1855–1897) into the immortal epigram "Beauty is in the eye of the beholder." This, in turn, was elaborated on by the American novelist Lew Wallace (1827–1908) and became "Beauty is altogether in the eye of the beholder." All three were saying that the discovery of beauty, whether in people or things, is a *subjective* process.

oblique (o bleek´) *adj.* The literal meaning of *oblique* is "slanting." A line that is neither vertical nor horizontal is *oblique*. Figuratively, *oblique* is used in the sense of "indirect, not straightforward, devious, underhand." An *oblique* observation or remark or accusation is not direct but intentionally obscure, with the implication of innuendo. An *oblique* answer to a simple question is a devious one, intended to evade the issue. An *oblique* glance is sidelong, one that avoids looking you straight in the eye.

obscure (əb skyoor—*oo* as in *book*) *vb.*, *adj.* To *obscure* something is to conceal it, in the way clouds *obscure* the moon, or to conceal the meaning of something, in the way unclear language *obscures* the meaning of a story or a message or a poem. As an adjective, *obscure* has a variety of uses. An *obscure* corner of a room is somewhat hidden, not clearly in view. *Obscure* language fails to express its meaning clearly. An *obscure* little village is remote, out of the current of world affairs. An *obscure* poet is one who has not gained recognition, whose work is hardly known. An *obscure* reason for doing something is puzzling, one that seems hardly to justify the action. In all these senses *obscure* evokes the image of dimness, whether literal or figurative. *Obscurity* (əb skyoor ih tee—*oo* as in *book*) is indefiniteness. *Obscurity* of language is ambiguity. The *obscurity* of much contemporary poetry leaves most readers puzzled and often irritated. *Obscurity* of motivation is a problem for psychologists. *Obscurity* can be used in the sense of "lack of fame." Most people live their lives in *obscurity*, far from the public eye. A person who wins a million-dollar lottery is plucked by chance from *obscurity*, and wins a short-lived fame.

obsolete (ob' sə leet) *adj.* *Obsolete* means "out of use," and can refer to words, equipment, machinery, processes, theories, systems. The use of the word *obsolete* indicates that the thing described was once, but is no longer, in current use. Blood-letting is an *obsolete* medical treatment. Blue laws in many states are now *obsolete*. The hoop skirt is an *obsolete* style. A related adjective is *obsolescent* (ob sə les' ənt), which describes things that are becoming *obsolete*, passing out of use. The bow and arrow and spear still used by primitive tribes are *obsolescent* among these people, *obsolete* in the civilized world. *Obsolescence* (ob sə les' əns) is the state of being *obsolescent*, i.e., of passing out of use. *Built-in* or *planned obsolescence* applies to the unethical commercial process of constructing appliances and automobiles of inferior or substandard materials so that they deteriorate rapidly and have to be replaced faster than they normally should; it may refer also to frequent changes of design that render older cars or appliances *obsolete* because the parts for them are no longer available.

obstinate (ob' stə nit) *adj.* An *obstinate* person clings firmly to his position or opinion and refuses to yield to persuasion. An *obstinate* disease does not respond readily to treatment. *Obstinate* weeds are hard to control. *Obstinate* children are difficult to train. The noun is *obstinacy* (ob' stə nə see), which expresses stubbornness in holding to one's position no matter what. The stubborn mule has become a symbol of *obstinacy*. The Irish playwright George Bernard Shaw (1856-1950) gave the true flavor of *obstinate* in these words: "not courageous, only quarrelsome; not determined, only *obstinate*; not masterful, only domineering." The English novelist Anthony Trollope (1815-1882) described a character as "so stupid and so *obstinate* that it was impossible to get him to do or understand anything." It is commendable to be steadfast in one's convictions and faith, but objectionable to be *obstinate*.

ominous (om' ə nəs) *adj.* *Ominous* describes anything threatening, anything that warns that all is not well. An *omen* (o' mən—*o* as in *go*) is a sign of something that will happen, whether for good or bad, but the related adjective *ominous* (note the different pronunciations of *o* in the noun and the adjective) relates only to the bad. (Is this because more bad things happen than good?) When the boss walks in with an *ominous* scowl, look out! An *ominous* dark cloud bank indicates, to the wise, that they had better postpone their picnic plans. When one is lost in the woods, silence can be *ominous*.

onus (o′ nəs) *n*. An *onus* is a burden, a responsibility, with the implication that the burden is a heavy one, involving difficulty and strain. Society is faced with the *onus* of caring for the elderly and disabled. In a trial, the *onus* is on the plaintiff to prove his case; this is called the *burden of proof*. It is the *onus* of every teacher to add to the sum total of each pupil's knowledge. Shirking may be defined as attempting to shift the *onus* onto somebody else's shoulders. The related adjective is *onerous* (on′ ər əs—*o* as in *got*, o′ nər əs—*o* as in *go*). An *onerous* task is a burdensome one, one that presents difficulties or causes hardships. Some professionals prefer to free-lance rather than submit to the *onerous* routine of an employee. *Onerous* taxes imposed by the British on the American colonists were one cause of the Revolutionary War.

opt (opt) *vb*. To *opt* is to exercise a choice. If you have to decide between two courses, for example, you may *opt for* one or the other, or *opt to* take one or the other. To *opt out* of something is to reject it. Fewer pupils are *opting for* the classics these days. Many Puerto Ricans *opt for* American statehood. The hippies *opted out* of conventional society. *Opt* is related to the noun *option* (op′ shən), the right to choose, or a choice given, like the *option* to stay or go. *Opt* is also related to the adjective *optional* (op′ shə n'l), describing something left to one's choice, something one can take or leave, like *optional* (elective) courses at school, or *optional* formal dress at a dinner party.

opulent (op′ yə lənt) *adj*. Applying to people, *opulent* means "wealthy"; describing places, it means "luxurious." It was the *opulent* industrialists of the nineteenth century who built the *opulent* mansions and endowed the foundations and libraries. The noun is *opulence* (op′ yə ləns), meaning "wealth." In *The Affluent Society*, the American economist and diplomat John Kenneth Galbraith (born 1908), discussing the "unevenness of . . . blessings" in American society, wrote of "private *opulence* and public squalor." *Opulent* and *opulence* imply not only wealth, but great, showy wealth and an abundance of all the good things of life.

ordeal (or deel′, -dee′ əl) *n*. An *ordeal* is a severe experience, an extremely trying test of endurance or trial of character. Sir Edmund Hillary (born 1919), the first man to achieve the ascent of Mt. Everest, spoke of "recovery from the *ordeal* of that climb." Final examinations at school are *ordeals* that all students must experience. World War II was a terrible *ordeal* for all the nations involved. Waiting for the jury's verdict must be an almost unbearable *ordeal* for the accused.

orient (or´ ee ent—*o* as in *go*, aw-) *vb.* To *orient* a person is to acquaint or familiarize him with his surroundings, or the surrounding circumstances of a situation. New recruits and draftees are *oriented* with the aid of films and lectures. When you first arrive in a new city, it is a good idea to study a map in order to *orient* yourself. It takes some time on the part of the authorities to *orient* freshmen to the trials and tribulations of college life. *Orientate* (or´ ee en tate—*o* as in *go*, awr-) is a variant of *orient*, and is the normal British form; it is hardly ever used in the United States. *Orientation* (or ee en tay´ shən—*o* as in *go*, awr-) is the process of *orienting*, adjustment to a new situation. *Orientation* films and lectures are often used by the armed services for recruits, and by large companies for new employees.

ornate (or nate´) *adj.* An *ornate* piece of seventeenth-century Spanish furniture, or the *ornate* interior of a millionaire's mansion, is richly adorned, with the implication of showiness and ostentation. An *ornate* style of writing is flowery and highflown. The residential architectural style of the Victorian age was characterized by *ornate* "gingerbread" and other ornamentation. It is usually more effective, in court, to keep one's arguments short and to the point, rather than *ornate*, florid, and full of literary allusions. The *ornate* style of the English poet John Milton (1608-1674) makes the meaning of his work obscure to many modern readers.

oust (oust—*ou* as in *mouse*) *vb.* To *oust* someone is to drive him out, expel him, from whatever place or position he occupies. Hecklers are sometimes *ousted* from public meetings. When an infiltrator is spotted in a union or an antigovernment movement, he is immediately *ousted*. Dictators make sure to *oust* potential rivals from office or any position of power. The discovery of an early scandal might *oust* a public figure from the high station he occupies. Foreign "diplomats" who turn out to be secret agents are summarily *ousted* by the offended government.

outspoken (out spoe´ kən) *adj.* *Outspoken* means "frank." *Outspoken* people say what's on their mind. *Outspoken* criticism is frank, unreserved, candid, straight from the shoulder. To *speak out* is to express oneself openly and freely, without hedging. *Outspoken* describes those who have the courage and strength to *speak out*. The forthright comments of the American humorist Will Rogers (1879-1935) on the affairs of the day were good-humored even though *outspoken*. The abolitionists were *outspoken* in their opposition to slavery. It is difficult to be *outspoken* without giving offense.

outstanding (out stan´ ding) *adj.* *Outstanding* has several quite distinct meanings. An *outstanding* scholar is exceptional, prominent in his field; an *outstanding* example is a striking one. Putting men on the moon was the *outstanding* achievement of our times. Marx, Freud, and Einstein were *outstanding* in their influence on modern thought. Used another way, *outstanding* means "still existing, still to be attended to." One's *outstanding* debts are those that remain to be paid. If a person's *outstanding* debts are greater than the value of his assets, he is insolvent. One's *outstanding* duties are those that still have to be attended to. One's *out-*

standing responsibilities are sometimes hard to face. The *outstanding* stocks and bonds of a company are those that have been issued and sold.

overbearing (o vər bare´ ing) *adj.* An *overbearing* person is domineering, arrogant, determined to bend others to his will. An *overbearing* attitude is haughty, rude, dictatorial. Benito Mussolini (1883-1945), *Il Duce*, is the perfect image of the *overbearing* dictator whose word is law. In sentimental Victorian novels, the father—the bewhiskered, haughty, intolerantly *overbearing* head of the family— is a frequent fixture ("Never darken my door again!" etc.).

overt (o´ vurt, ə vurt´—*u* as in *fur*) *adj.* Anything *overt* is out in the open, plain to see, openly done, not concealed. Its opposite is *covert* (kuv´ ərt, koe´ vərt), meaning "concealed, secret." *Overt* action is open to view, clearly visible, unconcealed. *Overt* hostility is a phrase often used in the discussion of international relations. The Germans, before America entered World War II, accused Franklin D. Roosevelt of an act of *overt* hostility in the lend-lease of ships to England. Under the American legal system, a person cannot be convicted for his beliefs or intent, but only for an *overt* act in actual preparation for the illegal objective.

overwhelm (o vər hwelm´) *vb.* Literally, to *overwhelm* is to crush with superior force, to destroy, as the Germans *overwhelmed* Poland and the Polish army in the early days of World War II. Figuratively, to *overwhelm* a person is to dumfound and stagger him, to overcome him in feeling or mind. When someone has been exceedingly kind to you, you may feel *overwhelmed* by his kindness and *overwhelmed* with gratitude. A person can be *overwhelmed* with work, or *overwhelmed* by troubles, or *overwhelmed* by sorrow. Hearing great music or seeing great art for the first time can be an *overwhelming* experience. *Overwhelming* (o vər hwel´ ming), as an adjective, can apply to anyone or anything that *overwhelms*, that is overpowering or stupendous, like an *overwhelming* victory on the field of battle or in sports, or an *overwhelming* majority in an election. Any emotion—joy, grief, relief—can be *overwhelming*, or *overwhelmingly* great. When Abraham Lincoln wrote a letter of consolation to Mrs. Bixby on the loss of her sons in the Civil War, he spoke of her "grief from . . . a loss so *overwhelming*."

pacific (pə sif´ ik) *adj. Pacific* means "peaceful, peace-loving." *Pacific* peoples reject the use of force. The Charter of the United Nations speaks of making "recommendations to the parties with a view to the *pacific* settlement of the dispute." This language harks back to that of the Kellogg Peace Pact of 1928, by which the signing nations renounced war and agreed "that the settlement . . . of all disputes or conflicts . . . [should] never be sought except by *pacific* means." (No comment.)

There are warlike periods and *pacific* eras in the history of a nation. It takes a calm and *pacific* frame of mind to deal reasonably with opposition. Ferdinand Magellan (1480–1521) named the ocean he discovered in 1520 the *Pacific* Ocean because it looked so calm and peaceful when he first caught sight of it. Beware of first impressions: The *Pacific* can be anything but *pacific*!

palatial (pə lay′ shəl) *adj.* This adjective is formed from the noun *palace*. Anything *palatial* is magnificent, stately, like a *palace* or fit for a *palace*. The very rich live in *palatial* homes, full of *palatial* furnishings, and are served *palatial* meals on *palatial* china. If they are very, very rich, they sail the seas in *palatial* yachts. It does not speak well for the distribution of wealth that some live in *palatial* residences while others, perhaps a short distance away, lead wretched existences in hovels. Old Hollywood films were fond of showing poor little rich girls, lonely and sad amid *palatial* surroundings, including the predictable *palatial* limousine.

pallid (pal′ id) *adj.* A *pallid* face is wan, pale, ill-looking. After a long illness, most people have a *pallid* look. Figuratively, *pallid* can mean dull, uninteresting, unexciting, lacking in vigor or sparkle. Even the best of plays will seem dull after a *pallid* performance. Most of what is shown on television is *pallid* fare and can hardly be called entertainment. A friend in need is a friend indeed: superficial "friends" make only *pallid* efforts on your behalf when you're in trouble. *Pallor* (pal′ ər) is the noun related to *pallid* in its literal sense. The faces of people recently released from prison are marked by *pallor*. Fear can drain the blood from a person's cheeks and cause unnatural *pallor*.

pamper (pam′ pər) *v.* To *pamper* someone is to treat him with an excess of attention and kindness, to overindulge him, to be too solicitous, to "spoil" him (in the way one speaks of a "spoiled child"). It is unwise to *pamper* children to the point where they resent the slightest discipline. A *pampered* pet can be an awful nuisance. Sometimes it's fun to *pamper* oneself by sleeping late. The English poet John Dryden (1631–1700) wrote of "the Jews . . . God's *pampered* people," a peculiar notion in view of their centuries of oppression. General Douglas MacArthur (1880–1964) said: "Patiotism . . . cannot be provided by *pampering* or coddling an army, and is not necessarily destroyed by hardship, danger or even calamity." *Pampering* elderly rich relatives is routine procedure for would-be legatees.

pander (pan′ dər) *n., vb.* A *pander* is a pimp. The noun is not much used nowadays; *pimp* or *procurer* is preferred (if one can "prefer" any name for a practitioner of this nasty business). The verb is in common use, however, in a figurative sense, and is usually followed by *to*; to *pander to* someone is to seek to gratify his loose and vulgar tastes, in order to gain his favor. One can be said to *pander to* the person, or to his tastes. Writers and producers who stoop to pornography are *pandering to* the low tastes of readers and moviegoers. There are "romantic" magazines that *pander to* the sentimentality of young women. Comic books *pander to* the uneducated masses. A great deal of contemporary "art" *panders to* the desire of a certain segment of the public to be considered avant-garde.

parlay (par´ lee, par´ lay) *n., vb.* A *parlay* is a bet of an original stake and its subsequent winnings, or a risking of an original investment plus its earnings. There are courageous or lucky people who have turned a *parlay* of a small sum into a fortune. Technically, the verb to *parlay* is to bet the amount of a prior successful bet, plus its winnings, on a subsequent sports (or other) event. Informally, the word is used to cover any situation in which someone cleverly turns a modest initial stake into a fortune. Aristotle Onassis *parlayed* a small sum into one of the world's great shipping fortunes. Senator Joe McCarthy (1908-1957) *parlayed* his anticommunist oratory and drive into blessedly short political prominence. There was once a company that advertised "100 ways to *parlay* a good idea and a little cash into a fortune." Do not confuse *parlay* and *parley*, a conference, usually between leaders of opposing forces.

parody (par´ ə dee—*a* as in *hat*) *n., vb.* A *parody* is a takeoff, a burlesque, a humorous imitation of serious writing, music, acting, a person, a happening. Professional mimics or "impressionists" ("I will now do my impression of . . .") specialize in *parody*. In these cases, the *parody* is intentional; but *paraody* is used in another way, to describe an unintentionally poor and weak imitation. When someone tries to ape the manners of his betters, his conduct is a *parody* of the original. A mediocre painter influenced by a master turns out *parodies* of the other's works. Sadly, the acting of the American actor John Barrymore (1882-1942) in his later years was only a *parody* of its former greatness. The verb to *parody* shares both meanings of the noun. Depending on the context, it may mean either to "imitate humorously," in order to ridicule a person or a style, or to "imitate poorly and unsuccessfully," because of a lack of talent. Children trying to "grow up" too fast *parody* the mannerisms of their elders. It is a fine thing to select a great person as a model, but be careful not to imitate and *parody* his personality.

parry (par´ ee—*a* as in *hat*) *n., vb.* *Parry* is a technical term for a defensive move in fencing, when one of the contestants wards off a thrust from the other. The term is used in boxing to describe the fending off of a blow. The verb to *parry*, in its technical sense, is common in fencing, but it also has a more general, figurative use: to evade, dodge, or sidestep. An adroit witness does his utmost to *parry* the cross-examiner's questions. Children have a way of changing the subject in order to *parry* their parents' inquiries about the decrease in the cookie supply. The art of *parrying* embarrassing questions is a skill worth developing.

passé (pa say´—first *a* as in *hat*) *adj.* This term, borrowed from the French, is used to describe anything or anyone that is dated, outworn, past his or its prime, behind the times. Slang often has a short life; the "with-it" lingo of today can become embarrassingly *passé* before you know it, kiddo! The fashion world sees to it that styles become *passé* with each passing season. In this age of the pocket calculator, simple arithmetic is fast becoming a *passé* skill. Early movies exhibit emotional acting techniques so *passé* as to seem comic.

peer (peer) *n.* A *peer* is an equal, a person of the same class or standing or ability or qualifications. Under the common law, a person is entitled to be judged by a jury of his *peers*. Youngsters tend to conform to the customs of their *peer* group. *Peer* can apply to things as well as people: as a conductor of electricity, copper, at normal temperatures, is *without a peer*. An adjective formed from *peer* is *peerless*, meaning "without equal, unsurpassed, matchless." Laurence Olivier (born 1907; now Lord Olivier) is known for his *peerless* acting. Shakespeare is the *peerless* dramatist. A special use of the noun *peer* is to designate a member of the British and Irish nobility. The Scottish biographer and novelist John Gibson Lockhart (1794–1854) combined the special and general meanings of *peer* in an epitaph for one Patrick ("Peter") Lord Robertson: "Here lies that *peerless peer* Lord Peter,/Who broke the laws of man and God and metre."

perceive (pər seev´) *vb.* To *perceive* is to become aware of someone or something, or to understand or grasp something. If you *perceive* that you can't win, you surrender. You don't have to spend a long time in a man's house to *perceive* whether or not he is a person of refined tastes. What you can *perceive* is *perceptible* (pər sep´ tə b'l) to you. Rome's ancient glory is quickly *perceptible* from a glance at her ancient monuments. Subtle changes in another's mood are *perceptible* to a sensitive person. A *perceptive* (pər sep´ tiv) person is keenly aware of what he sees; he has insight and quickly understands people and gets the point of situations. A *perceptive* person entrusted to report on a situation will present a *perceptive* analysis and appropriate recommendations.

perceptible (pər sep´ tə b'l) *adj.* See perceive.

perceptive (pər sep´ tiv) *adj.* See perceive.

permissive (pər mis´ iv) *adj. Permissive*, meaning "tolerant," is the word used by adults who believe in discipline to describe the relatively tolerant and indulgent way in which other families live and bring up their children. There are those who attribute widespread crime to *permissive* parents or *permissive* schools or the *permissive* attitudes of a *permissive* society. Such people equate the words *permissive* and *lax*; they use *permissive* in a disparaging way. *Permissive* upbringing is thought to be unduly lenient, with parents, schools, and courts shutting their eyes to current social changes like greater sexual freedom, looser law enforcement and censorship, etc. A correct balance must be found between reasonable understanding and unreasonable severity in the training of the young and the enforcement of the law; then perhaps society may discover the correct degree of *permissiveness*, which would then cease to be a derogatory term.

perplex (pər pleks´) *vb.* To *perplex* someone is to puzzle or confuse him. A *perplexed* person is bewildered, filled with doubt and uncertainty; a *perplexed* state of mind is one that is confused and puzzled by what is not grasped or clearly understood. There are lecturers who *perplex* their audiences by assuming that the listeners know more than they actually do; when too much remains unexplained, the audience is *perplexed*. Anything baffling or bewildering or causing doubt and confusion can be described as *perplexing*. There are many *perplexing* questions nowadays about the disturbed condition of the world. A new environment, like college or the army, can be a *perplexing* experience. *Perplexity* (pər plek´ sih tee) is confusion, the state of being *perplexed*. The ever-growing maze of new laws and regulations fills the business community with confusion and *perplexity*.

persist (pər sist´, -zist´) *vb*. When a person *persists* in something, he sticks to it, refuses to make a change despite opposition, stands fast no matter what. When a condition *persists,* it lasts, endures, continues to exist. Despite the mass of medical evidence that smoking is harmful, millions *persist* in the habit. Against all reason, millions *persist* in superstitious beliefs that guide their lives. Churchill rightly *persisted* in the certainty that the Allies would be victorious. Without historical support, there are legends that *persist* for centuries. Migraine is an ailment that *persists* in spite of all attempts at finding a cure. The noun is *persistence* (pər sis´ təns, -zis´-). *Persistence* in the face of hardship and discouragement has won many a battle. The *persistence* of family characteristics through the generations is brought about through the genes. *Persistent* (pər sis´ tənt, -zis´-) is the adjective. A *persistent* door-to-door salesman can be very annoying. There are substances that leave a *persistent* odor long after they are removed. There are *persistent* memories that continue to haunt one long after the events have occurred.

personify (pər son´ ə fy) *vb*. To *personify* something is to typify it, to be an example of it. Scrooge, in *A Christmas Carol,* by the English novelist Charles Dickens (1812–1870), *personifies* miserliness; he is greed and gloom *personified*. *Personification* (pər son ə fə kay´ shən) is the noun, meaning "embodiment." One can express the same thought in several ways: Hitler *personified* evil; Hitler was evil *personified*; Hitler was the *personification* of evil. (It is gratifying to express that thought in three ways!) Winston Churchill was the *personification* of dogged determination and courage. Cf. **embody**.

perspective (pər spek´ tiv) *n*. *Perspective* has several uses. As a technique, *per-* is the art of representing volume and space relationships on a two-dimensional surface so that the viewer gets the impression of both third dimension and distance. A proper drawing or painting or blueprint is done in *perspective*. The concept of the "right relationship" carries over into the more general use of the word, where *perspective* pertains to seeing things in their correct relationship. When you hear a report of a situation, you must visualize it *in perspective,* or *in true perspective,* or in the right or proper *perspective,* i.e., without bias or distortion and without overemphasizing any one aspect of the matter. A judge, particularly, must view the parties, their relationships, and the facts in proper *perspective*. A scientist must view all relevant data in their right *perspective*. A distorted *perspective* will always lead to wrong conclusions.

pertain (pər tāne') *vb.* When something *pertains* to anything, it relates to it, bears upon it, has something to do with it, has some connection with it. In arguing, avoid bringing up matters that do not *pertain* to the point under discussion. In a trial, remarks that do not *pertain* to the case will not be admitted in evidence. Most women are interested in anything *pertaining* to clothes. The adjective is *pertinent* (pur' tə nənt)—*u* as in *fur*). Anything that *pertains* is *pertinent*, relevant. On hearing about a new vacation resort that sounds interesting, one should write for the *pertinent* details. In context, *pertinent* can have the force of the phrase *applicable to today's world*. There are books written centuries ago that are as *pertinent* today as the day they were written. See **irrelevant** and **impertinent**.

phenomenon (fih nom' ə non) *n.* A *phenomenon* is, literally, anything that is observed, as in the expression *the phenomenon of nature*; for example, the *phenomenon* of the "shooting star." But the word has a special use: to describe something or someone impressive, remarkable, extraordinary, one for the book, one in a million. (Note that the word is *phenomenon*; *phenomena* is the plural and should never be used as a singular!) Wolfgang Amadeus Mozart (1756–1791), the Austrian composer, who was writing and playing his own compositions at the age of four, was truly a *phenomenon*. *The Reader's Digest*, published in many languages and with a subscription list in the millions, is a publishing *phenomenon*. The adjective *phenomenal* (fih nom' ə n'l) follows the special sense of the noun: "extraordinary, exceptional, amazing." Bjorn Borg accomplished the *phenomenal* feat of winning six Wimbledon championships in a row. There are books seemingly of no great merit that nevertheless achieve a *phenomenal* sale. Louis Armstrong (1900–1971) was a *phenomenal* trumpet player. It is said that the English historian Thomas Macaulay (1800–1859) had a memory so *phenomenal* that he could memorize a whole page of print at a glance.

pilfer (pil' fər) *vb.* To *pilfer* is to filch, steal in small quantities, practice petty theft. *Pilfering* is petty thievery. It is not unusual for employees to *pilfer* stamps, pencils, and the like from the company. Students have been known to *pilfer* from others in the dormitory. In Shakespeare's *Henry V* (Act I, Scene 2) the Archbishop of Canterbury assures King Henry, who is worried about marauding Scots, that the forces on the border "Shall be a wall sufficient to defend/Our inland from the *pilfering* borderers," whom Henry refers to as the "coursing snatchers," i.e., the petty raiders who "snatch" and run. One would never accuse big-time thieves of *pilfering*; the image is always one of petty theft.

pique (peek) *n., vb. Pique* is annoyance, resentment, particularly a feeling of damage to one's self-esteem, wounded pride. To be *in a pique* or a *fit of pique* is to be in a huff, to take offense. To sit for hours in a doctor's waiting room, or be ignored by a waiter or a salesperson, is enough to put most people *in a pique*. To *pique* someone is to nettle, annoy, offend him, to wound his pride by slighting him. Indifference *piques* most people. It *piques* one not to be invited to a big party given by an old friend. A cliché in domestic comedies is the wife *piqued* by the husband's failure to remember their wedding anniversary.

pittance (pit´ əns—*s* as in *so*) *n.* A *pittance* is a scanty allowance or income or pay, barely enough to scrape by on. Despite minimum-wage laws, there are still sweatshops where people slave day and night for a *pittance*. In these days of inflation, it is difficult to get along on a *pittance*. There are millionaires who spend more in a day than other people's annual *pittance*. Pay scales vary greatly according to profession; teachers' salaries, compared to doctors' incomes, are mere *pittances*.

placid (plas´ id) *adj.* *Placid* describes things and persons that are calm, serene, untroubled, peaceful. The most characteristic aspect of Buddha is his *placid* expression. It is exhilarating to sail over *placid* waters in a stiff breeze. The American poet Elinor Wylie (1885-1928) wrote of "a *placid* lamb lying fast asleep." The American poet Walt Whitman (1819-1892) wrote, "I think I could turn and live with animals, they are so *placid* and self-contain'd. . . ." What is more *placid* than a babe in arms? The *placid* look of the Madonna in old paintings is her most touching feature. *Placidity* (plə sid´ ih tee) is the noun. Lake Placid soon loses its *placidity* in a squall, like the not-so-pacific Pacific Ocean in a gale.

plagiarize (play´ jə rize, -jee ə-) *vb.* To *plagiarize* is to pirate another author's work and pass it off as one's own, to "lift" passages from somebody else's literary efforts. The act is called *plagiarism* (play´ jə riz əm, -jee ə) and the stolen passage a *plagiarism*; the offender is a *plagiarist* (play´ jə rist, -jee ə-). It is one thing for a writer to show the influence of another writer, but quite a different matter to *plagiarize* him. The American humorist Wilson Mizner (1876-1933) said: "When you steal from one another, it's *plagiarism*; if you steal from many, it's research." Imitation may be the sincerest form of flattery, but *plagiarism* is outright theft.

plausible (plaw´ zə b'l) *adj.* This adjective describes anything like an argument, theory, excuse, or alibi that makes sense, is believable, has the ring of truth, whether or not actually true or correct. (See **implausible**.) The Big Bang Theory is a *plausible* explanation of the origin of the universe. Self-defense is often pleaded as the most *plausible* justification of violence. Attending a grandmother's funeral is no longer automatically accepted as a *plausible* excuse for the office boy's absence.

plebeian (plə bee´ ən) *n., adj.* A *plebeian* is one of the common people, as opposed to the aristocracy or upper class. *Plebeian,* as an adjective, describes such a person, but it is used in a more general way to describe anyone or anything common, commonplace, everyday, undistinguished, or vulgar. Most of what comes out of the mouths of politicians is directed at the *plebeians*. The *plebeians* are the backbone of the nation. Most TV commercials are directed at *plebeian* tastes. *Plebeian* jokes are not suitable at aristocratic dinner parties. Our fast-food chains cater to *plebeian* appetites.

plentiful (plen´ tih fəl) *adj.* *Plentiful* describes anything that exists in great quantities, with the implication of overabundance. Ideal weather conditions produce a *plentiful* supply of grain. Aluminum is one of the world's most *plentiful* elements.

The adverb is *plentifully* (plen′ tə fə lee). The *plentiful* meals consumed by our Victorian forefathers produced *plentifully* padded stomachs. In good times, the public contributes *plentifully* to the many charity appeals. *Plenteous* (plen′ tee əs) means the same thing as *plentiful,* but it is somewhat too literary for everyday speech and is better kept for high-flown prose.

plight (plite) *n.* A *plight* is a serious situation or state or condition, a fine mess, a fine kettle of fish, a mess. People who don't think ahead and plan often find themselves in a sorry *plight.* The *plight* of the millions of refugees all over the world is enough to make one despair of the human race. What can be done about the *plight* of the homeless whom we see on our city streets? Robinson Crusoe made the best of a *plight* that would have defeated most men.

ploy (ploy) *n.* A *ploy* is a maneuver or tactic to gain advantage over one's opponent in a game, or to embarrass or frustrate the other person in a conversation; an exercise in gamesmanship or one-upmanship. The English humorist Stephen Potter (1900-1969) wrote books illustrating these techniques. He suggests, for instance, that after just a few moves in a chess game, you use the *ploy* of resigning, with a knowing glance at your superior opponent, in order to lead him to think you've figured things out a dozen moves ahead (when in fact you haven't the least idea what's going on). He also recommends the *ploy* of letting a superb passing shot in tennis go by, with a comradely wink at the other player to indicate that you refrained from hitting it so as not to spoil his fun (you didn't have a prayer of hitting it anyway). There are other *ploys* you can use, at parties, for instance, during some endless discussion among wine experts, exotic cheese devotees, jet-setters, etc.: Invent the name of a nonexistent wine or cheese or South Sea island, and confound the others by affecting astonishment at their having slipped up on that one. All these *ploys* are quite unfair, of course, but they are so satisfying!

poignant (poyn′ yənt, -ənt *adj. Poignant* applies to anything distressing, heart-rending, deeply moving. Though *poignant* can describe any deeply felt emotion, like *poignant* regret or *poignant* disappointment, the most common use is in connection with events or scenes that play on one's heartstrings. In times of sadness, one suffers from the *poignant* recollections of happier times. Charlie Chaplin symbolized the *poignant* figure of the homeless tramp. Old-fashioned Victorian melodrama contrived one *poignant* scene after another, vulgarly known as tear-jerkers. Fallen women, homeless waifs, reunited long-lost parent and child—these were the stock characters of those *poignant* scenes. The noun is *poignancy* (poyn′ yən see, -en-), equivalent to *pathos.* The *poignancy* of the condition of millions of refugees has appealed to the conscience of the favored nations of the world.

poise (poyz) *n. Poise* is quiet self-possession, self-confidence, composure, particularly in a difficult situation. Children tend to be shy in the presence of strangers; *poise* may develop with maturity. It takes a lot of self-control for a person not to lose his *poise* under any circumstances. The *poise* of a football quarterback under a blitz attack is difficult for a layman to comprehend. To be *poised* can mean several things. *Poised* may mean "composed": A *poised* person will not "lose his cool" in a tight spot; an experienced actor will remain *poised* despite a disturbance in the audience. *Poised* means "balanced" when one speaks of a ball or a billiard cue kept motionless on a juggler's forehead; a bird is *poised* in flight when it hovers in the air. To be *poised for* something is to be on the verge of it. A man *poised for* an important step in his career is about to take that step.

polish (pol'ish) *n., vb.* Apart from its common use as both noun and verb in matters referring to making surfaces shiny, *polish* has to do with refinement and elegance. *Polish,* in this latter sense, refers to superiority in manners and education, elegance of dress and behavior, and refinement generally. True *polish* exists when crude manners and ignorance are absent. *Polish* can also refer to the quality of an artistic performance. *Polish* is an ingredient in the work of truly great actors, singers, musicians, and dancers. In this connection, we know that a serious artist is continually at work *polishing* his or her skill in order to be able to give a *polished* performance. If someone has neglected a skill and wants to recover it, he *polishes up on* it. Before going to France, a person with a smattering of French would do well to *polish up on* it.

polygamy (pə lig'ə mee) *n.* See **monogamy**.

ponder (pon'dər) *vb.* To *ponder* something is to consider it carefully and seriously, to weigh it thoughtfully, to think long and hard about it. Before taking an important step, a person should *ponder* all the alternatives. A witness under oath should *ponder* his answers. *Ponder* implies quiet, sober, deep thoughts, and when followed by *over, upon,* or *on,* suggests serious meditation. In many of life's situations, one must take into account not only the legal considerations; one must also *ponder over* the moral issues. As a person grows older, he often *ponders upon* earlier incidents that shaped his life. The American poet and short-story writer Edgar Allan Poe (1809–1849) began his famous poem "The Raven": "Once upon a midnight dreary, while I *pondered* weak and weary,/Over many a quaint and curious volume of forgotten lore. . . ." *Ponder* was used again in the context of night, fatigue, and deep and serious thought by the English painter and poet William Morris (1834–1896) in his poem "Sir Galahad": "It is the longest night in all the year, . . ./Six hours ago I came and sat down here,/And *ponder'd* sadly, wearied and forlorn."

populace (pop'yə ləs) *n.* See **populous**.

populous (pop'yə ləs) *adj. Populous* describes any densely populated, thickly settled community or region. New York used to be the most *populous* state in the union, but it has now been overtaken by California. Japan is the most *populous* (most densely populated) country in the world. The English poet Percy Bysshe Shelley (1792–1822) wrote:

Hell is a city much like London—
a *populous* and smoky city.

Populous is also used at times as the equivalent of *numerous*. American Indians are said to be more *populous* now than they were at the time of the white man's first appearance. Do not confuse *populous* with *populace*, which is pronounced in exactly the same way, and means "the general public, the masses." The American poet Walt Whitman (1819–1892) described "the *populace* [rising] . . . against the never-ending audacity of elected persons." President John Adams (1735–1826) wrote: "The law . . . is . . . inflexible, . . . 'tis deaf . . . to the clamors of the *populace*."

portray (pore tray´, pawr-) *vb.* A *portrait* painter *portrays* the subject; a novelist *portrays* a scene by vivid description; an actor *portrays* a character. In all these cases, to *portray* is to *represent* people or things, by one means or another, and the noun is *portrayal* (pore tray´ əl, pawr-). The Puritan statesman Oliver Cromwell (1599–1658) told the Dutch painter Sir Peter Lely (1618–1680) that he wanted to be *portrayed* with all his "roughnesses, pimples, warts, and everything as you see me." (Cromwell's words are usually misquoted as "warts and all.") Most great actors aspire to *portray* Hamlet. A true *portrayal* on the stage must show the audience the essence of the characters being *portrayed*. The English novelist Charles Dickens (1812–1870) vividly *portrayed* the hardships suffered by the London poor. Experienced war reporters chill their readers with detailed *portrayals* of the horrors of the battlefield.

poseur (poe zur´—*u* as in *fur*) *n.* A *poseur* is an affected person, who pretends to be what he isn't in order to impress other people. *Poseurs* assume attitudes, opinions, manners, mannerisms, dress, and elegance that are not genuine. They *pose* as connoisseurs of art, or as gourmets with a taste in fine food and wine, or as experts in fashion and design. *Poseurs* are cultural phonies; it must be very satisfying to unmask one.

precedent (pres´ ih dənt) *n.* A *precedent* is a previous instance or situation that serves as a justification for subsequent action. When in doubt about what action to take, people normally look for a *precedent*. The prior instance *sets a precedent*. When someone decides to do something the way it was done previously, he is *following a precedent*. In law, court decisions are usually made in accord with previous decisions, which are known as *precedents*. The earlier decision is said to *set a precedent*. The later one is *supported by a precedent*.

precise (prih sise´) *adj.* The adjective can be used in a number of ways. *Precise* instructions are exactly stated; *precise* measurements are absolutely correct. The *precise* moment is the exact time. Why does the telephone ring at the *precise* moment that I am going out the front door? A *precise* person is a very careful one, determined to make no mistakes. The noun *precision* (prih sizh´ ən) partakes of all the meanings of the adjective. In general, *precision* means "accuracy." The noun is sometimes used as an adjective in expressions like a *precision instrument* (one that works *with precision*), or *precision flying, precision marching* (team exercises in *precise* formation). The adverb *precisely* (prih sise' lee) follows the meanings of the adjective. Used alone as a response, it shows agreement with a statement made, meaning "Exactly!" or "Right!"

preclude (prih klood'—*oo* as in *boot*) *vb*. To *preclude* something is to prevent it from happening, to make it impossible, rule it out. Children's illnesses sometimes *preclude* an athletic career. Clear statements on both sides of an argument will *preclude* misunderstanding. Bad weather often *precludes* traveling. Intense devotion to one's work *precludes* a great deal of social activity. The noun *preclusion* (prih kloo' zhən—*oo* as in *boot*) means "prevention, forestalling." Getting a corner on the market results in the *preclusion* of an adequate supply to other dealers.

prejudicial (prej ə dish' əl) *adj*. To *prejudice* someone is to cause him to have an opinion about someone or something (a letter may *prejudice* the reader in your favor or against you); to *prejudice* something is to act to its disadvantage (an inadequate childhood diet *prejudices* one's chances for robust health). *Prejudicial* follows the latter meaning of the verb: Anything *prejudicial* is harmful, damaging, detrimental, and acts to the disadvantage of the person or thing involved. Smoking is *prejudicial* to health. Lack of education is *prejudicial* to one's career. Poor reviews are *prejudicial* to a show's chances of success.

preliminary (prih lim' ə nerr ee) *n., adj*. *Preliminary*, as an adjective, describes things that come first and lead up to the principal matter. Speakers usually get down to the main subject after a few *preliminary* remarks. When one is embarking on a venture, whether a business matter or a vacation trip, there are always *preliminary* steps that have to be taken. A *preliminary* boxing match is a minor affair preceding and leading up to the main event. The match can be described as a *preliminary*, using the word as a noun. *The preliminaries* is an expression describing the actions or measures to be taken before getting down to the main business. Conferees spend a great deal of time attending to the *preliminaries* before settling down to a discussion of the actual subject matter of the conference. In the SALT talks, the delegates seem to devote an astonishing amount of time to wrangling about the agenda and other *preliminaries* (while those buttons remain within frighteningly easy reach of nervous fingers).

premise (prem' iss) *n*. A *premise* is a statement or an assumption on the basis of which a conclusion is reached. All horses have four feet; Man-o'-War was a horse; therefore, Man-o'-War had four feet. "All horses have four feet" is a *premise*, a basis for the conclusion that that particular horse had four feet. It's cold in December (at least in the north); this is December 21; so baby, it's cold outside. "It's cold in December" is a *premise* leading to that conclusion. In the plural, *premises* means a parcel of land or the buildings on it. "These *premises* are protected by the Jones Alarm Co." ought to keep the burglars out. A tenant with too much space tries to sublet part of the *premises*.

prepossessing (pree pə zes´ ing) *adj*. *Prepossessing* describes anyone or anything that makes a favorable impression and tends to please. It is pleasant to enter a building with a *prepossessing* interior. A rosy-cheeked young person with sparkling eyes cuts a *prepossessing* figure. A *prepossessing* person is immediately attractive, and not only is pleasing in appearance, but somehow gains your confidence as well. One doesn't have to be good-looking to be *prepossessing*: one of the most *prepossessing* characters in the theater is poor old Cyrano de Bergerac of the mighty nose, in the play by the French dramatist Edmond Rostand (1868-1918). *Prepossessing* comes from *prepossess*, a verb not in common use except in the *-ing* form.

preposterous (prih pos´ tər əs, -trəs) *adj*. *Preposterous* is another way of saying "absurd, ridiculous, senseless." Baron von Munchausen (1720-1797), the German adventurer, became famous as the teller of *preposterous* tales. When *preposterous* things happen in fiction, don't hold it against the author; remember that truth is still stranger. Hitler and his adoring public subscribed to the *preposterous* racial theory of "Aryanism." It seems to many that astrology is a *preposterous* guide to life. The English poet Samuel Butler (1612-1680) invented a *preposterous* form of *preposterous* in his "Satire upon the Weakness and Misery of Man":

> The best of all our actions tend
> To the *preposterouest* end.

prerequisite (prih rek´ wih zit) *n., adj*. *Prerequisite* applies to anything required beforehand as a condition for something else. College entrance examinations are *prerequisite* (or *a prerequisite*) for admission to most universities. Certain basic courses are *prerequisites* for taking advanced courses on the same subject. A valid passport is *prerequisite* (or *a prerequisite*) for travel abroad. A deep understanding of human nature is a *prerequisite* for anyone entering the practice of psychiatry. Good health is a *prerequisite* for a career in sports. A *prerequisite* can be a technical requirement, like a passport, or a requirement in the very nature of things, like health for a sports career.

prestige (preh steezh´, -steej´) *n*. *Prestige* is the respect that comes with achievement and success, and the accompanying distinction and influence. *Prestige* is status and clout. Public success, whether in politics, the theater, television, the movies, the sciences, or the financial world, brings with it glory and *prestige*. One must avoid the kind of scandal that may result in a loss of *prestige*. A distinguished address, or the ownership of a very expensive automobile, can confer *prestige* among those who are automatically swayed by that type of status symbol. Those who hanker after *prestige* and influence agree with Julius Caesar (100-44 B.C.) who said, according to the English philosopher Francis Bacon (1561-1626), "that he had rather be first in a village than second in Rome."

pretense (prih tens´, pree´-) *n. Pretense* is pretending. When a person acts *under a pretense*, he is only pretending, making a false show. Flag-waving profiteers act under only a *pretense* of patriotism. A self-seeking person will do small favors under a *pretense* of friendship. In another context, a *pretense* can mean a false excuse or justification: An unfaithful husband may "stay in town" on a *pretense* of important business. In law, it is a crime to obtain money *under false pretenses*, i.e., by deception of any sort, like making false statements about the quality of merchandise, or claiming to be qualified when one is not, etc. The related adjective, *pretentious* (prih ten´ shəs), has a different twist and is usually understood in the sense of "pompous, showoffish." The newly rich have a habit of moving into *pretentious* homes. Old-fashioned politicians had a way of indulging in *pretentious* oratory. There are *pretentious* critics who are not worth one little finger of the works they *pretentiously* slam. The opposite of *pretentious* is, not surprisingly, *unpretentious*, which describes people and things that are simple and unaffected. Abraham Lincoln, like many great people, was a straightforward, *unpretentious* man. One feels comfortable in a quiet, cozy, *unpretentious* home.

pretentious (prih ten´ shəs) *adj.* See **pretense**.

pretext (pree´ tekst) *n.* A *pretext* is a subterfuge, a false reason given to justify an action, in order to conceal its true purpose or motive. "A previous engagement" is the usual *pretext* for turning down an invitation from people you can't stand. Hitler invaded Poland under the *pretext* that she was menacing Germany's border. Philandering husbands use the *pretext* of a crowded business schedule to justify staying in town after office hours. The Irish statesman and orator Edmund Burke (1729–1797) wrote: "Tyrants seldom want [i.e., lack] *pretexts*."

prevail (prih vale´) *vb. Prevail* has a number of uses. When it is said that the color green *prevails* in the countryside, *prevail* is a way of saying "is common, widespread, the dominant note." When the teacher walks into the classroom, the hum of conversation stops and silence *prevails*, i.e., exists throughout the classroom. When people heard of the death of Franklin D. Roosevelt, sadness *prevailed* all over the country, i.e., was widespread. *Prevail* may also mean to "be victorious, to triumph." To *prevail* over an opponent is to win out: The Allies *prevailed* over the Axis in World War II. In the long run, virtue *prevails* over evil. To *prevail upon* someone is to *persuade* or convince him: We often read that a mother *prevails upon* her fugitive son to surrender to the police. If your friend has had one too many, do your best to *prevail upon* him to let someone else do the driving. *Prevailing* can be used as an adjective meaning "current" or "usual" or "predominant." Each region has its *prevailing* winds. The *prevailing* fashion in skirts is mini, wide, or maxi, depending upon the whims of the designers. It is the *prevailing* opinion of those in power, alas, that the nations have to go on building atomic weapons. At the end of the Vietnam War, a *prevailing* wave of disillusionment swept the United States. *Prevailing* can often be interchanged with *prevalent* (prev´

ə lənt), meaning "widespread, generally accepted," as in *prevalent style, prevalent opinion, prevalent attitude.* Sadly, smoking is still *prevalent* among the youth.

prevalent (prev´ ə lənt) *adj.* See prevail.

primary (pry´ merr ee, -mər-) *adj.* What is *primary* is first in importance. The *primary* goal in life is happiness. The *primary* aim of this book is to enrich your vocabulary. *Primary* may also express the concept of *first in time,* i.e., *original.* A word has a *primary* meaning, and often develops secondary meanings. The *primary* meaning of *kiss* is clear to everyone. In phrases like *the kiss of death* or *to kiss someone* or *something off, kiss* has developed secondary meanings. The family unit is the *primary* social organization. It is obvious from these examples that in certain cases, *primary* can, at one and the same time, express both concepts: *first in time* and *first in importance.* The adverb *primarily* (pry mar´ ə lee—*a* as in *Mary,* pry´ merr ə lee) means "chiefly, principally." Interior decorators are *primarily* interested in the colors of the bindings, rather than the contents of books. The importance of the city of Detroit derives *primarily* from automobile manufacturing. Kansas was once *primarily* an agricultural state, but now manufacturing is its main activity.

problematical (prob lə mat´ ik əl) *adj.* Also *problematic* (prob lə mat´ ik). *Problematical* is a description of anything involving uncertainty or doubt, anything questionable or dubious. After all the effort that has been made to bring peace to the Middle East, its future remains *problematical.* Whether the United States should have become involved in the Vietnam War is *problematical.* The success of any of the conflicting economic theories now current is *problematical.*

procrastinate (proe kras´ tə nate) *vb.* To *procrastinate* is to delay action, to keep putting things off. (The second syllable, *-cras-,* is Latin for *tomorrow.* Don't *procrastinate*—never put off till *tomorrow,* etc.) At the first sign of a potentially serious ailment, don't *procrastinate*—call a doctor before it's too late. The English statesman and author Lord Chesterfield (1694–1773) wrote: "One yawns, one *procrastinates,* one can do it when one will, and therefore one seldom does it at all." The noun is *procrastination* (proe kras tə nay´ shən). According to the English poet Edward Young (1683–1765), "*Procrastination* is the thief of time." The American novelist and poet Don Marquis (1878–1937) put it this way:

> *procrastination* is the
> art of keeping
> up with yesterday

(This is a maxim of Archy, the cockroach, who was too light to depress the shift key on the typewriter for capitals and punctuation marks.)

procure (proe kyoor´—*oo* as in *look*) *vb.* To *procure* is to obtain, especially with special care, effort, or means. When a lawyer is preparing for trial, he does his best to *procure* all possible evidence that bolsters his case. There are special bookshops that will go to great lengths to *procure* out-of-print books for their customers. *Procure* has a special meaning in the field of sex: to obtain prostitutes for men. The noun *procurer* (proe kyoor' ər—*oo* as in *look*) reflects this latter, ugly sense: a *procurer* is a pimp.

profound (prə found´) *adj. Profound,* generally speaking, means *"deep,"* and like *deep,* can be used in a variety of ways. When you listen to a speaker with *profound* interest, you are deeply attentive. To take a *profound* interest in someone's career is to follow it closely. Loyal cooperation through thick and thin deserves *profound* gratitude. A *profound* treatment of a subject is one that goes into it thoroughly. A *profound* thinker is one who enters deeply into the matter at hand. A person of *profound* insight sees the crux of the subject and covers all the angles. The noun is *profundity* (prə fun´ dih tee). The *profundity* of Einstein's thought baffles even intelligent minds. The noun is not in common use, but the adverb *profoundly* (prə found´ lee), in the sense of "deeply," though rather formal, is heard fairly often: The winning candidate was *profoundly* grateful for the hard work of his campaigners; the president of the company found the latest sales reports *profoundly* disturbing.

profuse (prə fyoos´—*oo* as in *boot*) *adj.* Anything described as *profuse* is plentiful or abundant. South Africa is well known for its *profuse* variety of valuable minerals. English gardens make a *profuse* show of colorful flowers. On arriving late for a dinner party, a polite guest may embarrass his hostess by offering *profuse* apologies. Applied to a person, *profuse* takes on the meaning of "extravagant" or "lavish." When a critic sees truly great potential in a young artist, he should be *profuse* in his praise in order to encourage him in his efforts. The noun *profusion* (prə fyoo´ zhən—*oo* as in *boot*) means "abundance." Wild flowers grow in *profusion* in the countryside. It is amusing to poke around in an antiques shop where the merchandise is piled in disordered *profusion.* The English novelist Evelyn Waugh (1903–1966), in his travel book *Labels,* praised the meals on his ship, describing a table "laden with every kind of Scandinavian delicatessen, smoked salmon . . . cold game . . . sausage . . . salad . . . cold asparagus in almost disconcerting *profusion.*" When you walk into the cosmetics department of a shop, you are greeted by a *profusion* of odors. (Ditto for the cheese department.)

prophecy (prof´ ih see) *n.;* **prophesy** (prof´ ih sy) *vb.* Note the difference in spelling and pronunciation between the noun and the verb. *Prophecy* is the prediction (in general) of things to come. *Prophets* have the gift of *prophecy.* A *prophecy* is a particular prediction. The French astrologer Nostradamus (1503–1566) is famous for his *prophecies* of things to come. (Today we have to cope with Jeanne M. Dixon.) To *prophesy* is to predict or foretell. Weathermen *prophesy* tomorrow's weather. Hitler *prophesied* that the Third Reich would last a thousand years. His *prophecy* turned out to be wrong by 990 years or so. Both *prophecy* and *prophesy* are based on the noun *prophet* (prof´ it), which, apart from its Biblical meaning, applies to anyone who predicts what is to come. From *prophet* we get the adjective *pro-*

phetic (prə fet´ ik), describing statements or events that foretell what is to happen. The utterances of Jeremiah were *prophetic* of the woes that were to befall Israel. Black clouds are *prophetic* of a coming storm. The American poet James Russell Lowell (1819–1891) gave this advice: "Don't never *prophesy*—onless ye know." (The grammar and spelling are—intentionally, of course—bad, but the advice is good!)

prospect (pros´ pekt) *n.* This word is usually found in the plural, meaning "outlook." In every recession, the administration likes to emphasize the *prospects* for an early recovery. In 1937 and 1938, the *prospects* of war were ominous. In the singular, *prospect* can be used in a variety of ways. It can mean "expectation": the family waits anxiously for the doctor to announce the *prospect* of the patient's recovery. *In prospect* means "expected": a sudden drop in unemployment is not *in prospect* during a recession. What is *in prospect* for you at the moment? What is the *prospect* of your paying me an early visit? *Prospect* can be used to mean "potential customer" or "client": A customer (or client) who seems about to take the bait is a *good prospect*; a doubting Thomas is a *poor prospect*. The adjective *prospective* (prə spek´ tiv) means "likely" or "potential"; it describes something that will happen one day, or someone who, it appears, will occupy a certain position in the near future. The *prospective* earnings of a company are a most important factor in determining the price of its shares. The person with the best chance of nomination is the *prospective* candidate. A fiancée is a *prospective* bride.

providential (prov ih den´ shəl) *adj.* Providence is God's care of His creatures. Literally, *providential* describes anything pertaining to that care, or resulting from it. Thus, a *providential* recovery from illness or a *providential* escape from disaster is a recovery or escape attributed to divine intervention. But the word has been extended to mean "lucky" or "timely" in general, without reference to God. The *providential* winning of a lottery may save a person from bankruptcy. A *providential* storm at sea was accountable for the English defeat of the Spanish Armada in 1588. A *providential* peek into this book may save you from an embarrassing blunder.

provisional (prə vizh´ ə n'l) *adj.* Anyone or anything *provisional* is temporary, existing or serving for the time being, to be replaced in due time. A *provisional* government will serve for the present, until order is restored and proper election arrangements can be made. A *provisional* remedy is one that, it is hoped, will prevent further deterioration until a proper cure can be found. *Provisional* arrangements are acceptable for the moment and the existing situation, but are always meant to be nullified in favor of final arrangements as soon as circumstances permit.

provoke (prə voke´) *vb.* Provoke has several shades of meaning. To *provoke* a person is to make him angry, or at least to annoy him greatly. The same is true of *provoking* an animal: Don't *provoke* a dog if you don't want to be nipped. *Provoke* has a much milder use when it means simply "cause" or "arouse." Continued warm, humid weather *provokes* a feeling of languor and laziness. The sight of a person slipping on a banana peel is sure to *provoke* amusement. Shouting "Fire!" in a crowded auditorium will *provoke* panic. One can *provoke* a person into doing something. An impudent manner can *provoke* anger. *Provocation* (prov ə kay′ shən) is the act of *provoking*, or anything that *provokes*, i.e., annoys or angers or, less specifically, causes something to happen. Some people get angry at the slightest *provocation*. When you are *provoked*, what you do is done under *provocation*. *Provocation* is a technical defense in criminal law. It may be used, for instance, to demonstrate that a homicide was committed not deliberately, but in hot anger as a reaction to something infuriating. The adjective is *provocative* (prə vok′ ə tiv), describing anything that tends to arouse anger, hot argument, or interest. A *provocative* remark may enrage the other person, or at least result in angry discussion. Applied to female charms, *provocative* takes on the more specific nuance of "suggestive": *Provocative* dress, comment, or makeup, or a way of moving, or conduct generally, can induce a male to make advances.

prudent (proo′ d'nt—*oo* as in *boot*) *adj.* A *prudent* person is wise and cautious; a *prudent* act or decision is made after careful consideration of all the angles. Every business needs a *prudent* manager. *Prudent* spending will conserve one's assets. Ignore the get-rich-quick route and select only *prudent* investments. *Prudence* (proo′ d'ns) is careful forethought, good judgment, regard for one's own interests. *Prudence* in the management of one's affairs is the best way to avoid complications. William Ralph Inge (1860-1954), the Dean of St. Paul's Cathedral in London (known as the "Gloomy Dean"), said: "We can dream that the future will realize all our hopes, though *prudence* might suggest that as it [the future] is not yet born, it is too early to baptize it." "Look before you leap" is the most common motto in praise of *prudence*—but remember: nothing ventured, nothing gained!

pungent (pun′ jənt) *adj.* This adjective, describing smells or tastes, means "sharp, tart, acrid"; applied to remarks, it means "stinging, caustic, biting." There are many who enjoy the *pungent* sauces used in Mexican cooking. Who, even among confirmed smokers, can stand the *pungent* reek of a cheap cigar? The American journalist William Allan White (1868-1944) was noted for his *pungent* editorials. S. J. Perelman, the American humorist (1904-1979), was a master of *pungent* satire. *Pungent* wit is that which stimulates the mind. The two Irish dramatists Oscar Wilde (1854-1900) and George Bernard Shaw (1856-1950) wrote plays full of *pungent* wit. The noun is *pungency* (pun′ jən see). Audiences are stirred by the *pungency* of witty dialogue.

purist (pyoor′ ist—*oo* as in *look*) *n.* A *purist* is a stickler who insists on correct practice, especially in language. Depending on the point of view, a *purist* is a devoted guardian of correct language usage or a pedant showing off his learning, but there is a wide difference between the two. *Purists* offend people who aren't as fussy as they. "It's me" is good enough for most; the *purist* might insist on "It's I," though it sounds awkward. *Whom* is going out of style; the *purist* uses it when it is grammatically proper. The activity of *purists* is *purism* (pyoor´ izm—*oo* as in *look*), and it is all too often used as a term of abuse, like *pedant*. One hundred percent *purism* is practically nonexistent, according to the British lexicographer W. H. Fowler (1858-1933), who wrote: "Almost every man is potentially a *purist* and a sloven [sluv´ ən: a slipshod person] at once to persons looking at him from a lower and a higher position . . . than his own." The term *purist* is often flung by those whose own level gives them no right to criticize. Language is not the only area in which the *purist* operates: It can be in any field, from cooking to sailing. Polonius, giving advice to his son, Laertes, in Shakespeare's *Hamlet* (Act I, Scene 3), might have added: "Better a *purist* than a sloven be." (Apologies to W. S.)

pursuit (pər soot´—*oo* as in *boot*) *n. Pursuit* has a number of uses. In the physical sense, *pursuit* is chase. In the sport of fox-hunting, the hounds run in *pursuit* of the fox. In the field, cats are skillful and persistent in *pursuit* of mice. *Pursuit* of criminals is the theme of many a TV show. *Pursuit* can mean "effort to achieve," as in "life, liberty and the *pursuit* of happiness." The *pursuit* of knowledge is one of the man's greatest endeavors; the *pursuit* of pleasure, one of his least. A third meaning is "occupation" or "field of activity." Literary *pursuits* are usually less profitable than a career in business. Among the professions, medicine and law are more lucrative *pursuits* than teaching. The related verb *pursue* (pər soo´—*oo* as in *boot*) shares all the meanings of the noun. Cops *pursue* robbers; people *pursue* pleasure; men and women *pursue* various professions. *Pursue* has the figurative meaning of "follow," when we say that bad luck has *pursued* a person all his life, or a criminal record can *pursue* one wherever he goes.

quack (kwak) *n., adj.* A *quack* is a person who dishonestly claims qualifications and skills, particularly in the medical field. There are *quacks* in many kinds of medical practice, from quick weight reduction to plastic surgery to cancer cures. *Quack* usually means "phony doctor," but both as noun and adjective, it can apply to fraudulent pretending in any field. As a general term, *quack* applies to anyone claiming to be an expert in a field that he knows little or nothing about. There are *quack* scientists, *quack* politicians, *quack* sociologists. We are constantly being offered *quack* remedies for the ills of the world. One must do one's best to distinguish between *quacks* and experts.

quadruped (kwod´ roo ped—*oo* as in *look*) *n.* See **biped**.

quail (kwale) *vb.* To *quail* is to shrink with fear, to cower, to lose heart in the face of danger, difficulty, or a show of strength. Even her strongest courtiers *quailed* before an angry look from Queen Elizabeth I of England. The youth David never *quailed* before the giant Goliath. Sailors *quail* at the sight of angry clouds and the sound of howling winds. As the market plunges, speculators *quail* at the prospect of financial ruin. This expressive verb has nothing whatever to do with the little game bird that sportsmen love to shoot.

quest (kwest) *n.* A *quest* is a search, whether a physical *quest* for something material, like gold, or a mental *quest* for something abstract, like knowledge or peace of mind. The Gold Rush of 1849 was a disorganized, greedy mass *quest* for sudden wealth. The *quest* for the Holy Grail is the source of many legends about the Knights of the Round Table. Birds of all species go off in *quest* of food for their young. The *quest* for knowledge is one of the great activities of man. Sir William Osler (1849-1919), the Canadian physician, said: "The *quest* for righteousness is Oriental, the *quest* for knowledge Occidental." The United Nations was established in *quest* of a lasting peace.

quiver (kwiv´ ər) *n., vb.* To *quiver* is to tremble, to shake, to flutter. A *quiver* is a trembling or fluttering. As a great actor makes his first entrance, the audience *quivers* with anticipation; one can feel the *quiver* in the air. In *The Lady of Shalott*, Alfred, Lord Tennyson (1809-1892) wrote:

> Willows whiten, aspens *quiver*,
> Little breezes dusk and shiver
> Thro' the wave that runs forever
> By the island in the river
> Flowing down to Camelot.

The wings of a moth *quiver* so rapidly that they become almost invisible. The *quivering* hummingbird, sipping from a blossom, is one of the most beautiful sights in nature. One can *quiver* from fear, from excitement, from joy, from any deep emotion.

radiate (ray´ dee ate) *vb.* To *radiate* something is to emit *rays* of it, as a stove *radiates* warmth, or an electric bulb *radiates* light. The verb is used figuratively in the sense of "spread" or "project," in the way that the image of Santa Claus *radiates* good cheer, merriment, and love, or eyes *radiate* happiness and contentment, or a leader *radiates* courage and enthusiasm. It is not only cheer and joy that can be *radiated*: A slum scene *radiates* hardship and gloom, the figure of Judas *radiates* deceit and treachery. But the related adjective *radiant* (ray´ dee ənt) describes only looks that shine with happiness, love, and hope. The Madonna, in paintings, is shown with a tender, *radiant* face. The English-born (now American) poet and novelist Christopher Isherwood (born 1904) described a character as "*radiant*, like a schoolboy who has received an unexpectedly large tip." F. Scott Fitzgerald, the American novelist (1896–1940), wrote of "gray eyes, full of a *radiant* curiosity."

radiant (ray′ dee ənt) *adj.* See **radiate**.

radical (rad′ ih kəl) *n., adj.* A *radical* change of policy is a fundamental, thorough, extreme shift. Literally, *radical* means "from the root," and a *radical* change or shift is "from the root," i.e., from the ground up. The adverb *radically* (rad′ ih kə lee) means "thoroughly." Abraham Lincoln felt that slavery was *radically* immoral. Economic theories differ *radically*. *Radical* has a special use in political theory: The *radical* view is in favor of fundamental economic and social reforms. The American poet Robert Frost (1874–1963) wrote, "I never dared be *radical* when young / For fear it would make me conservative when old." *Radical* is also used as a noun, to designate a person holding such views. A *radical* is in favor of overthrowing the current social order. The term *radical* is at times applied to a person holding extremist views in any situation or environment. A college professor who wants to eliminate all examinations might be called a *radical*, regardless of his political views.

rancor (rang′ kər) *n. Rancor* is deeply felt, long-lasting, bitter resentment and ill will, deep-seated enmity. It was the *rancor* between the Capulet and Montague families, in Shakespeare's *Romeo and Juliet*, that led to the final tragedy. In Act II, Scene 3, Friar Laurence is willing to help the young lovers, "For this alliance may . . . turn your households' rancour [British spelling] to pure love." The Spanish philosopher and journalist José Ortega y Gasset (1883–1955) wrote: "*Rancor* is an outpouring of a feeling of inferiority." Psychologists attribute Hitler's implacable *rancor* to his deep-seated inferiority complex. The *rancor* of Lenin and Trotsky and their followers against the aristocracy led to the Russian revolution. A person full of *rancor* is *rancorous* (rang′ kər əs), meaning "resentful, bitter, unforgiving." The *rancorous* emotions displayed in the heat of political campaigning seem to dissipate soon after the elections.

random (ran′ dəm) *adj. Random* applies to anything done without system or definite method. Some people have systems in playing roulette or choosing lottery numbers; others simply indulge in *random* selection. *Random*-width floorboards make a more interesting pattern than boards of uniform width. To test the condition of merchandise purchased in bulk, buyers resort to *random* sampling. English country lanes follow the *random* paths originally taken by cattle. The expression *at random* means "haphazardly," and applies to things done without method or specific arrangement. German bombers returning home from their missions in World War II unloaded their unused bombs *at random* as they flew back over enemy territory.

rational (rash′ ə nəl) *adj.* To be *rational* is to be sane, sensible, reasonable, logical. When we say that man is a *rational* animal, we mean that human beings have reasoning power. A *rational* way of doing things is a sensible, reasonable way. *Rational* behavior is a sensible way of conducting oneself. The Civil Defense authorities are charged with the duty of formulating *rational* evacuation plans. A *rational* explanation of a situation is one based on reasoning. *Rational* can be used as a synonym for *sane* or *lucid*, as distinguished from *insane*, in describing a patient is the psychiatric ward. Civilized life is the triumph of the *rational* over the emotional side of mankind. The American poet and novelist Elinor Wylie (1885–1928) wrote of a man with "a mind so purely *rational* that it had . . . received absolute divorce from his naturally impetuous heart." See also **irrational**.

ravage (rav′ ij) *n., vb. Ravage* is destruction, devastation, but the noun is not often found in the singular. It is commonly used in the plural, denoting the destructive effects or ruinous damage caused by an event or the passage of time. *Ravage* is pretty serious stuff. We are all too familiar with the *ravages* of war, the *ravages* of floods or forest fires, the *ravages* of centuries on the great palaces and monuments of antiquity. As a verb, to *ravage* is to destroy, work havoc. Hitler's retreating armies were ordered to *ravage* everything along their path. The Black Plague *ravaged* Europe in the sixteenth century. Who has not recoiled at the sight of a once fine face now *ravaged* by drink?

ravish (rav′ ish) *vb.* This verb has some startlingly different meanings: To *ravish* someone is to enchant or to fill him or her with delight, but to *ravish* a woman can also mean to "carry her off by force," or even to rape her. The two meanings, "enchant" and "carry off by force," come together in the sense that, in either case, a lady on the receiving end of the action is "carried away." The rape part, however, cannot be very enchanting. *Ravishing,* used as an adjective to mean "enchanting, bewitching," is by far the commonest form of this word. It was the *ravishing* beauty of Helen of Troy that, according to legend, brought about the Trojan war. The *ravishing* views of Capri and Sorrento have lured millions of tourists to southern Italy.

realm (relm) *n.* Literally, a *realm* is a kingdom, as in the *realm* of England or the *realm* of Saudi Arabia. In England, one hears the expressions *defence of the realm* (note British spelling of *defence*) or a *Peer of the Realm. Realm* is used figuratively in the sense of "region." They say that a perfect world belongs only to the *realm* of the imagination. *Realm* can also denote the specialty or sphere of someone or something: Einstein's work lay in the *realm* of mathematics. It is difficult at times to know whether certain facts are in the *realm* of sociology or that of politics. The American poet William Cullen Bryant (1794–1878) described the afterlife as "that mysterious *realm*"; John of Gaunt, in the famous eulogy in Shakespeare's *Richard II* (Act II, Scene 1), speaks of his native land as ". . . This royal throne of kings, this scepter'd isle,/ . . . This blessed plot, this earth, this *realm,* this England. . . ."

rebuff (rih buf′, ree′ buf) *n.,* (rih buf′) *vb.* A *rebuff* is a blunt, contemptuous rejection or refusal, a cold shoulder, a snub. To *rebuff* is to give a *rebuff* to someone. Don't take a job as a door-to-door salesperson unless you can bear the impact of one *rebuff* after another. (This, despite the advice in the poem by the English poet Robert Browning [1812-1889], to "... welcome each *rebuff*/That turns earth's smoothness rough ...," on the theory that pain and strain are good for the soul.) It is unkind to *rebuff* invitations from people you don't like; just plead a previous engagement. A presidential veto is a specialized type of *rebuff*; if Congress overrides the veto, the *rebuff* becomes mutual.

rebuke (rih byook´—*oo* as in *boot*) *n., vb.* A *rebuke* is a sharp, severe disapproval, criticism, or reprimand; to *rebuke* someone is to express such a disapproval, to bawl him out. Top sergeants are usually depicted as experts in the art of the *rebuke*. Sharp parental *rebukes* often cause more tears than enlightenment. The English poet and novelist Rudyard Kipling (1865-1936) wrote: "He who *rebukes* the world is *rebuked* by the world." Winston Churchill (1874-1965) advised: "It is hard, if not impossible, to snub a beautiful woman—they remain beautiful and the *rebuke* recoils."

rebut (rih but´) *vb.* To *rebut* is to disprove, by argument or by offering evidence to the contrary. It has been said that the best way to *rebut* the assertion that something cannot be done is to do it. The English naturalist Charles Darwin (1809-1892) evolved the theory of natural selection to *rebut* the literal interpretation of Genesis. The noun is *rebuttal* (rih but´ əl). In a debate, A argues, B replies, then A is allowed a *rebuttal*. *Rebuttal* is a term common in debates and lawsuits, but it can be used to describe the offering of evidence or the making of an argument in opposition to what has already been offered or argued. When economists join in a roundtable discussion, the *rebuttals* fly around like a swarm of wasps.

recede (rih seed´) *vb.* To *recede* is to move back from the observer, or from a previous position. When the tide *recedes,* we can see various kinds of little creatures among the tangled seaweed. It is a happy thing when floodwaters *recede*. If an artist is skilled in perspective, he can make the objects in the background appear to *recede* as they do in nature. When you sail out to sea, those on shore appear to *recede*. A *receding* hairline is one that exposes an area of baldness at the front of the head. A *receding* chin or forehead is one that slopes back. *Receding* prices are declining prices. The literal meaning of the noun *recession* (rih sesh´ ən) is "withdrawal," but it is most commonly used to describe an economic turn for the worse, with the slackening of industry and business generally. The current (1983) world *recession* has caused an alarming rise in unemployment.

recount (rih kount´) *vb.* To *recount* is to narrate, tell (a story), give a report (of something). The use of this verb implies that the narration or report was given in some detail. When someone returns from a journey to faraway, exotic places, he is asked by his friends to *recount* his adventures. Listening to someone's dull *recounting* of his disputes with a neighbor over the maintenance of a common fence can be extremely boring. The English poet John Milton (1608-1674) also found it boring, as he states in *The History of England,* to read the works of fellow historians who saw fit to *"recount"* the "bickerings" of previous generations; he himself considered such details no more worthy of note than "the wars of kites or crows flocking and fighting in the air." There are also the verb *recount* (pronounced differently: ree´kount), to count again, and the noun *recount* (ree´kount), a second count, the kind demanded by the losing candidate when the vote is close ("I demand a recount!").

recuperate (rih koop´ ə rate—*oo* as in *boot*) *vb.* to *recuperate* is to recover from illness or exhaustion, to get back one's health, or to recover from financial loss. It takes a long time to *recuperate* from certain virus infections. Businesses hit by a long recession are fortunate if they are able to *recuperate* at all. *Recuperation* (rih koop ə ray´shən—*oo* as in *boot*) is the noun. The rate of *recuperation* usually depends on the patient's general constitution. In Germany and Japan, *recuperation* from the effects of World War II was surprisingly fast.

recurrent (rih kur´ ənt—*u* as in *fur* or *but*) *adj.* To *occur* is to happen; to *recur* (rih kur´—*u* as in *fur*) is to happen again and again, i.e., repeatedly. From *recur* we get *recurrent,* describing anything that *recurs,* that happens repeatedly, periodically. The purchase of a house is a *nonrecurrent,* i.e., one-time, expense; the payment of rent is a *recurrent* expense. The twentieth century has been plagued by *recurrent* outbreaks of war all over the globe. The building of the Aswan High Dam in Egypt has put an end to the *recurrent* floods along the banks of the Nile. *Recurrent* invasions of the gypsy moth have caused the repeated defoliation of trees in some areas. Based on its literal meaning, *recurrent* should be applicable to happy events as well as unhappy ones, but it seems usually to tie in with unpleasant events (wars, floods, gypsy moths, fits of depression)—somehow one rarely hears of *recurrent* gifts, periods of peace, times of prosperity, or other things that bring happiness. This is not the fault of the word, but of the world.

redundant (rih dun´ dənt) *adj.* Anything described as *redundant* is superfluous, unneeded. Although this word has come to apply to anything that exceeds what is essential, its original and best use is to describe excess or superfluous words, like the word *free* in the all too common (and abhorrent) expression *free gift.* If it's a gift, it's free, by definition; there's no such thing as an "unfree" gift. It is *redundant* to say that the game was tied at 10 to 10; *tied at 10* is enough. To declare that a resolution was unanimously adopted by the entire meeting is to speak *redundantly*: If adoption was unanimous, it had to be by all present. *Redundancy* (rih dun´ dən see) is the noun, applying both to the superfluous use of words and to an example of that use. According to W. H. Fowler (1858-1933) in *Modern English Usage,* to predict something *in advance* is a *redundancy*: when you predict, it's always "in advance." To perpetuate something *for all time* is another example of *redundancy:* if something is perpetuated, it has to be "for all time," doesn't it? The use of *redundant* has been extended to cover anything *abundant,* like the vegetation in the jungle, but the word is best restricted to superfluous words, as in Fowler's example.

refrain (rih frane´) *vb*. To *refrain* from doing something is to hold oneself back voluntarily, to abstain from doing it. *Refrain* gives the idea of checking an impulse or an inclination to do something that, on second thought, the person thinks better of. It is a good idea to *refrain* from attempting to separate fighting dogs. It is often difficult to *refrain* from saying "I told you so" to someone who gets into trouble by not heeding your advice. The American philosopher, essayist, and teacher Irwin Edman (1896-1954) said: "I have . . . tried, not very successfully, to *refrain* from muttering proudly, when the brighter young minds among contemporaries are mentioned: 'Former student of mine!' " It is advisable to *refrain* from spitting in a public place. The English philosopher and mathematician Bertrand Russell (1872-1970) said: "No tolerable parent could *refrain* from praising a child when it first walks and when it first says an intelligible word." This verb *refrain* has nothing to do with the noun *refrain*, the lines of a song or poem repeated, usually at the end of each verse or stanza. The noun comes from an entirely different root.

refute (rih fyoot´—*oo* as in *boot*) *vb*. To *refute* a statement, an argument, or an opinion is to prove it false or mistaken. The noun *refutation* (ref yoo tay´ shən—*oo* as in *look*) means "disproof." The psychiatrists brought in by the opposing sides in a criminal trial spend a great deal of time in the attempt to *refute* each other's testimony. The best way to *refute* the accusation of laziness is to work hard. The English historian and statesman Thomas Macaulay (1800-1859) declared, in an attack on a fellow statesman: "Some of his blunders seem rather to deserve a flogging than a *refutation*." The Irish philosopher Bishop Berkeley (1685-1753) developed a theory of the nonexistence of matter. James Boswell (1740-1795), the Scottish companion and biographer of the English author and lexicographer Samuel Johnson (1709-1784), remarked to Johnson that though they knew Berkeley's theory wasn't true, they couldn't *refute* it. Johnson kicked against a large stone until his foot rebounded, and replied, "I *refute* it thus!" The same Johnson said: "Shakespeare never had six lines together without a fault. Perhaps you may find seven, but this does not *refute* my general assertion." Some things are hard to *refute*. The English philosopher the Rev. William Paley (1743-1805) asked, "Who can *refute* a sneer?"

regrettable (rih gret´ə b'l) *adj*. To *regret* something is to feel sorry about it. One *regrets* having forgotten one's wedding anniversary; one *regrets* being unable to help a friend in need. Usually, tacking the suffix *-able* onto a verb brings in the concept of *ability*; something *conceivable*, for instance, is *able to be conceived*. But in the case of *regrettable*, there is a difference; *regrettable* doesn't mean "able to be regretted," but rather "to be regretted, cause for regret," i.e., "unfortunate, a pity." *Deplorable* is built the same way; so is *lamentable*. Their meaning is similar to that of *regrettable*, if somewhat stronger. When you speak of *regrettable* table manners, you are criticizing the uncouth diner for exhibiting faulty behavior at the table. You're planning a picnic, and the *regrettable* dark clouds gather up above. "It is *regrettable* that . . . " means "It's too bad that . . . " or "It's a pity that . . . " or "It's a shame that . . . " It is *regrettable* that the arms-limitations talks are proceeding so slowly. Do not confuse *regrettable* with *regretful* (rih gret´ fəl), meaning "feeling *regret,* sorrowful."

reiterate (ree it´ ə rate) *vb.* To *reiterate* something is to repeat it, with the implication that the repetition is endless and boring. There is a word *iterate,* which means about the same thing, but the form *reiterate* is far commoner. Since *iterate* means "repeat," it would seem that the *re-* in *reiterate* is superfluous; it got there, most likely, as an echo of the *re-* in *repeat,* and in all the other *re-* words whose *re-* has the force of *again.* Those repetitious commercials on television not only *reiterate,* they irritate. *Reiteration* (ree it ə ray´ shən) is the noun, meaning "repetition." *Reiteration* seems to be a primary technique in advertising (one advertising agency lived by the rule: "Say it three times!").

rekindle (ree kin´ d'l) *vb.* To *kindle* a fire is to start it. In its figurative use, to *kindle* something is to rouse it, stir it up, get it going, like a pep talk that *kindles* the team's hope of victory. To *rekindle* shares both the literal and figurative meanings of *kindle:* To *rekindle* a fire is to get it going again; to *rekindle* hopes is to rouse or stir them up once more. War always *rekindles* patriotism. A good sermon should *rekindle* noble thoughts. The New Year often *rekindles* old resolutions. Reading through this book should *rekindle* your urge to improve your vocabulary.

relentless (rih lent´ lis) *adj.* Anyone or anything *relentless* is pitiless, mercilessly harsh and unyielding, remorseless. Many plots have been built around the hero's *relentless* pursuit of a wrongdoer, or the triumph of a *relentless* avenger. A *relentless* person never gives up or gives way to softer feelings. The Axis Powers (Germany, Italy, Japan) in World War II found out that they were dealing with *relentless* foes. If not caught in an early stage, cancer is a *relentless* disease. To *relent* is to soften up, become less severe, more compassionate and forgiving. A *relentless* person does none of those things. Macduff, in Shakespeare's *Macbeth,* rises to the heights of dramatic *relentlessness* in his pursuit and killing of the villainous Macbeth.

relevant (rel´ ə vənt) *adj.* What is *relevant* is to the point, has a bearing on the matter under discussion. **Pertinent** is a synonym, and **irrelevant** is the opposite. A judge should admit in evidence only testimony and documents that are *relevant* to the case. Scientific analysis should exclude all facts and observations that are not *relevant* to the investigation in question. Whenever there is a large conference, it is difficult to keep the discussion *relevant* to the main topic. The noun *relevance* (rel´ ə vəns) or *relevancy* (rel´ ə vən see) expresses a relationship to the matter under consideration. The American chemist and educator James B. Conant (1893–1978), president of Harvard University (1933–1953), said: "A scholar's activities should have *relevance* to the immediate future of our civilization." *Relevant* and *relevance* were favorite catchwords of rebellious student groups in the 1960s when they objected to the failure of academicians to devote courses to social issues.

relish (rel′ish) *n., vb.* This is a versatile word. In food terms, *relish* brings to mind chopped sweet pickles, but the term includes any little appetizing extra like olives or pickles. In general use, a *relish* for something is a liking for it (some people have no *relish* for the theater; others have no *relish* for active sports) or a pleasing quality (some activities lose their *relish* as one grows older). The verb to *relish* means to "enjoy, get pleasure from." People who don't *relish* cold weather head south in winter. The true gourmet *relishes* the right wine with his food. Lazy folk don't *relish* early-morning appointments.

reluctant (rih luk′tənt) *adj.* A *reluctant* person is an unwilling one; to be *reluctant* to do something is to be disinclined to undertake it. Shy people are *reluctant* to make public appearances. *Reluctant* candidates have to be drafted. It is a sad commentary on our age that passersby are *reluctant* to come to the aid of people in obvious trouble. The Roman playwright Terence (190-159 B.C.) wrote (Loeb Classical Library translation): "There is nothing so easy but that it becomes difficult when you do it *reluctantly*." The noun is *reluctance* (rih luk′təns). The American humorous poet Ogden Nash (1902-1971) wrote:

> Dogs display *reluctance* and wrath
> If you try to give them a bath.

remarkable (rih mark′ə b'l) *adj.* Anything or anyone described as *remarkable* is out of the ordinary, unusual, noteworthy. Diet and exercise can work a *remarkable* change in one's appearance. Some elderly people are *remarkable* for their vigor and activity. Mozart (1756-1791) was *remarkable* not only for the greatness of his work but for the enormous volume of music he composed before dying so young. Putting men on the moon was the most *remarkable* event of the age. The adverb *remarkably* (rih mark′ə blee) is the equivalent of *notably* or *unusually*. Californians seem to do *remarkably* well in professional tennis. The Polish-born writer Joseph Conrad (1857-1924) and the Russian-born writer Vladimir Nabokov (1899-1977) wrote *remarkably* well in their adopted language, English. Both *remarkable* and *remarkably* contain the implication that what is being described is not only out of the ordinary, but, in most cases, somewhat unexpected or surprising. Note also that *remarkable* is built on the verb to *remark*, in its sense of to *note*, plus the suffix *-able*. As in the case of **regrettable**, the *-able* does not denote *ability*, but rather *necessity*: a *remarkable* achievement is not one *able* to be remarked upon, but one that is so unusual that it *must* or at least *should be* remarked upon. *Remarkable* can apply to persons as well as things: Einstein was a *remarkable* man.

reminisce (rem ə nis′) *vb.* To *reminisce* is to think and talk about past happenings and experiences. When old friends meet for the first time in years and talk about the good old days, they are *reminiscing*. A lot of *reminiscing* goes on at class reunions. The noun is *reminiscence* (rem ə nis′ əns). *Reminiscence*, generally, is the act of *reminiscing*; a *reminiscence* is the memory of a particular experience; *reminiscences* are remembered experiences, or the narrative of them, as in titles like *Reminiscences of a Schoolteacher, Reminiscences of an Old Artilleryman*, and the like. The English dramatist George Bernard Shaw (1856–1950) gave this line to a character in *Heartbreak House*: "*Reminiscences* make one feel so deliciously aged and sad." The American poet Walt Whitman (1819–1892) wrote of Abraham Lincoln: He leaves for America's history and biography . . . its most dramatic *reminiscence*. . . . " The adjective *reminiscent* (rem ə nis' ənt) applies to anything that brings to mind old experiences or triggers a related memory. A middle-aged man sees a little swimming hole and, recalling his youth, murmurs, "This is *reminiscent* of my boyhood." If a writer follows somebody else's style too closely, a critic might say, "This is *reminiscent* of So-and-so's style." A night at a glamorous restaurant, complete with all the right wines and chamber music, might prove *reminiscent* of old Vienna.

remiss (rih mis') *adj.* To be *remiss* is to neglect one's duties. Doctors and lawyers complain that many people are *remiss* in paying their bills. Landlords *remiss* in supplying heat to tenants may be penalized by municipal authorities. (I've just taken a tea break, and after dawdling too long, jumped up feeling very *remiss* in my writing schedule; now I'm back.) *Remiss* is from the Latin word *remissus*, meaning "relaxed," literally "sent back," which brings to mind the modern slang expression "laid back." *Remiss*, however, is more than just *relaxed*: It means "*too* relaxed," in other words, *negligent*.

remorse (rih mors'—*o* as in *horse*) *n. Remorse* is bitter regret and distress arising from a sense of guilt for past misdeeds. One should suffer from *remorse* for having failed to help a friend in need, when it was possible to do so. *Remorseful* (rih mors' fəl—*o* as in *horse*) is the adjective. Today can be ruined by *remorseful* feelings about the events of yesterday. One must watch one's words in an argument; feeling *remorseful* later won't cure wounds. The related word *remorseless* (rih mors' ləs) goes off in a different direction: To be *remorseless* is to be pitiless, merciless, ruthless; in certain contexts, unrelenting. Hitler was a creature of *remorseless* sadism. The condition of man is changed daily by the *remorseless* drive of technology. A *remorselessly* ambitious person is driven so hard that he has no time to be *remorseful*.

renounce (rih nouns'—*s* as in *see*) *vb.* To *renounce* something is to give it up. A hermit *renounces* all contact with society. People who lose their faith *renounce* religion. A king who abdicates *renounces* the throne. How much better a world it would be if all nations *renounced* forever the use of nuclear arms! *Renounce* can mean "disown" or "repudiate" in certain instances. A parent may *renounce* a child for marrying outside the faith. Fathers have been known to *renounce* sons because they have turned to crime. The noun is *renunciation* (rih nun see ay' shən, -shee-). King Edward VIII's *renunciation* of his throne for the woman he loved came as a shock to the world.

repercussion (ree pər kush' ən) *n.* A *repercussion* is an aftereffect, usually indirect and unexpected, sometimes immediate, sometimes remote, of a previous act or event. This word, almost always used in the plural, implies that the aftereffects were widespread and far-reaching. The *repercussions* of the assassination of President Kennedy changed the course of history. The mass production of the automobile initiated by Henry Ford had *repercussions* that altered social conditions all over the world. Do not use *repercussion* simply as a substitute for *consequence*: The implication of *repercussion(s)* is that the consequences are not only unforeseen but, in most cases, unpleasant. Henry Ford's invention increased mobility but also brought about pollution, to say nothing of urban traffic jams and terrible highway death statistics. *Repercussion(s)* also evokes the concept of multiplying effects, like ripples caused by throwing a pebble into a pond.

repudiate (rih pyoo' dee ate—*oo* as in *boot*) *vb.* *Repudiate* can be used in a number of ways. When the communists took over in Russia, the new government *repudiated* the foreign debt (i.e., refused to recognize or pay the obligation). The Bulgarians have *repudiated* responsibility for the attempt to assassinate Pope John Paul II (i.e., denied the charge as unfounded). To *repudiate* a child or an old friend is to declare that one will have nothing further to do with him. The Russian-born painter Marc Chagall (born 1887) has *repudiated* (i.e., declared to be fakes) a number of paintings imitating his style and bearing his alleged signature.

repugnant (rih pug' nənt) *adj.* What is *repugnant* is offensive, objectionable, in increasing degrees from *distasteful* to *repulsive* and *loathsome*. What is more *repugnant* than the sight of a cockroach in a dirty restaurant? The Nazi views on race are both ridiculous and *repugnant* to enlightened men and women. The customs of self-mutilation among certain African tribes like the Ubangi are *repugnant* to the civilized world. The noun *repugnance* (rih pug' nəns) means "strong distaste." Sensitive people feel a great *repugnance* at accepting welfare instead of employment. Cultured people feel a great *repugnance* at any show of vulgarity.

resemble (rih zem' b'l) *vb.* When people or things *resemble* each other, they look alike. Children usually *resemble* one parent or the other. People may *resemble* each other in one particular, like complexion or voice, but not in others, like size. Buildings planned by the same school of architecture tend to *resemble* one another. The noun *resemblance* (rih zem' bləns) is used mainly to point out a similarity of appearance between people or things. Some brothers bear a striking *resemblance* to one another. If people or things are described as bearing "a certain *resemblance*" to each other, it means that—whether or not they really look alike—each somehow reminds you of the other. People often speak of a *family resemblance*. When two people or things are quite different, one commonly says that there is *no resemblance* between them.

resolve (rih zolv') *n., vb.* To *resolve* is to determine, to decide firmly. In the famous Gettysburg Address, Abraham Lincoln used the stirring words: "We here highly *resolve* that these dead shall not have died in vain." George Washington told his army: "We have . . . to *resolve* to conquer or die." When courageous men commence upon a course of action, they *resolve* that nothing will hold them back. Every young hero of a novel by the American writer of boys' books Horatio Alger (1834-1899) *resolves* to succeed in life. To *resolve* is more than merely to decide: The word usually appears in situations where high aims are involved. As an adjective, *resolved* means "determined." When one is determined to do something, fixed upon a course of action, he is *resolved* to do it. Napoleon was *resolved* to rule all of Europe. Columbus was *resolved* to find a sea route to India. *Resolve* is a common term in the minutes of committee or corporate meetings: "*Resolved*, that this company enter into an agreement with. . . ." The result is a *resolution* (rez ə loo´ shən—*oo as in* boot), as, for instance, a corporate *resolution* authorizing the vice-president to sign checks. As a noun, *resolve* is determination, firm purpose. Nothing could shake the conspirators' *resolve* to kill Julius Caesar. Churchill's high *resolve* to beat the fascists inspired his countrymen and their allies.

respond (rih spond´) *vb.* The primary meaning of *respond* is to "reply" or "answer" with words, as one *responds* to a letter or a question; but the term is widely used to indicate action in answer to something, or reaction generally. A disease *responds* well to the right treatment. A kind person will usually *respond* to a plea for help. When you're tickled, you *respond* with laughter. When irritated, you *respond* with anger. The answer or reaction is a *response* (rih spons´). An unanswered letter is one without a *response*. In a small community, an appeal for help for a family in distress usually meets with a generous *response*. The related adjective *responsive* (rih spon´ siv) is used to describe a person who readily *responds* or reacts to people and situations, especially to influences, suggestions, and the like. Most people are *responsive* to a show of kindness or affection. A *responsive* person is sympathetic and sensitive to what is going on around him. *Nonresponsive* and *unresponsive* appropriately describe answers that are not to the point and evade the issue. "What shall we do about taxes, Mr. President?" "We'll have to wait and see." Do not confuse *responsive* with *responsible*.

reticent (ret´ ə sənt) *adj.* A *reticent* person is uncommunicative and reserved, inclined to keep his thoughts to himself. That famous conversation "Where have you been?" "Out." "What were you doing?" "Nothing." is typical of a *reticent* schoolboy. The typical Yankee farmer is always depicted in fiction and drama as a *reticent*, chin-stroking character. The noun is *reticence* (ret´ ih səns), denoting restraint in communicating. Puritans and Quakers are usually typed as persons of reserve and *reticence*. *Reticence* marks those who are timid about expressing themselves in company.

retort (rih tawrt´) *n., vb.* A *retort* is a sharp, to-the-point, witty comeback that neatly disposes of someone's statement, argument, or theory, especially one that turns the first speaker's statement against him. Example: Lady Astor said to Winston Churchill, "If I were married to you, I'd put poison in your coffee." Churchill's *retort*: "If you were my wife, I'd drink it." The Irish playwright George Bernard Shaw (1856–1950) sent Churchill two tickets to an opening night with a note: "Bring a friend—if you have one." *Retort*: "Busy that night. Would like two for second night—if there is one." (Or words to that effect.) To *retort* is to answer back sharply, make a quick comeback, "give as good as you get," as Churchill did on both the occasions reported above; each of his answers could have been introduced with the words: "*Retorted* Churchill . . ." One of the most famous and ill-timed *retorts* in history was the one usually, and improperly, attributed to Queen Marie Antoinette of France (1755–1793) who, on being informed that her people had no bread, is supposed to have replied, "Let them eat cake."

retrench (rih trench´) *vb*. To *retrench* is to economize, to cut down on expenses. Unfortunately, in times of recession, companies *retrench* by dismissing workers. People *retrench* one year in order to save up for next year's vacation. The noun is *retrenchment* (rih trench´ mənt). When statesmen want to warn their people of the need to *retrench* because of hard times ahead, they use lofty terms like "austerity" or heart-to-heart expressions like "cutting down," instead of the more ominous-sounding word *retrenchment*. "Peace, *retrenchment*, and reform" was the slogan of the British Liberal party in 1829.

retribution (reh trə byoo´ shən—*oo* as in *boot*) *n*. *Retribution* is eventual punishment for evil deeds; also known as "just deserts." Judgment Day is sometimes called the "day of *retribution*." *Retribution*, deserved punishment, is the theme of many a play and novel, wherein the villain gets what's coming to him. Virtue always triumphs in the movies; the unwritten law specifies *retribution* for the bad guy. In view of the prevalence of crime nowadays, it appears that evildoers don't give much thought to *retribution*, divine or man-made.

reverberate (rih vur´ bə rate—*u* as in *fur*) *vb*. To *reverberate* is to re-echo, re-sound. Voices tend to *reverberate* in a large, empty room, especially if the walls and floor are of stone and uncovered. During rehearsals in an empty theater, the actors are sometimes bothered by the *reverberation* (rih vur bə ray´ shən—*u* as in *fur*) of their voices. Apart from its literal meaning, *reverberate* has been used figuratively to describe the persisting influence of great thoughts. The words of Abraham Lincoln continue to *reverberate* through history. Sayings of the sages in the Book of Proverbs have *reverberated* through the ages.

revere (rih veer´) *vb*. To *revere* is to have deep respect for someone or something, to regard the person or the object with the deepest respect and awe. Deeply religious people *revere* not only the saints, but their idols. This author still *reveres* the great scholarship and academic skills of his old teachers. Robert Burns (1759–1796), the Scottish poet, writing of his native land, described it as "loved at home, *revered* abroad." The name and figure of Abraham Lincoln will be *revered* forever. The noun is *reverence* (rev´ ər əns, rev´ rəns), a feeling of deep respect mixed with awe. To *hold* someone or something *in reverence* or to *show* or *have reverence for* someone or something is to regard the object of one's *reverence* with the deepest respect. According to the Greek dramatist Aeschylus (524–456 B.C.), " '*Reverence* for parents' stands written among the three laws of most *reverend* righteousness." (Honor thy father and thy mother.) The English poet Alfred, Lord Tennyson (1809–1892) wrote of "*reverence* for the laws ourselves have made."

ritual (rich' oo əl—*oo* as in *boot*) *n.* A *ritual* is the established procedure for any ceremony, religious or other. There are set rules governing the *ritual* of church service in each denomination. There is a strict *ritual* for the opening of every new Congress. Stockholders' meetings tend to follow a procedural *ritual*. Apart from such fixed rules, *ritual* can apply to any set pattern of behavior, like the *ritual* of tipping one's hat to a lady, or the elaborate *ritual* of cleaning and lighting a pipe. W. Somerset Maugham, the English playwright and novelist (1874–1965), described a character as "busy among her pots and pans, making a *ritual* of her household duties." Thus, *ritual* can be applied to ceremonies as austere as the Catholic Mass, and to acts as humble and routine as the cleaning of pots and pans.

robust (roe bust', roe' bust) *adj.* One thinks of a *robust* person as hale and hearty, brimming over with good health and vigor. Anyone or anything that is *robust* is healthy, vigorous, and strong. Young growing boys are notorious for their *robust* appetites. Deeply religious people can be described as having *robust* faith. The juices flow as the *robust* aroma of frying bacon and eggs flows from the kitchen on Sunday morning. The American philosopher Morris Cohen (1880–1947) wrote of "the *robust* skepticism of science." *The New Yorker* magazine commented upon "splendidly *robust* soups and stews," using the word in the sense of "strong and full-bodied." It is clear that *robust* is a versatile and handy word with which to describe anyone or anything full of vim and vigor.

rudimentary (roo də men' tə ree, -tree—*oo* as in *boot*) *adj.* The *rudiments* (roo' də ments) of anything are its first steps or basic elements, as in the *rudiments* of arithmetic or the *rudiments* of grammar. The usual meaning of the adjective *rudimentary* is "basic, elementary, fundamental." Franklin D. Roosevelt deplored "conditions which do not meet the *rudimentary* standards of decency." The grammar school gives one only a *rudimentary* education. There are many jobs, like operating an elevator or manning a highway toll booth, that require only *rudimentary* skills. The best one can hope to achieve through a foreign-language course, without living in the country itself, is a *rudimentary* use of the language.

rummage (rum' ij) *n., vb.* A *rummage* is a thorough search through a hodgepodge of things in the attempt to find whatever happens to be of interest. To *rummage* for something is to ransack a space, like a desk or a shop, in search of whatever you're looking for, to sift through its contents in the hope of finding something. Untidy people are always *rummaging* through stacks of papers to find whatever they need at the moment, like a receipt or an address. *Rummaging* brings to mind the image of a disorderly attic containing a jumble of things you never want to see again but can't bear to throw away. When you suddenly need something (for instance, for a children's costume party), you *rummage* through the attic. *Rummage* has been used figuratively as well: One can speak of *rummaging* through one's mind for a forgotten name or word or title. A *rummage* sale is a sale of odds and ends contributed to raise money for charity, or of unclaimed goods in public storage.

ruse (rooz—*oo* as in *boot*) *n.* A *ruse* is a trick, a tricky, deceitful tactic or way of doing or getting something, a subterfuge. A familiar type of *ruse* is a feint, a movement made to deceive an opponent, used in boxing, fencing, or military strategy. As a *ruse* to obtain money unlawfully, one may pretend to be soliciting for a legitimate charity. To gain admittance to a house, a thief sometimes adopts the *ruse* of claiming to be a representative of the telephone or other utility company. Debaters sometimes resort to the *ruse* of bringing up a new subject in order to get away from a point on which their side is unconvincing. During war, the "leaking" of false information is a favorite *ruse* to deceive the enemy. *Ruse* evokes the image of a wily opponent with an honest face and a false heart.

rustic (rus´ tik—*u* as in *but*) *adj.* *Rustic* is used in a favorable sense to characterize a person, his manners, his speech, and his dress as countrified and therefore plain, simple, unsophisticated, and unaffected. It is used in an unfavorable sense to describe a person who is unrefined, uncouth, and boorish. In the early movies, and in much of literature (in the novels of the English writer Charles Dickens [1812–1870], for example), the *rustic* hero or heroine is shown as a pure, simple, unspoiled soul. A *rustic* scene is a country scene, especially one portraying the simple life. *Rustic* speech or manners, on the other hand, may be understood, in context, as rough, crude, unpolished, or even boorish. As applied to buildings or bridges or furniture (a *rustic* bench), *rustic* indicates rough workmanship. *Rustic* garden seats, for instance, are made of unplaned, unfinished sections of tree trunks and branches. The context must determine whether *rustic* is used in a favorable or unfavorable sense.

ruthless (rooth´ lis—*oo* as in *boot*) *adj.* A *ruthless* person is cruel and merciless, willing to do anything to attain his end without consideration for anyone else. (Believe it or not, there is a word *ruth*, meaning "pity" or "compassion.") One who is *ruthless* knows no pity or compassion. Ivan the Terrible (1530–1584), the first Czar of Russia, is depicted in history as a *ruthless* tyrant. Hitler is the supreme example of a *ruthless* despot. What is more *ruthless* than a policy of genocide? Trade wars arise from a *ruthless* determination on the part of a company or country to capture the market. President Grover Cleveland (1837–1908) said, in his second Annual Message: "When more of the people's sustenance is exacted through . . . taxation than is necessary to meet the just obligations of government . . . such exaction becomes *ruthless* extortion. . . ." (Bless you, Grover Cleveland!)

sacrilege (sak′ rə lij) *n*. *Sacrilege* is an act that violates or is disrespectful of anything that should be held sacred. The adjective *sacrilegious* (sak rə lih′ jəs, -lee′-) describes such an act. (Note the spelling of the adjective, which is often misspelled as a result of understandable confusion with *religious*.) Vandalism of a church or mutilation or stealing of an altarpiece is obvious *sacrilege*, but the term has been extended in a somewhat jocular and grossly exaggerated way to include anything that violates good taste. It is *sacrilege* to pour ketchup over scallopini prepared by a great Italian chef! One of the most *sacrilegious* sights ever seen by the author is a miniature reproduction of the Venus de Milo with a clock in the middle of her belly. Gourmets go so far as to say that it is *sacrilegious* to serve red wine with fish. How about wearing a flashy necktie to a funeral?

saddle (sad′ l) *vb*. We all know what a *saddle* is; to *saddle* a horse is to prepare it to bear the weight of a rider on its back. From this the verb to *saddle* derives its figurative meaning: to "burden." To *saddle* somebody with something is to impose a heavy burden or responsibility on him. An overworked employee groans under the tasks with which the boss has *saddled* him. The bachelor's carefree existence comes to an end when he finds himself *saddled* with a wife and a dozen children. Now *she* is *saddled* with *him* and the kids; once she, too, was footloose and fancy-free! The public is not happy about being *saddled* with sales taxes in addition to the income tax.

satire (sa′ tire—*a* as in *hat*) *n*. *Satire* is the use of sarcasm and irony to hold a person or society and its follies up to ridicule. A *satire* is a particular piece of writing or speech or acting that does this. A writer of *satire* is known as a *satirist* (sat′ ər ist). *Satirical* (sə tihr′ ih kəl) is the adjective. It describes a writer, actor, etc. who uses *satire*, and any writing or other activity that does so. To *satirize* (sat′ ə rize) is to attack someone or something through the use of *satire*. *Gulliver's Travels*, by the English writer and clergyman Jonathan Swift (1667–1745), is a *satire* holding up to ridicule the vices and weaknesses of society. Swift is one of the most famous *satirists* in history. The usual purpose of *satirical* writing is to expose and correct human vices or follies. Swift wrote: "*Satire* . . . [if] leveled at all [people], is never resented . . . by any." He also wrote: "*Satire* is a sort of glass [i.e., mirror], wherein beholders do generally discover everybody's face but their own." Lord Byron, the English poet (1788–1824), wrote: "I'll publish, right or wrong:/Fools are my theme, let *satire* be my song." The English author Lady Mary Wortley Montague (1689–1762) warned: "*Satire* should, like a polished razor keen,/Wound with a touch that's scarcely felt or seen."

saunter (sawn′ tər, sahn-) *n.*, *vb*. A *saunter* is a leisurely stroll; to *saunter* is to walk in that fashion, in a quiet, unhurried way. It is fun to *saunter* along window-shopping to pass the time of day. How nice to get away from it all and *saunter* through the woods, looking for wildflowers! Start out early for an appointment, so that you can *saunter* along the last stretch instead of hurrying and arriving late or out of breath. *Saunter* evokes the image of hands-in-pocket ease, calm, daydreaming, not a care in the world. There ought to be more of it and less hustle and bustle.

scamper (skam′ pər) *vb.* To *scamper* is to run off quickly, to scurry or scoot, to be off like a shot; or, in context, to run about playfully. A thief, suddenly interrupted in his unlawful activity, will *scamper* off unceremoniously. Small animals, like rabbits and mice, *scamper* and vanish when frightened. Children and their pets love to *scamper* about in their merry play. Squirrels *scamper* skillfully from branch to branch.

scandalous (skan′ də ləs) *adj.* A *scandal* is a shameful or disgraceful act or situation. It is also the harmful and malicious gossip that often follows it, thanks to the shameful activities of *scandalmongers* (skan′ d'l mung gərs, -mong-), those who delight in dishing the dirt. Society divorces involving mutual charges of sexual irregularities always create *scandals*, in both senses of the word. From *scandal* we get *scandalous*, meaning "disgraceful" or "shocking." History and fiction are full of examples of *scandalous* behavior. The matrimonial history of King Henry VIII of England (1491–1547) is a record of one *scandalous* act after another. Imperialist nations have been guilty of *scandalous* treatment of the natives in occupied areas. There are *scandalous* episodes in the history of every country: The most recent example in America was the administration of Richard M. Nixon.

scant (skant) *adj. Scant* and *scanty* (skan′ tee) mean about the same thing: "barely enough" or "barely large enough." Children all too often have *scant* regard for their parents' advice. Pupils who pay *scant* attention to teachers' instructions usually come to grief at examination time. *Scant* is somewhat more formal than *scanty*. *Scant* seems to be preferred in certain phrases like *scant regard* and *scant attention*, but *scanty* is the more usual term. Restaurant customers grumble when the portions are *scanty*. A *scanty* bathing suit on a well-proportioned young lady stirs up a lot of interest at the beach or swimming pool. A *scanty* wheat crop can upset the economics of a whole country. With the exception of the phrases mentioned, use *scanty* in preference to *scant*.

scathing (skay′ thing—*th* as in *this*) *adj. Scathe* is an almost never used verb meaning to "attack with harsh criticism." From it we get *scathing*, meaning "severe, harsh, biting." Critics seem at times to take sadistic delight in writing *scathing* reviews. The American author and critic Dorothy Parker (1893–1967) was famous for her *scathing* remarks. When an acquaintance stepped aside to allow her to go through a door first with the words "Age before beauty," she countered with "Pearls before swine," and sailed on through. Winston Churchill was a master of the *scathing* retort; see **retort** for some examples. People can be withered by a *scathing* look.

scrounge (skrounj—*ou* as in *house*) *vb.* To *scrounge* is to scrape up, cadge, "beg, borrow, or steal." Those sad people who live and sleep on the streets *scrounge* whatever they can find in litter bins. A familiar figure in American literature of the early 1900s is the hobo *scrounging* food at anybody's back door. There are those who give up smoking except for the cigarettes they can *scrounge* from their friends. Mayors and governors make frequent appeals to Washington in the attempt to *scrounge* as much money as possible for local needs. To *scrounge* around is to poke around in the search for whatever you can pick up. A *scrounger* is a habitual sponger or "borrower" who hasn't the slightest intention of returning what he *scrounges*.

scruple (skroo′ p′l—*oo* as in *boot*) *n.* A *scruple* is a qualm or twinge of conscience, a moral consideration that inhibits action. The word is usually found in the plural. Some people have no *scruples* about sponging on their friends. Some men are not overburdened with *scruples* when it comes to seducing naive young ladies. Literary *scruples* keep authors from plagiarizing. A *scrupulous* (skoo′ pyə ləs) person is one who has *scruples*: he is careful to follow his conscience at all times. Businessmen, alas, are not always *scrupulous* in their dealings. *Scrupulous* judges will always avoid political influence. In extended use, *scrupulous,* quite apart from its moral and ethical significance, means "precise, exact, correct to the tiniest detail." A first-rate musician will perform with *scrupulous* fidelity to the score. *Scrupulous* sometimes takes on the meaning of "painstaking": A careful lawyer will be *scrupulous* in considering every conceivable angle of the case. *Unscrupulous* (un skroo′ pyə ləs) people have no *scruples* and are not bothered or restrained by conscience; they suffer from total lack of moral standards; they are rogues who stop at nothing to gain their ends. Shakespeare's villainous Macbeths were *unscrupulous* in their drive for the throne. His Iago *unscrupulously* lied to Othello about Desdemona. Hitler and his gang were *unscrupulous* to the point of madness.

self-effacing (self ih fay′ sing) *adj.* See **efface.**

serene (sə reen′) *adj.* Anyone or anything *serene* is calm and peaceful. One thinks of the shepherd watching over his flock as the most *serene* of people. The *Mona Lisa* is known worldwide for its subject's *serene,* mysterious expression. The English poet William Wordsworth (1770–1850), in his poem "To a Young Lady," predicted for her "an old age, *serene* and bright." The American poet Oliver Wendell Holmes (1809–1894) told us to "Learn the sweet magic of a cheerful face;/Not always smiling, but at least *serene.*" The noun is *serenity* (sə ren′ ih tee). The English novelist Jane Austen (1775–1817) wrote of "the *serenity* of a mind at ease with itself and kindly disposed towards everyone." The English novelist James Hilton (1900–1954) praised "the austere *serenity* of Shangri-La."

sever (sev′ ər) *vb.* To *sever* is to cut, especially to cut a part of something away from the whole. The guillotine and the executioner's ax *severed* the head from the body. *Sever* is commonly used in the expression to *sever connections,* i.e., "break off relations." An offended nation recalls its ambassador and *severs* diplomatic relations with the offending country. After a divorce, it does not always happen that one *severs* ties with the ex-spouse's family. Bad weather often *severs* telephone communications. To *severe,* by itself (without an object), means to "break": a rope or cable bearing too much weight may *sever.* The noun is *severence* (sev´ ər əns, -rəns). One can speak of the *severance* of relations or connections, or the *severance* of a rope or cable. *Serverance pay* is money paid to an employee on termination of his employment.

severe (sih veer´) *adj.* This word has numerous meanings, depending upon the noun with which it is used. A *severe* teacher is a strict one. *Severe* laws are harsh. *Severe* criticism is stern. A *severe* look or a *severe* face is grim and unyielding. A *severe* illness is a serious one. *Severe* dress or style is extremely plain, without ornament. *Severe* manners are restrained and rigid. *Severe* weather is harsh and uncomfortable. A *severe* test or competition requires skill. A *severe* pace requires endurance. To speak *severely* is to speak harshly. When Noah was loading the ark, according to the English poet and novelist Rudyard Kipling (1865-1936), he had trouble with the typically obstinate donkey. Kipling describes the struggle in dialect: "Thin [then] Noah spoke him fairly, thin talked to him *sevariely* [*severely*],/ An' thin he cursed him squarely .../ ... an' the Donkey wint [went] aboard." The noun *severity* (sih ver´ ih tee) shares the many meanings of the adjectives. The *severity* of a teacher can be frightening. The *severity* of a landscape may make it unpleasant. The *severity* of a long, hard winter often has a depressing effect on people. *Severity* in dress is characteristic of the Quakers. Whatever the context, *severe* has an unpleasant flavor.

shackle (shak' l) *n., vb.* Technically, a *shackle* is one of a pair of metal rings joined by a chain, arranged so as to fasten a prisoner's wrists or ankles. *Shackles* are fetters. To *shackle* someone is to put *shackles* on him. Figuratively, *shackles* are anything that restrains a person, preventing freedom of action, expression, thought, etc.; to *shackle* someone is to prevent him from acting freely. Many feel that the government has put too many *shackles* on free enterprise. Hubert Humphrey (1911-1978) said that "we must release ourselves from the *shackles* of yesterday's traditions and let our minds be bold." The poor are usually *shackled* by illiteracy and superstition. The English poet William Cowper (1731-1800) wrote:

> Slaves cannot breathe in England, if their lungs
> Receive our air, that moment they are free;
> They touch our country, and their *shackles* fall.

shatter (shat´ ər) *vb.* To *shatter* something is to break it, with one sudden and crushing blow, into small fragments, the way a windshield is *shattered* by a flying rock. *Shatter* is used figuratively, meaning "destroy." The health of many people has been *shattered* by war. People can be *shattered* by a terrible experience. The legend of American invincibility was *shattered* by the Vietnam fiasco. An earthquake is a nerve-*shattering* experience. A pneumatic jackhammer makes an ear-*shattering* noise. After the seas have been searched for days, hopes of finding survivors are *shattered* by gale-force winds. One's composure is *shattered* by bad news. The peace of the countryside is *shattered* in time of war. Shatter can be used without an object: A windshield hit by a pebble may *shatter*. One's peace of mind, when bad news comes, may *shatter*.

shoddy (shod' ee) *adj. Shoddy* is the name of an inferior fabric made from reclaimed wool. As a noun, it has come to apply to anything inferior or imitation, and as an adjective to describe anything of poor quality, especially if made to resemble an article of superior quality. There is less and less genuine craftsmanship in the world these days; we are increasingly offered *shoddy* machine-made merchandise. Expensive garments come apart at the seams because they are stitched with *shoddy* thread. Workmen charging exorbitant prices add insult to injury by doing *shoddy* work. *Shoddy* can take on the meaning of "shabby, run-down," when used to describe secondhand apparel, well-worn draperies, or the broken-down armchairs in the lobbies of third-rate hotels (how depressing!). An unacceptable, flimsy excuse can be described as *shoddy*; so can the conduct of a tinhorn dictator like one who enriched himself while plunging the country into economic ruin—and then ran off with the furnishings of the presidential palace. *Shoddy* conduct is shabby, shameful behavior, unacceptable to decent people.

shortcoming (short' kum ing) *n.* A *shortcoming* is a defect, a failure, a flaw or imperfection, a weakness. The word is usually found in the plural. Most business failures can be traced to either inadequate capital or the *shortcomings* of management. Inferiority complexes are usually the result of one's sense of one's own *shortcomings*. The word implies a failure to come up to an expected or required standard, and is based on the image of *coming short* of a goal. The German mathematician Karl Friedrich Gauss (1777-1855) said: "It may be true that people who are merely mathematicians have specific *shortcomings*; however, that is not the fault of mathematics, but is true of every exclusive occupation." Critics are generally apt to stress the *shortcomings*, rather than the virtues, of a performance.

shun (shun) *vb.* To *shun* is to avoid deliberately, to keep away from something or someone, with the implication that one is taking great pains to avoid the contact. A hermit *shuns* society. Shy people *shun* publicity. St. Anthony (250-350) *shunned* temptation by the Devil. A scientist should *shun* speculation and stick to the observable facts. The English poet and statesman Lord Chesterfield (1694-1773) wrote this "Advice to a Lady in Autumn": "The dews of the evening most carefully *shun,* /Those tears of the sky for the loss of the sun." According to the Roman statesman, soldier, and writer Cato the Elder (234-149 B.C.), "wise men *shun* the mistakes of fools." *Shun* implies not only deliberate but also habitual avoidance.

significant (sig nif' ə kənt) *adj. Significant* means "meaningful, important." The Fourth of July is a *significant* date in our history; it is important and meaningful. If we say that something exists in a *significant* amount, or occurs to a *significant* extent, we mean that whatever it is, there is a lot of it, or that whatever is occurring is widespread. *Significant* can also indicate that what it describes has a special or disguised meaning or a suggestive twist. If someone gives you a *significant* look, he is "trying to tell you something." The verb is *signify* (sig′ nə fy), to "be a *sign* of," to "mean." A *significant* shrug or a *significant* wink is a meaningful gesture; it *signifies* something. The noun is *significance* (sig nif′ ə kəns). The *significance* of the Fourth of July should not be lost on Americans. A *significant* wink is a hidden sign and *signifies* something that the other person is trying to convey; it has a special *significance* or meaning. *Significance* can also mean "importance." The discovery of penicillin was a medical advance of the greatest *significance*.

signify (sig′ nə fy) *vb.* See **significant**.

sinister (sin′ ə stər) *adj.* Anything *sinister* threatens harm and trouble, the likelihood of bad luck to come. A deep, dark cave has a *sinister* atmosphere. There are cheerful rooms, full of sparkling light, and others that are gloomy and *sinister* and give one the shivers. Villains in early movies specialized in *sinister* leers and looks. The *sinister* purposes of Adolf Hitler were clearly revealed in his book, *Mein Kampf* [My Struggle]. Dark clouds have a *sinister* look, threatening bad weather ahead.

skeptical (skep′ tih kəl) *adj. Skeptical* people are those who are by nature inclined not to believe, who question the accuracy or truth of statements and claims. A *skeptic* (skep′ tik) doubts and questions the truth or validity of what others may take for granted. *Skepticism* (skep′ tih sizm) is doubt, the attitude of a *skeptic.* The *skeptical* attitude is summed up in the words: "Show me! I'm from Missouri!" "Doubting Thomas" (from St. Thomas, the apostle who doubted: John 20:25) is a popular name for a *skeptic*. A *skeptical* listener with a *skeptical* look makes the speaker uncomfortable. The American editor Francis P. Church (1839–1906), in his famous editorial "Is There a Santa Claus?" wrote: "Virginia, your little friends are wrong. They have been affected by the *skepticism* of a *skeptical* age. They do not believe except they see. . . . No Santa Claus! Thank God he lives, and lives forever." Not all *skepticism* is bad. According to the American poet James Russell Lowell (1819–1891), "A wise *skepticism* is the first attribute of a good critic."

skittish (skit′ ish) *adj.* What comes to mind when one meets this word is a *skittish horse*, one that is easily excitable, hard to control, quick to shy or start; but *skittish* can also be applied to human beings who are restless, easily excitable, jumpy. Cautious people who tend to shy away when faced with the need to make a decision can be described as *skittish*. A fickle, irresponsible, restless person who keeps changing his mind is *skittish,* and very hard to deal with. Shakespeare used the word to mean "fickle" in *Twelfth Night* (Act II, Scene 4), when Duke Orsino says that "all true lovers are . . . *skittish*" in everything but "the constant image of the . . . beloved."

sleazy (slee′ zee) *adj. Sleazy* is an expressive way to describe anything flimsy, unsubstantial, tacky, chintzy, junky, trashy, shabby, or shoddy. Fortune-tellers in their tents at country fairs are usually dressed in *sleazy* clothes and surrounded by *sleazy* décor. Nothing is as depressing as a *sleazy* rooming house in the slums of a big city. People who have done something wrong think up one *sleazy* excuse after another. *Sleazy* little pickpockets frequent crowded places. Charles Dickens, the English novelist (1812–1870), vividly described the *sleazy* conditions in which the nineteenth-century poor lived and worked.

slipshod (slip′ shod) *adj.* Anything *slipshod* is **slovenly** (see the next entry), careless, untidy, slapdash, sloppy. *Slipshod* work is careless, hasty, sloppy, with no thought for neatness and precision. One of the purposes of this book is to prevent the *slipshod*, careless choice of words, which leads to inexactness of expression and often of thought. A great deal of messy, *slipshod* work is done today by "craftsmen" who should know better. Conscientious workers have nothing but contempt for *slipshod* work. Many of today's youth dress in a sloppy, *slipshod* way.

slovenly (sluv′ ən lee—*u* as in *but*) *adj.* A *slovenly* person or appearance or way of doing things is messy, sloppy, and **slipshod** (see the previous entry). The noun *sloven*, describing such a person, is rarely used. See **purist**, for a mention of *sloven*. Careless craftsmen do *slovenly* work. Pupils who turn in *slovenly* homework are properly reprimanded by their teachers. People who are *slovenly* in their habits are not reliable. *Slovenly* grammar and pronunciation are all too common nowadays. In a sermon on dress, the English theologian John Wesley (1703–1791), founder of Methodism, preached: "*Slovenliness* is no part of religion. . . . Cleanliness . . . is next to godliness."

smug (smug) *adj. Smug* people are self-satisfied and excessively sure of their own superiority; they tend to be narrow-minded and lacking in imagination. Such people live lives of *smug* self-assurance. They wear a *smug* smile. They know they're right, and they have a favorite saying to prove it: "I told you so." In Shakespeare's *The Merchant of Venice* (Act III, Scene 1), Shylock describes Antonio, now presumably suffering the loss of his fortune, as "a bankrupt . . . a beggar, who used to come so *smug* [*smugly*] upon the mart [into the marketplace]." *Smug* and *complacent* are very close in meaning, but there is a shade of difference; *smugness* always includes a feeling of superiority and satisfaction with oneself while *complacency* implies satisfaction with one's situation. The English essayist Charles Lamb (1775–1834) describes the "*complacency* and satisfaction that beam in the countenance of the newly married." In this he echoes Shakespeare's own characterization in *King Lear*, in which the King declares (Act IV, Scene 6): "I will die bravely, like a *smug* bridegroom." But some authorities say that here, Shakespeare used *smug* in the sense of "spruce."

sojourn (so′ jurn) *n.*, (so′ jurn, so jurn′—*o* as in *go*, *u* as in *fur*) *vb.* A *sojourn* is a temporary stay; to *sojourn* is to stay for a while. This is a handy word, with the built-in connotation of *temporariness*. It is pleasant and enlightening to *sojourn* in a foreign country. The British in India enjoyed summer *sojourns* in what they called "stations," located on higher and cooler ground. In Psalms 39:1, King David the Psalmist sings: "For I am a stranger with thee; and a *sojourner,* as all my fathers were. . . ." Here, *sojourner* refers to the fact that everyone's life is but a temporary visit. The Roman philosopher and emperor Marcus Aurelius (121–180) used *sojourn* in the same way: ". . . Life . . . is a battle and a *sojourning* in a strange land. . . ." These quotes may suggest that *sojourn* is an exclusively literary word, but this is not so. The word has great importance in tax law, in distinguishing between a temporary visit and a permanent domicile.

solemn (sol′ əm) *adj.* Anything described as *solemn* is of a serious nature, said or done with a full sense of its importance and meaning. *Solemn* is the opposite of *casual.* Church music is *solemn,* and puts us in a grave and thoughtful mood. A judge sitting high up at the bench is a *solemn* figure commanding our attention and respect. *Solemn* assurances are to be taken seriously and relied upon. A funeral is a *solemn* occasion. The Allies entered World War II with *solemn* dedication to the cause of democracy and freedom. *Solemnity* (sə lem′ nih tee) is the noun, meaning "gravity, seriousness." College graduates receive their diplomas with full realization of the *solemnity* of the ceremony. The world was deeply impressed by the *solemnity* of John F. Kennedy's state funeral. To *solemnize* (sol′ əm nize) is to perform (a ceremony) with the usual rites; the word is commonly used of the marriage ceremony. The Archbishop of Canterbury *solemnized* the marriage of Princess Elizabeth to Prince Philip.

somber (som′ bər—*o* as in *got*) *adj. Somber* describes a mood or an atmosphere as being gloomy and dismal, a facial expression as grave and serious, a color as dark and dull. The continuous increase in nuclear weapons paints a *somber* picture of the future of our planet; it causes *somber* thoughts and leaves us in a *somber* mood. If a person comes toward you with a *somber* look, be prepared for bad news. People wear *somber* clothes at funerals. It is comforting to sit by a roaring fire on a *somber* December day.

sordid (sawr′ did) *adj. Sordid* conduct is vile and contemptible; *sordid* methods or motives are immoral, base, and more often than not prompted by self-interest; *sordid* living quarters are squalid and filthy. The exact meaning of *sordid* will depend on the context. The English novelist Charles Dickens (1812–1870) described the *sordid* living conditions of the poor. The *sordid* and treacherous conduct of Iago in inventing lies about Desdemona's chastity is the mainspring of the action in Shakespeare's *Othello.* The Irish poet and playwright Oscar Wilde (1854–1900) commented on "the *sordid* perils of actual existence." Lord Chesterfield, the English statesman and author (1694–1773), wrote a letter about "a very covetous [greedy], *sordid* fellow [William Lowndes (1652–1774), a former Secretary of the Treasury]," who used to say, "Take care of the pence, for the pounds will take care of themselves." In whatever sense *sordid* is used, whether as *mean, base, foul, degraded,* or *squalid,* the effect is unpleasant, and the person or thing described is the very opposite of clean, sparkling, generous, noble, or honorable.

sparse (spars—*a* as in *ah,* both *s*'s as in *so*) *adj. Sparse* means "scanty, thinly scattered." The majority of people in the Third World have to get along on extremely *sparse* rations. In hard times, contributions to charities tend to be *sparse*. Some of the American states in the Far West have only *sparse* populations. Chinese beards are typically *sparse*. The adverb is *sparsely* (spars´ lee—*a* as in *ah,* both *s*'s as in *so*). The homes of the poor are usually *sparsely* furnished. Soldiers in retreat are almost always *sparsely* clothed and equipped.

speculate (spek´ yə late) *vb. Speculate* has two entirely different, unconnected meanings. In matters of the mind, to *speculate* is to ponder, to engage in thought, to meditate and form opinions. In the field of finance, to *speculate* is to buy and sell goods, securities, real estate, or an interest in a business, entering into the transaction with a risk of loss and a chance of profit. The noun *speculation* (spek yə lay´ shən) and the adjective *speculative* (spek´ yə lay tiv, -lə´) share both meanings of the verb. A great deal of *speculative* thought, or *speculation,* goes into the predictions of our future. A *speculator* (spek´ yə lay tər) is a person who gambles on the market; in a theatrical context, he is a ticket scalper. In view of the nuclear threat, many people are *speculating,* fearfully and gloomily, upon the future of our planet. In planning outdoor activities, we *speculate* on the weather.

spirited (spihr´ ə tid) *adj.* A *spirited* person or animal is one full of *spirit,* courage, vim, and vigor. A *spirited* attack is one made with courage and enthusiasm. A *spirited* defense or reply is vigorous and gives as good as it gets. *Spirited* conversation is animated, lively, and full of wit. A *spirited* debate is vigorous and energetic and keeps both sides on their mettle. *Spirited* is often used in combination form: a *high-spirited* tomboy, a *high-spirited* horse; a *public-spirited* citizen; a *mean-spirited* slander. The American poet and diplomat James Russell Lowell (1819–1891) deplored "what is essentially vulgar and *mean-spirited* in politics."

spontaneous (spon tay´ nee əs) *adj.* Anything unplanned, unpremeditated, said or done on the spur of the moment or on impulse, is *spontaneous*. The noun is *spontaneity* (spon tə nee´ ə tee). When a good Samaritan sees a person or an animal in trouble he is instantly ready with *spontaneous* help. A good public speaker knows how to ad lib when necessary; he is always right there with *spontaneous* remarks. Cautious people think long and hard before they speak; they seldom say anything *spontaneous*. To act with *spontaneity* is a sign of a free soul. *Spontaneous* combustion is the burning of any material resulting from chemical reactions within the material, without external ignition.

sprightly (sprite´ lee) *adj.* A *sprightly* person is lively and merry, frisky and spry, jaunty and light-hearted. A *sprite* is an elf; *spright* is an old spelling; hence *sprightly*. A song or dance or a style can be *sprightly* as well. The English poet William Wordsworth (1770–1850) wrote of ". . . a host of golden daffodils/. . . Ten thousand saw I at a glance,/Tossing their heads in *sprightly* dance." Puck, in Shakespeare's *A Midsummer-Night's Dream,* is as *sprightly* a figure as can be imagined. People in a happy mood tend to walk with a *sprightly* step. The American critic Henry Seidel Canby (1878–1961) wrote: "Readers prefer *sprightly* trash to dull excellence." (How about *sprightly* excellence, readers?)

spry (spry) *adj.* A *spry* person is nimble, lively, agile, chipper, full of energy. A really *spry* one was Jack of the old nursery rhyme: "Jack, be nimble,/Jack, be quick,/Jack, jump over the candlestick." But *spry* is generally reserved for those fortunate older people who have managed to retain their vigor and youth—who, at an advanced age, are *still spry*. The American novelist Hervey Allen (1889–1949) describes the "*spry,* youthful vigor and unimpaired strength" of an aging character.

squeamish (skweem' ish) *adj.* One can be *squeamish* (disgusted or nauseated) at the sight of blood or filth, or *squeamish* (prudish or easily shocked) at immodesty, or *squeamish* (scrupulous) about a moral lapse. People who are *squeamish* at the sight of blood (they don't belong in medical school) or at contact with anything physically unpleasant, like filthy, horrible living conditions (they shouldn't become social workers) are said to "have a weak (or delicate) stomach." Those who are *squeamish* at the expanse of skin revealed by a daring bikini would be classified as prudes or prigs, and should stay off European bathing beaches. Those who are *squeamish* about a breach of ethics are upright and highminded and don't belong in politics.

stagnate (stag' nate) *vb.* When applied to water, air, etc., to *stagnate* means, literally, to "stop flowing, stop moving," and consequently, to become *stagnant* (stag' nənt), or stale from standing, like a pool of water that has no outlet. *Stagnate* and *stagnant* are both widely used figuratively. To *stagnate,* in this sense, is to stop developing and become sluggish because of inactivity; *stagnant* describes the result. A mind or body that is not kept busy will *stagnate* and become *stagnant.* TV-addicted youngsters *stagnate* mentally and physically. In a recession, business soon becomes *stagnant.* The term *stagflation* was coined to describe an economy stopped in its tracks, i.e., *stagnating,* because of inflation. Let's hope that word becomes obsolete in the very near future!

stalwart (stawl' wərt) *n., adj.* A *stalwart* person is solidly built, strong, and brave. In context, *stalwart* can also describe those who are determined, firm, resolute, steadfast, loyal. According to the legend, the Knights of the Round Table were typically *stalwart*; it would take a *stalwart* fellow to wear such heavy armor and participate in the dangerous game of tilting, full speed ahead! The noun, too, is *stalwart*: The *stalwarts* of today play football, become commandos, or join the police force. Every far-seeing person must be a *stalwart* supporter of the United Nations, despite its weaknesses. In politics, the party *stalwarts* are the party faithful, those who loyally support the party and can always be counted on in a campaign.

stationary (stay' shə nerr ee) *adj. Stationary* describes any person or thing that is still, motionless, or, in context, unchanging. *Stationary* machinery is fixed in place, not portable. A person in terror may flee or remain *stationary*. When a moving vehicle collides with a *stationary* vehicle, the one in motion is usually considered to be at fault. A *stationary* (i.e., "unchanging") population is one that remains at the same level. A *stationary* price is one that has not changed for a certain period. Do not confuse *stationary* with *stationery*. Stationery is pronounced in the same way, but it means "writing paper," or, more broadly, includes related materials like pens, pencils, erasers, etc. The difference in the ending results from the derivation: *Stationary* comes from *station,* in the sense of a fixed place; *stationery* comes from *stationer,* a seller of writing materials.

stature (stach' ər) *n.* Literally, *stature* means "height"; figuratively, it means "level of attainment, standing, rank." A person of great *stature* is one who has made his mark, whose "place in the world" is assured. No one questions the *stature* of Abraham Lincoln in history. The English physician Edward Jenner (1749–1823) and the American virologist Jonas Salk (born 1914) achieved great *stature* through their discoveries of the vaccines against smallpox and poliomyelitis (infantile paralysis, or "polio") respectively. As a result, these diseases, which used to break out in terrible epidemics, now occur rarely. Great achievements endow a person with great *stature*. St. Luke, in his Gospel (2:52), wrote of Jesus: "Jesus increased in wisdom and *stature,* and in favor with God and man." According to the Swiss psychiatrist Carl Gustav Jung (1875–1961), ". . . love alone can give her [woman] her full *stature.* . . ." (There are those who differ.)

status (stay' təs, stat' əs) *n.* A person's *status* is his position or standing, as related to others of his class or profession. It is important to consider a man's professional *status* before engaging his services. *Status,* generally, is an established position in society. Many people go through life seeking *status*. A *status symbol* is any object or activity that, in the opinion of the majority, confers status on a person. Examples are impressive addresses, big cars, yachts, unlisted telephone numbers, expensive travel, being seen in the "right" restaurants and clubs. *Status* can mean "state of affairs" in relation to an ongoing situation. People are worried about the *status* of disarmament negotiations. The *status quo* (kwo: *o* as in *go*) is Latin for "the existing condition." One is often well advised not to take the risks of a radical change in one's job or way of life, and to remain content with the *status quo*. The adjective *static* (stat' ik) means "at rest, unchanging." A *static* relationship is one that does not change. Concern about the world supply of food has led to a campaign for a *static* population.

staunch (stawnch, stahnch) *adj.* A *staunch* friend is firm, constant, faithful, loyal, trustworthy, **steadfast** (see the next entry); he will see you through thick and thin. A *staunch* Democrat or Republican will always support his party and its candidates. A *staunch* believer in a doctrine will cling to his beliefs. A good lawyer will do his utmost in *staunch* defense of his client's interests. The American poet Henry Wadsworth Longfellow (1807–1882) applied *staunch* to a ship: "Build me straight, O worthy Master!/*Staunch* and strong, a goodly vessel,/That shall laugh at all disaster,/And with wave and whirlwind wrestle!"

steadfast (sted´ fast—*a* as in *hat* or *arm*, -fəst) *adj.* *Steadfast* is another word for "firm, unwavering, staunch." What is more valuable than a *steadfast* friend? A truly religious person is *steadfast* in his faith. Joan of Arc *steadfastly* maintained that she had heard the voices of saints. An opinionated man will be stubborn, and *steadfast* to his principles; his mind's made up—don't confuse him with the facts! *Steadfast* takes on the meaning of "steady, fixed" in the expression *steadfast gaze*. It is difficult not to turn your eyes away from a *steadfast gaze*.

stem (stem) *vb.* Literally, to *stem* is to check, restrain, or stop. It is vital, after a wound, to *stem* the flow of blood. A dam *stems* the flow of a river. Figuratively, *stem* is often used to describe the making of headway against the surge or tide of popular opinion, or the quelling or curbing of a wave of emotion. After the failure of the attempt to rescue the hostages in Iran, President Carter went on the air to *stem* the tide of despair among the American people. To their sorrow, the French aristocracy in the late eighteenth century took no steps to *stem* the wave of popular indignation.

stigma (stig´ mə) *n.* A *stigma* is a mark of shame, disgrace, or infamy. A person born out of wedlock in one of those states that still note illegitimacy on the birth certificate will go through life bearing that *stigma*. Healthy young males (sometimes even conscientious objectors) who do not serve in the armed forces in time of war may bear the *stigma* of cowardice ("What did you do in the war, Daddy?"). For years after the abolition of slavery, the newly freed continued to bear the *stigma* of their previous bondage. To *stigmatize* (stig´ mə tize) someone is to brand him, to set some mark of shame on him, to characterize him scornfully. Tell a few fibs, and you will be *stigmatized* as a liar for all time. People who make a lot of money are often *stigmatized* by the less successful as "materialistic." The English novelist and critic Aldous Huxley (1894–1963) used *stigmatize* mockingly to mean "designate" or "brand" when he said, "I wish . . . that the fates had not *stigmatized* me 'writer.' "

stint (stint) *n., vb.* One's *stint* is one's allotted work or chore. Each of us is expected to do his daily *stint*. It is a good feeling to relax after having done one's *stint* for the day. In old-fashioned families, children were given chores to do and were not free to play until each had completed his *stint*. For a professional musician, six hours of practice is not an unusual *stint*. *Stint* goes off in another direction in the expression *without stint*, where *stint* means "limit" or "restriction." To work *without stint* is to spare no efforts. In moments of crisis, good neighbors will pitch in *without stint*. President Truman said, "During the war years we . . . expended our resources . . . *without stint*." As a verb, to *stint* is to be frugal, get along on little. Conscientious parents will *stint* for years on end in order to save up for their children's education. If an unexpected guest shows up, the family will *stint* on their portions at table (family hold-back, sometimes abbreviated as *f.h.b.*).

straggle (strag' əl) *vb.* To *straggle* is to roam or ramble. A member of a moving group who strays from the line of march is said to *straggle*. When an army retreats in disorder, it is common for soldiers to *straggle* in search of food. Cattle on their way to and from pasture often *straggle* and have to be pulled into line. Sheepdogs keep the flock from *straggling*. The English poet Robert Greene (1560-1592) wrote of "flocks that *straggling* feed." *Straggling* (strag' ling) is used as an adjective to describe things spreading in an untidy or disorderly fashion. A *straggling* town or village, which "growed like Topsy," may sometimes be more interesting than one planned from scratch. A *straggling* beard grows unevenly and often looks unkempt. Untrimmed *straggling* vines give a place a messy look.

strategy (strat' ə jee) *n. Strategy*, in general, is overall planning and maneuvering for the purpose of achieving a specific result. It is the concept of an operation (what Richard Nixon liked to call the "game plan"), as opposed to *tactics*, the carrying out of the steps that make up the plan. In military usage, *strategy* is generalship, the manipulation of military movements. Political candidates employ experts to devise the *strategy* of their campaigns. Advertising agencies devise market *strategies* for their clients. An earnest suitor works out a careful *strategy* for winning the hand of his fair lady (who often has formulated her own *strategy* long in advance). A *strategy* is the step-by-step design of an overall plan. A *stratagem* (strat' ə jem) is a particular trick or ruse for surprising and getting the advantage of an adversary or competitor. A *strategy* may well include a number of *stratagems*. Nixon's *stratagems* finally emerged as "dirty tricks." A diversionary attack or feint is a *stratagem* for deceiving the foe. *Strategic* (strə tee' jik) is the adjective relating to *strategy*. A *strategic* move in war or games is an integral part of the overall *strategy*. A *strategic* retreat or withdrawal is part of the general *strategy*; so is *strategic* bombing. Strategic can mean "essential" in describing material that is necessary for waging war or for conducting any campaign. Copper is only one of many *strategic* materials in time of war. Medical supplies are *strategic* during an epidemic. The OSS (Office of *Strategic* Services), established during World War II, was the forerunner of the CIA (Central Intelligence Agency).

stratum (stray' təm, strat' əm, strah' təm) *n.* A *stratum*, in geology, is a layer of rock or other material in the earth's crust. In social matters, a *stratum* is a class of society relating to education, wealth, birth, etc. The plural is *strata*. Never use *strata* as a singular—or *phenomena*, or *data*, or *media*! (*Agenda* is an exception.) Nowadays, university students come from every *stratum* of society. Those people in India who used to be called "the untouchables," and whom Gandhi (1869-1948) renamed "the children of God," remain, despite the name change, the lowest *stratum* of the caste-ridden Indian society. Remember, *strata* is plural only. There are numerous financial *strata* in society, from paupers to billionaires.

strenuous (stren' yoo əsz—*oo* as in *boot*) *adj. Strenuous* describes anything that involves or needs vigorous exertion. Difficult tasks require *strenuous* efforts. Farming is a *strenuous* occupation. Mountain climbing is a *strenuous* pursuit. Tennis singles is a *strenuous* game. It is wonderful to relax before a roaring fire after a *strenuous* day's skiing. It takes *strenuous* measures to keep a step ahead of the criminal element. *Strenuous objections* is a common phrase, meaning "strong objections." From a physical standpoint, dictionary-writing is not a demanding profession; as a nervous and mental activity, it is a *strenuous* one. The adverb, *strenuously* (stren′ yoo əs lee—*oo* as in *boot*), means "strongly, vigorously." The abolitionists campaigned *strenuously* for an end to slavery. The adverb is often found in the expression to *object strenuously*: there are numbers of exclusively male clubs that, to their shame, *object strenuously* to the admission of female members.

stress (stres) *n., vb*. We hear a lot about *stress* resulting from worry and the rat race. In that context, *stress* means "pressure, strain, tension," both physical and emotional. Wars and recessions are times of *stress*. Family financial worries cause *stress* that can impair health. People may act desperately under *stress* of poverty or ambition. A quite different meaning of *stress* is "importance, significance": to *lay stress upon* something is to give it importance and significance. The armed forces lay *stress* on spit and polish. Foremen lay *stress* on promptness and attention to work. Still another meaning of *stress* refers to the accent or emphasis on a syllable: In the word *importance*, the accent or *stress* is on the second syllable; in *impotence*, the *stress* is on the first syllable. To *stress* is to emphasize. Fire-drill manuals *stress* the importance of walking, not running, to the nearest exit. To *stress* a point in an argument is to emphasize it, to give it importance. I cannot too greatly *stress* the point that it is of great importance to use language correctly.

stun (stun—*u* as in *fun*) *vb*. To *stun* someone is, depending on the context, physically to knock him out or daze him, or psychologically to astonish or amaze him. A blow to the head sufficient to *stun* a boxer may cause brain damage. Bad news may temporarily *stun* a person. The rush of events in times of crisis can *stun* an entire population. One is always *stunned* to hear of the sudden death of a friend. People are sometimes *stunned* by the amount of a doctor's or lawyer's bill. The form *stunning* has become an adjective meaning "strikingly beautiful" as when one exclaims, "Look at that *stunning* woman!" or "What a *stunning* dress!" *Stunning* is appropriate not only to ravishing women and their attire and adornments, but also to stage or film productions, art exhibits, and the like. But one wouldn't use it to describe an awe-inspiring cathedral or castle or mountain; *splendid* or *majestic* would be more appropriate.

stupefy (stoo′ pə fy, styoo′-, *oo* as in *boot*) *vb*. Literally, to *stupefy* someone is to make him incapable of clear thought, to render him senseless, the way drink benumbs the brain. The English poet Robert Browning (1812–1889) wrote of "good, strong, thick, *stupefying* incense-smoke." Figuratively and more generally, to *stupefy* someone is to overwhelm him with astonishment, daze him, *strike* him dumb, "take his breath away." In this latter sense, *stupefy* comes very close to the figurative meaning of **stun**. A *stupefying* amount of work goes into the writing and publishing of an unabridged dictionary (to say nothing of this little effort). People are *stupefied* at their first sight of the Grand Canyon. The noun *stupefaction* (stoo pə fak'shən, styoo-, *oo* as in *boot*) means "amazement." Newly arrived travelers gaze upon the Taj Mahal with awe and *stupefaction*.

subdue (səb doo´, -dyoo—*oo* as in *boot*) *vb.* To *subdue* is to overcome, repress, bring under control. In building its empire, Great Britain had to *subdue* nations and tribes scattered all over the world. Cowboys *subdue* wild colts; animal trainers *subdue* lions and tigers. People in control of their emotions *subdue* their impulses and feelings. In other contexts, to *subdue* is to tone down: It is often agreeable to *subdue* the light in order to make a room feel cozier. The form *subdued* is used as an adjective meaning "quiet" or "toned down." People are often *subdued* after an emotional outburst or a violent argument. *Subdued* lighting is favorable to people's appearances, especially when they are wearing harsh makeup. *Subdued* tones (*pianissimi*) are often very effective in singing.

subject (səb jekt´) *vb.* We are familiar with *subject* (sub´jikt) as both noun and adjective. As a verb, *subject* is accented differently and has other meanings. To *subject* a country to one's rule is to bring it under control; to *subject* a person to one's influence is to dominate him. To *subject* someone to ridicule is to expose him to that unpleasant experience. The Irish playwright Oscar Wilde (1854–1900) was *subjected* to shame and virtual exile after his conviction and imprisonment for homosexual practices. *Subjected* also means "exposed" in cases when a person is *subjected* to severe strain, or a textile is *subjected* to hard wear, or a metal to intense heat. To catch errors, an author should *subject* his manuscript to close scrutiny. The noun is *subjection* (səb jek´ shən). The *subjection* of the American Indians took many years and cost many lives. Hitler kept not only Germany but much of the rest of Europe in *subjection* for many years.

subjective (səb jek´ tiv) *adj.* See **objective**.

submissive (səb mis´ iv) *adj.* To *submit* (səb mit´) to someone or to some superior force is to yield, surrender, give in, end resistance. This is known as an *act of submission*. George Washington addressed his army in these terms: "Our cruel and unrelenting enemy leaves us only the choice of brave resistance or the most abject *submission*." A *submissive* person is inclined to *submit*, to yield to the authority of another person or a superior force; he is humble and easily dominated; he seeks peace at any price; he can be described as "milk-toast." A gesture or look indicating surrender can be described as *submissive*. *Submissive* behavior was expected of wives in the days of yore. (You've come a long way, baby.)

subscribe (səb skribe´) *vb. Subscribe* has a number of literal uses: one can *subscribe* (agree to contribute money) to a charity or a church fund, *subscribe* for shares in a corporation, *subscribe* to a magazine or newspaper, etc. Figuratively, to *subscribe* to someone's belief, view, or opinion is to agree with it, share it, adopt it, endorse it. People of independent minds do not automatically *subscribe* to popular opinions; they like to investigate and think things out for themselves. In olden times, everybody *subscribed* to the fallacy that the sun revolved around the earth. In communist countries, it is very much safer to *subscribe* to the Marxist doctrine than to dissent.

subsequent (sub' sə kwənt) *adj.* A *subsequent* event is an event that follows another, one that happens later. Anything that occurs on January 2 is *subsequent* to anything that happened on January 1. The opposite of *subsequent* is *previous*. In early times, the practice of medicine was, by modern standards, extremely crude; in *subsequent* generations, important discoveries were made and great skills developed. The adverb *subsequently* (sub' sə kwənt lee) means "later, afterward." Students who neglect to study a subject in high school may *subsequently* have trouble with it in college. Deforesting a hilly area will lead to erosion and *subsequently* to the loss of topsoil.

subside (səb side') *vb.* When flood waters *subside,* they sink to a lower level. When land *subsides* because of mining operations, it sinks. Buildings sometimes *subside,* i.e., settle lower in the ground, if shrinkage occurs in the subsoil. *Subside* is often used to mean "quiet down," when it applies to things like noise, applause, laughter, weeping, emotions, etc. After prolonged clapping, the speaker signals for silence, and the applause *subsides.* It takes a few minutes for laughter to *subside* after the telling of a good joke. A raging fever will *subside* after proper medical treatment. When storms, winds, or high seas *subside,* they die away.

substantial (səb stan' shəl) *adj. Substantial* has several meanings, depending on the context. It may describe size. A *substantial* amount of anything is a lot of it. A substantial sum or bank balance is a considerable one. A *substantial* meal is an ample one. A *substantial* improvement in one's health, work, manners, etc., is an important or noticeable one. A *substantial* company is one that is in strong financial shape. *Substantial* can also be used to designate degree. If we are in *substantial* agreement, we agree in the main, we are together on the essential points. A *substantial* reason for doing something is a good, solid reason. The adverb is *substantially* (səb stan' shə lee). If your efforts have contributed *substantially* to the success of an enterprise, you have participated in a big way, made an important contribution to the overall effort. Here, *substantially* means "considerably." To be *substantially* in agreement is to agree on the main points, with only minor details to be cleared up. In this context, *substantially* means "practically" or "in the main."

substantiate (səb stan' shee ate) *vb.* To *substantiate* something, such as an accusation, a claim, or a theory, is to prove it, to present facts in support of it. It is easy enough to make a charge, but quite a different matter to *substantiate* it. If you reject a claim I make against you, I may have to take you to court in order to *substantiate* it. A person spreading damaging stories about someone had better be prepared to *substantiate* them if he wants to avoid damages for defamation of character. *Substantiation* (səb stan shee ay' shən) is proof through the presentation of facts in support of a claim, a charge, a theory, etc. A series of time-lapse photographs showing a ship disappearing or "sinking" below the horizon could be offered in *substantiation* of the theory that the earth is round.

subterfuge (sub´ tər fyooj—*oo* as in *boot*) *n*. A *subterfuge* is a dodge, excuse, or ruse used in order to evade or get around a rule, regulation, or anything one doesn't want to face or do. Malingering is a common *subterfuge* used in order to avoid work or other responsibility. "A previous appointment" and "We can't get a babysitter" are handy *subterfuges* for turning down an unwelcome invitation. "I gave at the office" is a favorite *subterfuge* to get around making a contribution when the charity representative comes to the door. If you can't get anywhere in a difficult situation by being open and frank, you can always resort to a *subterfuge*.

subtle (sut´ l) *adj*. This useful adjective can have any one of several meanings, depending on the context. A *subtle* flavor or odor, or a *subtle* smile, is one difficult to describe, hard to pinpoint or put one's finger on. A *subtle* distinction is a fine distinction, one that is somehow felt but may be extremely difficult to explain in precise terms. A *subtle* shade of difference or of meaning is a delicate one, one that requires real perception to understand. A *subtle* mind is sensitive, keen and shrewd, discriminating, blessed with insight. A *subtle* explanation is one that sees and touches on all the fine points and sets them forth in a meaningful way. A *subtle* argument is clever, ingenious, usually complex. A *subtle* approach to a problem is a careful, delicate, sensitive one, one that considers all the aspects. When an actor gives a *subtle* performance, he has mastered all the details of the character and has been able to project just what the author had in mind. *Subtle* can at times take on the meaning of "crafty" or "wily"; Iago, in Shakespeare's *Othello*, is a *subtle* liar, able to make his lies seem truer than the truth. We are told in Genesis (3:1) that "the serpent was more *subtil* [*subtle*] than any beast of the field." *Subtlety* (sut´ l tee—*u* as in *but*) is the noun, sharing all the meanings of the adjective, but used more commonly to describe the quality of being *subtle*, or to mean "mental acuteness, the ability to draw fine distinctions." It takes close reading to enjoy to the full the *subtlety* of the humor of the American writer Mark Twain (Samuel Langhorne Clemens, 1835–1910). Only a person of *subtlety* can understand and explain the complex problems of today's world. *Subtlety* often appears in the plural, meaning "fine points," the *subtleties* of logic, the *subtleties* of life.

succinct (sək singkt´) *adj*. A *succinct* report, message, memorandum, or narrative is expressed in few words; it is brief and to the point, terse, concise, compact, "short and sweet." *Succinct* language omits unnecessary words. The British poet William Cowper (1731–1800) gives excellent advice on this type of writing:

> A tale should be judicious, clear, *succinct*;
> The language plain, the incidents well-link'd;
> Tell not as new what ev'ry body knows;
> And, new or old, still hasten to a close.

An excellent example of *succinct* communication is the message radioed by an American carrier pilot in World War II: "Sighted sub, sank same." Another famous instance is the monosyllabic answer sent by an American general (who was in a tough spot) to the German commander who had ordered him to surrender. "Nuts!" replied he. A tale of rather more doubtful authenticity concerns the British general Sir Charles Napier (1782-1853). The telegram he is reputed to have sent from India, announcing that he had subdued the province of Sind, read simply, "Peccavi." What a risk he took, relying on the classical scholarship of the headquarters in London! Did he really expect them to translate the Latin *peccavi* into the English "I have sinned," and then, by making a pun on that, to decode the real message as: "I have Sind"?

suffice (sə fīse´, -fīze´) *vb*. To *suffice* is to be enough, to "fill the bill, do the trick." Four to six hours a day may *suffice* as practice time for a professional musician. Fifteen percent *suffices* as a tip for waiters and cab drivers. When you are dealing with sensitive people, a hint will usually *suffice*. If you trust someone, you can trust his word; his promise will *suffice*. *Suffice* can also mean "be enough *for*," i.e., "satisfy." The English poet Christina Rossetti (1830-1894) wrote:

> In the bleak mid-winter
> A stable-place *sufficed*
> The Lord God almighty,
>   Jesus Christ.

Even *suffice* we get *sufficient* (sə fish´ ənt), meaning "enough, adequate for the purpose." When you organize a picnic, you must be sure to take along *sufficient* food. People traveling abroad should always be provided with *sufficient* money for the expenses of the trip. We are told that a word to the wise is *sufficient*, and St. Matthew (6:34) tell us: "Take . . . no thought for the morrow [tomorrow]. . . . *Sufficient* unto the day is the evil thereof." The noun is *sufficiency* (sə fish´ ən see). A *sufficiency* of something is enough of it to meet the needs of the situation. Every community should have a *sufficiency* of shelter for the homeless.

suitable (soo´ tə b'l—*oo* as in *boot*) *adj*. *Suitable* means "fitting" or "appropriate"; it describes anyone or anything that *suits* the purpose or the occasion, meets the need, fills the bill, is just what the doctor ordered. People below the poverty level often find it impossible to purchase food *suitable* for human consumption. It is great fun to come upon a beach *suitable* for swimming. Movies are rated according to whether they are *suitable* for children. When attending a function, like a banquet or a wedding or a funeral, remember to choose clothing *suitable* for the occasion. There are roles in the theater for which it is hard to find a *suitable* actor. We are all faced with occasions when it is difficult to summon up the word *suitable* to express one's exact thought, or to describe a scene or an emotion.

sullen (sul´ ən) *adj*. A *sullen* person is gloomily and silently ill-humored, resentful, morose; a *sullen* look is peevish, grumpy, a look of irritation and bad temper.

People who are unsociable in a peevish, ill-humored way can be described as in a *sullen* mood. A silent, resentful audience in disagreement with a speaker proposing an unpopular program expresses its disapproval through *sullen* looks. The Scottish poet Robert Burns (1759-1796) emphasized the resentment factor in his poem *Tam O' Shanter*, writing of ". . . our . . . *sullen* dame,/Gathering her brows like gathering storm,/Nursing her wrath to keep it warm."

sultry (sul´ tree) *adj*. A *sultry* day is hot and muggy, oppressive, sweltering; *sultry* days are dog days. A *sultry* woman is passionate, sensuous, voluptuous, tempting. The English poet Lord Byron (1788-1824) touched on both aspects in *Don Juan*: "What men call gallantry, and gods adultery,/Is much more common where the climate's *sultry*." Many of the novels of the English writer Graham Greene (born 1904) are set in remote *sultry* islands. Old-fashioned movie vamps like Pola Negri were famous for their *sultry* glances. In Shakespeare's *Hamlet* (Act V, Scene 2), Hamlet, toying with the fool Osric (who has bowed low, making a sweeping gesture, hat in hand), tells him to "put [his] bonnet to his [its] right use: 'tis for the head." Osric protests: ". . . . 'tis very hot." Hamlet says: ". . . . 'tis very cold." Osric agrees, then Hamlet says, "But yet methinks [I think] it is very *sultry*. . . ." The toadying Osric agrees again: "Exceeding, my lord; it is very *sultry*. . . ." (Apparently, the confused Osric blows hot and cold.)

summarize (sum´ ə rize) *vb*. A *summary* is a brief recapitulation, a brief restatement and concise summing up of the main points. To *summarize* is to give a *summary*, to *sum up* in concise form. After a lecture or speech, or an argument in court, it is helpful to the audience or court to *summarize*, and in that way to bring the main points to mind—especially if the lecture or argument has been a long one. It is a rule of reporting to *summarize* the story in the opening sentence, and then proceed with the details.

summon (sum´ ən) *vb*. To *summon* someone is to send for him, to demand his presence. A principal who gets a bad report about a pupil's conduct will *summon* him to his office. A stockholders' meeting is initiated by a notice *summoning* the stockholders to attend at a certain time and place. To *summon* someone to do something is to call upon him to do what is required. A congressional committee can *summon* a person to appear before it as witness. A commanding officer may *summon* the enemy to surrender. To *summon up* one's courage, energy, or strength is to gather or muster it up in the face of a demanding situation. A person has to *summon up* his courage to get out of bed and investigate a mysterious noise in the middle of the night. Toward the end of a long race, a runner must *summon up* the last ounce of energy to stay the course. In Shakespeare's *King Henry V* (Act III, Scene 1), the King, *summoning* his army to prepare for battle, cries: ". . . when the blast of war blows in our ears,/. . . stiffen the sinews, *summon up* the blood. . . . " Another meaning of *summon up* is "recall, recollect, conjure up." Under the stimulus of a particular musical passage, one often *summons up* a past experience. A whiff of fragrance can *summon up* scenes of one's youth or the images of friends long gone. In Sonnet 30, Shakespeare, reminiscing, wrote: "When to the sessions of sweet silent thought/I *summon up* remembrance of things past. . . . "

sumptuous (sump´ choo əs—*oo* as in *boot*) *adj.* What is *sumptuous* is lavish, costly, magnificent, splendid, dazzling. The Rockefellers and the Vanderbilts built themselves *sumptuous* homes. The leading citizens of ancient Rome were famous for their *sumptuous* feasts. One is overawed by the *sumptuous* interiors of the baroque churches of Europe. The royal palaces of Europe were *sumptuously* furnished from basement to attic. In *The Young Visiters* [sic], the English author Daisy Ashford (1881–1972) described a residence as "a *sumpshous* [sic] spot all done up in gold with plenty of looking glasses." (Daisy used the right word, even if she spelled it wrong.)

superfluous (soo pur´ floo əs—first *oo* as in *book*, *u* as in *fur*, second *oo* as in *boot*) *adj.* Anyone or anything *superfluous* is unnecessary, more than is needed or wanted. In the current expression *free gift*, the word *free* is *superfluous* (a gift is always free). Cf. **redundant**. Labor conflicts have developed because of management's desire to eliminate *superfluous* personnel, like the fireman on a diesel locomotive. The American novelist Herman Melville (1819–1891) pointed out that "armed ships allow nothing *superfluous* to litter up the decks." A *superfluity* (soo pər floo´ ə tee—both *oo*'s as in *boot*) of something is an excess of it, an oversupply, an amount that is more than is necessary or needed. The rich often have a *superfluity* of the good things of life. There are novels in which the action is stopped by a *superfluity* of description. There is no such thing as a *superfluity* of happiness.

supersede (soo pər seed´—*oo* as in *boot*) *vb.* To *supersede* is to replace, supplant, take the place of, eliminate the need for. Airplanes have *superseded* ships as the principal mode of long-distance passenger travel, just as trucks have *superseded* trains for the movement of freight. Modern medical treatment has *superseded* the use of leeches and bleeding. The test tube will never *supersede* the old-fashioned method of creating the next generation. The English historian and author Thomas Macaulay (1800–1859) wrote a letter containing this sentence: "I shall not be satisfied unless I produce something which shall for a few days *supersede* the last fashionable novel on the tables of young ladies." If you've completed the sixth draft of something but want to hold on to the fifth, better write SUPERSEDED in big letters across the face of the fifth. *Supersede* would not normally be used in situations where people are involved, i.e., where one person replaces another (see the next entry).

supplant (sə plant´) *vb.* To *supplant* is to displace, replace, **supersede** (see the previous entry); to step in the shoes of (someone else), to take the place of or to succeed (someone or something else). Planes have *supplanted* ships in ocean travel. Plastics have *supplanted* wood and metal in many articles. One would use *supersede* rather than *supplant* in a case where a new statute nullifies an old law, but *supplant* rather than *supersede* in a situation where a new love crowds out the old one. When people are involved, in matters of love or favor, *supplant* often implies a campaign of scheming or wily maneuvering that succeeds in ousting a former favorite.

supple (sup′ əl) *adj*. *Supple,* in its literal use, means "pliable, easily bent," like the twigs of a willow tree. The *supple* stem of a young tree can grow into a stout and rigid trunk. Thin leather, like kidskin, is *supple* and will not crack when bent. Applied to people, *supple* means "limber," like an athlete or gymnast. A ballet dancer must have a *supple* body. The English poet Ralph Hodgson (1871-1962) wrote of

> Eve, with her body white,
> *Supple* and smooth
> To her finger tips.

supplement (sup′ lə ment) *n*., (sup′ lə mənt) *vb*. The term *supplement* applies to anything added to something to complete it or give it a special quality. The term often applies to sections added to reference books, to supply more recent information. The "Sunday supplements" are separate sections added to newspapers covering specific fields, like the book-review section, the travel section, etc. *Supplements* are added to foods to provide vitamins or other aids to a balanced diet. As a verb, to *supplement* (note different pronunciation of last syllable) is to make an addition to something. Some professional people *supplement* their earnings by giving lectures. People on long hikes can *supplement* their provisions by picking berries and shooting game. Martin Luther King, Jr. (1929-1968), said: "Nonviolent action, the Negro saw, was the way to *supplement,* not replace, the process of change. . . ."

suppress (sə pres′) *vb*. *Suppress* is a versatile word. In general, to *suppress* something is to put an end to its existence or activity or use. To *suppress* a political party is to stop its activities, in the way that Generalissimo Franco (1892-1975) *suppressed* the communist party in Spain. To *suppress* a custom is to abolish it, in the way that Kemal Ataturk (1881-1938) *suppressed* the wearing of the veil for women in Turkey. To *suppress* a book or a newspaper is to ban its publication, as Juan Peron (1895-1974) *suppressed* newspapers in Argentina. When one *suppresses* a smile or a feeling or an impulse or a cough or a belch, one holds it in, represses it. When an uprising or a revolution is *suppressed,* it is crushed, "put an end to." The Irish statesman and author Edmund Burke (1729-1797), writing of the English general and statesman Oliver Cromwell (1599-1658), said that he "was a man in whom ambition had not wholly *suppressed,* but only suspended, the sentiments of religion." The Roman statesman and orator Cicero (106-43 B.C.) stated: ". . . the historian . . . shall never dare utter an untruth and shall *suppress* nothing that is true." The noun is *suppression* (sə presh′ ən). The Constitution of the United States forbids *suppression* of free speech.

surge (surj—*u* as in *fur*) *n., vb.* A *surge* is an onrush, a strong forward sweep. All who have sailed on a windy day have experienced the *surge* of the sea. It is terrifying to watch the *surge* of floodwaters. On the TV these days, we witness the *surge* of angry crowds in one country after another. *Surge* is used of things other than floods and crowds. You experience a *surge* of anger when you see an animal mistreated. A *surge* of pity overwhelms any sensitive person at the sight of hungry children in backward countries. As a verb, to *surge* is to swell forward like rushing waves. At the end of a game, the milling crowd *surges* out of the stadium, like floods *surging* over a valley. Organ music *surges* through a church. Anger *surges* up when one hears of gross injustice.

surly (sur´ lee—*u* as in *fur*) *adj.* A *surly* person, manner, voice, remark, or answer is unfriendly, rude, bad-tempered, cantankerous. *Surly* is the opposite of *friendly, polite, cheerful, warmhearted.* A *surly* person just doesn't want to be bothered, and lets you know it. Scrooge, in *A Christmas Carol* by the English writer Charles Dickens (1812–1870), starts out ("Bah! Humbug!") as the *surliest* of characters, but softens up at the end. A *surly* waiter can spoil a whole meal. A *surly* manner won't win friends and influence people.

susceptible (sə sep´ tə b'l) *adj.* A *susceptible* person is impressionable, easily influenced. The word is used in a variety of ways. To be *susceptible* to flattery is to respond to it easily, and allow oneself to be affected and influenced by it. We are always aghast on discovering that a public official has been *susceptible* to bribery. To be *susceptible* to colds is to catch them easily. A special use of *susceptible* (a *susceptible* young man or young lady) is to describe someone who easily—and frequently—falls in love. *Susceptible* followed by *of* has the special meaning of "capable": An ambiguous passage is one *susceptible of* various interpretations, i.e., capable of being taken or understood in more than one way. The oracle at Delphi in ancient Greece gave answers and prophecies that were intentionally ambiguous. The phrase *Delphic utterance* has come to mean any statement *susceptible of* different meanings. Aesop, the sixth-century B.C. author of the *Fables,* told stories with a hidden moral; hence the expression *Aesopian language,* that is, language with a hidden meaning for those in the know, like members of a conspiracy; in other words, language *susceptible of* other than the literal meaning.

sustain (sə stane´) *vb. Sustain* can be used in quite a variety of ways. To *sustain* a roof or a shelf or a burden is to bear its weight, to support it. It takes strong brackets to *sustain* the weight of a crammed bookshelf. *Sustain* can mean "support" in another sense: Private charities *sustain* needy families. To *sustain* an effort is to keep at it. Devotees of historic buildings have made *sustained* efforts to keep real estate developers from demolishing old landmarks. When a court *sustains* a claim or an objection, it upholds it. "Objection *sustained*" is a common expression during a trial in court. When a singer *sustains* a note, he "holds" it, prolongs it, keeps it going. To *sustain* a defeat or a loss or a hardship is to suffer it. The use of *sustain* to mean "suffer" in expressions like *sustain injury* or *sustain* *a broken leg* is not recommended; *suffer* or *experience* will do, without the implication of *endure* that attaches to *sustain*. The noun is *sustention* (sə sten′ shən).

symmetry (sim′ ih tree) *n*. The term *symmetry* is applied to excellence of balance or proportion generally, and especially to evenness and matching of parts on opposite sides of a design. A clear example of *symmetry* in architecture is a Greek temple, with its perfectly matching rows of columns along either side. Beauty in a human face involves *symmetry*; a marked difference between the two sides spoils it. The English essayist Charles Lamb (1775-1834) thundered against "*borrowers of books*—those mutilators of collections, spoilers of the *symmetry* of shelves, and creators of odd volumes." The adjective is *symmetrical* (sih meh′ trih kəl). A design or object that is balanced, with a regular arrangement of its corresponding parts on either side, is called *symmetrical*. The human body is basically *symmetrical*, despite the varying functions of the two sides of the brain, and movie stars' assertions about their "better profile." Snowflakes are always *symmetrical*.

synonym (sin′ ə nim) *n*. *Synonyms* are words that have the same meaning. Examples: *big, large*; *joyful, happy*; *sad, unhappy*; *little, small*. *Synonymous* (sih non′ ə məs) is the adjective that describes such pairs (or groups—there may be groups of more than two that have the same meaning: *huge, vast, tremendous, enormous*). The basic or general meaning of words that are *synonymous* may be the same, but often the *synonyms* have different shades of meaning and varying associations and implications. In the words of the English writer Aldous Huxley (1894-1963): "Non-scientific writers are free to use a variety of *synonyms* to express the same idea in subtly different ways." A word that means the opposite of another word is its *antonym* (an′ tə nim). Examples: *big, small*; *happy, sad*; *fast, slow*; *pretty, ugly*. With *antonyms*, too, delicate shades of meaning must be taken into consideration, although the basic meanings are opposite.

tacky (tak′ ee) *adj*. This adjective has several entirely different meanings. In context, it can mean "sticky," like fresh paint or varnish that is not yet quite dry. Otherwise—and again depending on the context—anything described as *tacky* is either shabby, seedy, sleazy, down at the heel; or dowdy, tasteless, unfashionable; or (though this is an uncommon use) vulgarly flashy or gaudy. *Tacky* is a versatile and useful word, but must be used carefully, because its interpretation can vary so much. A *tacky* house is shabby, jerry-built. A *tacky* dress or outfit is out of fashion, dowdy, poorly designed, and badly made. The American writer Carson McCullers (1917-1967) described a character as "that pasty fat girl with those *tacky* pigtails." If someone is described as showing up at an afternoon tea party flashing a lot of cheap imitation jewelry and wearing a *tacky*, overly elaborate cocktail dress, *tacky* will take on the meaning of "flashy" rather than its more usual meaning of "dowdy."

tamper (tam′ pər) *vb.* To *tamper* is to meddle. To *tamper* with a lock or a piece of machinery is to meddle or monkey around with it, usually with the implication that the interference ruins the mechanism. *Tampering* with a letter or a manuscript involves improper, unlawful alteration. To *tamper* with a product, like a medicine, is to adulterate or contaminate it. To *tamper* with the evidence is to falsify it. *Tampering* with a witness or a juror involves illegally influencing him. The early publishers of Shakespeare's plays often *tampered* with the texts, producing variations among the different editions. Proof that either side has *tampered* with documentary evidence, or a witness or a juror, results in a mistrial, and the *tamperer* is guilty of a criminal offense. There has been a nationwide scare as the result of someone's having *tampered* with a popular medicine; consequently, *tamper*-proof packaging is now required.

tantalize (tan′ tə lize) *vb.* To *tantalize* someone is to make his mouth water by raising false hopes or exciting desires that cannot be realized, or to tease him by raising and repeatedly disappointing his expectations. Movie sirens of old *tantalized* men by acting as though they were more available than they were. Many advertisements *tantalize* unwary customers by extravagant promises. The American humorist and publisher Bennett Cerf (1898-1971) wrote of authors who "*tantalize* their publishers by submitting synopses that sparkle." (Presumably, the finished book never materalized, or if it did, fell short of expectations.) *Tantalizing* (tan′ tə ly zing) is used as an adjective to describe anything that arouses hopes, expectations, or desires that, at least for the moment, lie beyond reach. A *tantalizing* woman is provocative. A *tantalizing* restaurant window full of delicious-looking food starts the juices flowing. There is an interesting story behind this word. The mythical Tantalus was the son of Zeus and a nymph, and King of Phrygia. As punishment for divulging the secrets of the gods, and for even more heinous crimes, he was condemned to stand forever in a river in hell. The water below him receded when he stooped to drink, and the fruit-laden branches above him pulled away when he tried to eat. Sounds pretty *tantalizing*! A *tantalus* (tan′ tə ləs) is a locked rack containing visible bottles of wine or liquor. What an appropriate name!

tedious (tee′ dee əs, tee′ jəs) *adj. Tedious* activities or people are tiresome, wearying, dull, boring, uninteresting. The daily routine of housework is one of the most *tedious* tasks in the world. A *tedious* office or factory job can deaden the soul. A *tedious* lecture or sermon can put you to sleep. An endless cross-examination can be a *tedious* experience for judge and jury. In Shakespeare's *King John* (Act III, Scene 4), Lewis, the French prince, cries: "Life is as *tedious* as a twice-told tale/Vexing the dull ear of a drowsy man." These words of Shakespeare echo those of the ancient Greek poet Homer (c. 700 B.C.), who said in his *Odyssey*: "It is *tedious* to tell again tales already . . . told." The French novelist Anatole France (1844-1924) stated: "All the historical books which contain no lies are extremely *tedious*." The Roman poet Virgil (70-19 B.C.) wrote: "Let us go singing. . . . The road will be less *tedious*." The noun is *tedium* (tee′ dee əm). The English lexicographer H.W. Fowler (1858-1933) wrote in *Modern English Usage*: ". . . pretentious quotations [are] the surest road to *tedium*."

teem (teem) *vb.* To *teem* with something is to abound in it, be alive with it. Fishermen are fond of rivers that *teem* with trout or salmon. Hot countries tend to *teem* with insects of all kinds. A forest *teeming* with birds is pleasant to walk in. England *teems* with historic buildings and sights. The inventive mind of Thomas Alva Edison (1847-1931) *teemed* with brilliant ideas. The phrase *teeming with* means "swarming with, alive with." At noon on a sunny day in the city, one has to make one's way along *teeming* streets (i.e., teeming with people). The English poet John Keats (1795-1821) feared that he might die before he had turned into poetry all the thoughts in his *"teeming* brain." The famous inscription on the Statue of Liberty, by the American poet Emma Lazarus (1849-1887), starts: "Give me your tired, your poor,/ The wretched refuse of your *teeming* shores. . . ." (*teeming* with those fleeing from poverty and hunger). As a description of the weather, *teem* has a special, entirely different meaning: to "pour." It's no fun walking about on a *teeming* wet day, when the rain is *teeming* down. "What's it doing out?" "It's *teeming*!"

telling (tel´ ing) *adj.* We are all familiar with the verb to *tell*. The form *telling* is used as an adjective to mean "effective, impressive, forceful, striking." The incidence of cancer among smokers is a *telling* argument against smoking. It was the *telling* attack of the newscaster Edward R. Murrow (1908-1965) on Senator Joe McCarthy (1909-1957) that precipitated the latter's downfall. The American patriot Patrick Henry (1736-1799) made a *telling* appeal for revolution when he declared, "Give me liberty or give me death!" The English nurse Florence Nightingale (1820-1910) advocated reform of hospital procedures and conditions with *telling* effect.

tenacious (tə nay´ shəs) *adj. Tenacious* describes anything that holds fast, keeps a firm grip, won't let go; or anyone who is stubborn, dogged, persistent, won't give up. It is unpleasant to meet up with someone who holds you with a *tenacious* grip on your shoulder. False ideas a person may get in his early training are apt to be so *tenacious* that he can't get free of them in later years. Columbus was motivated by a *tenacious* determination to discover a direct route to the riches of India. It is very helpful to have a *tenacious* memory. The noun is *tenacity* (tə nas´ ə tee). It is hard to argue against the superstitions that primitive peoples hold on to with such *tenacity*.

tentative (ten´ tə tiv) *adj.* A *tentative* step is one that is taken experimentally, as a trial, to see what effect it will have; a *tentative* report is a temporary one, to be superseded by a final report; a *tentative* suggestion is one that can be withdrawn as the situation clears up. People draw up a *tentative* program or plan of action, which will be changed and improved as time goes by. An offer or proposal may be *tentative*, subject to alteration. A *tentative* acceptance of a proposition may be withdrawn as circumstances develop. One may come to a *tentative* conclusion, subject to later findings. An offer may be accepted *tentatively*, subject to investigation. *Tentative* may be used in a different sense, to mean "uncertain, hesitant." When a person is doubtful about his position, he may put on a *tentative*, almost apologetic smile. A *tentative* look is one of uncertainty, of not quite knowing which way to turn; a doubting, unsure look, the look of a person in need of assurance.

tepid (tep′ id) *adj. Tepid* means "lukewarm." It can be used literally to describe physical temperature, usually of a liquid; or figuratively to describe anyone or anything halfhearted, lacking in enthusiasm, passion, or conviction. *Tepid* water may be relaxing to bathe in, but it is not attractive to drink, nor are the *tepid* seas off tropical islands as invigorating to swim in as the cooler waters of the north. Fidel Castro got a *tepid* reception, to say the least, when he visited New York soon after his revolution. A weak election turnout indicates disillusionment and *tepid* interest on the part of the voters. A *tepid* audience reaction will result in an early closing notice in the theater. *Tepid* praise is faint praise.

threshold (thresh′ old, -hold—*o* as in *go*) *n*. A *threshold*, literally, is a doorsill or the entrance to a building; figuratively, it is used to mean "point of beginning" or "outset." The *threshold* of adulthood is an important milestone in a person's life. Many serious decisions must be made at the *threshold* of one's career. With the death of Queen Victoria, England stood at the *threshold* of a new era. *Threshold* is used in another way, in psychology and physiology, to denote the point at which a stimulus begins to produce an effect. The *threshold* of pain differs widely from person to person (different people suffer pain at different degrees of intensity). The *threshold* of consciousness is the point at which a person is aware of what is happening around him. Dreams are below the *threshold* of consciousness; fantasy is above it.

thrive (thryve) *vb*. To *thrive* is to prosper, flourish, grow strong and healthy, succeed. The past tense is *thrived* (thryv′d) or *throve* (thrōve); to *have thrived* can also be written to *have thriven* (thriv′ ən). A business cannot *thrive* with insufficient capital. People *thrive* on a balanced diet. It is difficult for industry to *thrive* under excessive government restrictions. Some people seem to *thrive* better when the going gets rough. An obscure English poet whose dates are uncertain wrote, in 1639:

> He that would *thrive*
> Must rise at five;
> He that hath *thriven*
> May lie till seven.

The American poet Robert W. Service (1874–1958) wrote a famous poem about the Yukon:

> This is the Law of the Yukon, that
> only the strong shall *thrive*;
> That surely the weak shall perish,
> and only the fit survive.

throng (throng) *n., vb*. A *throng* is a crowd; to *throng* is to crowd. Dictators like Mussolini and Hitler addressed numberless *throngs* of followers who shouted their approval. The American poet Henry Wadsworth Longfellow (1807–1882) wrote: "Not in the clamour of the crowded street,/Not in the shouts and plaudits of the *throng*,/But in ourselves, are triumph and defeat." *Throng* can apply to things other than people, like the *throngs* of ants that spoil picnics, or the *throngs* of ideas that clutter your brain when you're trying to fall asleep. It's slow business trying to make one's way through people *thronging* the exits after a major sports event, or *thronging* the aisles at a well-advertised sale.

thwart (thwart—*a* as in *raw*) *vb.* To *thwart* is to frustrate, foil, or obstruct, to prevent (something) from happening or (someone) from succeeding. When the Scottish poet Robert Burns (1759–1796) wrote, "the best laid schemes o'mice an' men/Gang aft a-gley [often go astray]," and the Japanese philosopher Ihara Saikaku (1642–1693) said (in translation), "There is always something to upset the most careful of human calculations," and the German churchman Thomas à Kempis (1380–1471) wrote (in translation), "Man proposes and God disposes," and Mr. Murphy (whoever he was) formulated Murphy's Law, they were all referring to the *thwarting* of human plans, aims, and ambitions. Franklin D. Roosevelt was *thwarted* in his plan to "pack" the United States Supreme Court by increasing the number of justices from nine to fifteen and appointing new liberal members. The defeat of the French army at Moscow *thwarted* Napoleon's aim to rule all of Europe. Bad weather often *thwarts* picnic plans.

tirade (ty´rade, ty rade´) *n.* A *tirade* is a long, bitter speech, a prolonged denunciation, a vehement harangue, a tongue-lashing. Hitler was famous (or infamous?) for his frenzied *tirades* against the Allies and the Jews. The American poet Robert Lowell (1917–1977) wrote of his wife's ". . . *tirade*—/loving, rapid, merciless—/that breaks like the Atlantic Ocean on my head." The *tirades* of Senator Paul Douglas (1892–1976) on the floor of the Senate helped ultimately to bring about the official censure of Senator Joseph McCarthy (1909–1957).

tiresome (tire´səm) *adj.* Anything or anyone *tiresome* is, in the literal sense, wearying; in a figurative sense, tedious, boring, dull; or, in context, annoying. A *tiresome* companion is the very opposite of interesting. A *tiresome* job is boring. When noisy children are said to be *tiresome,* they are annoying, bothersome, pesky. Preparing one's income-tax figures is a *tiresome* job, in all senses of the word. Suburbanites complain of *tiresome* daily commuting. The English novelist and playwright W. Somerset Maugham (1874–1965) wrote of "a nagging, *tiresome* woman." The American humorist Mark Twain (Samuel Langhorne Clemens, 1835–1910) commented on "the *tiresome* chirping of a cricket." What is more *tiresome* than having to sit through a poorly acted amateur performance of a play starring your cousin's darling daughter?

trait (trate) *n.* A *trait* is a distinguishing quality, characteristic, feature. Generosity is a *trait* of the American people. One of Greta Garbo's most fascinating *traits* was the air of mystery that clung to her. It is a *trait* of a really great man that;

despite the heights to which he may have risen, he remains tolerant of and accessible to his fellow men. Courage and wit were Churchill's most engaging *traits*. Conflicting *traits* may indicate a split personality.

tranquil (trang′ kwil) *adj*. Anything or anyone that is *tranquil* is peaceful, calm, quiet, serene, placid. Many people leave the noisy, jarring city for a *tranquil* life in the country. What is more *tranquil* than a rural church on a Sunday afternoon? The noun is *tranquillity* (trang kwil′ ə tee), also spelled *tranquility*. How sweet the *tranquillity* that follows the completion of a job well done! The English poet Percy Bysshe Shelley (1792-1822) wrote:

> I love *tranquil* solitude.
> And such society
> As is quiet, wise and good . . .

The American essayist Ralph Waldo Emerson (1803-1882) "heard with admiring submission the experience of the lady who declared that the sense of being well-dressed gives a feeling of inward *tranquillity* which religion is powerless to bestow." The English poet Roden Noel (1834-1894) wrote:

> After battle sleep is best,
> After noise, *tranquillity*.

To tranquilize (trang′ kwə lize) is to make (someone) *tranquil*. *Tranquilizers* (trang′ kwə ly zərs) are supposed to do just that.

trauma (trou′ mə—*ou* as in *house*, traw′-) *n*. In medicine, *trauma*, as it refers to the body, is an injury; as a term in psychiatry, a *trauma* is an emotional shock or startling experience that has a lasting effect. The plural is either *traumata* (trou′ mə tə—*ou* as in *house*) or *traumas* (trou′ məz—*ou* as in *house*). The British medical magazine *Lancet* wrote of "injuries . . . such as strains, bruises, fractures, dislocation, concussion—indeed, *traumata* of all kinds." In the psychiatric field, we are told that the separation of a young child from its mother is the most serious *trauma* of all. The adjective is *traumatic* (trə mat′ ik, traw-, trou-, *ou* as in *house*). Literally, *traumatic* describes any effect of a wound or injury; figuratively, it applies to any experience so distressing and unforgettable as to produce a psychological *trauma*. The loss of a loved one is a *traumatic* experience. Facing the danger of imminent death can have a *traumatic* effect that can never be shaken off. To *traumatize* (trou′ mə tize—*ou* as in *house*, traw′-) is to injure, either physically or emotionally. To say to a child, "Stop crying or the bogeyman will get you" can *traumatize* him for the rest of his life.

trifling (try′ fling) *adj*. A *trifle* (try′ fəl) is anything of little value or importance. To *trifle with* someone is to deal with him without respect or the proper degree of seriousness. An important person is not to be *trifled with*. A decent man will not *trifle with* a girl's affections. The form *trifling* (see also **trivial**) is used as an adjective meaning "unimportant, insignificant, trivial, picayune." To be out a few cents in figuring your bank account is a *trifling* error. When someone is telling a long story, he should not stop to figure out such a *trifling matter* as the exact date of a minor event. "It's no *trifling matter*" means "It's serious." Imitation jewelry is of *trifling* value compared with the real thing.

trite (tryte) *adj.* Anything described as *trite* is hackneyed, stale, "old hat," too familiar. *Trite* usually applies to commonplace remarks, opinions, ideas, plots, conversation, advice, and the like. The boy-girl movie plot—they meet, they fall in love, big misunderstanding, it all clears up, big reconciliation—is about as *trite* as you can get. That first letter from summer camp—"I like my counselor, we went canoeing, I need some money"—is usually a pretty *trite* affair. Most commencement addresses are unbearably *trite*. It is hard to stay awake during a *trite* sermon. The chairman's introduction of "A man who . . ." at a political meeting is outworn and *trite*. Even the best and most original prose and poetry can become *trite* through overuse: *A rose by any other name*; *Water, water, everywhere*; *A bird in the hand*; *All's well that ends well*.

trivial (triv´ ee əl) *adj. Trivial*, like *trifling*, means "insignificant, unimportant, of little value." The two words come from different sources: *Trifling* derives from the very old English word *trufle* meaning "idle talk"; *trivial* comes from a Latin word denoting a crossroads where the three roads meet, and presumably people stop for petty conversation. Illegal parking is a *trivial* offense. People who keep raising *trivial* objections to every proposal are themselves objectionable. It is best not to bother the boss with *trivial* matters. The noun is *triviality* (triv ee al´ ə tee), often found in the plural, meaning "*trivial* matters, insignificant things." At cocktail parties, even the chatter of important public figures is full of *trivialities*. *Trivialities* make up the daily life of most people.

tumult (too´ məlt, tyoo´-, *oo* as in *boot*) *n. Tumult* is uproar, and suggests crowds making noisy commotions and disturbances. Anyone who has been at the front line in war is all too familiar with the *tumult* of battle. Newsreels of the Russian revolution of 1917 show enormous crowds in *tumult*. In the famous poem "Recessional" by the English poet Rudyard Kipling (1865-1936) appear the lines: "The *tumult* and the shouting dies;/The Captains and the Kings depart;/ . . . Lord God of Hosts, be with us yet,/Lest we forget—lest we forget!" *Tumult* is used figuratively to describe mental agitation or emotional disturbance. A person *in tumult* is in a confused and deeply upset state of mind. The English essayist and poet Hilaire Belloc (1870-1953) wrote of a woman who "stood bewildered, her soul in a *tumult*." Similarly, the English poet T.S. Eliot (1888-1964) spoke of those who "seek refuge in religion from the *tumults* of a strong emotional temperament." The adjective is *tumultuous* (too mul´ choo əs, tyoo-, all *oo*'s as in *boot*), meaning "disorderly and noisy." Football victories are often followed by *tumultuous* celebrations. Returning heroes are greeted with *tumultuous* ovations. National political conventions seem to become more *tumultuous* every four years. (See the next entry.)

turmoil (tur´ moil—*u* as in *fur*) *n*. *Turmoil* is a state of commotion, agitation, disturbance. Like **tumult,** *turmoil* can be used both literally and figuratively. Traffic is in *turmoil* while a new subway is being built. While the enemy pursues, the retreating army rushes to and fro in *turmoil*. William R. Inge (1860–1954), the "Gloomy Dean" of St. Paul's, London, said that "the child's inner life is often a *turmoil* of terrors and anxieties." Those in high places face the *turmoil* of making decisions that may affect the fate of millions. *Tumult* and *turmoil* may sometimes be interchangeable, but in general, it is best to use *tumult* where noise and clamor are involved, and *turmoil* where violent inner conflict takes place.

uncanny (un kan´ ee) *adj*. *Uncanny* suggests the mysterious, the unexplainable, the disconcertingly strange and frightening. Nostradamus (1503–1566), the French astrologer, had an *uncanny* knack of foretelling the distant future. Now and then, one finds a mathematical genius who has the *uncanny* ability to do enormously complex problems in his head. Some theatrical producers show *uncanny* skill in judging the public taste. At night, one worries about the *uncanny* sounds that fill the house. The English novelist Sir Arthur Quiller-Couch (1863–1944) used the comparison "as *uncanny* as the shadows of unfamiliar furniture on the walls of an inn." The films of the English director Alfred Hitchcock (1899–1980) were marked by an *uncanny* atmosphere of suspense. The American poet Edgar Allan Poe (1809–1849) was a master of the *uncanny*.

underhand (un´ dər hand), sometimes **underhanded** (un´ dər han dəd), *adj*. Apart from its use to describe the throwing of a ball (in softball, football, etc.) with the palm upward, *underhand* is used as a description of discreditable conduct, and means "deceitful, sly, dishonorable, not open and aboveboard, shady, corrupt." Unscrupulous people stoop to all kinds of *underhand* methods to gain their ends. Nixon's dirty tricks were an *underhand* strategy to besmirch opposing candidates. Corrupt politicians sometimes make *underhand* deals with notorious criminals. Spying is an *underhand* system of gaining information about enemies, real or potential. In Shakespeare's *As You Like It* (Act I, Scene 1), Oliver says to Charles, the wrestler, whom Oliver's younger brother Orlando has challenged: "I . . . have by *underhanded* means laboured to dissuade him from it, but he is resolute."

undoing (un doo´ ing—*oo* as in *boot*) *n*. A person's *undoing* is his ruin or destruction, or the thing that causes it. Literally, to *undo* something is to untie it (like shoelaces, packages), to erase, reverse, or do away with it (as a bad government *undoes* the good done by a previous regime). Figuratively, to *undo* someone is to ruin him; but this is a rather old-fashioned use. "I am *undone*!" cries the wronged heroine in Victorian melodrama. And in Shakespeare's *Two Gentlemen of Verona* (Act II, Scene 5), Launce says to Speed: " . . . a man is never *undone* till he be hanged. . . . " The noun *undoing*, however, is in current use. The obstruction of justice and cover-up were Richard Nixon's *undoing*. Overexpansion has been the *undoing* of many a company. The charms of a *femme fatale* have been the *undoing* of many families. Drugs are the *undoing* of thousands of our youth. Shakespeare uses the word in *King Henry VIII* (Act V, Scene 3) when Archbishop Cranmer, told by the Bishop of Winchester that he is to be imprisoned, says: "I see your end [purpose];/'Tis my *undoing.*"

uneasy (un ee´ zee) *adj.* One who is *uneasy* is troubled, anxious. An *uneasy* conscience is a troubled one; an *uneasy* sleep is fitful; to pass an *uneasy* night is to sleep poorly. There are two nouns: *unease* (un eez´) and *uneasiness* (un ee´ zee nəs). A well-known use of the adjective is the line spoken by the King in Shakespeare's *Henry IV, Part 2* (Act III, Scene 1): "*Uneasy* lies the head that wears a crown." (The King was sleepless: "uneasy lies" means "uneasily sleeps.") In view of widespread unemployment, college graduates are *uneasy* about their future. When you're waiting for someone who's long overdue, you begin to feel *uneasy* about him. Newcomers to a school or social group experience *uneasiness* until they feel that they are accepted. Almost everyone is familiar with the *uneasiness* of the first day on a new job.

uniform (yoo´ nə fawrm—*oo* as in *boot*) *adj.* Uniform means "the same." Two (or more) suits of *uniform* cloth and pattern are identical. When something is *uniform*, it does not vary. A board of *uniform* thickness is the same thickness throughout. If something is to be kept at a *uniform* temperature and humidity, those conditions must not vary. A factory geared to *uniform* output produces at an unvarying rate. The meaning of the adjective *uniform* explains the noun *uniform* (e.g., army *uniform*, school *uniform*)—the same distinctive outfit for all members of a group. The noun is *uniformity* (yoo nə fawr´ mih tee), meaning "sameness." U.S. Supreme Court Justice Benjamin Cardozo (1870-1938) wrote of the "certainty and *uniformity*" of legal precedents on which "men have shaped their conduct." *Uniformity* of legal decisions is desirable, but *uniformity* of TV commercials and sitcoms is boring in the extreme.

unique (yoo neek´—*oo* as in *boot*) *adj.* Anyone or anything *unique* is one of a kind, stands alone, has no like or equal. In the words of the English lexicographer H. W. Fowler (1858-1933), *unique* describes things "the precise like of which may be sought in vain." *Unique* is not the equivalent of *exceptional* or *rare* or *wonderful* or *outstanding*; the qualities these words express are all relative, they exist in greater or lesser degrees. But there are no degrees of *uniqueness*; things either are or are not *unique*; *uniqueness* is an absolute. Something may be *almost unique*, but it cannot be a *bit unique, very unique, more unique, most unique,* or similar nonsense. Shakespeare's position in literature is *unique*. The mortality caused in Europe by the Black Death (bubonic plague) of 1665 is *unique* in medical history. The adverb is *uniquely* (yoo neek´ lee—*oo* as in *boot*). One's first view of the Taj Mahal at Agra, India, is a *uniquely* moving experience.

unkempt (un kempt´) *adj.* *Unkempt* hair is uncombed. Anything else described as *unkempt* is messy, untidy. An *unkempt* lawn is uncut and packed with weeds. *Unkempt* clothes are uncared-for, wrinkled, full of stains. (Believe it or not, the adjective *kempt*, meaning "neatly kept, trim," does exist, but it is practically never used.) We meet *unkempt* in "The Old Vicarage," by the English poet Rupert Brooke (1887–1915):

> Here tulips grow as they are told;
> *Unkempt* about those hedges blows
> An English unofficial rose.

Nothing is more *unkempt* than a retreating army, fleeing in disorder.

unpretentious (un prih ten´ shəs) *adj.* See **pretense**.

unscrupulous (un skroo´ pyə ləs) *adj.* See **scruple**.

unwitting (un wit´ ing) *adj.* *Unwitting* means "unknowing, unaware," or "unintentional." The latter use is the common one. It occurs in phrases like *unwitting error, unwitting offense* or *cruelty* (one would not speak of an *unwitting person*). Children, because of their frankness, are often guilty of *unwitting* cruelty. The adverb *unwittingly* (un wit´ ing lee) is used more frequently than the adjective, to mean "unintentionally." A frank and honest criticism can *unwittingly* give offense.

upbraid (up brade´) *vb.* To *upbraid* someone is to scold him severely, give him a piece of one's mind. General George Patton (1885–1945) was in the habit of *upbraiding* any soldier who showed the slightest sign of weakness. It is embarrassing for bystanders to hear a married couple *upbraid* each other publicly. Top sergeants, if we can believe the fictional prototypes, are specialists in the *upbraiding* of awkward raw recruits. In its censure (December 1954), the U.S. Senate *upbraided* Senator Joe McCarthy (1909–1957) for conduct unbefitting a member of that august body.

upstart (up´ start) *n.* An *upstart* is a person who has suddenly risen from a lowly status to power, wealth, or a higher position, and has become objectionably arrogant and cocky as a result. *Upstarts* who have suddenly made fortunes are careful to seek publicity for their charitable works. The *upstarts* of today may turn out to be the ancestors of the gentlemen of tomorrow. *Upstarts* are often blackballed when they apply for membership in exclusive clubs. In typical Hollywood movies, the loudmouthed *upstart* rides to an inevitable fall.

urbane (ur bane´—*u* as in *fur*) *adj.* An *urbane* person has the polish, sophistication, and elegance characteristic of social life in a big city. Such a person has *urbane* manners and *urbane* tastes. Anyone described as *urbane* is cultivated, poised, and well traveled, feels comfortable in society, fits gracefully into the highest circles.

One thinks of an *urbane* person as impeccably dressed, feeling at ease everywhere, knowing all the best restaurants and their headwaiters, belonging to the best clubs—the absolute opposite of a hick. The noun is *urbanity* (ur ban′ ə tee). David Niven, Ronald Colman, and William Powell played characters that were the very soul of *urbanity*, flawlessly smooth, always graceful, with never a false move or a jarring note.

utilize (yoo′ tə lize—*oo* as in *boot*) *vb.* To *utilize* something is to make use of it, find a use for it. People are now *utilizing* solar heat to produce energy. For centuries, man has *utilized* river currents as a source of power. Experienced people know how to *utilize* their contacts to get ahead in the world. Before the invention of machinery, primitive people had to *utilize* manpower to build great monuments. Robinson Crusoe had to *utilize* what was at hand to sustain life. The noun is *utilization* (yoo tə lə zay′ shən—*oo* as in *boot*). The *utilization* of all of a nation's resources is important in times of austerity. One is told that people who raise pigs see to the *utilization* of every part of the animal—including the squeal.

utmost (ut′ most—*o* as in *go*) *n., adj.* As an adjective, *utmost* means "greatest." Motorists should use the *utmost* care when driving on snow and ice. It is of the *utmost* importance to remain calm in a crisis. Confidences made to a minister, doctor, or lawyer must be preserved with the *utmost* secrecy. One should not be treated by a physician unless one has the *utmost* confidence in him. As a noun, *utmost* means "the greatest amount or degree, the most possible." After a spell of hard work, one should try to relax to the *utmost*. One should do one's *utmost* to help a friend in need. Hotels and resorts like to advertise that they offer "the *utmost* in comfort."

valiant (val′ yənt) *adj.* A *valiant* person is brave, stout-hearted, bold and fearless, dashing and dauntless; a *valiant* effort is a brave effort, a boldly courageous effort. D'Artagnan and the three musketeers, in the novels of the French writer Alexandre Dumas (1802–1870), were a *valiant* band. The epitaph of Margaret, Duchess of Newcastle (1624–1673), in Westminster Abbey reads: "Her name was Margaret Lucas, [of] a noble familie; for all the Brothers were *Valiant*, and all the Sisters virtuous." In Shakespeare's *Julius Caesar* (Act III, Scene 2), Brutus, addressing the crowd after the assassination, tells them: "As he [Caesar] was *valiant*, I honour him; but, as he was ambitious, I slew him." The *valiant* defense of London by the Royal Air Force during the Battle of Britain is a glorious chapter of English history. One rarely meets with the nouns *valiance* (val′ yəns) and *valiancy* (val′ yən see); *valor* (val′ ər) is the common form.

valid (val′ id) *adj.* The basic meaning of *valid* is "sound." A *valid* reason for doing something, or a *valid* objection to an argument or action, is a sound one, well founded. A *valid* contract or a *valid* marriage is one that fulfills the legal requirements and is therefore effective. A season ticket *valid* for six months is one that is good for that period. The noun is *validity* (val id´ ih tee). When you enter a foreign country, the immigration officer looks into the *validity* of your passport. One objection to the *validity* of a contract is that it was entered into under duress. To *validate* (val´ ih date) something is to make it *valid* and effective. It takes certain signatures and seals to *validate* visas. Affidavits are *validated* by the signature of a notary public or other official authorized to take oaths. *Invalid* (in val´ id) is the opposite of *valid*; an expired driver's license is *invalid*; a will executed by an incompetent person is *invalid* and without legal effect. Note the accent on the second syllable. This accent differentiates the adjective *invalid* from the noun *invalid* (in´ və lid), signifying a sick person, and its adjective *invalid*—same pronunciation—describing someone who is ill and unable to take care of himself.

vanquish (vang´ kwish, van-) *vb*. To *vanquish* is to conquer, overcome, defeat, crush. One can *vanquish* not only a foe in battle or an opponent in tennis or in a dispute, but also one's fears, inhibitions, baser impulses, and other emotions. In Shakespeare's *Antony* and *Cleopatra* (Act IV, Scene 13), the doomed Antony says that his death will not be ignoble because he will die " . . . a Roman by a Roman/Valiantly *vanquished*." The English poet Oliver Goldsmith (1728-1774), describing the local personalities in *The Deserted Village*, wrote of the parson who was so skillful in arguing that "even though *vanquished*, he could argue still." The Greek poet Sappho (c. 612 B.C.) could not go on with her weaving because at the loom, she was "*vanquished* by desire for a youth." The Allies *vanquished* Germany in World War I and again in World War II. Bjorn Borg, the Swedish tennis star, *vanquished* all opposition in five successive Wimbledon tournaments.

vegetate (vej´ ə tate) *adj*. To *vegetate* is to lead an entirely passive life, to be sluggish, dull, to stagnate, to "live like a *vegetable*" (in a general sense—not to "be a vegetable" in the medical sense), without initiative or intellectual activity or interests. There are those who are content to lead an uneventful, humdrum existence, without mental or intellectual stimulus, in a word, to *vegetate*. The English essayist Charles Caleb Colton (1780-1832) gave this advice: "If you would be known and not know, *vegetate* in a village; if you would know, and not be known, live in a city." A contemporary of Colton's, the English essayist William Hazlitt (1778-1830), wrote: "When I am in the country, I wish to *vegetate* like the country." We agree with Hazlitt; to *vegetate* (in the country or anywhere else) for a short period may be nothing more than to rest body and mind; but keep both busy the rest of the time!

venom (ven´ əm) *n*. In its literal sense, *venom* is the poisonous fluid injected by some snakes and insects into their victims. Figuratively, *venom* is hate, spite, malice—emotions that have "poisonous" effects. The *venom* of jealousy has poisoned many a relationship. To spout *venom* is to say hateful things. The adjective is *venomous* (ven´ ə məs), meaning "deadly, spiteful." One can die from the bite of a *venomous* snake. Nothing is more wounding than a *venomous* tongue. Toward the end of a political campaign, political rivals have been known to hurl *venomous* attacks at each other.

versatile (vur´ sə til—*u* as in *fur*) *adj.* A *versatile* person is one with a wide range of skills, an all-around, many-sided person. A *versatile* tool or material is one that has many different uses. A *versatile* actor can turn easily from tragedy to farce; a *versatile* musician can perform many different kinds of music (from Bach to boogie-woogie) or can play a number of instruments. A *versatile* painter is skillful at portraiture, landscape, and still life. Unlike the proverbial jack-of-all-trades who is master of none, a *versatile* person is one who is master of several. Plexiglas is a *versatile* material. The noun is *versatility* (vur sə til´ ə tee). People of great *versatility* are much sought after in small businesses. A combination screwdriver-hammer is a tool of useful *versatility*. The *versatility* of the inventions of Thomas Alva Edison (1847-1931) staggers the imagination.

vestige (ves´ tij) *n.* A *vestige* is a trace, a small surviving bit of evidence of something that no longer exists. Archaeologists spend their lives digging for *vestiges* of civilizations now lost in history. Some ancient temples are remarkably well preserved; others have vanished, and the only *vestiges* that remain are bits and pieces of stone, scattered at random. Many Southern mansions today show only *vestiges* of their former magnificence. One can sometimes still detect a *vestige* of former beauty in the face of an aged woman. *Vestige* may also be used like *trace*, to mean "tiny amount" or "least bit," as when a person loses the last *vestige* of self-respect, or no longer possesses any *vestige* of his youthful prowess.

vicarious (vy kar´ ee əs—*a* as in *dare*) *adj.* A *vicarious* experience is one you feel by putting yourself in the place of somebody else who is actually going through the experience. If you have come to take for granted the beautiful mountain landscape outside your home, you can see it with renewed *vicarious* pleasure and enthusiasm when you show it to a first-time visitor; you see it through his eyes and participate in his reaction. When you experience an emotion—joy, excitement, fear, or any other deep feeling—through participating in the experience of another person, you are undergoing the other person's experience *vicariously*. An emotional response to the action of a novel is based on *vicarious* identification with the characters and imagined participation in the plot. People in seclusion often lead *vicarious* lives through reading and watching television.

vigilant (vij´ ə lənt) *adj.* A *vigilant* person is watchful, on the lookout for danger. In Shakespeare's *King Henry IV, Part 1* (Act IV, Scene 2), Falstaff proclaims himself to be "as *vigilant* as a cat [stealing] . . . cream." A person must be *vigilant* in order to protect himself from physical danger (when climbing a mountain or walking in a rough neighborhood); he should be equally *vigilant* in order to protect his civil rights or to maintain his solvency. In his First Epistle General (4:8) St. Peter tells us: "Be sober, be *vigilant*; because your adversary, the devil

... walketh about. . . . '' The noun is *vigilance* (vij´ ə ləns). Abraham Lincoln wrote to a general: "Beware of rashness, but with energy and sleepless *vigilance* go forward and give us victories." The Irish politician John Curran (1750-1817) declared: "The condition upon which God hath given liberty to man is eternal *vigilance* . . . ,'' a statement attributed also to Thomas Jefferson (1743-1826) in the form: "Eternal *vigilance* is the price of liberty." Later, the American radio commentator Elmer Davis (1890-1958) adapted this sentiment in the words: " . . . freedom can be retained only by the eternal *vigilance* which has always been its price." So—better be *eternally vigilant* where your freedom is concerned!

vindicate (vin´ də kate) *vb.* To *vindicate* someone is to clear him of an accusation; one can *vindicate* the person, or his honor, his reputation, etc. To *vindicate* a person's judgment or policy is to prove it right, to justify it. It was through the efforts of the French novelist Emile Zola (1840-1902) and especially through his letter to the French President (*J'accuse*—"I accuse') that the good name of Alfred Dreyfus (1859-1935)—the French army officer charged with treason and later acquitted—was finally *vindicated*. The noun is *vindication* (vin də kay´ shən), signifying freeing from guilt or blame. Abraham Lincoln said: "Truth is generally the best *vindication* against slander." The *vindication* of one person falsely accused is a justification of all the complicated and time-consuming safeguards provided by our legal system.

vindictive (vin dik´ tiv) *adj.* A *vindictive* person or disposition is vengeful, moved by a thirst for revenge and a desire to hurt. The English detective-story writer A. Conan Doyle (1859-1930), creator of Sherlock Holmes, described a corpse whose "features were convulsed into a spasm of *vindictive* hatred." The history of Sicily is crowded with tales of never-ending feuds among *vindictive* families. The American philosopher Morris R. Cohen (1880-1947) believed that convicted criminals should be given rehabilitation rather than "punishments . . . essentially *vindictive* in their nature." Hitler's orders to burn Paris were purely *vindictive* and had no real military purpose. Judging by the fact that St. Paul, in his Epistle to the Romans (12:19), attributed the statement "Vengeance is mine, I will repay" to the Lord, the apostle must have believed God to be a *vindictive* deity. *Vindictive* persons never forget, and avenge themselves without mercy.

virtual (vur´ choo əl—*u* as in *fur*, *oo* as in *boot*) *adj. Virtual* and the adverb *virtually* (vur´ choo ə lee—*u* as in *fur*, *oo* as in *boot*) have meanings unrelated to *virtue* and *virtuous*. The *virtual* head of a firm, for instance, is the unstated real boss, the operating boss, the head man in effect, though not so recognized by title. Anything described as *virtual* is effectively so, though not formally so. The evacuation at Dunkirk in World War II, though hailed at the time as a great success, was a *virtual* collapse of the British forces. When someone is accused and remains silent, the silence is a *virtual* confession, in the sense that (although not a word is spoken) silence under these circumstances practically amounts to an open confession. *Virtually* means "just about, practically, for all practical purposes." A man with only a dollar to call his own is *virtually* penniless. A first-rate writer who has achieved great artistic success and has been enthusiastically received by the critics may nevertheless remain *virtually* unknown, alas, to the general public.

vivacious (vih vay shəs, vy-) *adj*. A *vivacious* person, performance, dance, piece of music, etc., is lively, full of spirit, animated, sprightly; the opposite of *languid*. The role of Puck in Shakespeare's *A Midsummer-Night's Dream* must be played in a *vivacious* manner. Orangutans look sad and lethargic; chimpanzees are *vivacious* and full of fun. The noun is *vivacity* (vih vas´ ə tee, vy-). The entrance of one person full of enthusiasm and *vivacity* can lighten the mood of a dull party. What is more endearing than the *vivacity* of children at play?

vivid (viv´ id) *adj*. *Vivid* has a number of uses, all connected, in one way or another, with the concept of liveliness. A *vivid* color is intense, extremely bright (she was wearing a *vivid* pink dress; a *vivid* flash of lightning can be quite frightening); a *vivid* personality is one full of spirit; a *vivid* painting is a realistic one; a *vivid* account of an adventure is exciting, full of spirited detail; a *vivid* impression is clear, distinct, unmistakable; a *vivid* imagination is one full of striking images. Travel books full of *vivid* description can give you the feeling that you're actually there. The best witnesses are those with *vivid* recollections of the subject matter involved. Churchill's *vivid* personality made an unforgettable impression on all who met him.

vocation (voe kay´ shən) *n*. A person's *vocation* is his business or profession, his calling. Abraham Lincoln's *vocation*, in his youth, was the legal profession. People often change their *vocations* in later life: the Russian composer Alexander Borodin (1834–1887) changed his *vocation* from chemistry to music. (The author changed his *vocation* from law to lexicography.) In Shakespeare's *King Henry IV, Part 1* (Act I, Scene 2), young Prince Hal (later King Henry V) taunts the rascally Falstaff with being a purse-snatcher. Falstaff remonstrates: "Why, Hal, 'tis my *vocation*, Hal; 'tis no sin for a man to labour in his *vocation*." An *avocation* (av ə kay´ shən) is a hobby, or an occasional activity that is not a person's regular *vocation*. Both Churchill and Eisenhower took to painting as an *avocation*. The American poet Robert Frost (1874–1963) wrote: "My object in living is to unite/My *avocation* and my *vocation*. . . . " (Nice work, Robert, if you can get it.)

wallow (wah´ lo, waw´-) *vb*. To *wallow*, literally, is to roll around, the way pigs *wallow* in mud, or goats in dust. Figuratively, to *wallow* is to revel or take sensual delight (in something). Rakes and roués *wallow* in sensual pleasures. People who are too rich for their own good and have nothing in the world to do *wallow* in self-indulgence and luxury. The audiences at Victorian melodramas *wallowed* in sentimentality. When the nation began to grow suspicious as more and more revelations piled up, Nixon told his "fellow Americans" that it was time to "stop *wallowing* in Watergate" and get down to more serious matters.

wanton (won' t'n—*o* as in *gone*) *adj.* *Wanton* has several different meanings, all related, however, to the concept of lack of restraint. *Wanton* destruction is vandalism; *wanton* cruelty is savage and senseless; a *wanton* insult is uncalled-for, provocative, made without regard to another person's feelings. Applied to conduct or a person, *wanton* means "immoral, lewd, and lascivious," and describes someone who is unrestrained in sexual matters. Hitler ordered the *wanton*, arbitrary destruction of Paris, which was not a military target. There are self-centered people who act with *wanton* disregard of the rights of others. President John Adams (1735-1826) wrote: "The law . . . will preserve a steady . . . course; it will not bend to the uncertain wishes, imaginations and *wanton* tempers of men. . . . " Because of the double standard in matters concerning sexual morality, the adjective *wanton*, in the sense of "lewd," has almost always been used of women only. For the same reason, the noun *wanton*, though defined in some dictionaries as "a lewd or lascivious person," is defined in several others as "a lewd and lascivious person" with the added qualification "especially a woman"; still others define *wanton* simply as "an unchaste woman." (Most lexicographers are men.)

wary (war' ee—*a* as in *dare*) *adj.* A *wary* person is on his guard, ever watchful. Mothers sending little children off to school tell them to be *wary* of strangers who may approach them. One should always be *wary* of hurting people's feelings. People speak a foreign language slowly, *wary* of making mistakes. In Shakespeare's *Julius Caesar* (Act II, Scene 1), Brutus says: "It is the bright day that brings forth the adder;/And that craves [requires] *wary* walking." The noun is *wariness* (war' ee nis—*a* as in *dare*), meaning "watchfulness, caution." Extreme *wariness* is necessary when walking the dimly lit streets of a city at night.

waver (way' vər) *vb.* When things are said to *waver*, they move around uncertainly, like flames, foliage in the wind, a distant beam of light. Prices, too, can be said to *waver* or fluctuate. When people *waver*, they hesitate, show uncertainty or doubt. People often *waver* in their courage, resolution, or determination when the going gets really tough. Vacillation, the inability to make a choice or a decision, is another form of *wavering*. People have been known to *waver* between marrying for love and marrying for money (it is said that those who choose the money *earn* it the hard way). Gifted people often *waver* in their choice of a profession.

weather (weth' ər—*th* as in *this*) *vb.* This verb is a different kind of *weather* from the one that everybody talks about but nobody does anything about. To *weather* a storm is to bear up under it and come through successfully. In adventure stories, the hero *weathers* crisis after crisis but always triumphs in the end. During a depression, the people find it hard to *weather* all their troubles. The British *weathered*

World War II with magnificent courage. Pitifully few Jews were able to *weather* the atrocities of the Third Reich.

weigh (way) *vb.* Literally, to *weigh* something is to find out how heavy it is by putting it on a scale. Figuratively, *weigh* has another use: To *weigh* a suggestion or a proposal or a theory is to consider it carefully. One should *weigh* the pros and cons of a proposition before coming to a decision. It is important to *weigh* the consequences rather than act impulsively. On the witness stand, one must *weigh* one's words beforehand instead of blurting out an answer. After a presidential speech, experts go on the air to *weigh* its significance. The English philosopher Francis Bacon (1561–1626) told us to "read not to contradict . . . nor to believe and take for granted, . . . but to *weigh* and consider." In connection with this figurative use of *weigh*, the noun *weight* (wate) is also used figuratively in the sense of "importance" or "significance." The decisions of the United States Supreme Court carry *weight*, nationally and even internationally. In this same vein, the adjective *weighty* (way′ tee) means "important, critical." The negotiations for nuclear disarmament are the *weightiest* in history.

whim (hwim, wim) *n.* A *whim* is a passing fancy, a sudden idea, an odd notion, a mood of the moment that comes out of nowhere. It has been noted that women, when pregnant, develop *whims* for strange foods that they normally never hanker for. A person may be struck by a *whim* to take a walk in the rain, or to look up an old friend he hasn't thought about for years. People who suddenly come up with a strange, unreasoning notion say, "The *whim* struck me" or "The *whim* seized me." *Whimsy* or *whimsey* (hwim′ zee, wim′-) is an odd, fanciful sort of humor, like that written occasionally by G. K. Chesterton (1874–1936), the English novelist and poet:

> The gallows in my garden, people say,
>   Is new and neat and adequately tall.
> The strangest *whim* has seized me. . . . After all
>   I think I will not hang myself today.

The adjective *whimsical* (hwim′ zih kəl, wim′-) means "fanciful" or "pixyish," and describes these lines by the English poet Hilaire Belloc (1870–1953):

> The Devil, having nothing else to do,
>   Went off to tempt my Lady Poltigrue.
> My Lady, tempted by a private *whim*,
>   To his extreme annoyance, tempted him.

wile (wile) *n.* A *wile* is a trick, a deception, a bit of cunning. The plural, *wiles*, is the common form, meaning "trickery" in general. Impressionable ladies of wealth are sometimes taken in by the *wiles* of unscrupulous fortune hunters. Many a sermon has been delivered warning the congregation of the *wiles* of the Devil. The adjective *wily* (wy′ lee) means "tricky, crafty," or "foxy" (in the original sense).

It is all too easy to be taken in by the *wily*, high-pressure chants of pitchmen on the sidewalk. *Wiliness* (wy' lih ness) is the noun. The proverbial crafty rug dealer is the personification of *wiliness*.

willful, wilful (wil' fəl) *adj.* A *willful* person is obstinate, headstrong, pigheaded, determined to have his own way. The mule is the proverbially *willful* animal. It is difficult to curb a *willful* child. President Woodrow Wilson (1856–1924) was frustrated by a filibuster when he wanted to arm American merchant ships in 1917. He angrily characterized his opponents as "a little group of *willful* men reflecting no opinions but their own." The American novelist and critic Bernard De Voto (1897–1955) said, tongue-in-cheek: "Possibly a few *willful* people might deny that Vermont is the most beautiful state." A *willful* crime is deliberate and intentional. *Willful* killing is first-degree murder. The English poet Ann Taylor (1782–1866) gives this sound advice: "And *willful* waste, depend upon't,/Brings, almost always, woeful want." Ignorance of the law is no excuse, but *willful* violations bring harsher penalties.

wistful (wist' fəl) *adj.* A *wistful* mood is one marked by sadness and longing, yearning, and vague, unfulfilled desires. The American poet and humorist E.B. White (born 1899) wrote of "Those *wistful* little ads which the lovelorn . . . place in the classified columns." A *wistful* look comes into the eyes of a person recalling the happy times of years gone by. The Irish poet and dramatist Oscar Wilde (1854–1900) wrote, in "The Ballad of Reading Gaol":

> I never saw a man who looked
> With such a *wistful* eye
> Upon that little tent of blue
> Which prisoners call the sky.

People think nostalgically about lost opportunities and *wistfully* about unattainable goals.

withstand (with stand'—*th* as in *this* or *thing*) *vb.* To *withstand* (an attack, a pressure or temptation) is to hold out against it. A good Harris tweed will *withstand* decades of hard wear. The British proved that they could *withstand* anything Hitler sent them. According to the Greek poet Homer (c. 700 B.C.), Ulysses was able to *withstand* the fatal song of the sirens and ultimately to return home by putting wax in his seamen's ears and lashing himself to the mast. One wonders at the Eskimos' capacity to *withstand* the rigors of an Arctic winter. The engine of a car is likely to outlast the body, since the body often cannot *withstand* rust.

zealous (zel′ əs) *adj.* The noun *zeal* (zeel) means "fervor, ardent diligence." A person driven by *zeal* is *zealous*, full of enthusiasm for the task at hand, gung-ho. Martin Luther King, Jr. (1929–1968) was the most *zealous* civil-rights leader of modern times. An epitaph on an ancient gravestone reads:

> A *zealous* locksmith died of late
> And did arrive at heaven [sic] gate.
> He stood without and would not knock,
> Because he meant to pick the lock.

This being the last word of the "1000," I trust the reader will agree that the author has been *zealous* in his task.

WAKE TECHNICAL COLLEGE LIBRARY
9101 FAYETTEVILLE ROAD
RALEIGH, NORTH CAROLINA 27603

DATE DUE			
MAR 2 0 2008			
APR 2 0 2008			
MAY 2 6 2008			
APR 2 3 2009			
MAY 2 1 2009			
MAR 1 8 2013			
DEC 1 2 2023			